Providing Internet Services via the Mac OS

Carl Steadman and Jason Snell

Foreword by Peter N Lewis

Addison-Wesley Developers Press

Reading, Massachusetts • Menlo Park, California • New York
Don Mills, Ontario • Harlow, England • Amsterdam
Bonn • Sydney • Singapore • Tokyo • Madrid • San Juan
Paris • Seoul • Milan • Mexico City • Taipei

Many of the designations used by manufacturers and sellers to distinguish their products are claimed as trademarks. Where those designations appear in this book, and Addison-Wesley was aware of a trademark claim, the designations have been printed in initial capital letters or all capital letters.

The authors and publisher have taken care in the preparation of this book, but make no expressed or implied warranty of any kind and assume no responsibility for errors or omissions. No liability is assumed for incidental or consequential damages in connection with or arising out of the use of the information or programs contained herein.

Library of Congress Cataloging-in-Publication Data
Steadman, Carl.
    Providing internet services via the Mac OS / Carl Steadman
  and Jason Snell; foreword by Peter Lewis.
        p.   cm.
    Includes index.
    ISBN 0-201-48998-8
    1. Internet (Computer network) 2. Macintosh (Computer)
  I. Snell, Jason. II. Lewis, Peter. III. Title.
  TK5105.875.I57S75   1996
  005. 7' 136—dc20   96-11104
                                           CIP

Sponsoring Editor: Kim Fryer
Project Manager: John Fuller
Production Coordinator: Ellen Savett
Cover design: Ann Gallager
Set in 11.5 point Minion by Greg Johnson, Art Directions

1 2 3 4 5 6 7 8 9 -MA- 0099989796
First printing, April 1996

Addison-Wesley books are available for bulk purchases by corporations, institutions, and other organizations. For more information please contact the Corporate, Government, and Special Sales Department at (800) 238-9682.

Find *Providing Internet Services via the Mac OS* at http://www.pism.com/

Find A-W Developers Press on the World Wide Web at: http://www.aw.com/devpress/

Contents

About the Authors

Who We Are

Carl Steadman is the co-producer of *Suck* <http://www.suck.com/>. Previously, he has worked as the production director for HotWired <http://www.hotwired.com/>, where he attempted to develop and evolve an infostructure that could contain the live and twitching content whipping through the site like a Bengali typhoon. Or something like that. He's also the Web editor for *CTHEORY* <http://www.ctheory.com/>, and has involved himself in other Web projects too numerous to mention here. A co-author of *Web Weaving: Designing and Managing an Effective Web Site* (Addison-Wesley, 1995), Carl's first book-length work of nonfiction, *Rats To Cats!,* should be available in late 1996. You can find out even more about Carl and his dead fish at <http://www.freedonia.com/~carl/>.

Jason Snell is an associate editor at *MacUser* magazine <http://www.zdnet.com/~macuser/>, where he covers the Internet and electronic publishing, and coordinates the magazine's online presence. He's also the founder and editor of *InterText,* <http://www.etext.org/Zines/InterText/>, an online fiction magazine that has been publishing since March 1991. He was editor in chief of his college newspaper at UC San Diego, and then spent two years earning a Master of Journalism degree from UC Berkeley. Together, these two facts suggest he may be first against the wall when the revolution comes. His collection of useless information about himself is located at <http://www.etext.org/Zines/InterText/jason.html>. He lives in San Ramon, California, with his wife Lauren.

What We Use

Carl Steadman

The most important feature ever to be added to BBEdit was word wrap. I used BBEdit to lovingly craft every other word in this book.

Screen shots were produced with the fabulous shareware utility, Snapz, and cropped in Photoshop. BBEdit, Snapz, Photoshop, and the servers I wrote about ran on a PowerBook 540c, which is a few pounds too heavy, but is otherwise a nice machine, with built-in Ethernet: the small Dayna EasyNet transceivers are great, although I still hope to go wireless. Pages were revised from hard copy with a red Extra Fine Pilot Precise Rolling Ball—easily, my favorite pen: black for writing, red for editing.

Comfort was provided by Bigelow Raspberry Royale tea, Hostess Coffee Cake, and the usual—Cocteau Twins, Robyn Hitchcock. And I discovered Spiritualized Electric Mainline's Pure Phase. Thanks for the promo.

Jason Snell

I have five different word processors on my hard drive, and use them all from time to time. Most of the hard work was done in that bastion of the Evil Empire, Microsoft Word, though I've also spent quality time in Nisus Writer, BBEdit, and WordPerfect. Screen shots courtesy of Capture (now Captivate) and Photoshop. CPU power courtesy a Power Mac 7100/66 at work and a souped-up Powerbook 160 at home.

General good vibes provided by Crowded House, Peter Gabriel, Matthew Sweet, Sugar, and Marshall Crenshaw. Decaffeinated beverages (in bag form) by Lipton. Couch time caused by J. Michael Straczynski and Babylon 5.

Both of Us

When we exchanged e-mail related to the book, it was with Eudora as a client and AIMS as a server. When we exchanged files related to the book, it was with Anarchie or Fetch as a client, and FTPd as a server.

Acknowledgments

Carl Steadman

I'd like to thank Steve Dorner, Peter N Lewis, Glenn Anderson, and Matthias Neeracher for clueing me in when I needed it; Ben Koo and Jim Miner for doing the same on a much more personal level; Joey Anuff, for his insight into how to do a proper HTML tutorial and for writing more than his share of *Suck* <http://www.suck.com/> articles while I was working on this book; Melissa Pauna, for her assistance in obtaining and tracking the CD-ROM permissions; all the calm souls at *HotWired,* for humoring me when necessary; Gary Wolf, for a few well-placed reassurances leading not only to the completion of this book but also to the online version; Eric Tilton, for seeing the previous project through; Jason Snell, for being so shamefully competent; Matt Lee, who left a Macintosh at my apartment until I was willing to turn it on and deal with the weird GUI; and John Mowitt, under whose grand tutelage I earned a degree with which I could do anything.

Sean Welch, Director of Core Engineering for *HotWired* <http://www.hotwired.com> and the original maintainer of the comp.dcom.isdn FAQ, wrote a good part of Chapter 2 and made significant contributions to the Glossary. Sean also made sure to beat me at any game of pinball or pool we played together, thereby encouraging me to stay in the office and work on this book. Thanks, Sean.

Chuq Von Rospach, of Apple Computer World Wide Server Solutions <http://www.solutions.apple.com/> and Plaidworks Consulting <http://www.plaidworks.com/>, is List Mom for the Apple Internet Providers mailing list and a retired member of Usenet's infamous Backbone Cabal. Chuq was the technical reviewer for our project, and made *Providing Internet Services via the Mac OS* a much stronger book for his watchful eye. We owe you a pack of Post-it notes.

I'd also like to thank Kim Fryer at Addison-Wesley for putting up with me.

Also, it would only be appropriate if I were to extend an appreciative thanks to Albert F. Bayers III, for understanding.

My thanks and love to Andra, who believed in me when no one else would.

I'd like to dedicate my half of the book (lengthwise) to all those who contributed to my online FAQs, and to the regular contributers to the Apple Internet Providers and related lists, all of whom have my greatest respect.

Jason Snell

Thanks to Peter N Lewis, Mikael Hansen, Stephan "Obi-Wan" Somogyi, Marck Bailey, and Elizabeth Wasserman, and the ListSTAR team at StarNine for their good-natured donations of information; Geoff Duncan, my stalwart assistant editor at *InterText* for helpful tools, advice, and wisdom; Pam Pfiffner, editor-in chief of *MacUser,* for being a more understanding boss than I probably deserve; Carl Steadman, for deciding I'd be a good co-author after having never met me in person; and to all the members of the support mailing lists covering the products that I had the pleasure of profiling for this book—they're part of the sharing and openness that's such an integral part of the Internet.

Special thanks to Chuck and Crispin Holland, who got me interested in computers when I was a fourth-grader; my parents, for buying that first Commodore PET and encouraging me to learn about computers; and most of all to Lauren, whose love and support for me are matched only by her patience during those long weekends I spent writing.

Foreword

The Internet is about communication. This may seem obvious, but with all the hype around today, it's easy to think that the Internet is really about selling products and advertising or distributing pornography. It's all those and much much more, but primarily the Internet is about communication. And *that's* what makes it important.

Communication has always been important, and each new form of communication has been hailed as a breakthrough, leading ever onward. Written language, the printing press, newspapers, the telegraph and telephone, radio, and television—each one brought with it new ways of conveying information, and corresponding new groups of people who could use it to communicate.

Written language allows people to communicate without loss of information over distance or time. The printing press extended the audience from a select few to a much larger population. The telegraph and telephone allowed instantaneous communication, but only on a one-to-one basis. Radio and television extended that audience to the general population.

So what makes the Internet special, different from all these other forms of communication we already have? It's *bidirectional.* Every person on the Internet is in a position to become a publisher of information, not just a passive recipient.

Before the Internet, if I wanted to get my message to a large number of people, I would have had a very hard time. I could publish a book, but that requires either a large sum of money or the cooperation of a publisher. I could write a letter to the newspaper, but it might not publish it. I could try to get on a radio or television talk show, but the chances of that happening would be slim. I would be able to get my message across only with the grace of the powers controlling the mass media.

Now, on the Internet, I have lots of options. I can post a message to a relevant newsgroup. I can start a mailing list. I can set up an FTP server or Web site. My messages can be read by thousands of people around the world. If there's enough interest, we can form our own newsgroup. Other people can refer to my FTP or Web sites, and I can refer to theirs. All that's required is other people with similar interests anywhere in the world.

So on the Internet, you no longer need the assistance of media moguls to get your message across. The only real barrier is lack of knowledge. Just about anyone can "surf the Net" passively, looking at the information other people have provided, but in order to get all the benefits of two-way communication, you must know how to set up servers that provide information.

When I started on the Internet in 1990, only UNIX machines could really access the Internet. These machines are fine for computer geeks like me, but they're cryptic to the point of being useless for people who specialize in other fields.

I was already a Macintosh fanatic back then—in other words, I viewed computers as tools to help me, not complicate my life. Over the years, I've made it a personal crusade to bring Internet services to the Macintosh. There were already people doing fine work creating Internet clients for the Macintosh, but I felt (and still feel) that it is very important that people are empowered to provide information as well.

The Macintosh has proved to be an ideal platform for both clients and servers. The ease of use of a Macintosh means that you can now set up a mail server, mailing list, FTP server, or Web server on a Mac in a matter of minutes—a job that would take even a professional UNIX geek hours.

Of course, you still need to know what you're doing. The Internet was not designed by Apple—it isn't a plug-and-play environment, and there are little gotchas lurking everywhere. That's why it's great to see a book like this: one that shows you step by step how to be an information provider instead of just being a passive recipient.

Good luck getting your message across!

—Peter N Lewis
peter@stairways.com.au
<http://www.share.com/peterlewis/>
<ftp://ftp.share.com/pub/peterlewis/>

Peter N Lewis is the owner of Stairways Software and the author or co-author of countless Macintosh applications, including Anarchie, FTPd, Internet Config, SOCKS, Daemon, Script Daemon, Finger, MacTCP Watcher, TFTPd, Talk, and Chat. He lives in Booragoon, Western Australia. In 1994 he was honored for his Internet programming work by receiving Apple Computer's Cool Tools award and MacUser *magazine's Derek Van Alstyne Rising Star Award.*

## CHAPTER 1

Introduction: Internet Services via the Mac OS

It's hard to muster up enough fanaticism to properly introduce this book, but fanaticism is what this book requires. Not so much for the sake of the book itself—although we think it's a resource people will find useful—but for the reason that it's possible to write such a book, on how to provide Internet services via the Mac OS.

Only a short time ago, many of the services described here weren't available on any platform other than UNIX. And now they're all available via the Mac OS, with its true plug-and-play networking and point-and-click interface. No longer does providing Internet services require a fascination with the user-unfriendly complexities of UNIX or the significant amounts of time and money involved in purchasing and maintaining a UNIX workstation. With the Mac OS, Internet server applications can be as easy to use as your favorite word processor—and depending on which word processor you use, perhaps a good bit easier.

Since the Macintosh first debuted in 1984, networking has been part of the equation. It's appropriate, then, that the Mac is such a powerful and easy-to-use tool for providing Internet services. With the advent of the PowerPC chip and components of an updated operating system such as Open Transport, machines running the Mac OS have the robustness and horsepower to compete directly with UNIX workstations, while continuing to lead the industry in ease of use.

The second decade of the Macintosh has brought it new challenges, including an updated Microsoft Windows. While many of the failings of Windows 3.x have been addressed in this newest release of Windows, Windows 95 still can't offer the consistent interface of the Mac OS and its applications. And perhaps the Mac OS's biggest strength is the close-knit Internet software community built around it, which time and again has brought to the desktop the power of UNIX harnesssed in a friendly, point-and-click environment, several software development cycles ahead of similar Windows-based products.

And the benefits of the Mac OS go beyond having the right server applications on the right platform at the right time: the Mac OS also brings you the best tools for putting together the content that is provided via Internet services. Whether your services involve Gopher resources, Web pages, or FTP archives, whenever those services involve text, graphics, or sounds, the best tools exist on the Mac OS. From Photoshop to Painter to Illustrator to Director to SoundEdit to Acrobat to BBEdit, the premiere content creation tools exist first, if not only, on the Mac OS. Why? It comes from a platform that, to use words that have been used before, is insanely great: an OS that encourages developers to push limits and see what's possible.

The availability of Mac OS-based Internet servers opens up the world of Internet publishing to Mac users who never wanted to become UNIX gurus (or pay a bundle to hire one). It means that it now takes significantly less money, less time spent in training, and less time to set up and maintain Internet services.

What we soon expect to see is a revolution in Internet services akin to the Macintosh desktop publishing explosion of a decade ago, in which comparatively inexpensive, easy-to-use tools bring a previously esoteric, high-cost realm to the right people at the right price.

You may be one of those people.

Audience

This book was written with the small publisher or service provider in mind: an individual or organization with a vision to share, whether that be artistic, practical, commercial, or political. You might be putting up your own server, or a server for your K-12 school, your small business, or your department within a larger organization.

You might choose to provide e-mail services for the Chicago and San Francisco branches of your company, to allow for interoffice communications and to facilitate group work. You might choose to administer a mailing list for aficionados and collectors of Pez dispensers. You might make an FTP archive of your interactive presentations available, or allow people to make updates to your Gopher or Web site from across the country. You might put in place a Gopher archive of a collection of conference papers, in both text-only and Adobe Acrobat formats. You might make available a Web site to allow your elementary school's fourth grade students to have a place to publish their personal essays, while learning to how to develop content in an interactive, online medium. You might put up a chat server as a place to hold weekly discussion meetings for a postcolonial Algerian poetry reading group. To support any of these services, you might want to register your own domain name, so that if you're at Happy Valley High School, you can send mail to *yourname@happy-valley.hvsd.k12.ca.us*, or if you work for Pandemonium, Inc., you can use <http://www.pandemonium.com/> as your Web address. Whatever services you choose to provide, you can begin to run any of them on any Mac that runs the latest system software—System 7.5—using freeware or relatively inexpensive shareware packages.

We assume that you already have a good understanding of the Mac OS, and are familiar with at least a few Internet clients, such as Eudora, MacWeb, Netscape Navigator, Fetch, or Anarchie. If not, good introductory texts on the Mac OS are easy to find; Adam C.

Engst's *Internet Starter Kit for Macintosh* 3rd Ed. (Hayden Books, 1995) is highly recommended.

Organization

The first three chapters deal with the basics of setting up an Internet server: this chapter introduces the book; Chapter 2, Connecting to the Internet, gives a brief introduction to the Internet and the Internet Protocol, and on purchasing a full-time Internet connection; and Chapter 3, An Overview of Internet Services, discusses client/server architecture, the various Internet services discussed (and not discussed) in this book, and the type of hardware that might be most appropriate for your needs.

For the remainder of the book, we've assigned a chapter to each service we discuss—e-mail, mailing lists and auto-reply, FTP, Gopher, Web, and domain name services—except for those miscellaneous services described in Chapter 10—including Finger, Talk, and Chat—which we felt really didn't warrant their own chapters. We open each chapter with a brief discussion of the service and its protocols, with the exception of Domain Name System, which does require more than a cursory knowledge of the underlying mechanisms. What we've tried to do in most cases is allow the software we describe to do the work: the Mac OS does a good job of masking a lot of complexity through an easy-to-use and intuitive interface, which many of the applications described here take advantage of, and we didn't want to bog you down with too many of the whys or hows something worked: in reality, a separate book could probably be written on each of the services we describe here. Whether or not you would want to devote yourself to such in-depth discussions is another matter. We go on to discuss the setup and use of software running under the Mac OS that enables you to provide the service, and close each chapter with a listing of clients that can interact with the service, if appropriate, and some general tips on organizing and maintaining the service for the benefit of both you and your users.

The chapters progress from the most basic of services, electronic mail, to the more esoteric services—domain name services, and those miscellaneous services that might be important or necessary to only a few, such as Finger. We also devote a chapter to utilities that can help you administer your Internet server remotely, such as Timbuktu Pro.

Finally, the book closes with those niceties you've come to expect from high-quality books such as this one: a glossary, an index, and several appendixes. Appendix A covers Uniform Resource Locators, which should provide you with the information you need to refer to your services in a clear, concise, and universally recognized way. Appendix B covers character entities, which are used to display special and reserved characters within HTML documents. Appendix C contains descriptions of the software found on the CD-ROM (see the following section).

CD-ROM and Online Resources

Providing Internet Services via the Mac OS comes with a CD-ROM that includes most of the software discussed in the book. A lot of the software is freeware, but a good portion of it is unregistered shareware or demos, for trial and evaluation purposes only. We would like to insert a gentle reminder to pay your shareware fees if you do decide to use a shareware package. Although freeware carries no obligations, and commercial demo software has time limits or other restrictions that insure payment, shareware is on the honor system. Please, if you use shareware, pay your shareware fees.

The software included on the CD-ROM is briefly described in Appendix C. Please be sure to read the read me files describing usage and licensing terms, and covering any updates and revisions to the software that occurred between the time the book was completed and the CD-ROM was pressed.

Online resources to support this book are available via the Web at

```
<http://www.pism.com/>
```

These pages include (hopefully) up-to-date links to and/or archives of all the software packages mentioned here, as well as updates and revisions to the text, which is itself made available in full. Putting the full text online is a risky proposition for both us and Addison-Wesley; if the online resource cuts too deeply into sales of the book, Addison-Wesley won't see too much reason for an updated second edition, and we might not be able to afford the time necessary to keep the online materials up to date. What we're hoping for, of course, is an online resource that gives back to the community while fueling sales of the book, which in turn provides a useful bound reference, and is improved by the time we spend on online updates.

## CHAPTER 2

Connecting to the Internet

The Internet: Your Digital Connection

In order to provide services on the Internet via a computer running the Mac OS, you've got to connect that computer to the Internet. The Internet is a decentralized global computer network—there's no real "center." As a result, connecting to the Internet can be a good deal more confusing than connecting to commercial online services such as CompuServe or America Online.

People connect to the Internet via a service provider, a company that's a lot like your local phone or cable company. An Internet service provider can give you an Internet "dial tone," just as your phone company gives you a regular dial tone and the cable company gives you a selection of television channels. The difference is that there are usually several competing service providers in a given area, and their rates can often differ substantially. So there's a lot more choice involved in getting on the Internet than there is in hooking up cable TV.

If you're reading this book, there's a good chance that you're already on the Internet—either via a local service provider or via one of the commercial online services. Unfortunately, providing services via the Internet usually requires a level of connectivity that's beyond what normal online users have. With a few exceptions, if you want to become an Internet information provider, you'll need a 24-hours-a-day, 7-days-a-week connection to the Internet. That's a big jump, and it's a lot more expensive than just logging in once or twice a day to check your mail or surf the Web. Of course, if your company or school already has a full-time Internet connection, connectivity will probably be much less of a problem. But if you're planning on establishing service from scratch, you'll need to know a lot more about what's involved before taking the plunge.

In this chapter, we'll try to discuss the issues involved in making a connection to the Internet—what different connection options there are, diagnosing what your connectivity needs are, and how to shop for a service provider. We'll also try to give you a brief overview on how the Internet Protocol (IP) works, both in general and specifically on the Mac OS.

Types of Internet Connections

The first complication in connecting to the Internet is choosing the method you'll use to connect. Sure, you can connect via a modem over a standard phone line, just as you probably connect to online services today. But those lines can be slow, especially if you're going to be serving large files to several people at the same time. For that reason, there are other options you should consider when you're planning to hook up to the Net: ISDN, a means of using the standard copper phone lines in your house or office to make high-speed digital connections; Frame Relay, a connection to a high-speed, public, digital network; and the stratosphere of Internet connectivity, high-speed digital phone lines with names like PRI and T1.

Modem Connections

The most common way to make a connection to the Internet is via a modem line. But modems can't go very fast—even the fastest modems on the market can send and receive only 28,800 characters per second. That's fast enough for most of the Web surfers of today, but imagine trying to load several graphically rich Web pages all at once over such a line. The pace would be glacial at best. And since servers tend to send files to multiple users at the same time, even a fast modem line (and we're rapidly approaching the limits of modem technology when it comes to using old-fashioned voice telephone lines) isn't going to work very well.

That said, a modem connection to the Internet (via your service provider) might still be the best option for you, depending on what services you want to provide. If you're not expecting your site to get a lot of use, and you're serving mostly text (whether it's via the Web or Gopher or some other protocol), a modem link may be enough to handle your traffic. But if you expect your site to be popular, or you're planning on making lots of big graphics available, or if you're going to be letting people upload or download large files to your server, you may find your modem line overtaxed quickly.

As we mentioned in the introduction to this chapter, not all Internet services require you to have a 24-hours-a-day connection to the Net. If you want to put up a Web, Gopher, or FTP site, you'll need to be online all the time, or people won't want to visit your server. But if all you want to do is run mailing lists or a mailbot, a program that automatically replies to incoming e-mail messages based on their content, you can probably survive with only a sporadic Net connection (see Chapter 5). Likewise, a protocol called UUCP also makes it feasible for you to provide Internet e-mail services to yourself and others without a continuous connection (see Chapter 4).

Most service providers tend to charge an hourly rate for connecting to their system via a modem, because this is the best way to charge regular users. Chances are, those same providers offer a special flat rate for 24-hours-a-day connections. It'll cost a lot more than being connected sporadically, but the upside is that you'll be paying only a basic telephone rate, and all you'll need in the way of hardware is a fast modem.

ISDN

ISDN stands for Integrated Services Digital Networks. It's a means of using the copper wires that connect most homes and businesses to the telephone network to achieve high-speed data transmissions far beyond those offered by modems.

Here's now ISDN works: Standard telephone lines are analog in nature. They were designed to transmit voices across distance, and they do a pretty good job of this—after all, this is the telephone system most of us use every day. Now, we also use this same phone system to transmit digital information via modem—but we're still using an analog system to transmit this information. That's what a modem does—it translates (or modulates, the first half of the word modem) digital information into a series of sounds, which it then sends across the analog phone line. At the other end, another modem translates (or demodulates) the signal back into digital form.

ISDN uses those same copper wires, but it's a digital system. Everything that goes across an ISDN line has to be in digital form— even if it's a voice call. As a result, standard telephones (and modems) don't work on an ISDN line without an adapter, because they're made to work with the common analog phone lines.

Though ISDN has gained quite a bit of popularity in Europe, it's not as prevalent in the United States yet. As a result, ISDN can be an option for you only if you're lucky enough to live in an area serviced by a telephone company that's ISDN-savvy. Both of us are lucky enough to live in the San Francisco Bay Area, and our phone company, Pacific Bell, is on top of things when it comes to ISDN. In fact, an ISDN connection from Pacific Bell curently doesn't cost much more per month than a regular analog phone line. Unfortunately, ISDN rates vary widely across the country.

The world of ISDN is one filled with acronyms and other forms of jargon, so bear with us as we try to describe this. The most common form of ISDN is the BRI, the Basic Rate Interface. The BRI line has two B (or Bearer) channels; essentially, the B channel is akin to a digital version of a regular phone line. Since each BRI contains two of these, every ISDN line has the capacity to place two calls at once—or place one call with twice the bandwidth. You could, for example, be transferring a file over one B channel while chatting with a friend at the same time.

As we said, the 28.8 Kbps rate achieved by modern V.34 modems is nearing the upper limit of transmission speeds on analog lines. But each B channel on an ISDN can handle data rates up to 64 Kbps, and two B channels connected in a process called "bonding" can handle 128 Kbps of information—almost nine times the speed of that wicked fast 14.4 modem you bought a couple of years ago.

ISDN is a great way to get a high-speed line into a home office, small business, or school. The only real problems with ISDN are availability (as we discussed) and price. In addition to paying your ISDN set-up fee and your monthly fees to the phone company, you have to buy hardware that can handle ISDN. The most important piece of hardware is the NT1, or network terminator. The NT1 is a device that connects to the digital telephone network and serves as the gateway between the outside world and your equipment. You'll also need to get either an ISDN terminal adapter to connect one CPU to the ISDN line, or an ISDN router to connect your local network to the line. You may also need an adapter to enable you to use analog devices like voice telephones with your ISDN line.

The good news is that the cost of ISDN hardware is coming down. You can now get an ISDN router for under $1,000, to which you can hook up several machines via Ethernet.

Now as with all the connectivity options we discuss, keep in mind that all of these costs still don't cover what you'll have to pay your Internet service provider to connect you to the Net via ISDN.

Frame Relay

Frame relay is a form of networking gaining in popularity because it's reasonably inexpensive for the speed it offers. At the heart of frame relay is a digital network. Subscribers sign up for a fixed access speed, typically between 56 Kbps and 1.554 Mbps. The speed through the provider's network is much faster, but you pay for the speed at which your data enters the port to the network. In addition to a speed, you specify a destination, a port somewhere else on the network. When you establish service, a permanent virtual circuit is set up between your port and the destination port. It's much like a physical circuit from the subscriber's point of view—all your traffic goes between the two ports, though the details of how it actually traverses the network are left up to the provider.

What makes frame relay interesting to many customers is that you aren't always limited to the amount of bandwidth you buy. If you sign up for 56 Kbps and access a frame relay network at 128 Kbps over ISDN, you can get your data to the network faster than you paid to have it transmitted. This is because, most of the time, a network isn't filled with traffic. A typical FTP server, for instance, uses the network only when people are transferring files to and from the server. When nobody is connected, an FTP server needs little to no bandwidth. But when someone wants to pull down a large file, the server will want as much bandwidth as it can grab.

Frame relay takes advantage of this by guaranteeing a minimum bandwidth to each customer, but allowing all customers to make use of unused bandwidth in the network. If your network is lightly loaded and your server suddenly starts serving files, you can use the extra, unused bandwidth. If another subscriber then needs some of its guaranteed bandwidth, your connection is dropped back down to the speed you've been guaranteed—but not below it.

Beyond: PRI, T1, T3

Beyond these connection types are high-speed lines that won't be needed for the person or organization setting up a Net presence for the first time—though if your services become popular enough, you might end up needing them one day. There's a type of ISDN called PRI, or Primary Rate Interface. PRI is a high-speed connection made up of 23 B channels—that's well over a megabyte per second. It offers high speeds, but it also costs a fortune.

The PRI has roughly the same bandwidth as the T1, a high-speed digital line usually used to connect large businesses to service providers. T1s run at 1.544 Mbps, about one sixth the speed of

Ethernet, but over a hundred times faster than your 14.4 Kbps modem. There's also another type of digital line, the T3, with a maximum transfer rate of 45 Mbps. If all the machines in your office already have Internet connectivity, there's a good chance that your office is connected to the Net via one of these high-speed lines.

If you're searching for Internet connectivity on your own, you probably won't need any of these at first. But it's always something to shoot for.

Selecting a Service Provider

In addition to figuring out how you're going to get that digital or analog dial tone, you'll also need to contact an Internet service provider to get you connected to the rest of the Internet.

Shop Around

The best advice we can give when it comes to finding a service provider can be boiled down to this: *shop around.* In most areas, there are multiple service providers fighting for customers. Usually, there will be one or two that can offer you the best deal, taking into account where you live, how much bandwidth you'll be using, and by what means you'll be connecting to them. Don't be afraid to shop around. Considering how much money you might be paying for these services, you'll want to find the best price. But at the same time, keep the stability of your potential service providers in mind. Choosing a fly-by-night provider that may not be in business long won't do any good, no matter how cheap their services are.

A Service Provider Checklist

There are several things you should keep in mind when you're shopping for an Internet service provider. First, know as much as you can about your needs. Be clear about what sort of services you're going to need—Web, Gopher, FTP, mailing lists, and so on. Have a good idea of how popular you expect your site to be, if at all possible. This will let you determine how much bandwidth you'll need.

Bandwidth

Determine how much bandwidth you're going to need, or at least how much to start, and make sure your provider can meet your needs. With the wide variety of connection speeds and media available, be sure that your provider can give you not only what you want today, but what you will probably need down the road when your services increase in popularity.

This doesn't just mean that if they can set you up with a large pipe to their office, they can meet your needs. Make sure that they aren't overselling the quality of *their* connection to the rest of the Internet. If your provider is connected to the Internet at a certain speed, they can't offer any more than that to their customers. If you pay them for a certain amount of bandwidth, be sure they can guarantee that amount, even when all their other customers need the bandwidth they've paid for at the same time.

Hardware

There is hardware involved in any connection to the Internet. Generally, this takes the form of a box at either end, be it a pair of modems, ISDN terminal adapters, or routers. Find out what brands your provider supports and what they recommend. Some providers have arrangements with hardware manufacturers such that if you buy through your provider you get special discounts. But if you already own network hardware, you may want to make sure you can interoperate with your provider. You also may want to ask how much technical support you might be able to expect per each variety of hardware solution.

In some cases, as part of the startup, you will need to purchase equipment at both ends of the connection. Be sure to find out where the hardware goes should you end service.

Whither the Server?

There are three different ways to provide services on the Internet, and you should keep all three methods in mind when talking to service providers. First, you can keep your connection up 24 hours a day and run a server on a machine in your home or office. This situation offers a number of advantages. There's a clear line between what is your responsibility and what is the provider's: you take care of everything from where the line into your office or home ends. The only time you should have to deal with your provider is when something is wrong, as opposed to every time you want to change something. On the other hand, if you'd rather leave the details to someone else, you might be better off with letting your provider do more of the work.

Second, you can run your services from one of your computers, but keep that machine connected at the offices of your service provider. This way, the machine is always connected to the Internet, but you don't have to deal with the hassles of keeping yourself connected to the Net 24 hours a day. The drawback? Your service provider will probably charge a pretty penny to store your machine, keep it cool, and make sure it's up and running. You'll also need to invest in some remote-maintenance software (see Chapter 11) to administer your server from a distance. But be sure to ask prospective service providers about this option; if you live where ISDN costs a bundle and you expect your server will need a high-speed connection to the Internet, setting up a machine at your service provider might be more economical than running it yourself.

Third, you can provide your services on your provider's hardware. This is an easy way of doing things, and it works for a lot of people. It's also usually pretty cheap. The big drawback is that service providers seldom provide those services via the Mac OS. Usually, their Web, Gopher, FTP, and mail servers are run on a workstation using UNIX. UNIX workstations are quite powerful, but they usually don't offer much in the way of an interface. They can be hard to use. And chances are good that if you're reading this book, you'd prefer to avoid this option. However, if all you really want to do is serve a few HTML pages, run a mailing list, or offer a few files for FTP transfer, you may want to ask a service provider how much it would cost to do it on their server.

Support and Trouble

Support is crucial when dealing with a provider, and a provider's support policy can give a great deal of insight into what you can expect in your relationship with them. Some providers offer start-to-finish "get you on the Net" service where they walk you through the entire process. Others will leave you with a line in your office and expect you to handle the rest. Be sure you understand what level of assistance you can expect. If you'll need a significant amount of support, be sure your provider has experience with Mac-based clients.

Even with support, though, things break, and you'll want to know how well your provider handles it when they do. Find out if they have a 24-hour service number, and if they do, check to see if it's just an answering machine, or if a live human being will be able to help you when your line goes down at 3 A.M. on a Sunday. Find out how they track trouble reports, so that you'll be able to easily find out the status of a report you've filed.

You'll also want to find their average trouble report turnaround time. If you are going to be running your services as part of a business, you can't afford to be kept waiting. If your provider can give a list of their current customers as references, that can help in determining how they handle problems. Providers who deal with commercial clients generally have a higher level of professionalism than those who deal primarily with end users, though they often charge more.

You might also want to visit your provider's office and ask to see their machine room. A well-kept, orderly, properly air-conditioned machine room is a good sign that you are dealing with a professional organization. A rat's nest of cables and machines is a sign that you are not. Remember, your connection to the Internet goes through

their setup, and if they have a hard time pointing out what everything is and what it does, imagine having to deal with them when
things aren't working.

Costs

Of course, in some cases, it all comes down to money. You'll want to
know all of the start-up costs. It's likely you'll have to pay the phone
company if they're involved in setting up the physical line to your
provider, be it an additional phone line, ISDN service, or a T1. Your
provider may have start-up costs for opening your account with
them and for anything they need to purchase on their end. You may
also have initial hardware costs in the form of a modem, an ISDN
terminal adapter, or even a router.

That's only the beginning. Monthly costs are where you have to be
especially careful. The various options you have in terms of bandwidth are not linearly related—if you double your bandwidth, you
may not end up paying exactly twice as much. Also, there is a great
deal of overlap in the various options; for example, you could get the
same bandwidth from an ISDN line as from a fractional T1 line, but
they won't cost the same. Be careful to watch for any charges *per
minute* or *per packet*. For instance, in some locations, ISDN is tar-
iffed at a certain rate per minute, which may make it more expensive
than a leased line. On the other hand, certain areas allow 24-hours-
a-day, 7-days-a-week connections for a flat monthly fee. Be sure to
check a variety of pricing models before picking one. And expect to
pay more than you expect to. There will always be costs that you've
forgotten to take into account.

Also, plan ahead. Some bandwidth and pricing solutions do not
scale well. A 28.8 modem is a good solution for some sites, but if you
need to increase your bandwidth at some point, it's much less
expensive to go with another type of network than to buy a roomful
of modems. Modems are increasing in speed, but buying new
modems every year isn't efficient. A T1 line can generally be provi-
sioned, so that you could start with some fraction of the full capability of a T1 and then expand as you need without having to reinvest

in additional hardware. In addition to clearing any expansion plans with your provider, be sure to consult your local phone company if it is involved in any way with the line.

Name Services

Chances are good that if you're providing Internet services, you'll want to have your own Internet domain name—for example, free-donia.com. Be sure to ask prospective service providers what they'll charge to register a domain for you and provide you with name services. (Alternatively, you can run a name server yourself. See Chapter 9 for details.)

Mail Services

If you're not planning to provide Internet e-mail to more than a handful of people, it might be easier to use your service provider's e-mail server than to set up one of your own (see Chapter 4). Gauge just how many e-mail accounts you might need, and ask prospective service providers how much it would cost to set up addresses for all of those users. If you have special e-mail needs, such as mailing lists or addresses that change on a regular basis, you may be better off handling mail on your own.

The Internet Protocol

All communications on the Internet happen by using the Internet Protocol, also known as TCP/IP. It's not necessary to know how TCP/IP works in order to provide Internet services, but it's usually helpful to know something about what's happening behind the scenes when you're downloading a file from a distant Internet server.

TCP/IP

Every machine on the Internet has an IP address assigned to it. IP addresses are a lot like street addresses—they're a short way of letting people know where they can find you. IP addresses are made up of four numbers, or quads, each of which can run from 0 to 255, separated by decimal points. So a sample IP address might be 128.25.255.8.

Addresses are given out in blocks, and these blocks come in three sizes, Classes A, B, and C. Class A networks are defined by the first quad, and have the rest of the numbers for particular machines. For instance, any IP address that starts with 13 is in the class A network at Xerox Palo Alto Research Center. Class A networks encompass millions of unique addresses, but there are only a small number of these networks.

Class B networks are defined by the first two quads, with the last two for individual machines. The University of California, Berkeley, has all addresses that start with 128.32 in their class B. Class B networks can have over 65,000 addresses in them.

Class C networks have the first three quads defining the network, and the last quad for each host, so there are many more class C networks, but each can only have 256 addresses. Addison-Wesley Publishing Company holds the 192.88.129 class C network. If you are planning on having a network in your home or office, this is the type of network you may initially have.

Of course, we know most machines on the Internet by names, not numbers, but those names all correspond to IP addresses like 128.25.255.8. A naming system was created because it's easier to remember www.freedonia.com than it is to remember 128.25.255.8. (For more information on this naming system, see chapter 9.)

When two machines on the Internet "talk," they use this four-number IP address to find one another. They converse by sending little bundles of information called packets back and forth. A packet contains a chunk of information, an identifier that lets the receiving computer understand in what sequence it was sent from the sending computer, the IP address of its target, and the IP address from which it came.

A sending computer creates a packet and sends it out across the Internet, where it bounces from router to router until it finds its way to the IP address of its target. There, the target computer receives the packet, sees where it goes in the sequence of packets it's receiving from the sender, and opens it. The individual packets can take any number of routes from the sender to the recipient—one could be routed through Great Britain, the other through Germany—but once the receiver gets the packets, sees where they fit, and opens them, it's as if one computer has sent a continuous stream of information directly to another. This can sound like an unreliable system, but in practice it works extremely well. And the best part is, it's all invisible to the user. All you have to do is set up your TCP/IP software.

TCP/IP Software for the Mac OS

In the DOS and Windows world, there are lots of software solutions that provide TCP/IP connectivity. But for years, the only way you could connect a machine running the Mac OS to the Internet was with a piece of software from Apple called MacTCP.

These days, MacTCP is on its last legs. Apple is in the process of replacing it with an easier-to-use, more efficient piece of networking software called Open Transport. When Open Transport was originally released, it worked only on Power Macintoshes that used the PCI bus architecture. But by the time you read this, Open Transport should be available for all machines that run the Mac OS.

Which should you use? Open Transport is a lot easier to configure, and most TCP/IP-based applications were Open Transport-compatible by early 1996. Open Transport also runs native on the PowerPC processor, unlike MacTCP—so if you're using a PowerPC-based system and software that's compatible with Open Transport, you should use Open Transport. But MacTCP is there if you need to be assured of software compatibility.

Also note that MacTCP has only 64 available connections to distribute among all incoming and outgoing requests. For very busy servers providing multiple services that use several connections each, it's possible to exceed this 64-connection limit, resulting in refused connections. If you're using MacTCP, keep the 64-connection limit in mind when setting maximum connection values in your server applications. Open Transport has not set upper bound on the number of available connections.

MacTCP

MacTCP is not a freely available piece of software; it initially was bundled with version 7.5 of the MacOS. It's also available on disks that come with many books, including the excellent *Internet Starter Kit for Macintosh* by Adam Engst (Hayden Books). You can also buy it directly from Apple.

Installing MacTCP

Installing the MacTCP software is a fairly straightforward process; just drop the MacTCP control panel into the Control Panels folder within your System Folder.

Then open the MacTCP control panel (see Figure 2.1) and configure it. To do this, you'll need to get information from your service provider. Ask for all the information you'll need to configure MacTCP (be sure to mention it by name). Among the information you'll need is:

- **Your IP address,** which you'll place in the IP Address box in the main MacTCP control panel window.
- **The service provider's gateway address,** which you'll place in the Gateway Address box in the window that appears when you click MacTCP's More button (see Figure 2.2).
- **The Subnet Mask,** which is a bit mask that separates the portions of the IP address significant to the network from the bits significant to the subnet. For example, for a class C address, the standard subnet mask is 255.255.255.0, which masks the first three bytes of the address and leaves the last byte available to identify machines on the subnet.
- **The address of the provider's domain name server or servers,** which you enter in the Domain Name Server Information boxes in that same window

FIGURE 2.1
The MacTCP
Control Panel

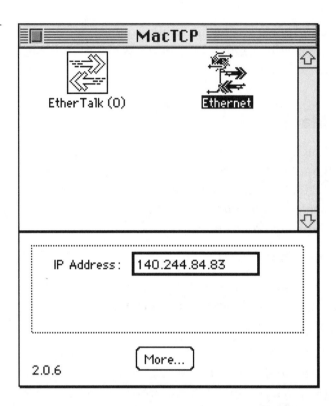

FIGURE 2.2
MacTCP's More
Window

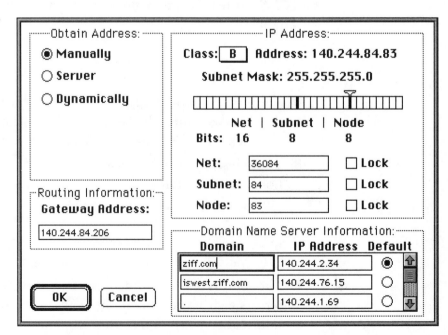

You'll also need some method of connecting to your service provider; ask what SLIP or PPP software they recommend. (SLIP [Serial Line Interface Protocol] and PPP [Point-to-Point Protocol] are means of connecting to the Internet via a modem.) Several free SLIP and PPP software packages are available on the Internet.

MacTCP is quite complicated to configure, and how you do so can vary depending on who your service provider is. If your service provider can't help you configure MacTCP, we recommend you purchase one of the many general Internet access books available on the market.

Open Transport

As we said, Open Transport is a much-improved Mac networking architecture. It affects more than just Internet connections; Open Transport controls all Mac networking functionality, right down to AppleTalk. It's Power Mac native and easy to configure—in many ways, it's Apple's apology for the difficult-to-use MacTCP control panel.

Installing Open Transport

Open Transport is installed automatically with all PCI-based Power Macintosh systems, and will be installed automatically, starting with a future release of Apple System Software. If you have an older Mac, Open Transport should be available by the time you read this, either for free on the Net or for a small fee from Apple. A handy installer program will install all the pieces of Open Transport automatically, just as if you were installing any other new software package.

The TCP Control Panel

The core of Internet connectivity in Open Transport is the simply named TCP/IP control panel (see Figure 2.3). In this control panel, there are no More buttons to push, no modal dialog boxes to become trapped in. The top pop-up menu, Connect via:, lets you select the type of connection you'll be using. This could range from Ethernet to AppleTalk to SLIP or PPP.

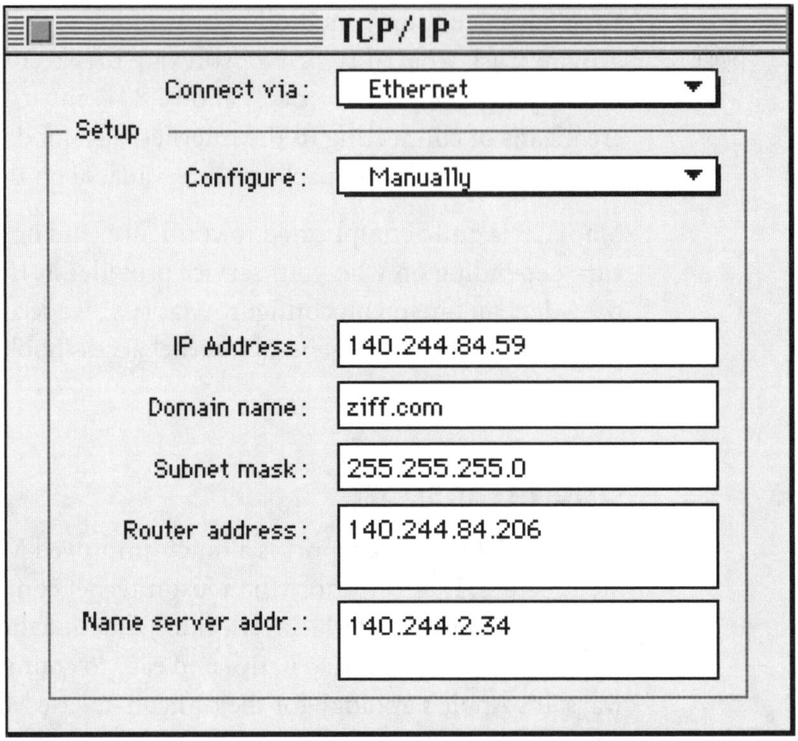

```
┌─────────────────────────────────────────────────────────┐
│ ▤▫▬▬▬▬▬▬▬▬▬▬▬▬▬▬▬▬▬  TCP/IP  ▬▬▬▬▬▬▬▬▬▬▬▬▬▬▬▬▬ │
├─────────────────────────────────────────────────────────┤
│          Connect via:  ┌─ Ethernet            ▼ ┐         │
│   ┌ Setup ──────────────────────────────────────────────┐│
│   │        Configure:  ┌─ Manually             ▼ ┐       ││
│   │                                                      ││
│   │                                                      ││
│   │       IP Address:  ┌ 140.244.84.59             ┐     ││
│   │                    └───────────────────────────┘     ││
│   │     Domain name:   ┌ ziff.com                  ┐     ││
│   │                    └───────────────────────────┘     ││
│   │     Subnet mask:   ┌ 255.255.255.0             ┐     ││
│   │                    └───────────────────────────┘     ││
│   │   Router address:  ┌ 140.244.84.206            ┐     ││
│   │                    │                           │     ││
│   │                    └───────────────────────────┘     ││
│   │  Name server addr.:┌ 140.244.2.34              ┐     ││
│   │                    │                           │     ││
│   │                    └───────────────────────────┘     ││
│   └──────────────────────────────────────────────────────┘│
└─────────────────────────────────────────────────────────┘
```

FIGURE 2.3 Open Transport's TCP/IP Control Panel

Below that, in the Setup section of the control panel, you can enter your network information. If you choose Using DHCP from the Configure pop-up menu, your information can be automatically entered when you connect to a server. The catch is that your server must support the protocol known as DHCP in order to escape entering a string of IP addresses.

However, even if you have a conventional connection that requires you to choose Manually from the Configure pop-up menu, things are easier than in MacTCP. Enter the IP address your service provider has assigned you in the IP Address box, enter your name server's domain name in the Domain name box, enter your router (or gateway) address in the Router address box, and enter the address(es) of your name server(s) in the Name server addr. box.

Open Transport: Friend or Foe?

Open Transport's debut when the Power Mac 9500 was released in the summer of 1995 was scarred by a series of bugs. Many industry observers feel that Open Transport was released to the public long before it was ready. This was much to the dismay of the people who bought those fresh new Power Macs only to find that their network connections were flaky at best.

But Open Transport's stability has improved. New versions of Internet applications that explicitly support Open Transport have appeared. The sheer speed of its Power Mac native code makes Open Transport an extremely appealing option, and we're sure that over time, it will be the final stake in the heart of MacTCP.

## CHAPTER 3

An Overview of Internet Services

I nternet services are provided with *servers*, which, in turn, provide services.* In this chapter, we discuss what a server is, what kinds of services you might offer, and the kind of hardware you'll need to offer your service.

Distinction between Clients and Servers

Most of the resources made available via the Internet—and all the major services discussed in this book—use a client/server architecture. The distinction between clients and servers is fairly straightforward:

Clients *request* information from a server for display on a monitor or other use by, or on the behalf of, a user. For example, a Web client—usually called a *browser*—will request information from a Web server, and then display the data it receives for a user.

Servers provide, or *serve,* information to clients. A Web server, for example, will listen for requests from clients, and, when it receives one, will send the requested data to the client that asked for it.

Servers, by their nature, require full-time connections (see Chapter 2, Connecting to the Internet). They always need to be available to

---

* Few servers, however, provide tautologies. The authors are kind enough to serve in this role instead.

answer clients' requests. Clients, on the other hand, need be connected to the Internet only when in use by a user or a user-agent, computer software acting on behalf of a user. Servers are sometimes also known as *daemons,* the name for any UNIX program that runs as a background process at all times.

In order for clients to communicate with servers, a *protocol* must be defined. Just like the protocols, or rules of etiquette, you learned as a child—rules governing your expected behavior in specific situations—Internet protocols are rules governing the expected behavior between servers and clients to guarantee the orderly exchange of data. Client/server protocols for Internet services sit atop the IP protocol—a lower-level protocol—described in Chapter 2.

Many client/server architectures on the Internet are also *distributed,* meaning that there is no one central server to which all clients must connect and depend upon. Distributed services improve reliability and performance. Reliability, in that there is no single point of failure; with multiple servers, if one server isn't available, others are. Performance, in that it is easier and cheaper to build a fast, efficient service using multiple servers and networks, instead of attempting to scale a service with faster and faster hardware for one, monolithic server. Distributed services can also be designed so that there is no longer a centralized authority for the service, allowing anyone to provide a service without going through a central registry or other potential arbiter of content. Most Internet services share this feature of a distributed architecture, with the notable exception of the Domain Name System, or DNS.

Types of Internet Services

There are many types of Internet services, each suited to particular tasks and particular audiences. In this book, we cover electronic mail, mail-based services, FTP, Gopher, the Web, and DNS, as well as various miscellaneous services.

Electronic Mail

Electronic mail combines the speed and convenience of the telephone with the accountability of postal mail. Most e-mail arrives within minutes of when it is sent but doesn't interrupt the recipient, and e-mail can be filtered, prioritized, and saved. E-mail is used for person-to-person communications, and for workgroup and discussion group activities. In the latter case, a single message can have multiple recipients, so that everyone within the group is part of the discussion.

Of course, if you're reading this book, chances are you're not only familiar with e-mail, it's likely you would have difficulty imagining your life, or at least your job, without it. Most of the discussions related to the writing, editing, and publication of this book occurred in e-mail. A screen shot of Eudora, an e-mail client, is shown in Figure 3.1

Mail-Based Services: Mailing Lists and Auto-Reply

A mailing list is a list of e-mail addresses available through a single e-mail address. When a message is sent to the mailing list's address, the message is "exploded" into the entire list, so that each member of the list receives a copy. Lists are usually large discussion groups devoted to a single narrow topic, although some lists are

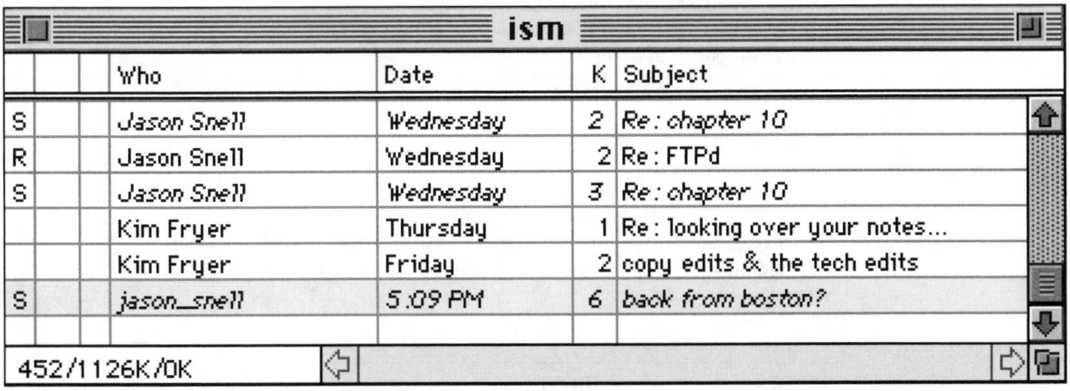

		Who	Date	K	Subject
S		*Jason Snell*	*Wednesday*	2	*Re : chapter 10*
R		Jason Snell	Wednesday	2	Re : FTPd
S		*Jason Snell*	*Wednesday*	3	*Re : chapter 10*
		Kim Fryer	Thursday	1	Re : looking over your notes...
		Kim Fryer	Friday	2	copy edits & the tech edits
S		*jason_snell*	*5:09 PM*	6	*back from boston?*

452/1126K/OK

FIGURE 3.1 A Eudora Mailbox

broadcast-only, such as company product announcement lists and newsletters. Discussion lists are also sometimes moderated in order to keep the signal-to-noise ratio low: in a moderated list, all messages sent to the list must first be approved by a moderator before being redistributed to the list.

An auto-reply service behaves as you might expect from its name: when a message is sent to a particular address, a reply is automatically generated and mailed to the original sender. The auto-reply might simply return a single message regardless of the content of the mail it receives, or it might attempt to interpret the sender's text as commands, and return a message appropriate to the original request. Although auto-reply is the most basic of information services, it shouldn't be overlooked as you consider other services to deliver your content, for the very reason that it is so basic. Although FTP, Gopher, and Web access are becoming more widespread, virtually everyone with any kind of connection to the Internet can be reached through e-mail. For short, informative, text-only resources, an auto-reply message can sometimes be the quickest, most efficient, and convenient way of delivering that content. Figure 3.2 is an example of an auto-reply.

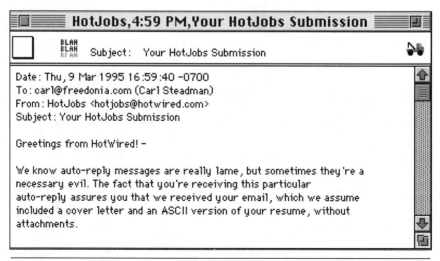

FIGURE 3.2 The beginning of the lame auto-reply message Carl got when applying for a job at *HotWired*.

File Transfer Protocol

The File Transfer Protocol, or FTP, is an Internet standard for transferring files to and from computers on the Internet. Anonymous FTP is probably the most common form of FTP, in which files are available for retrieval by anyone on the Internet who identifies himself or herself as the user "anonymous." Otherwise, FTP is restricted to users with an appropriate user name and password for a site. Figure 3.3 shows a popular FTP client, Fetch, in the process of retrieving a file. The in-progress chapters of this book were exchanged among its authors and editors using FTP.

FTP is an obvious choice for making executable programs available to the public, or for exchanging large data files among collaborators. It's far from ideal for publishing information in the traditional sense, however; users have only filenames to rely on for descriptive information on what files might contain, and, in order to view a document, users must download the entire file.

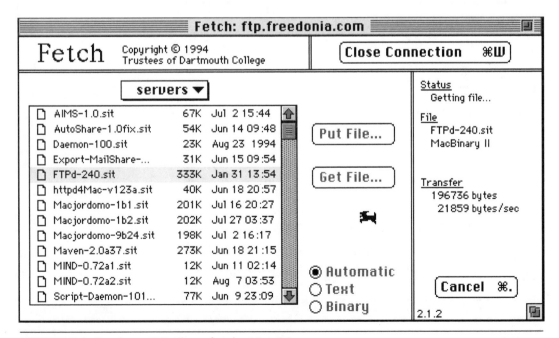

FIGURE 3.3 Fetch, an FTP Client for the Mac OS

Gopher

Gopher is a simple menu-based information service. Gopher clients present lists of items that can be downloaded and displayed (either within the client itself or with a helper application), as well as items that are links to other directories or servers. Figure 3.4 is a screen shot of TurboGopher, a Gopher client for the Mac OS.

The benefits of presenting information with Gopher are largely those of ease of use: the menu-driven interface of Gopher clients makes Gopher simple to use, and the absence of a specialized markup language or complex protocol makes Gopher sites fairly straightforward to set up and maintain. These benefits also become Gopher's drawbacks, however; since it doesn't have a standard formatting or markup language, and isn't able to handle multiple media types within one document, Gopher services are, by necessity, largely text-based. And Gopher's linking ability is limited to menu

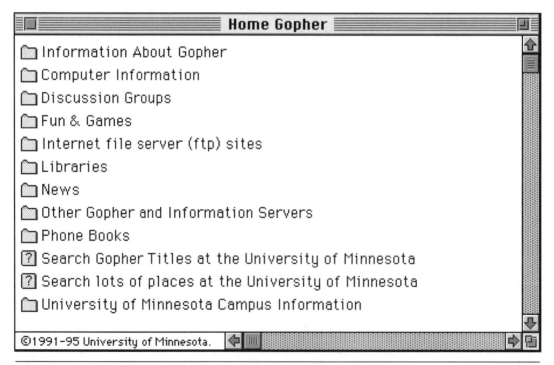

FIGURE 3.4 TurboGopher, a Gopher Client for the Mac OS

items; links from within documents that point to other documents aren't possible.

Although Gopher continues to be extended (Gopher+ includes forms support), and Gopher clients are being built with better integration between the Gopher client and other media players (such as the Adobe Acrobat reader), its appeal compared to Web-based services, described next, may be limited. At the same time, all Web browsers have the ability to access Gopher resources, and making existing documents available via Gopher may be the quickest or most economical way of placing your content on the Internet.

World Wide Web

Much like Gopher, the World Wide Web is a distributed information system, although many of the similarities end there. Most Web documents are written in Hypertext Markup Language, or HTML. HTML gives some page layout capabilities* to documents, including the inlining, or inclusion, of images, while making them available across a wide variety of platforms. HTML also makes it possible to place hypertext links anywhere within a document. The concept of hypertext has moved from the esoteric to the everyday in the past decade, but, to put it briefly, hypertext is text that is not constrained to be linear—text with links. Footnotes, which might provide additional information on a topic or refer to other texts on the same subject, are an example of hypertext in traditional media.

Outside of HTML, most Web browsers support a multitude of other formats, either directly within the browser itself or through the use of helper applications; in fact, almost any browser can be configured to use additional helper applications in a virtually seamless way. In addition, other description languages are being developed—such as Virtual Reality Markup Language, or VRML—for use on the Web, as well as client-side scripting languages for true distributed processing

---

* Of course, HTML theoretically describes *structure,* and not layout. In practice, however, those using HTML have cared a great deal about appearance and very little about the underlying structure. Such is life.

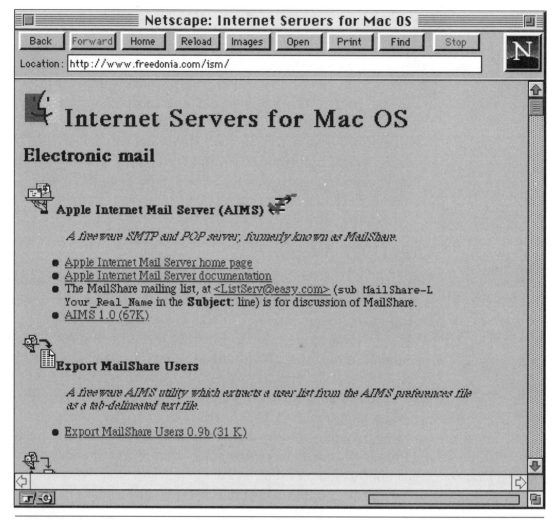

FIGURE 3.5 The Internet Services for the Mac OS page, shown in Netscape Navigator.

of multimedia applications, such as Sun's Java. Figure 3.5 shows the Internet Servers for the Mac OS page, which grew into this book, being displayed by Netscape Navigator for Mac OS.

Domain Name System

The Domain Name System, or DNS, resolves the names of computers—such as www.freedonia.com—into Internet Protocol, or IP addresses—such as 204.62.130.118. Every computer on the Internet is assigned an IP address, which computers use to locate other computers on the Internet. DNS is a naming scheme primarily intended for people to associate usually easy-to-remember names with almost always hard-to-remember numbers.

Depending upon your situation, it may not be necessary to run your own domain name server, however. In most cases, your Internet Service Provider (ISP) will provide DNS for you, and will usually perform such tasks as registering new domain names for a nominal fee. If your ISP is able to provide only primary or secondary service, but not both (DNS requires two servers per domain; see Chapter 9), or if your local network is large enough that local administration would be greatly simplified by running your own DNS, you may wish to run DNS under the Mac OS.

Miscellaneous Services

The miscellaneous services covered in this book—services not important or widespread enough to warrant their own chapters— are lumped together into a single chapter of this book. We cover Finger, Chat, Talk, and other services. See Chapter 10 for a description of each, to determine if any of these miscellaneous services might fill a particular need.

So, What's Missing?

News. At the time of this writing, there wasn't yet a news server available that ran under the Mac OS, although several companies have preannounced Mac OS-based servers. News is the online discussion forums available via Usenet, which is a network defined, suitably enough, as a collection of all the machines that carry and distribute news. (Though Usenet is largely congruous with the Internet, there are machines that are considered part of Usenet that aren't on the Internet.)

At the same time, news is a lot like DNS, in that, for most small organizations, news services (a "news feed") will be provided by the organization's Internet Service Provider.

Selecting the Proper Hardware for Your Services

Once you've selected the services you'd like to offer, you'll need to decide on the hardware needed to run them. Unfortunately, there's very little outside of anecdotal evidence as to what works and what doesn't.

The reason for this? The primary factor is that there are simply too many permutations of server applications, system configurations, network connections, and hardware platforms for anyone to measure it all.

The short answer is that any Mac shipping at the time this book is published—any machine running the Mac OS 7.5.x with Open Transport on a PowerPC CPU—will have ample horsepower to run all but the busiest of Internet sites. Unless you're in a university environment and hope to provide e-mail services for thousands of staff, faculty, and students, or you're providing some high-traffic resource on the Web in excess of 200,000 connections per day, you should have plenty of processing power to run your services. In almost all cases, a modern PowerPC-based machine running the Mac OS can handle the load.

Machines are often selected by different criteria from the above, however; the targeted machine is often that old Macintosh IIci that was replaced by a Power Mac a month back. So the question becomes, will that old Mac (IIci, or SE/30) be able to handle the load? Probably. Assuming the Mac in question has or supports the networking connection you need. And if it supports the latest system and network patches, and has a bare minimum of nonessential extensions, it can probably handle any number of server applications for low- and medium-traffic sites. And don't let "low- and medium-traffic" scare you; when we (don't) say *high*-traffic, we really do mean high traffic—usage that only a very small number of sites on the Internet actually see.

You will want to ensure that your hardware has adequate memory. You'll need enough real memory in which to run your Internet server applications comfortably; using virtual memory or RAM Doubler memory hurts performance and makes your server less reliable. Most of the server applications discussed here require about 1 megabyte of memory, with Common Gateway Interface (CGI) add-ons to Web services increasing that figure. Depending on the memory footprint of your system (which you can determine from the About This Macintosh menu item in the Apple menu), and the number of Internet server applications you hope to run, an 8-megabyte Mac may be fine, although a machine running the Mac OS with 12 or 16 megabytes of memory may be more appropriate.

It's unlikely you'll need to concern yourself with any of the subsystems of the Mac; as you can see from the theoretical maximum transfer rates in Table 3.1, even a very slow SCSI drive can outpace a T1 connection, which is considered a significant amount of bandwidth. Of course, more than the simple ability to saturate the link comes into play here: you'll also want to consider *latency,* or the amount of time between a user's request for a file and the server's response to that request. For applications like FTP or Gopher, this is seldom a real concern: the nature of the data returned—usually a single, large file—permits some latency without affecting the perceived speed of the server from the user's perspective. When multiple smaller files are retrieved to build a single document, however—as in Web documents using many inline graphics—seek times for a disk drive could, in theory, make a difference, although the amount of time MacTCP or Open Transport takes to set up the TCP/IP connection to answer each client request may be more significant. In most cases, drive speed simply shouldn't matter.

There are two steps you can take to help guarantee your hardware provides the most stable environment possible, described in the following subsections.

TABLE 3.1 Theoretical Maximum Transfer Rates

Approx. MB/sec	Medium
.018	14.4K modem (14.4 Kilobits/sec)
.036	28.8K modem (28.8 Kilobits/sec)
.07	56K leased line (56 Kilobits/sec)
.08	64K ISDN B-channel (64 Kilobits/sec)
.193	T1 (1.544 Megabits/sec)
1.25	Ethernet (10 Megabits/sec)
5	SCSI (5 Megabytes/sec)
5.593	T3 (44.746 Megabits/sec)
10	Fast SCSI (10 Megabytes/sec)
40	Fast & Wide SCSI (40 Megabytes/sec)

Use a Dedicated Machine

Although you can run server applications in the background of a machine that is running, say, PhotoShop in the foreground, that doesn't really give an environment robust enough for providing an Internet service, both in terms of stability and speed.

Also, the architecture of the current Mac OS is, frankly, far from ideal for running multiple applications providing Internet services.* Whatever application is in the foreground gets significantly more processing time than any other process running on the machine; until the release of a Mac OS with preemptive (versus cooperative) multitasking, you'll want to keep the server application in which speed matters most to you (usually, your Web server) in the foreground.

---

* Not that any desktop OS provides a better environment for server-type applications. The only desktop OS that claims to support preemptive multitasking and protected memory is Windows 95, but at the core of the newest version of Windows is 16-bit, nonprotected, nonmultitasking code.

Run the Latest System and Network Software and a Minimum of Nonessential Extensions.

Running the latest versions of your operating system should be obvious: as Apple fixes bugs and increases reliability and performance, you'll want to take advantage of these improvements. Installing a minimum of nonessential extensions should be fairly obvious, as well. Most extensions will add load to your system, slowing it down, and introduce additional layers of complexity, making your system less stable.

Multiple Servers

You can also take advantage of multiple machines serving the same content, if you use a round-robin domain name server, which will point first to one machine, then to another, for the same host name. For example, you can set up two machines as Web servers, both housing the same content with the same directory structure, named www1.freedonia.com and www2.freedonia.com, respectively. You can then configure your DNS to point first to www1.freedonia.com, and then to www2.freedonia.com, in turn, when clients request www.freedonia.com, effectively splitting the load between the two machines. The problem with this scheme? At the time of this writing, the software needed in order to mirror—or copy—the content of one server from another is still under development. Also, when using multiple machines to provide a single service, you'll need to deal with such issues as synchronization of user-submitted data, although this is often handled by making only one machine responsible for data processing and data storage.

## CHAPTER 4

Electronic Mail

Electronic mail is one of the most basic services provided via computers on a network. Being one of the most basic services makes it all that much more essential; however, e-mail is usually taken for granted by users until it doesn't work, at which time you'll certainly be notified immediately that there's something amiss—if the person having trouble can find your phone number. Luckily, setting up and maintaining mail services under the Mac OS can be fairly trivial, compared to doing the same under UNIX.

Typical uses for mail are for person-to-person communications and for facilitation of groupwork activities, through the delivery of messages to multiple recipients—a *mailing list*—and through the exchange of data files through the use of e-mail *attachments*. Small mailing lists can be created from within the software of individual users, but larger lists are best administered using specialized mailing list software, covered in the next chapter. By the same logic, although smaller data files can be transferred through e-mail attachments, larger files are best transferred using the File Transfer Protocol (see Chapter 6).

Mail User Agents and Mail Transport Agents

For those who deal with the vagaries of e-mail on a regular basis, an e-mail client is known as a *mail user agent,* or MUA, while an e-mail server is known as a *mail transport agent,* or MTA. While this undoubtedly shows a predilication for TLAs, or three letter acronyms, among the UNIX administrators and programmers who designed the Internet mail transport system as it exists today, it also makes the probably already obvious point that mail servers simply *transport* messages generated by other software.

A mail client, or mail user agent, then, allows users to compose, send, receive, and read electronic mail, as well as delete and file sent and received messages. See the upcoming section, Mac OS Mail Clients, for a brief description of some mail clients available for the Mac OS. A mail server, or mail transport agent, on the other hand, handles the delivery of mail to mail clients and the routing of mail between different servers.

The standard protocols that mail servers and mail clients use are the Simple Mail Transfer Protocol, or SMTP, and the Post Office Protocol, or POP. There exist many e-mail systems for local networks, such as QuickMail or Microsoft Mail, which use different, proprietary protocols, which can then be *gatewayed* in order to exchange information with servers that use the standards: see the upcoming section, Mail Gateways, for a short discussion.

SMTP: Simple Mail Transfer Protocol

Simple Mail Transfer Protocol, or SMTP, is an Internet standard designed to deliver electronic mail reliably and efficiently. SMTP works something like the postal service: an e-mail message is sent from a user's mail client to your mail server, which then forwards the message on to the addressee's mail server or to an intermediary host, taking any number of hops to reach the destination mail host. Once there, the destination server then delivers the message to its addressee.

When clients connect to your mail server, they speak SMTP to transfer their messages. Why, then, don't they just deliver the messages directly to the destination address? One reason will soon become apparent as you browse through your mail server log. Often, mail servers aren't as reliable as they should be; a server might not be available when the user sends his or her message. Your server, on the other hand, can repeatedly try to deliver a message at a specified interval for a specified number of days. Also, it's a lot quicker for the client to deliver all its outgoing mail to one place; it would take more time for the client to negotiate a connection to each destination address.

Finally, you can set up your server to send mail through a gateway mail host, in order to deliver mail to hosts to which, for one reason or another, your server can't directly connect.

SMTP assumes a full-time connection: there are no provisions within SMTP itself to deliver mail only at certain times—say, when a dial-up connection is up.

POP: Post Office Protocol

POP, or Post Office Protocol, is another Internet standard, designed to allow computers that may not be connected to the Internet at all times to receive mail via a *maildrop*, in a fashion similar to a box at a post office.

A POP server accepts mail for a user via SMTP, and then waits for the user to connect to the server with a POP client to transfer his or her mail from the server to his or her computer. Normally, the mail is deleted from the server after it's delivered to the client, but some clients allow the user to keep mail on the server. This can be useful in the case of someone who checks e-mail from more than one place; for example, when a user checks mail from home in the evening, the mail can be left on the server so that it can also be downloaded to ther user's work machine when he or she returns to work the next day (and only then is the mail deleted from the server)—so that all the mail can be stored in one place. Generally, however, mail stored on the server is there only for a short period of time, and server hard drive space can be planned accordingly. A good rule of thumb is 2 megabytes of hard drive space per user.

However, there will always be those users who don't check their mail or are on vacation. See the section on size limits later in this chapter for information on setting quotas for user accounts.

Mail Routing and the Domain System

The Domain Name System (DNS) is a naming scheme for dotted decimal Internet Protocol (IP) addresses. Every computer on the Internet has an IP address assigned to it; every domain name refers to an IP address.

When you send an e-mail message, you send it to a user at a host, which is usually expressed as a domain name: for example, a message addressed to *carl@hail.freedonia.com* is destined for the user carl at the host with a name of hail.freedonia.com. When a mail server attempts to deliver the message, however, it first needs to look up, or resolve, the domain name into the host's IP address. For example, the host hail.freedonia.com might have an IP address of 204.62.130.118. The Domain Name System calls the records that associate host names to IP addresses Address, or A, records.

However, because multiple hosts may share the same mail server—that is, because not all hosts can accept mail—the Domain Name System has a type of intermediary record to sit in front of the A records that resolve host names into IP addresses. These records are called *mail exchanger,* or MX, records. An MX record for a domain name provides the name of a host that, by prior arrangement, will accept mail for that domain. MX records can point to the same domain as the one queried—the domain name hail.freedonia.com might have an MX record which points to the host hail.freedonia.com—or to any other host that can accept mail for that domain (hail.freedonia.com could instead have MX records that point to mail.freedonia.com or mailhost.intertext.com).

In fact, it's possible for there to be multiple MX records for a given domain name, in which case the priority number assigned to each

MX record is referred to. The record with the lowest number is tried first, and then the next lowest, and so on, until a host is found that is able to accept mail for the domain in question.

It's also common for MX records to exist for domain names that don't represent an actual host on the Internet. While there may be no machine that is known as freedonia.com for other services— freedonia.com may have no A record—it's possible to have an MX record that points from freedonia.com to hail.freedonia.com.

Once a mail server's domain name resolver finds an MX record for the domain name it's attempting to deliver mail to, it then tries to retrieve the A record for that domain name. For example, a mail server, delivering a message to *carl@freedonia.com*, might first send a query to a domain name resolver for an MX record for freedonia.com, to which it might receive the answer hail.freedonia.com. It then needs to query for the A record of *hail.freedonia.com*, which might give the answer 204.62.130.118. Only then does the server have the necessary information to attempt to contact the recipient's mail host.

Some host names don't have MX records associated with them. For those hosts, a mail server would simply use the host's A record.

There's yet one more thing to be aware of with domain names and mail servers: a properly behaved server won't accept mail for a domain for which it hasn't been specifically instructed to receive mail. That means, for example, that even if you or your service provider creates an MX record to point mail addressed to freedonia.com to a host hail.freedonia.com, the server running on hail.freedonia.com needs to know that it should also accept mail addressed to freedonia.com, not just hail.freedonia.com.

Finally, some of the preceding examples of domain name resolution have been simplified; a resolver might request all the records for a given host at one time, versus doing separate queries for each record type. Refer to Chapter 9, DNS, for further discussion of the Domain Name System.

Apple Internet Mail Server

Apple Internet Mail Server, or AIMS, formerly known as MailShare, is an SMTP and POP server for the Mac OS from Apple Computer. AIMS also supports a password server, and includes NotifyMail support, both of which can be taken advantage of by Eudora, a Macintosh and Windows mail client. See the Mail Clients section for more information.

AIMS requires a Mac Plus or higher. AIMS also requires System 7.0 or later, and MacTCP 1.1.1 or later, although System 7.0.1 or later and MacTCP 2.0.4 or later are highly recommended. Network Software Installer 1.5 or later should also be installed. AIMS 1.0 is freeware.

Configuring Connections: Preferences

To begin using AIMS, you'll first want to be aware of the options available in the Preferences window, available from the Preferences item in the Server menu; see Figure 4.1. Any changes you make in Preferences don't take effect until you quit and restart AIMS.

Maximum Number of Connections

For each different service AIMS offers, you can specify an upper limit on the number of simultaneous connections allowed. For larger sites, you may need to increase the default maximum number of connections. If you don't want to allow a service, such as the Password Server (which allows a user with a client with password server support, such as Eudora, to change his or her password), you can set the maximum number of connections to zero.

The maximum number of outgoing SMTP connections is set in the Outgoing SMTP connections box. The default is 2. If you see your outgoing mail queue (see Outgoing Mail, page 58) with more than a few messages in it often, you can increase the number of Outgoing SMTP connections.

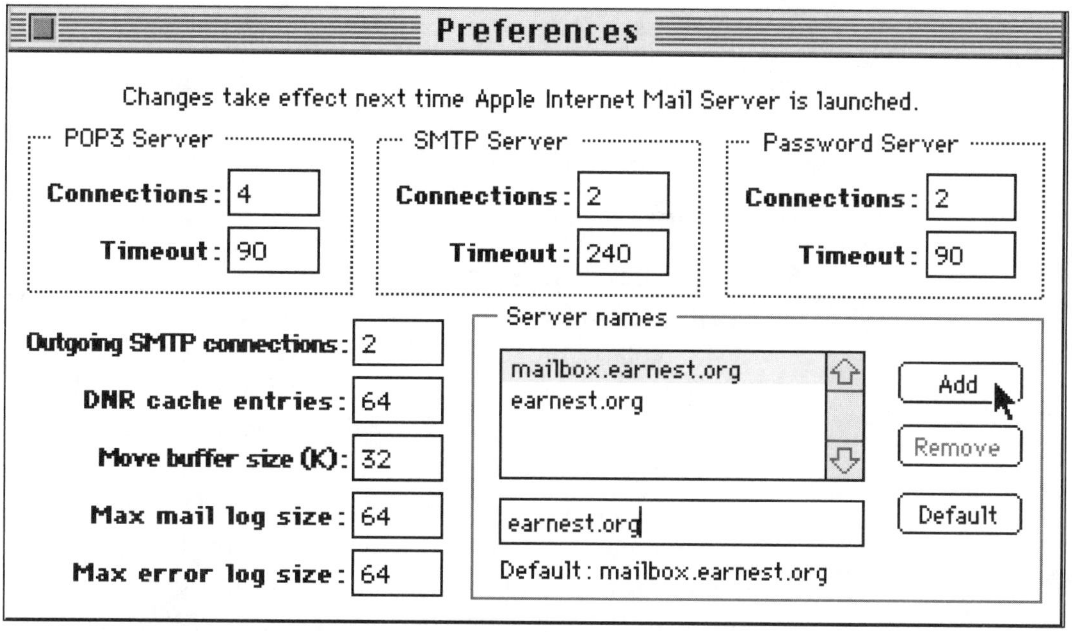

FIGURE 4.1 AIMS Preferences

If you're using MacTCP and not Open Transport as your TCP stack, remember MacTCP's upper limit of 64 connections, which all the TCP/IP applications on your server must share.

In addition to the connections you configure for POP, Password, and incoming and outgoing SMTP, AIMS uses a single connection for domain name resolution, and a second connection for sending NotifyMail (Finger) requests. See the MacTCP section (page 21) in Chapter 2, Connecting to the Internet, for more details on the 64-connection limit.

You may need to increase the amount of memory you allocate to AIMS as you increase the number of allowed connections. You can do this by quitting AIMS and adjusting the Preferred size: value in the Memory Requirements section of the application's Get Info box, as with any other application.

Timeout Values

Timeouts are measured in seconds, and may need to be increased if your users are on slow links, such as dial-up SLIP lines. In most cases, however, the default values should be fine.

Other Settings

- **DNR cache entries** specifies the number of entries to cache for AIMS's built-in Domain Name Resolver, which, for AIMS, replaces the resolver found in MacTCP or Open Transport. See the previous section, Mail Routing and the Domain System, for a brief overview of name resolution. AIMS keeps a cache of the lookups it has performed in order to increase performance and reduce load on your domain name server. By default, AIMS remembers the last 64 lookups, which should be appropriate for most sites. Each entry requires about 280 bytes of memory. AIMS's resolver does *not* consult a hosts file, if you have one.

- **Move buffer size** is the size, in K, of the memory buffer for moving messages internally within AIMS. If your users send many large messages (which you can monitor from the mail log; see The Mail Log, page 59), you may be able to improve perfomance by increasing this value.

- **Max mail log size** and **Max error log size** specify the file size, in K, of the mail and error logs, found in the Preferences folder of your System Folder as Internet Mail Server error log and Internet Mail Server mail log. When the file sizes of these logs reach the maximum size you give here, they are reduced by half. If you choose to write analysis tools for the logs, instead of using AIMS's scrolling windows for manual analysis, you may want to make these numbers arbitrarily large, and periodically rename and archive logs by date. Note that performance degrades as the logs become very large.

- **Date and Time Settings.** AIMS gets its date, time, and time zone settings from the Control Panels settings on your machine. To set the time zone, use the Map control panel to find your city, or change the value directly. Date and time are set from the Date & Time control panel (in pre-System 7.5 systems, from the General Controls control panel).

Server Names

AIMS does a reverse domain name lookup for the machine it runs on when it's first launched; it uses this value as the default server name. In Figure 4.1, although mailbox.earnest.org is the default server name, so that the server will accept mail in the form *user@mailbox.earnest.org,* we also want the server to accept mail addressed to *user@earnest.org.* To do so, we can type *earnest.org* in the lower input box and click the Add box to add it as a name for this host. Note that this tells the server to *accept* mail only for the given address; the domain name system needs to be aware of your machine's names in order to route the incoming messages to your server. See the previous section, Mail Routing and the Domain System, for more information.

AIMS will identify itself to other hosts using the default name, which you can set by highlighting a name, and then clicking the Default button.

Providing Mail Service for Multiple Domains

By adding multiple server names, you may provide mail service for multiple domains, provided, once again, that the Domain Name System is aware of your machine's names in order to route the incoming messages to your server.

You should be aware that AIMS's user name space remains global across domains; any accounts you create for one domain are equally valid for another served by the same copy of AIMS. For example, if you configure AIMS to accept mail for both foo.com and bar.com, the e-mail addresses *jdoe@foo.com* and *jdoe@bar.com* are equivalent, and delivered to the single account, jdoe. The user jdoe and her correspondants may use either address, although jdoe, if she belongs to the organization foo.com, may not even know about the organization bar.com being served by the same host. You may not run multiple copies of AIMS on the same host in order to avoid accounts sharing this global name space.

Unlike the default configuration of sendmail, the most common UNIX-based mail transport agent, AIMS does no rewrites of the From: or Reply-to: message headers based on the default domain for outgoing mail. From: and Reply-to: message headers are passed to a message's recipient(s) as written by the user's mailer.

Account Administration: Account Information

Account administration is performed from the Account Information item in the Server menu (see Figure 4.2).

<any-name> and Postmaster Accounts

You'll notice, when you first run AIMS, that you're given two default accounts: <any-name> and Postmaster. Postmaster is the server's

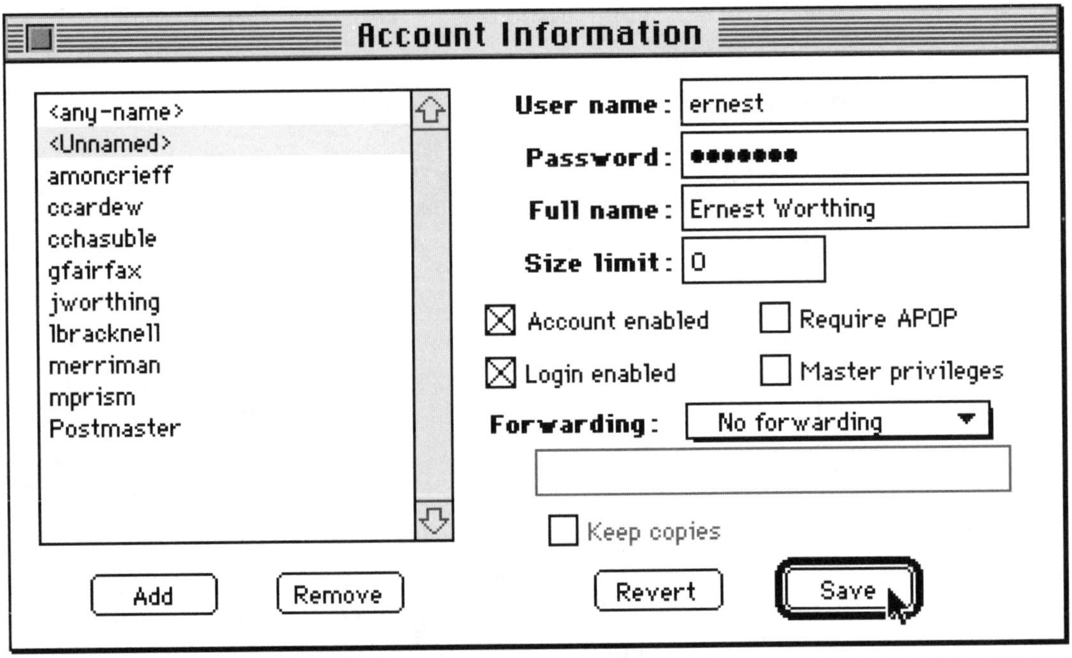

FIGURE 4.2 AIMS Account Information

most important account. It receives mail delivery failure messages from the server, and, most important, users' problems and complaints. The Postmaster account is required for all mail hosts. It's vital that someone regularly read the mail sent to Postmaster, either by checking mail under that account name, or forwarding mail to a user's account (see Forwarding Options, page 53).

<any-name> will accept mail for any account not defined in your user list. It's probably most useful to smaller, commercial sites that don't want to lose contacts due to misaddressed mail. Like the Postmaster account, you can forward the mail for <any-name> to another account in order to monitor it.

Postmaster is an example of an account that represents a function, rather than an individual. Consider setting up other accounts along functional units within your organization, which can then be forwarded to the appropriate individuals; for example, you might want to set up an account called editor, for which the e-mail address, *editor@myorg.org*, is placed on the masthead of your company's newsletter. This not only eases administration when an individual leaves your organization, it's also useful during short-term absences. When your editor is on vacation, for instance, you can forward the mail sent to *editor@myorg.org* to an appropriate staff member, while allowing mail of a more personal nature addressed to your editor to collect until his or her return.

Adding User Accounts

Account Names. To add a user, click on the Add button and supply a user name in the User name box. User names should contain no spaces or special characters, and are not case-sensitive. Smaller sites might allow each user to select a user name of his or her choice; larger sites might want to consider a more formalized naming scheme, such as using the user's first initial followed by his or her last name, to keep administration simpler. Also, on some UNIX systems, account names are limited to eight characters (although a longer alias can be created for the account); you may want to keep such a limit in mind if it's possible you may someday migrate to a UNIX system.

Passwords. You'll next want to assign your user a password. Some good rules for password creation are:

- Passwords should be at least six characters.
- Passwords shouldn't be either all letters or all numbers.
- Passwords should not be based on the user name spelled forward, backward, or any other way.
- Passwords should not based on known facts about a user, such as a birthdate or pet's name.
- Passwords should not be words that can be found in a dictionary, even a foreign dictionary, spelled backward or forward. Also, they should not be a word found in a dictionary with a number appended or prepended to it.
- Passwords should not be catch phrases from popular television shows or films.

Passwords should be changed periodically by either the mail administrator or by users using the Password server, and all users should be assigned a password.

Full Name. The next field to fill in is the Full name of the account. This is primarily to aid administration and ease record keeping. Specify the user's full name or the purpose of the account.

Size Limits. You can impose a Size limit on users. This can be useful in keeping a user's mail from filling your hard drive while he or she is away on vacation, or if the user has subscribed to several high-traffic mailing lists and fails to check mail for more than a few days. It can also prevent accounts from receiving excessively large messages that could cause clients to timeout during receipt, especially over a slow link. If an incoming message for the account exceeds the size limit, the message is permanently rejected. If an incoming message exceeds the amount of space left in an account (for example, an incoming message is 20 K for an account that has a 100 K limit, but currently only has 10 K free), it is only temporarily rejected. This number is in K; 0, the default, sets no size limit.

Account Options. You can then enable or disable several options:

■ **Account enabled** should normally be checked. If the box is unchecked, mail for the account will be rejected by the server (except when <any-name> is enabled: see the previous section), unless forwarding is enabled. This option does not affect forwarding.

■ **Login enabled** should be checked if you wish the user to be able to log in with a POP client to check mail. You might uncheck this box for accounts that have one of the forwarding options selected to reduce the number of passwords you need to monitor.

■ **Require APOP.** The POP protocol normally uses cleartext passwords, which can be a security risk. When this box is checked, POP sessions are authorized through an encryption scheme. If you do check this box, make sure your user's client supports APOP. (Eudora and Claris Emailer—see Mail Clients, page 63—include APOP support.)

■ **Master privileges** allows a user to connect to the server and perform remote administration with a planned remote administration package, which isn't yet available. Check this only if you plan on performing remote administration with this account.

Forwarding Options. Finally, you have several forwarding options, as shown in Figure 4.3.

■ **No forwarding** is the default. It allows the normal action of spooling incoming messages to a maildrop, which the user then checks with a POP client.

■ **Forward to . . .** allows incoming messages to be forwarded to another e-mail account. For accounts on the same mail server, you need only supply the account name—that is, for a server mailbox.earnest.org, you can simply forward to an account gfairfax; you don't need to type the entire *gfairfax@mailbox.earnest.org*. Beware of forwarding loops, in which a message is forwarded from account A to account

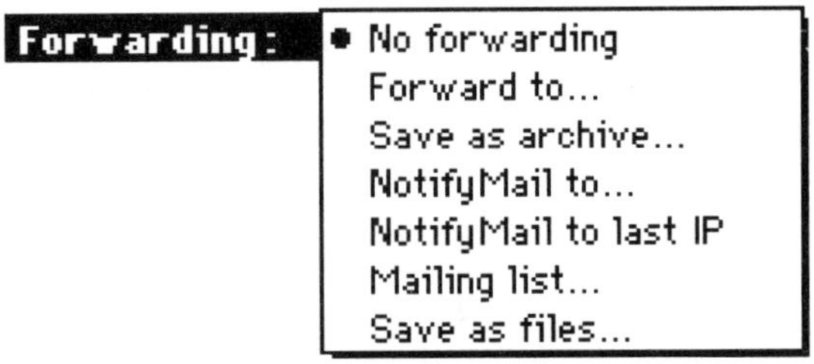

FIGURE 4.3
AIMS Forwarding
Options

```
Forwarding:   • No forwarding
                Forward to...
                Save as archive...
                NotifyMail to...
                NotifyMail to last IP
                Mailing list...
                Save as files...
```

B, which in turns forwards the mail back to account A. However, it is perfectly acceptable to forward from account A to account B, which in turn forwards to account C. Always verify that forwarding works as expected after a change.

- **Save as archive . . .** saves mail into a text file in BSD UNIX Mail format. This is the same format Eudora uses to store its mail, so that if you place an archive into the Eudora Folder in the System Folder of a machine that has Eudora installed, the next time Eudora is launched it should recognize the archive as an additional mailbox. You need to provide a destination filename: if you supply only a filename, the file will be saved in the same folder as the AIMS application. Alternatively, you can provide a full pathname; for a file called archive in the folder Folder of a hard drive Macintosh HD, you would type Macintosh HD:Folder:archive. If you check the Keep Copies box, mail will also be spooled to the POP maildrop, in addition to the archive.

- **NotifyMail to . . .** NotifyMail is a Macintosh extension that listens for a finger request, and, when it receives one, sends an AppleEvent to Eudora to check a user's mail. This option tells AIMS to send NotifyMail a finger request. You can either specify an IP address for the user's machine or the fully qualified domain name. For more information, see Mail Clients, page 63.

- **NotifyMail to last IP** is similar to NotifyMail to..., except that it sends the finger request to the last IP address from which a user checked his or her mail. This is useful for mobile users, and can also simplify administration, since you no longer need to track machine names or IP addresses. If you select this option, NotifyMail should be configured on the user's machine to check mail upon startup, so AIMS can record an initial IP address.

■ **Mailing list . . .** can be used to implement a simple mailing list in which a message sent to a single address is redistributed to multiple recipients. A mailing list is a plain text file, with one address per line in the format *user@host (optional comment)*. If you supply only a filename, the mailing list file is assumed to be in the Mail Folder in the System Folder. You can also provide a full pathname. This is a sample mailing list file:

```
ernest (Ernest)
amoncrieff (Algernon Moncrieff)
dgray@portrait.edu (Dorian Gray)
carl@freedonia.com (Carl Steadman)
```

Note that the addresses ernest and amoncrieff are local, and the full e-mail addresses, **ernest@mailbox.earnest.org** and **amoncrieff@mailbox.earnest.org**, don't need to be supplied.

■ **Save as files . . .** will spool the mail messages to a specified folder as separate text files, with line feeds removed. You should not include a trailing colon in your pathname— despite what you may think, this won't work. If no folder is given, AIMS will save the files in the same folder as the AIMS application. You can use Save as files... in conjunction with a utility or script in order to extend the capabilities of AIMS. If you check the Keep Copies box, mail will also be spooled to the POP maildrop. Save the account information by clicking on the Save button when you're done setting up the account. You can click on the Revert button to put the settings back to the way they were before you made any changes.

Removing User Accounts

To delete an account, highlight it in the scrolling account list, then click on the Remove button, and click OK when you're asked if you're sure. You can't remove the Postmaster and <any-name> accounts, although you can disable the <any-name> account by unchecking Account Enabled.

Delivering Mail via Other Hosts: Sending Setup

Routing via Other Hosts

You can use the Sending setup window, shown in Figure 4.4, to remap the domain information of outgoing messages. Most sites do not need to add any information to the Setting setup window, except, perhaps, the expiry value (described shortly) for the default domain.

One possible use of Sending setup is to handle BITNET addresses, which end in .BITNET—for example, *LISTSERV@JHUVM.BITNET*. Many LISTSERV addresses are still distributed in this format, although most machines with BITNET addresses have alternate, preferred Internet addresses as well. The use of *.BITNET domains is actively discouraged; however, a user may have a BITNET address and may not be aware of the Internet equivalent—or, more likely,

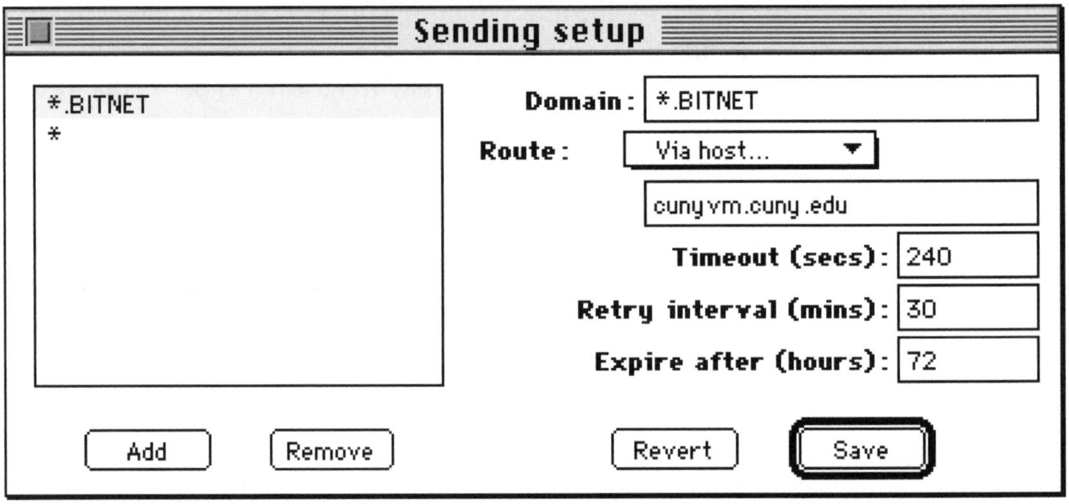

FIGURE 4.4 AIMS Sending Setup

simply doesn't want to know about the distinction between Internet and BITNET addresses, and just wants to send his or her mail. For these cases, you can set up a rule to reroute addresses that end in .BITNET. In Figure 4.4, we've asked AIMS to match any address that ends in .BITNET by first using the wildcard *, which will match any domain information, followed by .BITNET. We can then select to Route Via host, and specify a mail server that is connected to both the Internet and BITNET. In the example, the host cunyvm.cuny.edu has been given, but there's probably a more appropriate local host for you to route BITNET addresses to.

To configure AIMS as a simple mail relay, so that all mail is forwarded to another machine for actual delivery, you can route to another host for the * domain, which will match anything. For example, if all outgoing mail needed to go through a host relay.earnest.org, you could specify Route Via host, and enter relay.earnest.org.

You can also save the messages that match a particular rule with the Save as files... option from the Route popup menu. You might want to do this if you plan to use a batch script to deliver all the queued mail for a specific destination at a particular time of day, and if you have limited Internet connectivity.

Domains are checked down the list until a match is made. You can drag domains in order to change their order; * should usually be last in the list, as it will match any domain.

Timeouts, Retry Intervals, and Message Expiry

For each domain, including *, you can set a Timeout, a Retry interval, and the time in hours a message will Expire, or bounce, because delivery wasn't possible. You can set these values to shorter or longer intervals based on the known availability and reliability of the delivery routes being taken. Also, depending on the expectations of your users, you may want to set the expiry value to something other than 72 hours. In some organizations, a wait of three days before knowing that an e-mail can't be delivered may be too long, especially if critical communications take place via e-mail. In most cases, three days should be appropriate, however.

Monitoring AIMS: Outgoing Mail and Logs

AIMS includes several windows with which to monitor its programs, including the Outgoing Mail window, the Mail Log, the Error Log, the Connection Statistics window, and the Debug window.

The Mail Queue: Outgoing Mail

Outgoing mail shows the queue of all outgoing messages for AIMS. You'll want to monitor this queue, especially if you have the expiry for messages for the default domain (assigned in the Sending setup window) set to a high value, to catch problems with routing or your Internet connectivity before they begin to produce bounced messages.

The Outgoing mail window is made up of four fields, as shown in Figure 4.5: To, or the destination address of the message, the Size in bytes of the message, the message's Date arrived, and the Next try for delivery. For any highlighted message, you can select three options from the Message menu: Send now, Delete, and Forward to.... Send now will attempt to deliver the message immediately, regardless of the time set for the next try. Delete will delete a message from the queue; Forward to... will forward it to another

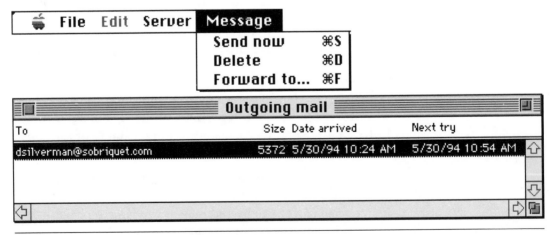

FIGURE 4.5 AIMS Outgoing Mail Window

address, with the options to continue to attempt delivery or to remove the message from the queue. Remember to be considerate when using the Delete and Forward to... options; don't arbitrarily delete or forward mail without informing users of your actions.

The Mail Log

The Mail log records all incoming and outgoing mail from AIMS. Its window is made up of six fields (only the first four are shown in Figure 4.6): Address, Size, Kind, Date, Message ID, and Internet address. These are all fairly self-explanatory.

All messages use at least two lines in the Mail log: one with a Kind of from, listing the originating address and the Date the message arrived at your server, and a to line, listing the destination address. Messages with multiple recipients can have multiple to lines.

Messages destined for a different host use an additional line, with a Kind of sent. You won't always see a sent immediately after a from/to pair, because sometimes immediate delivery isn't possible. Messages that can't be sent should be recorded in the error log.

The mail log is stored as a plain text file in the Preferences folder of your System Folder as Internet Mail Server mail log, and its size is limited by the maximum size specified in Configuring Connections: Preferences, discussed previously.

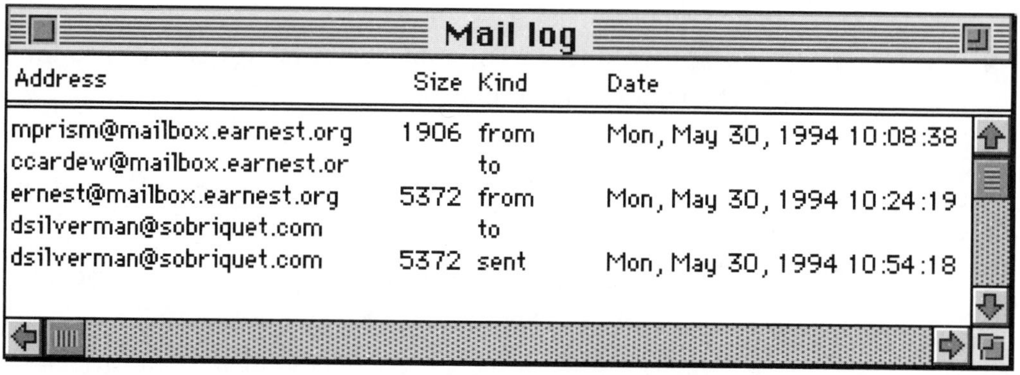

Mail log			
Address	Size	Kind	Date
mprism@mailbox.earnest.org	1906	from	Mon, May 30, 1994 10:08:38
ccardew@mailbox.earnest.or		to	
ernest@mailbox.earnest.org	5372	from	Mon, May 30, 1994 10:24:19
dsilverman@sobriquet.com		to	
dsilverman@sobriquet.com	5372	sent	Mon, May 30, 1994 10:54:18

FIGURE 4.6 AIMS Mail Log

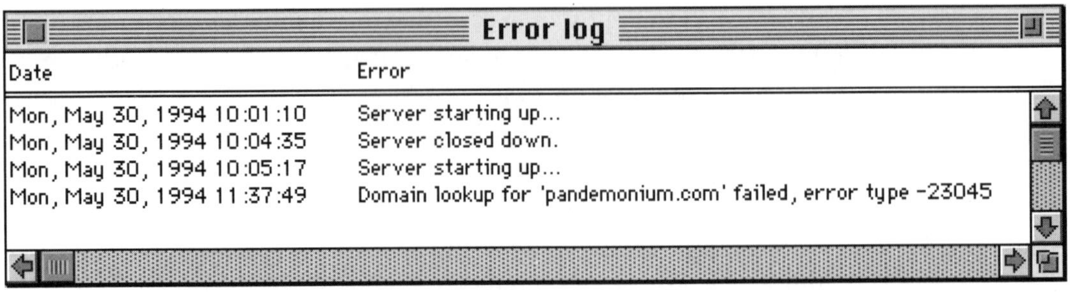

FIGURE 4.7 AIMS Error Log

The Error Log

The Error log records all errors AIMS encounters, and, because of this, you'll probably consult it more than any other log. Its window, shown in Figure 4.7, is made up of two fields: the Date on which the error occurred, and the Error message. Error messages you might encounter include:

■ Connection timed out to <IP address> (<domain name>).

■ Domain lookup for <domain name> failed:

  -23044: noNameServer: No name server answered the query or no name servers configured.

  -23045: authNameErr: The name does not exist.

  -23046: noAnsErr: No answers were returned that could be fully resolved.

  -23047: dnrErr: The name server being queried encountered an unexpected problem.

    1: rcodeFormatErr: Query formatting error.

    2: rcodeServerFailure: The name server has a problem processing the query.

    4: rcodeRefused: The query was refused for some security or policy reason.

  -23049: authNoAnsErr: Type does not exist for this name.

■ Error opening TCP stack.

- File/Mailing list error:

  -33: Disk full.

  -35: No such volume.

  -36: I/O error (something is probably wrong with your hard drive).

  -43: File not found.

  -49: The file is open in another application.

  -50: Parameter error.

  -120: Directory not found.

  -5025: The file specified is a directory.

- Server closed down: Lists the date and time when AIMS is quit. This isn't really an error, but it appears in the Error log.

- Server starting up...: Lists the date and time when AIMS is launched. This isn't really an error, but it appears in the Error log.

The Error log is stored as a plain text file in the Preferences folder of your System Folder as Internet Mail Server error log, and its size is limited by the maximum size specified in Configuring Connections: Preferences, discussed previously.

Connection Statistics

The Connection Statistics window, shown in Figure 4.8, gives both the current number of connections, and the maximum number of simultaneous connections for each service that AIMS offers. If the maximum number for any service is equal to the maximum number of allowed connections you've specified (see Configuring Connections: Preferences, page 46), you should consider increasing the value.

The Debug Window

The Debug window records detailed information on all the transactions AIMS performs. It has no scroll bar, and much of the information is logged in clearer form in the Outgoing, Mail, and Error logs,

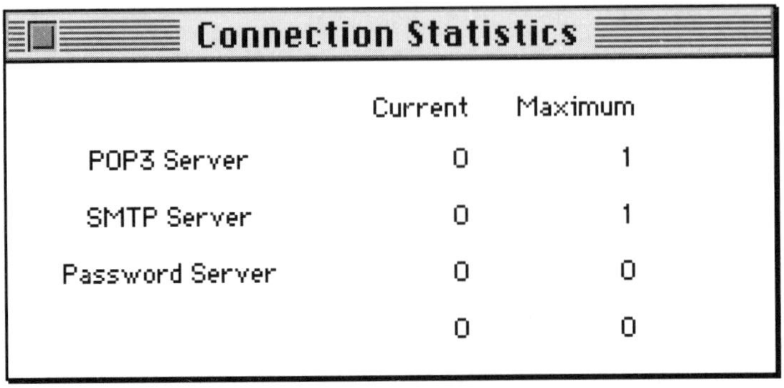

Connection Statistics

	Current	Maximum
POP3 Server	0	1
SMTP Server	0	1
Password Server	0	0
	0	0

FIGURE 4.8 AIMS Connection Statistics

but it's useful in order to both check the current status of AIMS and monitor problems as they occur.

You can save the debug information to a log file for later analysis by enabling Capture to File in the Debug window. This enables capture only for the current session; that is, if you quit and relaunch AIMS, the Capture to File option will default to off.

Mail Gateways

There are several mail gateway products available to gateway mail from proprietary systems to standard POP or SMTP format.

HoloGate is a commercial package from Information Access Technologies that can be used to gateway mail between SMTP, UUCP, First Class, Microsoft Mail, NovaLink, QuickMail, and SnapMail.

Mail*Link is a commercial gateway between SMTP and QuickMail, PowerShare, or Microsoft Mail, from Apple Computer.

MailConnect is a shareware PowerTalk/POP gateway from JBert.

PT/Internet is a commercial package from Apple Computer that can be used to gateway mail between a POP server and a PowerTalk mailbox.

AIMS Localtalk Bridge is a shareware AIMS utility by Chris Owens that provides a bridge between AIMS and Eudora clients in UUCP mode over LocalTalk, and includes a notification utility.

Mail Clients

This is a short list of mail clients for the Mac OS. AIMS, of course, can interact with a POP3-compatible client regardless of the platform it runs on; note that Eudora runs under both the Macintosh OS and Windows.

Eudora is a POP3-compatible Macintosh and Windows e-mail client by Steve Dorner of Qualcomm, Inc., and includes APOP support. Eudora also provides client support for Password, Ph, and Finger servers. It is a powerful, easy-to-use package, and is highly recommended. Eudora also provides MIME support, for dealing with character sets other than ISO Latin-1. Eudora for the Macintosh requires System 7.0 or later (an earlier version that will run under System 6.0.7 or later is available); Eudora for Windows requires Windows 3.1 or later. Both freeware and commercial packages are available.

POPmail is a POP3-compatible Macintosh e-mail client with an icon-driven interface, written by Dave Johnson and others at the University of Minnesota. It requires System 6.0.7 or later and MacTCP 1.1 or later. POPmail is freeware.

Claris **Emailer** is a POP3-compatible Macintosh e-mail client that can also check mail on several commercial online services, including America Online and CompuServe. The package can also be set up to deliver auto-reply messages, such as a vacation notice. (See Chapter 5.) Claris Emailer is commercial software.

NotifyMail is a Macintosh system extension by Scott Gruby that listens for a Finger request. When it receives one, it sends an AppleEvent to Eudora (or any other scriptable mail package) to check the user's mail. It can also be configured to run any application upon notification, and has an optional mail indicator/counter. It requires System 7.0 or later and MacTCP 1.1 or later, and is shareware.

## CHAPTER 5

Mail-Based Services

Mailing Lists and Other Mail Services

When people think of discussion groups on the Internet, they usually think of Usenet newsgroups, the large-scale discussion areas where everyone and their dogs can (and usually do) post messages on a variety of topics, both relevant and irrelevant.

Usenet newsgroups are quite popular, of course—but when it comes to creation of close-knit virtual communities, the place to go isn't a newsgroup like talk.politics or rec.arts.tv. It's a mailing list—usually a group of Internet users, ranging in size from a handful of people to several hundred or even a few thousand, covering highly focused topics by sending e-mail to one another through a central mail server.

While many mailing lists are discussion-oriented, they can also be one-way distribution channels. A mailing list's moderator can send out periodic information postings, press releases, or even e-mail-based magazines to a targeted readership via a mailing list. (One of the largest mailing lists on the Internet is of this type: the administrators of the Top Ten mailing list send out David Letterman's Top Ten List nightly after his television show is broadcast. At last count, well over 30,000 people were on that mailing list.[*])

---

[*]To subscribe, send an e-mail message to *listserv@clark.net* with "SUBSCRIBE TOP-TEN *your name*" as the first line in the body of your message.

Unlike Usenet newsgroups, on a mailing list, not just *anyone* can receive your messages—only the people whose e-mail addresses appear on your list. In that way, Usenet newsgroups are like television or radio (anyone with news-reading software can "tune in" and read postings), while mailing lists are a lot more like newspaper or magazine subscriptions.

In addition to being a medium that can foster small-group communication or wide-scale message distribution, e-mail can also be used to perform automated information exchanges. A *mailbot,* a comparatively recent Internet phenomenon, is any system that's designed to reply to incoming e-mail messages by itself, providing an information system that can be accessed by *anyone* with Internet e-mail access and that doesn't require the presence of a human being to process each incoming request.

Non-Mac List Servers on the Internet

While Internet mailing lists have been around for a long time, none of the Mac-based list software described in this chapter existed before early 1995. Until now, Internet users have needed to rely on powerful workstation-based systems to function as list servers.

Since these servers have been hard at work for many years, and since many of your future mailing list users will be familiar with the ins and outs of at least one of these systems (at least from the subscriber's perspective), let's quickly cover three of the most popular list processing packages on the Internet today.

LISTSERV

Originally designed as a list server that worked over the BITNET network, LISTSERV is ow a commercial product that supports regular Internet e-mail as well. LISTSERV runs on VMS, UNIX, and Windows NT servers. In LISTSERV, all mailing list commands are sent to a single mail processor, named listserv.

LISTSERV is the grandaddy of list processing packages, a workhorse that can serve huge amounts of mail at a time. It's also remarkable because all the public LISTSERV machines in the world are connected, talking to one another and keeping track of which sites are maintaining particular lists. Queries sent to *listserv@listserv.net* cover *every* public LISTSERV list in the world.

ListProc

Formerly known as UNIX Listserv, ListProc runs on machines running a version of the UNIX operating system. It comes in two versions–versions 6.0 and before are free, and versions 7.0 and beyond (known as CREN ListProc) are commercial. In ListProc, all mailing list commands are sent to a single mail address, named listproc.

Majordomo

Majordomo is a relative newcomer to the world of Internet mail servers, but its popularity has grown rapidly because of two important factors: it's free software (that's regularly updated by its authors), and it's written in Perl, a highly portable scripting language. Like LISTSERV and ListProc, Majordomo receives all mailing list commands at a centralized address, in this case named majordomo.

Apple Internet Mail Server: Broadcast Mailing Lists

The Apple Internet Mail Server (AIMS), Apple Computer's POP/SMTP server, is capable of serving mailing lists on its own (see Chapter 4). The catch is that AIMS will only send mail to a list of addresses kept in a plain text file on the AIMS server's hard drive. Users are unable to add or remove themselves from mailing lists; instead, all changes to the mailing list must be manually handled by the AIMS administrator.

If the mailing lists you wish to create are going to be quite stable, AIMS might have enough list processing power for you. But if you want to give mailing list users the ability to subscribe and unsubscribe from your mailing lists at will, you'll need either an add-on to AIMS or a dedicated list server and mailbot application.

AutoShare: Auto-Replies and Mailing Lists

AutoShare is an application that works as an extension to AIMS 1.x. AutoShare can work only with AIMS, because it actually uses the same folders and files that AIMS does. AutoShare knows where AIMS puts files containing incoming messages, and knows where to place files so that AIMS will automatically send them out.

AutoShare was initially conceived as a mailbot utility that would sense an incoming message to a certain account and respond without requiring any human intervention. AutoShare's auto-reply system works with any number of accounts on your AIMS server, and every account can have any number of different auto-replies (including BinHex enclosures, if desired) depending on what's in the incoming message's subject line.

While AutoShare's author, Mikael Hansen, was creating the program, he realized that rather than letting AutoShare remain a one-trick pony, he would give it even more power over mail accounts served by AIMS. AutoShare then blossomed into a fairly powerful mailing list server. AIMS 1.0 *does* support mailing lists, in the sense that you can create a text file with several names and addresses in it, and AIMS will forward all incoming mail to those addresses. But AIMS doesn't currently offer an interface to allow outside users to add and remove addresses, enumerate who is on a given mailing list, hide their subscription information from others, or give subscribers the option of receiving a regularly mailed "digest" instead of a stream of individually forwarded messages. In short, it doesn't have the features you'd find in a UNIX-based list server. AutoShare adds all those features to your AIMS server.

Of course, AutoShare must be run on a machine that's already running AIMS. If you aren't running (or can't run) your own POP/SMTP server with AIMS, you can't use AutoShare. If you have access to a non-Mac POP/SMTP server, you might consider using a client-oriented list server such as Michele Fuortes' Macjordomo or StarNine's ListSTAR/POP (discussed later).

Step by Step: Configuring AutoShare

Since AutoShare really doesn't offer much in the way of a user interface, it's useful to walk through how to configure and run AutoShare step by step.

First Steps

Before you begin:

- ■ Be sure your Map Control Panel is configured properly. This is where AutoShare gets its information about your time zone for use in e-mail headers.
- ■ Consider using Network Time, a control panel that automatically sets your Mac's clock based on information from an outside time server, so that your clock is always correct.
- ■ Make sure AIMS is fully set up and running.

Create AutoShare Folders

First, create an AutoShare folder for the AutoShare application and put AutoShare inside. Then create a folder (preferably inside your hard disk's root folder), which AutoShare will use to store its files. A sample version of this folder, called Auto, comes with the AutoShare distribution.

Inside the Auto folder (or whatever you choose to call it), you'll need to create Filed Mail, Documents, List Server, Filter, and Archive folders.

AutoShare Preferences

Now launch AutoShare and configure its preferences, found in the Preferences menu.

Folder Preferences

The Folders Preferences dialog (Figure 5.1) contains a list of several locations you'll need to choose by clicking on the Select button. The final choice will appear in the box next to it in "path" format. For example, if you've got a hard drive called HD, with the Auto folder on the top level of that hard drive, the path to that folder would be HD:Auto:. Except where noted otherwise, it's usually best to create these folders inside one overarching folder dedicated to AutoShare.

Filed Mail folder. This is the folder to which you'll save all your incoming mail.

Incoming Mail folder. This is not an AutoShare-created folder. Instead, it's AIMS's Incoming Mail folder. Most likely, this folder will be found in your System Folder, inside the Mail Folder, and will be called Incoming Mail.

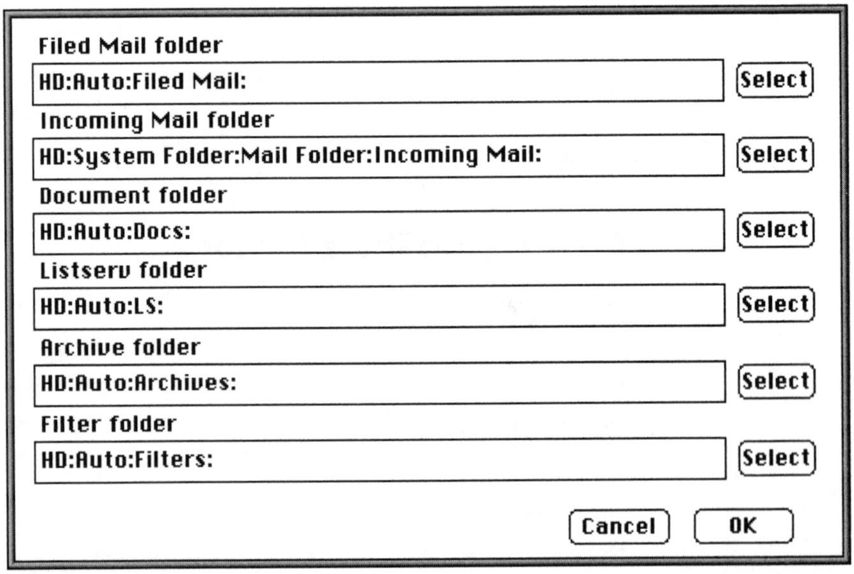

```
Filed Mail folder
HD:Auto:Filed Mail:                              [Select]
Incoming Mail folder
HD:System Folder:Mail Folder:Incoming Mail:      [Select]
Document folder
HD:Auto:Docs:                                    [Select]
Listserv folder
HD:Auto:LS:                                      [Select]
Archive folder
HD:Auto:Archives:                                [Select]
Filter folder
HD:Auto:Filters:                                 [Select]

                                   [Cancel]  [ OK ]
```

FIGURE 5.1 AutoShare's Folders Preferences Dialog

Document folder. This is the folder in which you'll store all of your auto-response messages. Within this folder, you'll create subfolders based on the names of all your auto-reply accounts.

Listserv folder. This is the folder that will store all your list files (containing the name and address of every list member for every list).

Archive folder. Archives of your mailing list can be created automatically by AutoShare. Within this folder you can create subfolders named after lists you are running on your server. Once archiving has been enabled, an archive file will be created and updated each time a new message appears on that list.

Filter folder. Filters can be used to prevent certain files from being automatically returned to certain people, sites, and so on. This folder is where AutoShare's filter files live.

Miscellaneous Preferences

The Miscellaneous Preferences dialog (Figure 5.2) is where you set the address of your AutoShare administrator, the format of your mailing list digests, and how AutoShare's list server processes list commands, among other options.

Address of the administrator. This is the e-mail address of the AutoShare administrator. At a user-specified time (set in the Preferences:Times menu, described later), this address will receive the AutoShare log.

Address of the bounce account. This is the address that will receive bounced mail. For example, the postmaster account might receive this mail. This address must be on your own AIMS server, or AutoShare won't run correctly.

Log. Logs are automatically mailed to the AutoShare administrator at a user-specified time. The log setting can be either Off (no logging will be done), Always (only important messages will be logged), Brief (a single line will appear in the log for each transaction), or Tech (every transaction will have detailed information). If you can't decide which you want, pick Brief. It's a good place to start.

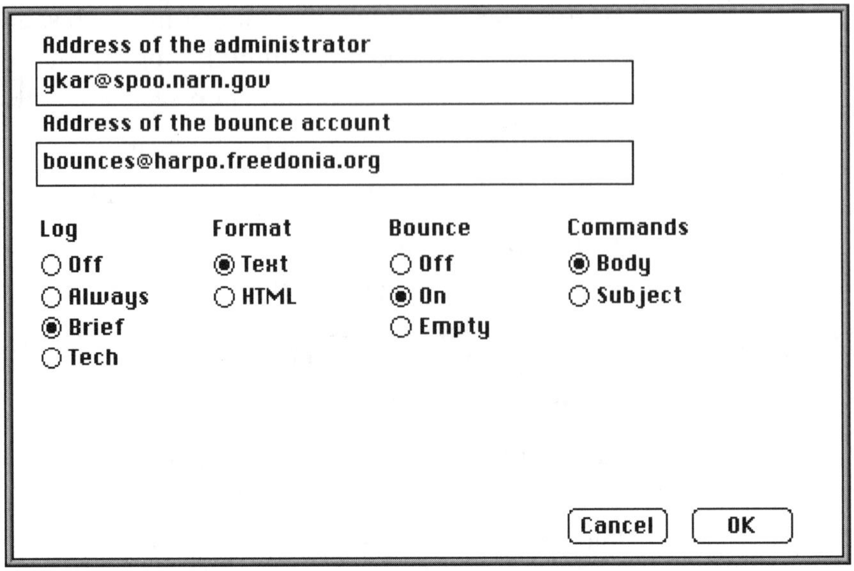

FIGURE 5.2 AutoShare's Miscellaneous Preferences Dialog

Format

Format will determine what your list archives (not the digest, which is always plain ASCII) are saved as. If you're not planning on running a mailing list, you can ignore this. Otherwise, choose either Text (plain ASCII text) or HTML (the Hypertext Markup Language, the standard on the World Wide Web).

Bounce

This setting determines whether the sender of your message is reset to direct bounced mail to one specific account. If Bounce is set to Off, nothing will be altered. If Bounce is set to On, all auto-responses and admin log mailings will be set so that if they're bounced back, they'll point to the Bounce address rather than to the originator of the mailing. If Bounce is set to Empty, no mail will bounce back to your server.

Commands

This setting tells AutoShare's list server whether to scan for list server commands in the Subject: line of an incoming message or in the message's body. Since most list servers scan the message body rather than the Subject: line, and since a subject can contain only one command whereas a message body can contain many commands, you should probably choose Body as your option.

Times Preferences

The Times Preferences dialog (Figure 5.3) lets you determine when and how often you want AutoShare to automatically send two different types of files.

Logs. Logs (see previous section) can be sent out to the AutoShare administrator after a certain span of time, which you determine in the Preferences:Times dialog. You can choose how often to send out the log, from every day to every week, and also at what local time the log is mailed. By checking the Now (besides scheduled) box, you'll cause AutoShare to immediately send the log to the Administrator address specified in the Miscellaneous Preferences (see previous section).

Digests. Digests are compilations of messages sent to a mailing list. The default format for most mailing lists, including the ones administered by AutoShare, is that each individual message sent to the list

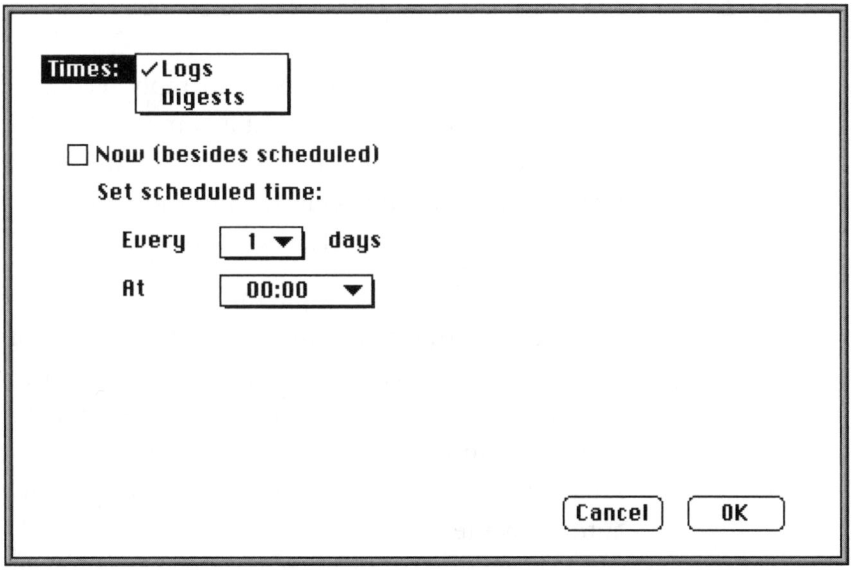

FIGURE 5.3 AutoShare's Times Preferences Dialog

will automatically be reflected to every other member of that list. Some people prefer to cut down on the volume of individual messages they receive, by receiving an omnibus of messages sent to them periodically in the form of a list digest.

AutoShare's digests are sent out after a certain span of time, which you determine in the Preferences:Times dialog. (To get to the Digests section, click on the pop-up menu in the dialog and select Digests.) You can choose how often to send out a digest, from every day to every week, and also at what local time the digest is mailed.

By checking the Now (besides scheduled) box, you'll cause AutoShare to immediately create a digest and send it out to those subscribed to the digest option of your mailing lists.

Analysis

This option creates a file titled AutoShare Analysis in the same folder as your AutoShare application. It includes configuration information about AutoShare, and is useful in troubleshooting AutoShare problems from a distance.

Step By Step: Auto-Reply Accounts

You're now able to create new auto-reply accounts in AIMS. To do so, create a new account, give it a name, and enable it (though you don't need to enable logins). Set your forwarding option as Save as files . . . and in the box below, enter the same path that appears in the Filed Mail folder preference in AutoShare (see Figure 5.4).

Be *sure* all paths in the Apple Internet Mail Server do *not* end with a colon, even if they're pointing to folders instead of files. Unlike AutoShare, which enjoys the colon, the Apple Internet Mail Server finds colons distasteful when placed at the end of a path. Using one there will cause AutoShare to stop working. That's all you need to do in AIMS to set up the account. Next you'll want to set up your auto-reply files.

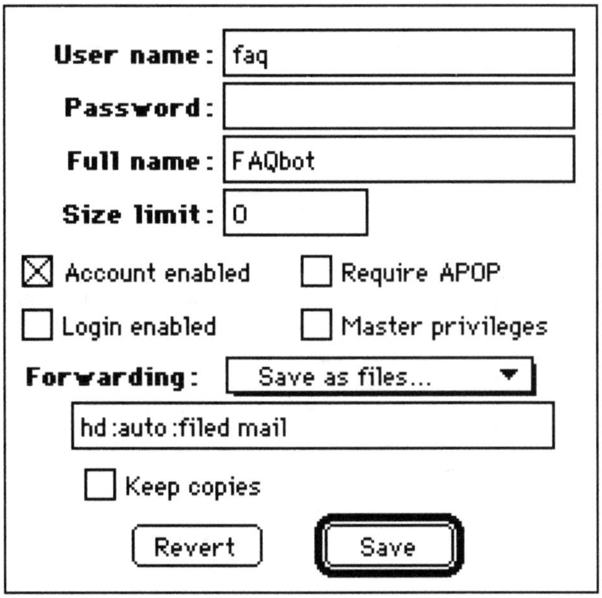

FIGURE 5.4
Setting up an auto-reply account in Apple Internet Mail Server. Be sure not to use a colon at the end of the path.

Setting Up

Go to the Documents folder you specified in AutoShare's preferences and create a new folder within it with the name of the AIMS account you just added. Within that, you'll need to create at least one text file: Default. This is the text file that will be returned in response to all messages that are sent to that account, unless you specify otherwise (see Figure 5.5).

This file needs to be a plain text file. There is one token you may place in that text file—it's there in case you want to quote the previous message at some point in your auto-reply. To do that, place:

```
/=original
```

at that point in the file.

You can also create other text files in this folder. Every text file you create will be sent back to all the messages that come in with the file's name in the Subject: line. (While AutoShare's list server can listen for commands in either the Subject: line or the message body, AutoShare's auto-reply function requires the keyword be in the

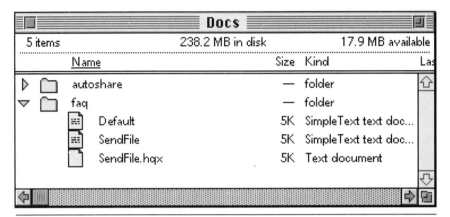

FIGURE 5.5 Create a file structure for your AutoShare auto-reply account.

Subject: line.) For example, if you create a file named INFO, then any message that comes in with the word info in it (AutoShare is case-insensitive) will receive that file back.

You can create as many of these as you want. Any message with a subject that doesn't match any of the filenames will receive Default instead.

File Enclosures

You can also add a BinHexed file enclosure to any or all of your auto-return documents. Simply create the BinHex (.hqx) file using a utility like Aladdin Systems' shareware DropStuff with Expander Enhancer or the free utility BinHex, and then name it with the same name as the text file you'll be sending back, with .hqx appended on the end. Therefore, if you're sending a file back with Default, your enclosure's name will be Default.hqx.

Step by Step: Vacation Notices

Since AutoShare can auto-reply to incoming messages, it can be used as a means of creating "vacation notices" for users of your AIMS server. This means that as users receive mail while they're on vacation, the folks who have sent them mail will receive small notes saying that they'll read their messages when they get back. The note might also point them to another person who is still in the office while the intended recipient is out climbing up the side of a Hawaiian volcano.

Here's how to set up a vacation notice for one of your AIMS users via AutoShare.

Modify the AIMS Account

Go into AIMS, select the user's account, and set the pop-up menu to Save as files . . . . Check the Keep Copies box, so that all the mail coming to that user will still be in his or her mailbox when he or she returns. Enter a path that leads to your AutoShare Filed Mail folder, as it appears in your Preferences:Folders dialog (see Figure 5.6).

Create a Folder for Your Vacationing User

In AutoShare's Documents folder, create a folder with the same name as your user's account name.

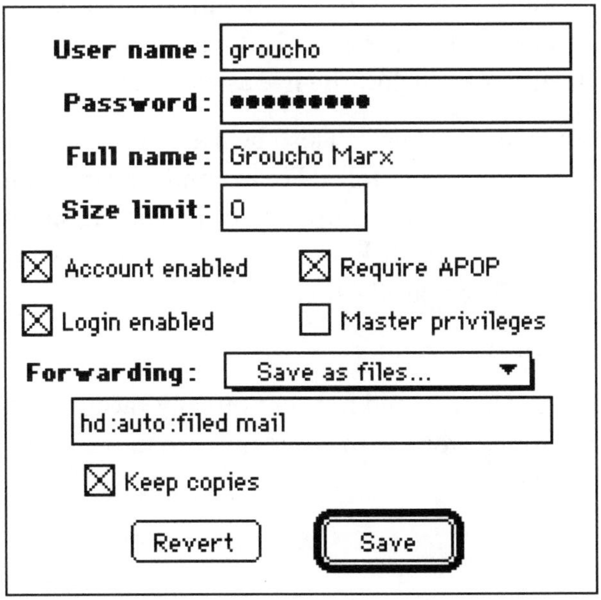

FIGURE 5.6 Enter a path in AIMS that leads to the Filed Mail folder.

Create a Vacation Announcement Text File

Ideally, you'll have the user create his or her own text file, with a personalized message, but the text file can also be generic; it doesn't matter too much. Save this file in the folder you created in the previous step, with the name Default.

Set Up a Filter

While the first three steps will create an auto-reply to any message that comes in, if your user is on a mailing list, every time he or she receives mail from that list, that list will receive the same form reply. You can see how that would become annoying in a hurry. As a result, AutoShare includes a facility to ensure that a person will receive a vacation message only once.

Create a text file with the same name as your user's account name, and place it in the Filters folder you defined in AutoShare's Preferences:Folders dialog. All the file needs to contains is five asterisks:

```
*****
```

and you've created a filter that will prevent AutoShare from sending out a vacation notice to the same person twice. (AutoShare manages this by appending the e-mail addresses of people who have written to the filters file below the five asterisks.)

AutoShare's filtering can also be used to prevent vacation messages from going to other folks. For example, if you wanted to prevent anyone at your own company from receiving vacation notices, because they already know who's on vacation, you could insert a line above the asterisks like this:

```
From: company.com
```

and AutoShare would not sent out any vacation auto-replies to messages from anyone with company.com in their e-mail address.

Remove the Vacation Processor When the User Returns

When your vacationaing user returns, be sure to turn off Save as files . . . for that account in AIMS and delete accumulated addresses after the five asterisks in that filter file, so that those people will be notified the next time your user goes on vacation.

Step by Step: Running a List Server

Here's how to create a list for your list server.

Be Sure the List Server Account is Operational

In AIMS, create a user with the name AutoShare, as if it were an auto-reply account. Be sure there's a folder within your Documents folder named AutoShare. Within that folder must be files named Default, Get, Help, Index, List, Release, Review, Set, Sub, Unsub, and Which, containing special tokens that cause AutoShare to modify mailing list files. An example of this folder, which you may modify and use yourself, is included in the AutoShare distribution. It is highly recommended you start with these sample files. For more information about the special processing tokens contained within those files, consult the main AutoShare documentation.

If you'd like to have a specialized file, say a FAQ, sent to users upon subscribing to a certain list, you can do so by creating a copy of the Sub file and renaming it Sub.[listname]—then AutoShare will send that file (which you can modify to include just about any text you like) to users who subscribe to that particular list. Subscription requests to lists without special Sub.[listname] files will receive the standard subscription reply found in the Sub file.

Check If You Need a Hosts File

If your mail server acts as more than one domain, you'll need an AutoShare hosts file. If you don't know what this means, you probably don't need to worry about it. The key is, if mail sent to more than one machine name ends up at your machine (for example, if you're both wackynet.com and wacky.net), you'll need to create a file that contains all the secondary machine names your Mac is posing as. Call it AutoShare Hosts, and put it in the AutoShare folder in your Preferences folder.

Create a List File

This needs to be a text file (it can be completely empty) in the folder you defined as your Listserv folder in the AutoShare preferences. The text file needs to be the name of the list you're creating, say, FUN-L. (The format for these text files is <address> (<name>). For an example of a mailing list field, see Figure 5.7.

Create a Mailing List in AIMS

In AIMS, you'll have to add three new accounts that are permutations of the name of your mailing list; in this example FUN-L.

First, create an account that's the exact name of your mailing list, and set AIMS to Save as files . . .. In the box below Save as files . . ., enter a path that points to the Filed Mail folder you configured in the AutoShare folder preferences (see Figure 5.8).

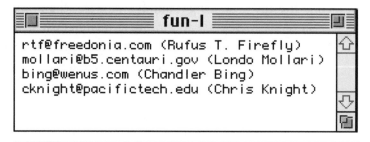

FIGURE 5.7 A mailing list text file

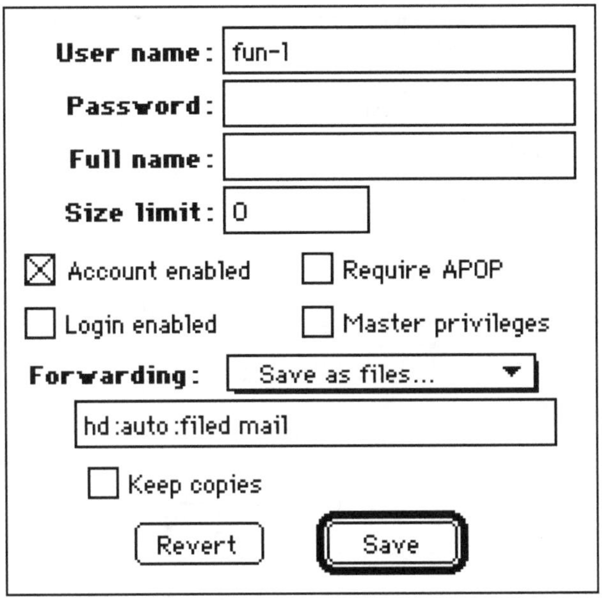

FIGURE 5.8
Configure a mailing list receiver in the Apple Internet Mail Server.

Second, create two new accounts with the exact name of your mailing list along with .m and .d appended on the end (FUN-L.m and FUN-L.d). Each of these should be set to Mailing list and pointed to the complete file path that leads to the Listserv folder, plus the name of the account (see Figure 5.9). Example paths might be

```
HD:Auto:LS:FUN-L.m
HD:Auto:LS:FUN-L.d
```

Before you test an AIMS-assisted mailing list, make sure the address of your bounce account is set to an account on your AIMS server. Otherwise, AutoShare will refuse to process your list files correctly.

Add More Lists

To add more lists, simply repeat the last two steps. Really.

Some List Server Hints

■ A common way new AutoShare admins test their new lists is by subscribing themselves and then sending mail to the list.

```
┌─────────────────────────────────────────┐
│  User name:  fun-1.d                      │
│                                           │
│  Password:                                │
│                                           │
│  Full name:                               │
│                                           │
│  Size limit:  0                           │
│                                           │
│  ☒ Account enabled    ☐ Require APOP      │
│                                           │
│  ☐ Login enabled      ☐ Master privileges │
│                                           │
│  Forwarding:  │  Mailing list...      ▼│  │
│               ┌─────────────────────────┐ │
│               │ hd :auto :ls :fun-1.d   │ │
│                                           │
│               ☐ Keep copies               │
│                                           │
│          [ Revert ]   [ Save ]            │
└─────────────────────────────────────────┘
```

FIGURE 5.9
Configuring a mailing list reflector in the Apple Internet Mail Server.

Since AutoShare by default sends a list message to everyone except the original sender of the message (this is called NOACK, and is described next), if you send a message to a list with only you on it, you'll never see a message come back. To make sure you can see messages you send to your list, send a message to AutoShare with the command SET [listname] ACK. Then you should be able to test your list to your heart's content.

■ AutoShare is careful not to allow people who don't subscribe to a list to post a message to that list. Because AutoShare is extremely finicky in the way it checks this, your users might complain that they can't post to the list. If you're not too afraid of "spamming" from nonlist members, you can deactivate this AutoShare feature by creating an empty file named All May Contribute in the same folder as your AutoShare application.

The AutoShare List Server from the Outside Looking In

While setting up a list server in AutoShare is as simple as the four-step process just outlined, in real life it's a little more complicated. Once you've got AutoShare up and running, you and your list members have to begin dealing with how AutoShare's list server processes commands via e-mail.

AutoShare's Command Set

AutoShare understands the following list server commands: LIST or LISTS; REVIEW or REV; RECIPIENTS or WHO; SUB or SUBSCRIBE; UNSUB, UNSUBSCRIBE, or SIGNOFF; SET; INDEX or IND; GET or SEND; WHICH; RELEASE; and QUERY. Let's go through them one by one, and see what they do. (Keep in mind that commands can be processed either in the message body or in the message's subject, depending on which radio button you checked in the Preferences:Miscellaneous dialog.)

LIST (or LISTS)

Usage:

```
LIST
LISTS
```

LIST or LISTS returns a message that displays all mailing lists available from your server.

REVIEW (or REV or RECIPIENTS or WHO)

Usage:

```
REVIEW fun-1
REV fun-1
RECIPIENTS fun-1
WHO fun-1
```

This command displays a list of all the subscribers to a particular mailing list and a count of how many total subscribers there are. If a user has decided to CONCEAL him- or herself (see later), he or she won't appear on this list, though the user will be counted among the number of concealed subscribers listed here.

SUB (or SUBSCRIBE)

Usage:

```
SUB fun-l Boutros Boutros-Ghali
SUBSCRIBE fun-l Boutros Boutros-Ghali
```

This command adds someone to a given list. The format is SUB [listname] [your full name]. You can't subscribe without giving your name after the name of the list.

UNSUB (or UNSUBSCRIBE or SIGNOFF)

Usage:

```
UNSUB fun-l
UNSUBSCRIBE fun-l
SIGNOFF fun-l
```

Use this command to remove yourself from a list. You don't need to give your name.

SET

SET is a command with multiple uses.

CONCEAL. This will remove you from the list of subscribers that's returned when someone sends a REVIEW [listname] command to the list server. Usage:

```
SET fun-l CONCEAL
```

NOCONCEAL. This will include you on the list of subscribers that's returned when someone sends a REVIEW [listname] command to the list server. This is the default setting. Usage:

```
SET fun-l NOCONCEAL
```

DIGEST. Instead of receiving individual messages as they're sent to the list, users who SET [listname] DIGEST will receive one omnibus message at an interval set by the AutoShare administrator. Usage:

```
SET fun-l DIGEST
```

NODIGEST. You'll receive individual messages as they come in to the mailing list, rather than a digest. This is the default setting. Usage:

```
SET fun-l NODIGEST
```

MAIL. You'll receive messages from the mailing list. This is the default setting. Usage:

```
SET fun-l MAIL
```

NOMAIL. With this setting, you'll be officially subscribed to the list (including having posting privileges), but you won't receive any mail from the list. This is good when you're on vacation or post from several different accounts while reading from only one. Usage:

```
SET fun-l NOMAIL
```

ACK. Every message you send to the list is automatically reflected to you, as well. Usage:

```
SET fun-l ACK
```

NOACK. Your own messages to the list are never reflected back to you. This is the default setting. Usage:

```
SET fun-l NOACK
```

INDEX (or IND)

Usage:

```
INDEX fun-l
```

This command gives you a list of archival files available for the given list. This allows you to retrieve digest files via e-mail with the GET command (see next).

GET (or SEND)

Usage:

```
GET fun-l. Current.html
```

Use this command to retrieve files listed by the INDEX command. The command structure is GET [listname] [filename].

WHICH

Usage:

```
WHICH
```

This command returns a list of all the mailing lists you're subscribed to on the AutoShare server.

RELEASE

Usage:

```
RELEASE
```

This command lets you know which version of AutoShare is running on the server.

QUERY

Usage:

```
QUERY fun-1
```

This command shows you what all your options are (ACK or NOACK, DIGEST or NODIGEST, MAIL or NOMAIL, CONCEAL or NOCONCEAL) for a given list.

AutoShare: For More Information

For more detailed information about AutoShare, consult Mikael Hansen's documentation, which is included with the AutoShare distribution on the CD that accompanies this book.

 # Macjordomo: POP-Based List Services

Although AutoShare works only on a Mac and also works as a POP/SMTP server via AIMS, Michele Fuortes' Macjordomo can work on a Mac running AIMS, on a Mac working in tandem with another Mac running AIMS, or even on a Mac working in tandem with a non-Mac POP/SMTP server. Because it can be used remotely, unattached to a full-time mail server, this also means that Macjordomo can be used to serve mailing lists even if the computer it runs on isn't connected to the Internet 24 hours a day.

Macjordomo was named in homage to the UNIX server Major-domo, but the two programs are related only in that they're both mailing list servers: Macjordomo was written from scratch as a Mac application, and boasts an interface that makes it very easy even for novice Mac users to quickly set up and operate a mailing list server.

Unlike AutoShare, which connects itself to AIMS's file system, AutoShare communicates with POP/SMTP servers via the Internet protocols POP and SMTP. Even if it's running on the same Mac as AIMS, Macjordomo will connect to AIMS just as if it were a remote user from the outside world. This somewhat limits Macjordomo's integration with AIMS, but by relying on standard Internet mail protocols, it makes Macjordomo flexible in dealing with non-AIMS environments.

Configuring Macjordomo

Macjordomo works by using multiple accounts on a POP server as maildrops. It needs at least two accounts in order to function: one account (usually called macjordomo) serves as the list processing account, the place users go to get information about the server, to subscribe and unsubscribe from mailing lists, and to change their mailing list options; the other account or accounts are for processing messages sent to an individual list. Macjordomo needs only one list processing account, but it requires one additional account for every mailing list you serve using Macjordomo. So, if you're going to serve five mailing lists via Macjordomo, you'll need six accounts on a POP/SMTP mail server.

Subscription List Configuration

The first item you should configure in Macjordomo is your list processing account. To configure it, select Subscription Lists . . . from the Lists menu and enter your information in the Subscription List dialog box (see Figure 5.10).

POP Address

This is the address of your list processing account itself. While macjordomo is a standard address name, you can choose any name for your account. Other common options are listserv, listproc, and majordomo.[*]

POP Password

This is the password of the list server's POP account. Be sure it's a good password—don't use a word that can be found in the dictio-

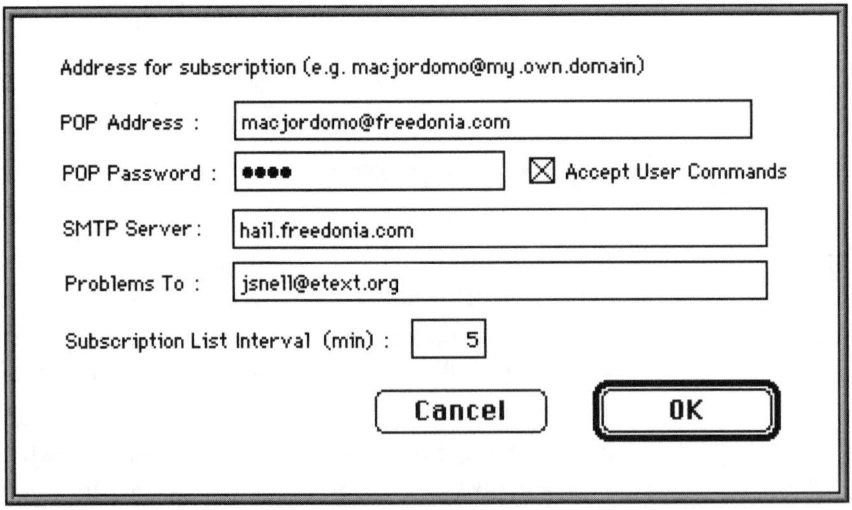

Address for subscription (e.g. macjordomo@my.own.domain)

POP Address : macjordomo@freedonia.com

POP Password : ●●●●   ☒ Accept User Commands

SMTP Server : hail.freedonia.com

Problems To : jsnell@etext.org

Subscription List Interval (min) :   5

Cancel   OK

FIGURE 5.10 Enter your information in Macjordomo's Subscription List dialog box.

---

[*] Since there are so many common list server addresses on the Internet, people running the only list server on a given POP/SMTP server might consider setting up addresses for *all* the common list server addresses (e.g., listserv, listproc, majordomo, autoshare, macjordomo) and forwarding all of them to one central mailbox.

nary (either forward or backward) or a friend's name. Best is a string of unrelated characters (including some punctuation marks or numerals). As of version 1.0, Macjordomo doesn't support APOP, a password-authentication protocol that makes POP password transactions much more secure. If you're using a server (like AIMS) that supports APOP, you'll have to turn APOP off for all Macjordomo accounts.

Accept User Commands

When this box is checked, users from the outside can send commands (like SUBSCRIBE and UNSUBSCRIBE) to the list processing account. When the box isn't checked, those users are locked out altogether. You can turn commands off for individual lists by turning off Accept Subscribers Commands in the list window (discussed shortly).

SMTP Server

This is the host name of the machine that's acting as your SMTP (mail sending) server for your list server account. Usually, this will be the same as your POP server, though in rare circumstances it might not be.

Problems To

Any problems that occur with the list server (such as bounced mail) will go to this address. Be sure this address is *not* the name of your list server, or damaging mail loops could result.

Subscription List Interval

This option selects how often Macjordomo checks your POP/SMTP server for new messages to the list server, in minutes. Scale this number up or down based on a couple of factors: how busy your lists are and how busy your mail server is. A busy mail server doesn't need the added strain of Macjordomo logging in and checking its mail every minute, and a busy mailing list won't be able to have interactive conversations if mail gets distributed only every two hours. You'll need to pick a number that's right for your situation. A serving interval of 5 to 15 minutes might be most appropriate.

Mailing List Configuration

Next let's create a sample mailing list for use with Macjordomo. Go to Macjordomo's Lists menu and choose New List. You'll be prompted with a List Info dialog box, as in Figure 5.11.

List Name

This is the name of the list. It doesn't need to equate with the address the list will use for list mail, though it might be better for your memory if the names were similar. This name must not include any spaces, so wacky list is unacceptable, but wacky-list is fine.

List Address

This is the address the list will use for all list mail. It needs to be a configured POP account on whichever mail server you're using with Macjordomo. This address should be entered in user@host format (such as, *wacky@freedonia.com*).

POP Password

This is the password for the list's POP account. As with all other passwords, it shouldn't be a word you can find in a dictionary, nor should it be a name.

Subscriber Only

If this box is checked, only people who are subscribed to your mailing list will be able to post to the list. All others will be turned away. This is a way to filter out "spam" messages sent to large numbers of mailing lists by people advertising products, or such, as well as being a way to prevent subscription requests from would-be subscribers to a list. When a message is sent by someone who isn't subscribed, it is returned to the sender and not passed on to the list. When this box is unchecked, anyone can post to a list.

SMTP Server

Just as with the list server account, this is probably the same machine as your mail server. However, if Macjordomo is serving several high-volume lists, you might choose to distribute list traffic

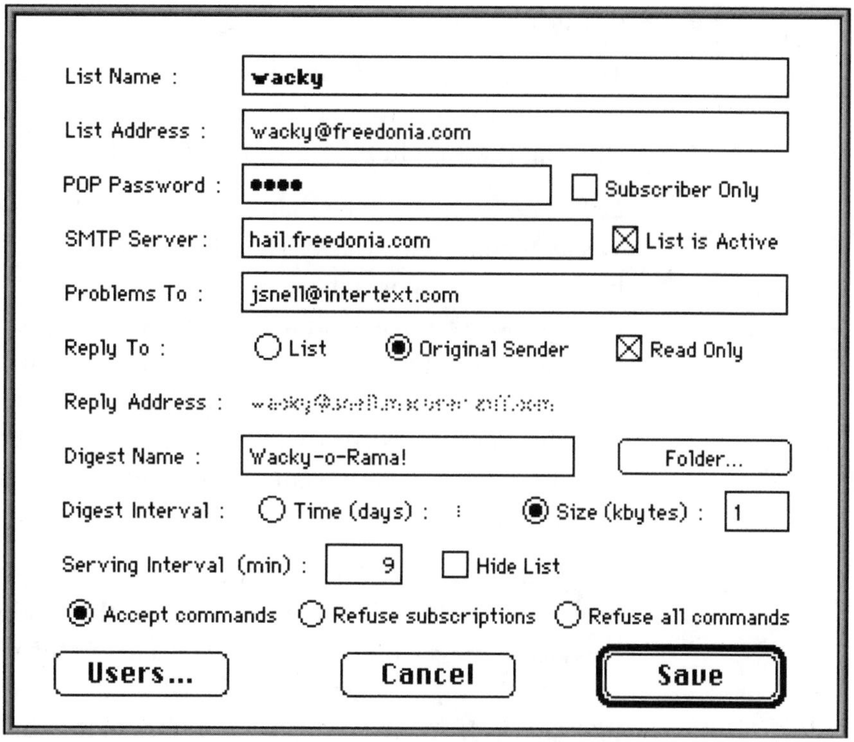

FIGURE 5.11 List data appears in the List Info dialog box.

over several local SMTP servers. Since you can specify a different SMTP server for each list, Macjordomo makes such distribution possible. But, in most cases, you'll just want to use the same mail server for all your POP and SMTP needs.

List Is Active

When this box is checked, the list is up and running—the list's mailbox on the POP server will be checked regularly, and any incoming messages will be processed and forwarded on to list members. If this box is not checked, the list won't check its box and won't process any mail.

Problems To

This is the administrator of your list. This address will receive all bounced mail and any other problem mail.

Reply To

This series of radio buttons determines which addresses appear in the Reply-To: and To: mail headers, which in turn determine to which address replies a message will be sent.

List. The To: line will be that of the mailing list itself (such as, To: Wacky mailing list <wacky@freedonia.com>), and the Reply-To: line will be that of whichever address is specified in the Reply Address box (discussed shortly). Unless a user specifically tells his or her mail reader to reply only to the individual who sent the e-mail message, the reply will by default go back to the "reply address" (usually, but not necessarily, the list itself). This is a good setting for administrators who want to foster lots of discussion on their mailing lists.

Original Sender. The To: line will still be that of the mailing list itself, but the Reply-To: line will be set to the original sender of the message. Unless a user specifically tells his or the mail reader to reply to the entire mailing list, the reply will by default go only to the original sender. If you're trying to keep idle chatter on your mailing list to a minimum, this is a good setting—it ensures that people will post only to your list when they intend to do so, and not as part of a quick, unthinking reply.

Read Only

This check box is for administrators who want to use their mailing lists as one-way distribution points only. When checked, the To: line will omit the actual list address (such as, To: Multiple recipients of list wacky from <jsnell@etext.org>). The Reply-To: line will point to the list administrator, so all replies will go to that person automatically.

Reply Address

This address is the one that will appear in the Reply-To: field of messages sent to a list with its Reply To option set to List. Usually, this will be the address of your mailing list proper. An administrator who wanted to moderate his or her list could point replies to his or her account, however, and then forward relevant postings on to the list itself. For first-time list administrators, this address should probably be identical to the one entered in the List Address window. If the Reply To option is not set to List, this box will be grayed out.

Digest Name

This will be the name of your mailing list digest (defined shortly). Most mailing lists use the same name for their digest as they do for their mailing list, but some more creative lists have come up with unique names. My favorite is the digest of the Crowded House mailing list.[*] Rather than calling it something dull like Crowded House Digest, it's called Tongue in the Mail, after a lyric in one of the band's songs. If you're feeling similarly creative, this is the place to give your digest a personality of its own.

Folder

Click on this button to select a folder in which to save your list digests for archival purposes.

Digest Interval

This setting determines how often your mailing list digest is sent out. The digest is for users who don't want to receive a message every time someone posts to a list; instead, they want to see a compilation of messages every once in a while. Users determine whether they receive individual messages or digests by sending a command to your list server account, or you can set the option for them in their user information box (discussed shortly).

Macjordomo offers two ways to determine how often messages are sent to the mailing list. If you select the Time radio button and enter a number into the accompanying box, a digest will be sent to subscribers after a predetermined number of days. This is a good setting for lists that aren't very busy, so that list members can see what's going on, even if there have been only a couple of postings over the course of a few days.

---

[*] To subscribe, send an e-mail message to <listproc@listproc.wsu.edu> with either "subscribe ch-digest *your name*" or "subscribe ch *your name*" as the first line in the body of your message.

If you select the Size check box and enter a number into the accompanying box, subscribers will receive a digest after it reaches a certain size cutoff. This is a good setting for busy lists, because digests appear sooner or later depending on how much traffic is happening on the list itself.

Serving Interval

This box contains the number of minutes that Macjordomo will pause between checks for new list messages on your POP server. This number should strike a balance between a low number, which will give the list the feel of an almost real-time conversation, and a high number, which will reduce the burden on a busy mail server. Five or ten minutes would be a good starting point.

Hide List

When checked, the list's name won't appear in the list of all available mailing lists when a user sends a LIST command to the list server address.

Accepting or Refusing Commands

This set of radio buttons lets you control which commands can be issued to the list server regarding a list. When Accept Commands is selected, users from the outside can send commands (such as SUBSCRIBE and UNSUBSCRIBE) to the list processing account for this list. When Refuse All Commands is selected, those users are locked out. When Refuse Subscriptions is selected, users can issue any command *except* SUBSCRIBE—in other words, the list is closed and won't accept any new subscribers, though the old ones will still be able to change their list options via the list processing account.

Users

This button sends you to the Users dialog, described next.

User Configuration

Clicking on the Users . . . button in a list dialog brings you to the Users dialog (see Figure 5.12), which lists all the subscribers to a

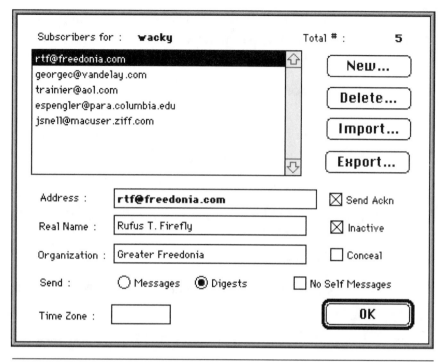

FIGURE 5.12 You can see all of a list's subscribers in the Users dialog.

given list and gives you the ability to add them, remove them, or change their preferences.

New

This button lets you add a user to the mailing list. You'll be prompted with a dialog box containing the fields found at the bottom of the Users window. Once the user information has been entered, you'll return to the Users window and your new user will appear in the user list.

Delete

This button will delete a selected user from the user list.

Import

Upon hitting this button, you'll be prompted to select a text file containing users you'd like to add your mailing list. This text file must contain a different user on each line, with the user's e-mail address appearing first, followed by his or her real name. The address and real name must be separated by either a space, tab, or comma.

Export

You can use this button to export your user list as a tab-delimited text file, with each user entry on its own line. A user's e-mail address appears first, followed by his or her real name.

Address

This window will contain the e-mail address of your user. All mail to the list will be resent to the user at this address.

Real Name

This should be the full name of your user. This is mostly for identification purposes.

Organization

This can be an organization your user is affiliated with. This is purely for identification purposes.

Send

These two radio buttons determine whether the user will receive copies of every message sent to the list (Messages) or a compilation of messages sent out periodically (Digests).

Send Ackn

If this box is checked, users will receive an acknowledgment when they send their message to the mailing list. If it's not checked, their list submission will be greeted with silence. (This can also be controlled by the user through the SET ACKN and SET NOACKN list server commands, defined shortly.)

Inactive

When this box is checked, a user is still officially on the mailing list, but no mail is sent to the account. This is good for people who have gone on vacation, or for people who post from multiple accounts and are on a list that limits list posting to subscribers only.[*] (This can also be controlled by the user through the SET INACTIVE and SET ACTIVE list server commands, defined shortly.)

Conceal

If this selection is checked, a user won't appear on the list of subscribers when someone sends a REVIEW command to the list server (discussed shortly). (This can also be controlled by the user through the SET CONCEAL and SET NOCONCEAL list server commands, discussed shortly.)

Forcing a List Check

If ou want Macjordomo to check all its accounts on the POP server, you can force it to connect by hitting Command-L or by selecting Connect Now from the File menu.

Customizing Macjordomo's List Messages

Like most list-serving packages, Macjordomo includes a host of generic messages that will be sent to users who send messages to the list server. You can customize these messages from within Macjordomo by selecting Edit Generic Messages . . . (for list processor messages, as well as generic messages that will be used when a list-specific message hasn't been created for a given list) or Edit List Messages . . . (for messages specific to a given list) under the Special menu.

Macjordomo gives you a large menu of documents, which you can customize to your heart's content. For a guide to how they're used, see Table 5.1.

---

[*] Those people would subscribe to a list under all their various posting accounts, but set all but one of the subscriptions to inactive via a SET INACTIVE command. That way, they could post from any account, but would receive only one copy of list messages.

TABLE 5.1 Auto-Reply Files You Can Configure in Macjordomo

Message Name	When It's Used
Generic Error	When a message sent to the list server address can't be recognized as a valid command. Lists the valid commands.
Help	When a message with the HELP command is sent to the list server address. Lists the valid commands.
List	When a message with the LIST command is sent to the list server address. Lists the names of all lists maintained by Macjordomo.
List not found	When a message sent to the list server refers to a list that doesn't exist on the server, this tells the user to use the LIST command to find available lists.
Get successful	When a message contains a GET command, this message precedes the attached file.
Get unsuccessful	When a message contains a GET command for a file that isn't found, this message is returned.
Index	When a GET command includes an invalid file name, this message is returned.
List refuses commands	When a command is sent regarding a mailing list that's been set not to accept user commands, this reply is sent.
Message redirected	When a message posted to a mailing list seems to contain a list server command, this message is returned.
Review	When a REVIEW command is received, this message is returned along with a list of users on a given list.
Search	Unknown
Set	When a list command is sent by a list member, this reply is sent back, telling them their command has been executed.
User already exists	When someone already subscribed to a list tries to subscribe again, this rejection message is returned.
User not found	When a user tries to issue a user command for a list, but isn't on that list, this error message is returned.
User subscribed	When a user subscribes to a list, this file is returned.
User unsubscribed	When a user unsubscribes from a list, this file is returned.
Info	Gives information about a given list

The Macjordomo List Server from the Outside Looking In

Once you've got AutoShare up and running, you and your list members have to learn the language that Macjordomo's list processor understands. Macjordomo can understand the following list server commands: LIST, REVIEW, SUBSCRIBE, UNSUBSCRIBE, SET (and eight SET-related subcommands), INDEX, GET, and HELP. The commands *must* appear in the body of a message; you can send several commands at once by putting them on successive lines of a message. For those who don't like typing long command strings, Macjordomo will also recognize the first three letters of any command or subcommand.

LIST (or LIS)

Usage:

```
LIST
LIS
```

LIST or LIS returns a message that displays all mailing lists available from Macjordomo.

REVIEW (or REV)

Usage:

```
REVIEW wacky
REV wacky
```

This command displays a list of all the subscribers to a particular mailing list and a count of how many total subscribers there are. If a user has decided to CONCEAL him- or herself (discussed shortly), he or she won't appear on this list.

SUBSCRIBE (or SUB)

Usage:

```
SUBSCRIBE wacky Rufus T. Firefly
SUB wacky Rufus T. Firefly
SUBSCRIBE wacky
SUB wacky
```

This command adds someone to a given list. The format is SUBSCRIBE [listname] [your full name]. Including your full name is optional.

UNSUBSCRIBE (or UNS)

Usage:

```
UNSUBSCRIBE wacky
UNS wacky
```

Use this command to remove yourself from a list. You don't need to give your name.

SET

SET is a command with multiple uses.

CONCEAL (or CON)

Usage:

```
SET wacky CONCEAL
SET wacky CON
```

This will remove you from the list of subscribers that's returned when someone sends a REVIEW [listname] command to the list server.

NOCONCEAL (or NOC)

Usage:

```
SET wacky NOCONCEAL
SET wacky NOC
```

This will include you on the list of subscribers that's returned when someone sends a REVIEW [listname] command to the list server. This is the default setting.

DIGEST (or DIG)

Usage:

```
SET wacky DIGEST
SET wacky DIG
```

Instead of receiving individual messages as they're sent to the list, users who SET [listname] DIGEST will receive one omnibus message at a regular time interval or after the digest file has reached a certain size, depending on what was set in Macjordomo's list dialog.

MAIL (or MAI)

Usage:

```
SET wacky MAIL
SET wacky MAI
```

You'll receive individual messages as they come in to the mailing list, rather than a digest. This is the default setting.

ACTIVE (or ACT)

Usage:

```
SET wacky ACTIVE
SET wacky ACT
```

You'll receive messages from the mailing list. This is the default setting.

INACTIVE (or INA)

Usage:

```
SET wacky INACTIVE
SET wacky INA
```

With this setting, you'll be officially subscribed to the list (including having posting privileges), but you won't receive any mail from the list. Good for when you're on vacation or post from several different accounts while reading from only one.

ACKN (or ACK)

Usage:

```
SET wacky ACKN
SET wacky ACK
```

An acknowledgment is sent that your message was received, but you don't receive the actal message you sent.

NOACKN (or NOA)

Usage:

```
SET wacky NOACKN
SET wacky NOA
```

Your own messages to the list are never reflected back to you, and you don't receive any acknowledgment message from the server. This is the default setting.

REPRO (or REP)

Usage:

```
SET wacky REPRO
SET wacky REP
```

Every message you send to the list is automatically reflected to you as well. This is the default setting.

NOREPRO (or NOR)

Usage:

```
SET wacky NOREPRO
SET wacky NOR
```

Your own messages to the list are never reflected back to you.

INDEX (or IND)

Usage:

```
INDEX wacky
```

This command gives you a list of archival files available for the given list. This allows you to retrieve digests and other files via e-mail with the GET command (see next).

GET

Usage:

```
GET wacky Wacky-o-Rama-#1
```

Use this command to retrieve files listed by the INDEX command. The command structure is GET [listname] [filename].

HELP (or HEL)

Usage:

```
HELP
HEL
```

This command sends a summary of all Macjordomo list commands.

Macjordomo: For More Information

More information about Macjordomo can be found at the Macjordomo Web site, located at <http://leuca.med.cornell.edu/Macjordomo>. A mailing list for the discussion of Macjordomo issues (administered by Macjordomo's author and run, appropriately enough, on a Macjordomo list server), is also available by mailing *macjordomo@afar.med.cornell.edu* with "subscribe Macjordomo-List [*your name*]" in the first line of the body of the message.

FireShare: An AppleScript Extension to AIMS

Jerry Stratton's FireShare is a shareware list server and mailbot written in AppleScript that works with AIMS 1.x. While its AppleScript nature makes FireShare a bit slower than AutoShare and Macjordomo, it also makes FireShare much more customizable for those who are adept at programming in AppleScript.

FireShare isn't for the timid—it's a lot harder to set up than Macjordomo, and even a little harder than AutoShare. FireShare doesn't really offer any sort of interface. You alter your preferences by editing text files placed in special folders within the FireShare folder. In fact, as Jerry Stratton writes in his documentation, to run FireShare "you'll need a brain, a heart, some courage, and a home." That about says it all.

Off to See the Wizard

In addition to AppleScript, FireShare requires several AppleScript scripting extensions to run. In addition to FireShare itself, you'll need to install the ACME Script Additions, the GTQ Scripting Library, and the TCP/IP Scripting Extension in the Scripting Extensions folder inside the Extensions folder in your System Folder. Power Mac users should be forewarned: at the time of this writing, FireShare was unstable when running on Power Macs.

FireShare is composed of six modules: AutoDrop, which receives text files (including BinHex files) and places them in a folder that's publicly accessible through FireShare's FileServer module; AutoReply, a mailbot; AutoFilter, a unique module that lets you filter incoming messages to one AIMS account and, based on various criteria you select, redirect those messages to various other e-mail addresses; Explode, a mailing list sender; ListManager, a very simple list server that works either with the Explode module or AIMS's regular mailing list functionality; and FileServer, an e-mail-based FTP server. In addition, you can modify FireShare modules or create your own if you feel comfortable enough with AppleScript.

Step by Step: Installing FireShare

After you've placed all the necessary extensions in the Scripting Extensions folder, you'll need to start creating accounts in AIMS for FireShare to use. To do this, create an account in AIMS (logins can be disabled; FireShare uses AIMS's file system à la AutoShare, rather than interacting via POP/SMTP like Macjordomo). Set the account to Save as files . . . and enter the path to the FireShare Drop folder, located within the folder containing the FireShare applet (see Figure 5.13). An example would be a path like:

```
HD:FireShare Folder:FireShare Drop Folder
```

Because we're dealing with AIMS, be sure not to end your path with a colon.

You configure the accounts FireShare uses (and which modules it uses on those accounts) by editing the FireShare Users text file, located in the Etc folder within the FireShare folder. The FireShare Users file comes preconfigured with three account names: files, submit, and aid. Submit is configured to use the AutoDrop module—

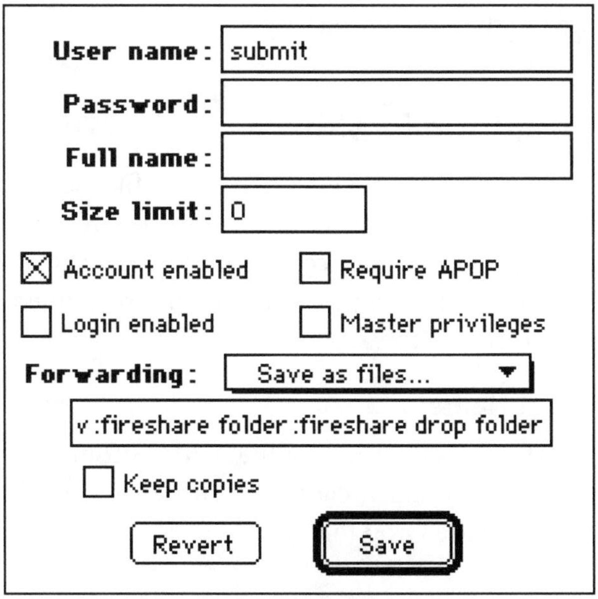

FIGURE 5.13
Configure Apple Internet Mail Server for use with FireShare.

any mail you send to the files account on your server will be saved out, with your subject line as its filename, in the Pub folder within the FireShare folder. Aid is linked to the AutoReply module: any message to aid will receive a copy of the file named help located in the Pub folder inside the FireShare folder. Files is linked to the FileServer module: if you send a message to files with a body of

```
ls
```

you'll receive a list of all files within the Pub folder; ls is the standard command for listing the contents of a directory when using FTP. FileServer also supports other FTP commands: GET [filename], which retrieves particular files; and CD [directory name], which changes directories. You can send a string of these commands to an account linked to FileServer. For example, a message body of:

```
cd ascii
get ITv5n3.etx
ls
```

would return the file ITv5n3.etx located within the ASCII folder, which is itself located within the Pub folder within the FireShare folder. Because that GET command is followed by an LS command, the file ITv5n3.etx would be followed by a listing of all the files located in the ASCII directory.

Configuring FireShare

You'll need to open the FireShare Users file (see Figure 5.14) in a text editor in order to create new accounts in FireShare. Each line of the file corresponds to one account, and each line includes four or five items delimited by commas. The items are defined in the following subsections.

Account Name

The first item is the name of the AIMS account that's to be used by FireShare. It should already be set to "Save as files . . ." and pointed to the FireShare Drop folder.

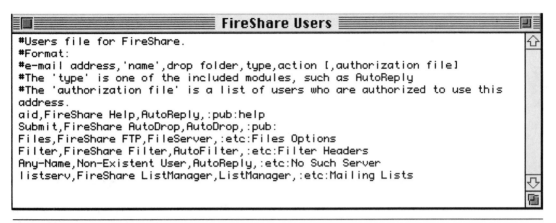

FIGURE 5.14 FireShare's Users File

User Description

This is the full name that corresponds to the account. It should probably be the same as the full name you entered for the account in AutoShare, though it doesn't have to be.

Module

The third item is the FireShare module that will be used with this account.

Configuration

This item will vary depending on which module is chosen for a given account.

AutoDrop. For AutoDrop accounts, this will be the folder where incoming messages will be dropped. It should be listed in path format—for example, a configuration line of:

```
:pub:wacky:ascii:
```

would mean files for that account would appear within the ASCII folder, within the Wacky folder, within the Pub folder, within the FireShare folder.

AutoFilter. For AutoFilter accounts, this would be the path leading to the filter file, such as:

```
:etc:specialfilters
```

with "specialfilters" as the name of the filter file (see later), located in the Etc folder inside the FireShare folder.

AutoReply. For AutoReply accounts, this is the path leading to the file that will automatically be returned to everyone who sends mail to the account.

Explode. For Explode accounts, this is the path leading to the file listing the e-mail addresses to which the incoming mail will be resent.

FileServer. For FileServer accounts, this will point to the configuration file for the files-by-email account.

ListManager. For ListManager accounts, this points to the file that describes the mailing lists.

Authorization File

The fifth item in a line is optional. Administrators who want to limit access to a certain account can enter a path in this space that points to a text file containing e-mail addresses. If this fifth item is present, only the users listed in that text file will be allowed to access the account. All other users will receive a rejection message.

The format of the authorization text file is that each individual user should appear on his or her own line. If a user has more than one e-mail address, all of his or her addresses should appear on the same line, delimited by a comma.

If only one person is allowed to access a given account, his or her e-mail address may be used as the fifth item instead of the path entry.

Filter Format

Filters are formatted with up to four different items on a single line, delimited by a | (straight up-and-down line) character, or "pipe." The items are defined in the following subsections.

Action Line

This item is the line of a message that will be scanned. Possibles are Subject and From. This item can also be Other. If Other is in the action line, then it must be followed immediately by an e-mail address. All mail that hasn't been directed with a previous filter will go to the e-mail address that follows the Other action line tag.

Logical Operator

The second item is a logical operator: is, contains, begins with, ends with, abovve, below, is not, does not contain, does not begin with, does not end with. This lets you more carefully define what you're scanning for.

Criteria String

The third item is exactly what you're looking for. It could be a keyword in a Subject line or a particular e-mail address or domain in a From line.

E-Mail Address

This is the e-mail address to which files fitting the criteria set up in the first three items will be sent. This could be an individual account, an AIMS mailing list, or even a FireShare account using the Explode module.

A Sample User

Say you wanted to set up an account called info that would automatically reply to any message sent to it with a file called information located in your Etc folder inside the FireShare folder. The line you'd enter into the FireShare Users file would be:

```
info,Info Server,AutoReply,:etc:information
```

 # FireShare: For More Information

For more information about FireShare, including details on FireShare's list manager and file server data files, see the FireShare home page, located at <http://cerebus.acusd.edu/html/FireBlade/FireShare/FireShare.html>.

ListSTAR: The Industrial-Strength Mail Processor

ListSTAR is a commercial package from StarNine that offers powerful and customizable mailbot and list processing services. ListSTAR is available in four forms: ListSTAR/SMTP, which (sort of like the AIMS/AutoShare combination) runs by itself as an SMTP server; ListSTAR/POP, which (like Macjordomo) runs as a POP/SMTP client interacting with other mail servers; and ListSTAR/QM and ListSTAR/MSM, which run as QuickMail and Microsoft Mail clients, respectively. Though they work with different protocols, the internal ListSTAR program is essentially the same in all versions.

Because ListStar's features are so broad and are well documented in the ListSTAR documentation, we won't attempt to give a step-by-step explanation of every feature in the product. (Demonstration versions of the ListSTAR software, as well as ListSTAR documentation in Adobe Acrobat format, are available on the CD that comes with this book. You can get a temporary serial number and use these demo copies for a limited time by going to StarNine's Web site at <http://www.starnine.com/>).

What we will do is give you an overview of just what ListSTAR does, how it works, and what it offers beyond the freeware and shareware mail software packages out there.

ListSTAR's Rules and Services

ListSTAR (in all its forms) is a rules-based system. You create a set of rules from the ground up (or modify generic rule sets that ListSTAR ships with the product) to create the kind of mailbot or list server you want. List servers from LISTSERV and ListProc to AutoShare and Macjordomo all have a particular way of handling lists. ListSTAR, on the other hand, allows you complete flexibility to handle mail in just about any way.

ListSTAR considers each e-mail address you use as a "service," and within each service can be any number of rules that interpret incoming messages and respond to them accordingly. Services can work together in many different ways. For example, you could have one service configured as a single list server account, taking subscription requests and adding or removing users from various lists, while other individual services do the work of the list itself, mailing out incoming messages to all subscribers. This is how most list servers operate.

But ListSTAR doesn't have to work that way. You could set up each mailing list as its own service, taking subscription requests from the same address as list postings. The first rules in such a service would filter out all list requests, and then the final rule would assume any message that hadn't already been filtered was a legitimate list posting and mail it out to subscribers.

Or you could set up your mailing lists as pairs, with a "list" service and a "list-request" service, matched addresses, one for posting to a list, one for handling list services. The advantage this tactic has over the previous one is that no subscription requests go to the main list address. This could be a problem if, for example, someone trying to subscribe to a list sent a message with a misspelled subject like "susbcribe"—this misspelling would probably fail to be caught by filters, and would be inadvertently passed on to the list's subscribers.

ListSTAR's flexibility also means that you don't have to limit subscription commands to either the subject or body of a message. You can pick one or both. You can choose which commands will work and which commands won't. In essence, you can build a list server or mailbot from the ground up—so be sure you know what you want before you go about creating it!

Sample List Services

To give you an idea of what ListSTAR can do, let's walk though the creation of a sample list server. In this example, we'll create a rudimentary mailing list service with a separate list-request service to handle subscriptions and other automated matters.

Enter Server Information

You start creating a service by clicking on the New . . . button in ListSTAR's Services window. You'll be prompted to give your service a name (pick one that makes it easy to identify) and enter information about what account your service will represent. (This will vary depending on what version of ListSTAR you're running; see the ListSTAR documentation for more detailed information.)

Once you've got that set, you can begin entering rules for this service, which will be for your list's request account. In ListSTAR, rules are processed one at a time, from top to bottom in the Rules window. Because of this, the order of your rules is important. For example, you wouldn't want to place a rule that passes any message on to all your list subscribers without preceding it with rules that make sure it's not a subscription request or an error message from another mail server.

A Subscription-Request Rule

The first rule we create will check for messages that come in with a subject that starts with the word subscribe, add the sender's name and address to our mailing list, and send that person back a confirmation letter.

ListSTAR's rules are split into six panes. The first is the Content Triggers pane (see Figure 5.15). In this pane, we can choose how ListSTAR reacts to a message based on information contained within that message. In this case, all we're doing is selecting that this rule will be activated if a message's subject begins with the word subscribe. A message with subjects of subscribe list, subscribe-list, and subscribe!!, would trigger this rule, but a message with the subject "sub" would not. (As your list gets up and running, you might want to start creating rules that look for misspelled words, shortened words, and the like, so that they also get processed.)

For now, let's skip over the Address Triggers pane (we'll come back to it in our next service) and go to the third pane, the Reply Actions pane (see Figure 5.16). This pane is where you set actions that

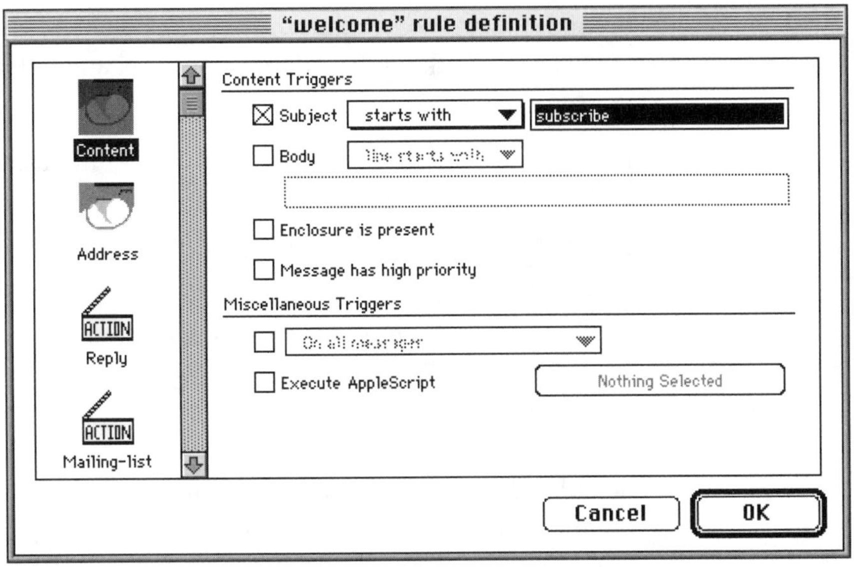

FIGURE 5.15 ListSTAR's Content Triggers Pane

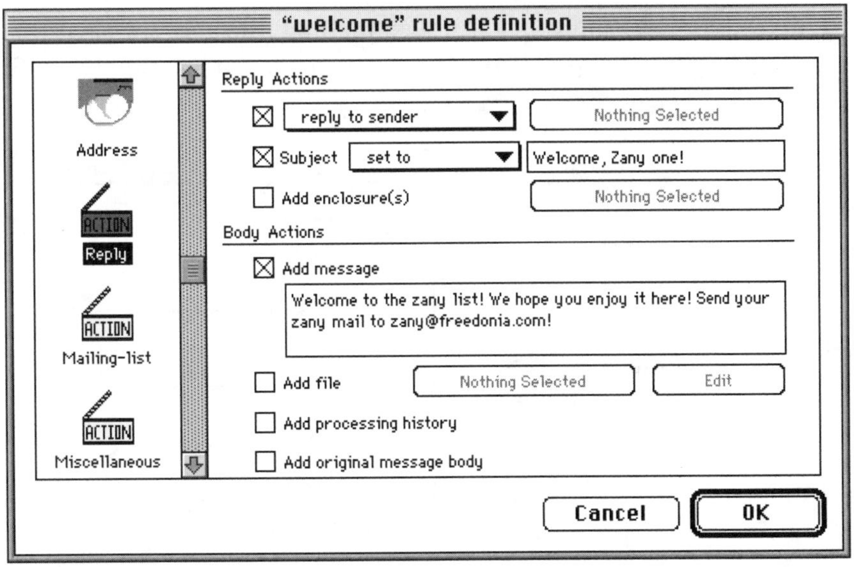

FIGURE 5.16 ListSTAR's Reply Actions Pane

involve sending replies back to messages sent to your service. In this case, we'll check three different options. We'll send a reply by checking the reply to sender option. We'll give our outgoing message a unique subject by checking the Subject box. And we'll add a brief message by checking the Add message box and entering in our message.

Now anyone who triggers this rule will automatically be sent a reply, with the subject we've set and a brief message reading that he or she has been added and how to post to the list.

The next pane we'll need is the Mailing-List Actions pane (see Figure 5.17). This pane is used for adding and removing people from mailing lists, forwarding incoming messages to mailing lists, and other actions related to mailing lists. In our case, we'll be selecting the second check box, which is listed as add "From" address to by default. This command adds the name and address of the sender of the message ListSTAR is processing to the mailing list or lists you select. This pop-up menu can also be remove "From" address from, which removes that person's name from the list or lists you select.

To the right of the pop-up menu is a button that, when clicked, brings up a list of all mailing lists and users within ListSTAR (see Figure 5.18). Here, we'll create a new mailing list file for our list and

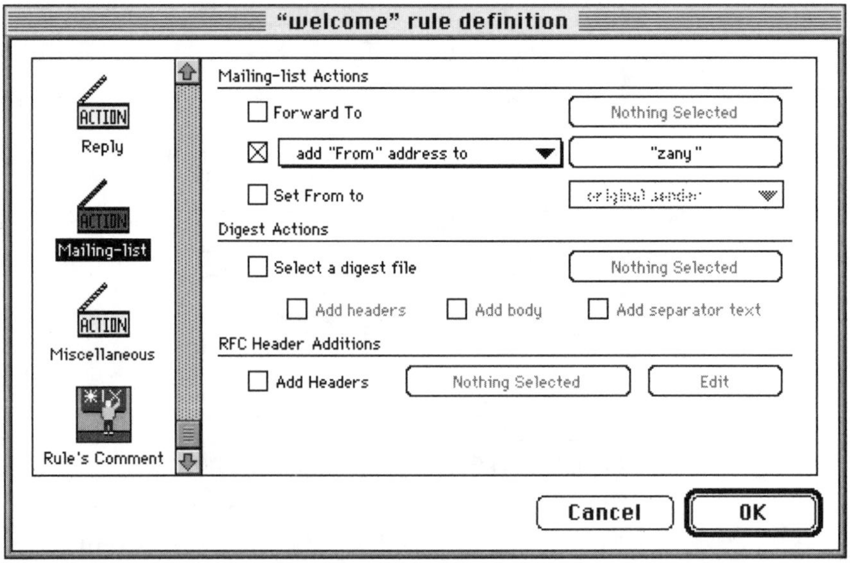

FIGURE 5.17 ListSTAR's Mailing-List Actions Pane

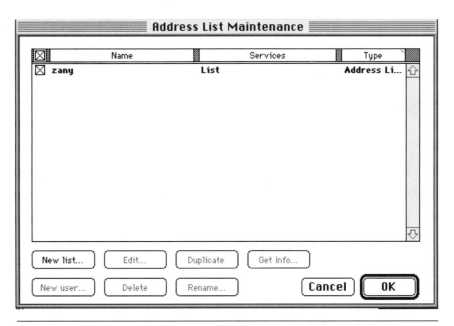

FIGURE 5.18 A List of All the Users and Mailing Lists in ListSTAR

select it by clicking on its check box. Now our rule is set: we'll add the person who sent the message we're processing to our mailing list.

Next, we go to the Miscellaneous Actions pane (see Figure 5.19) and check the Stop rule processing box. This prevents any other rules in this service from acting on the message we've just processed. Because we've already added this person to our mailing list and sent him or her a reply, we've done all we'll ever need to do. No more processing needs to be done with this message.)

Finally, we go to the Rule's Comment pane (see Figure 5.20), which doesn't perform any actions at all. But it's still important to enter a description of what your rule does in this pane, so that you and others will have a quick reminder of what your rule does.

In the end, this is what this rules does: it searches for a message with a subject starting with "subscribe," replies to that message with a welcome note, adds the recipient to the mailing list, and stops processing the message.

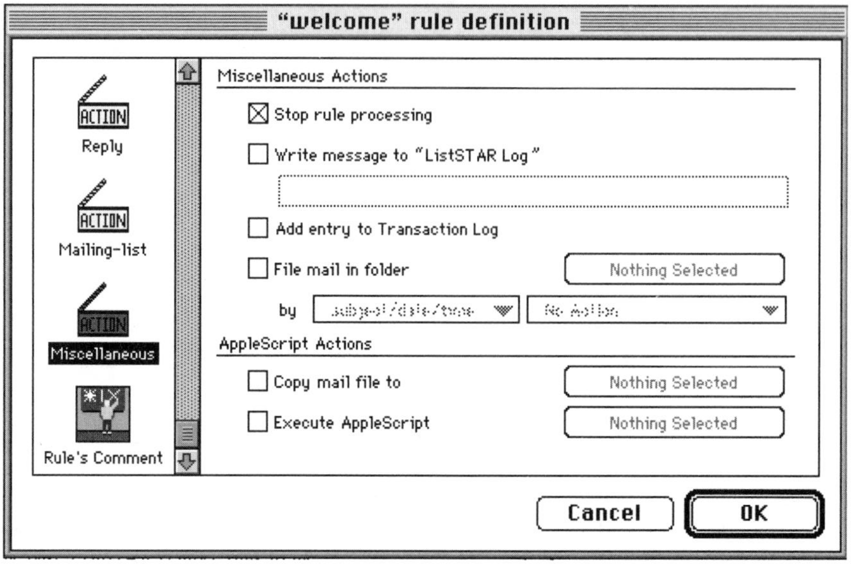

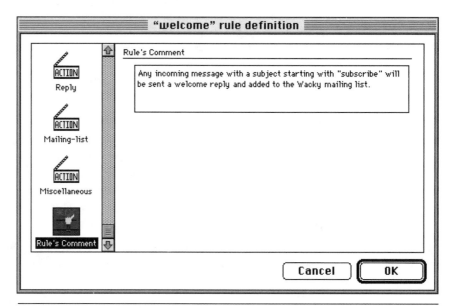

FIGURE 5.19 ListSTAR's Miscellaneous Actions Pane

FIGURE 5.20 ListSTAR's Rule's Comment Pane

Unsubscribing Users

The next rule you'll create will be one to unsubscribe people who send a message with unsub or unsubscribe as the subject of their message.

1. Create a new rule. Give it a name like unsubscribe.

2. Go to the Content Triggers pane and select Subject starts with, and enter unsub into the window.

3. Go to the Reply Actions pane and check reply to sender, which will send a reply to the message you've received.

4. In the same pane, check Subject set to and enter a subject like "You've been unsubscribed."

5. In the Body Actions section, click on Add message, and enter a brief message telling your user he or she has been unsubscribed and thanking him or her for being on the list.

6. In the Mailing-List Actions pane, select the second check box and set it to delete "From" address from. Click on the button to the right and select your mailing list. This will make ListSTAR remove your user from the mailing list when a subject starting with unsub (including unsubscribe) is received.

7. Go to the Miscellaneous Actions pane and check Stop rule processing.

8. Go to the Rule's Comment pane and enter a description of what this rule does: unsubscribe users who send a message whose subject starts with unsub.

Deal with the Rest

As with any service you create, you need to create one rule that takes care of any messages that haven't triggered *any* rules. This is how we'll do it for this service:

1. Create a new rule, and give it a name like no rules hit.

2. In the Content Triggers pane, select the first check box below the Miscellaneous Triggers header. From the pop-up menu,

select When no previous rules hit. This means if a message passes to this point in your rules sequence without having encountered a matching rule, it will automatically trigger this rule.

3. In the Reply Actions pane, select the first check box (Reply to sender).

4. In the same pane, check the Subject box and enter a subject like List Error in the corresponding window.

5. Still in the Reply Actions pane, click the Add message window and enter a brief message in the box that says something like: "Your message could not be processed. Please send your message to this address with a command in the subject line. Valid commands are SUBSCRIBE and UNSUBSCRIBE. If you have any questions, mail [*your name*] at [*your address*]." This will inform people what the valid commands are and give them a human being to write to if they're still having problems.

6. Go to the Miscellaneous Actions pane and check Stop rule processing.

7. Go to the Rule's Comment pane and enter a description of what this rule does.

Fend Off Daemons

You're almost done with this service, but there's one rule we still need to insert. Incoming e-mail messages will actually be error messages from other list servers or mailer daemons, programs that send back mail that can't reach its destination. If your list server were to reply to such a message, it would probably generate yet another return message, and so on, ad infinitum. This is called a *mail loop,* and mail loops are to be avoided at all costs. To do so, you need to write a rule, placed at or near the top of every one of your ListSTAR services, that filters out mail from list servers and mailer daemons, and forwards that mail to a list administrator.

1. Create a new rule, and give it a name like mailer-daemons.

2. In the Content Triggers pane select the check box next to From address is a list server/mailer daemon. This will automatically detect any message that's an error from another list server or mail server.

3. In the Mailing-list Actions pane, check the Forward To box, and click on the corresponding button. Create a new *user* (not a new list), and enter your own name and mailing address for that user. Then make sure its check box is selected and hit OK to return to the Mailing-list Actions pane. This will forward any error mail to your account, so you can see what the problem is and fix it. Often, the error will simply be a failed e-mail address, and the solution will be for you to manually remove a user from your mailing list so future mail doesn't also fail.

4. Go to the Miscellaneous Actions pane and check Stop rule processing.

5. Go to the Rule's Comment pane and enter a description of what this rule does.

Once you're finished with this rule, click OK. Then click on it in the Rules window and drag it to the top of the Rules list. This way, any list server or mailer-daemon mail will be intercepted before any of your other rules have a chance to process it.

Mission Accomplished

That's all there is to it. Now you've got a service that waits for list commands at a given address, forwards bounced mail to you, processes the requests it can, and automatically replies to the messages it doesn't understand. All that's left to do is create a service for the mailing list itself.

The List Service

We'll create a simple list service, one with only three rules. Your first rule will check to see if a message is coming from a member of your list, and if it *is* from a member, it will forward it to every other list member.

1. Create a new rule, and give it a name like Pass through list mail.

2. Go to the Address Triggers pane (see Figure 5.21). This is the area where you can filter a message based on what name or address it's coming from. Select the third check box, the one next to the phrase From address. Click on the corresponding button, and select your mailing list from the mailing list menu. This will verify that the incoming message is from a list member.

3. In the Mailing-list Actions pane, select the first check box (Forward To), click on the corresponding button, and select your mailing list. This will forward the incoming message to all the people on that list.

4. Go to the Miscellaneous Actions pane and check Stop rule processing.

5. Go to the Rule's Comment pane and enter a description of what this rule does.

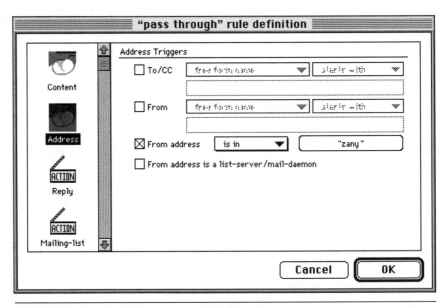

FIGURE 5.21 ListSTAR's Address Triggers Pane

Deny Access to Outsiders

Since that rule eliminates mail from people not on your list, you need to create another rule that handles that mail.

1. Create a new rule, and give it a name like Rejected mail.

2. In the Content Triggers pane, select the first check box below the Miscellaneous Triggers header. From the pop-up menu, select When no previous rules hit.

3. In the Reply Actions pane, select the first check box (Reply to sender).

4. In the same pane, check the Subject box and enter a subject like Message Rejected in the corresponding window.

5. Still in the Reply Actions pane, click the Add message window and enter a brief message in the box that says something like: "Your message could not be sent, because you are not a member of this list. To subscribe, send mail to [*list address*] with a subject of Subscribe. If you have any questions, mail [*your name*] at [*your address*]."

6. Go to the Miscellaneous Actions pane and check Stop rule processing.

7. Go to the Rule's Comment pane and enter a description of what this rule does.

Protect against Daemons

As before, protect yourself against daemons by creating the same rule as we did for the last message and placing it at the top of the rule list. Since ListSTAR supports copying and pasting of rules, you can go back to the other service, select that rule, copy it to the clipboard, return to this service, and paste the rule into the Rules window. After you've pasted it, be sure to turn on the list by clicking to the left of the rule's name. (When a rule is on, a check mark appears to the left of the name. When a rule is inactive, it appears in italics.)

<image data-ref-id="-1" data-missing="true"></image>

You've Made It!

That's it. You've created your own custom list server in ListSTAR. Of course, ListSTAR can do a lot more than this, from serving as a mailbot to performing complicated mail actions via AppleScripts. For more information, refer to ListSTAR's comprehensive documentation.

Claris Emailer: A Simple Mailbot

Claris Corporation has released an e-mail client, Claris Emailer, that also manages to work pretty well as a simple mailbot and auto-forwarding system, although it can't act as a list server.

Setting Up Emailer as a Mailbot

When you select Mail Actions from Emailer's Setup menu, a new window opens showing any message-filtering macros you've defined in Emailer (see Figure 5.22).

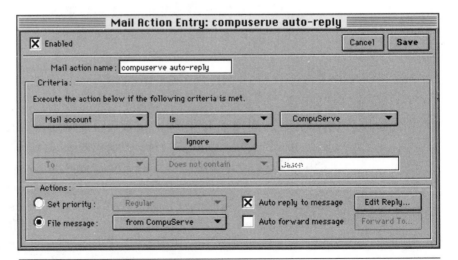

FIGURE 5.22 Emailer's Mail Actions Window

Click on Add to add a new action. You'll be prompted with a new window, the Mail Action Entry window (see Figure 5.23). From here, you can set up Emailer to automatically reply to an incoming message based on criteria such as subject, the sender's address, or even the POP account to which the message was originally sent. Then check the Auto reply to message box, click the Edit Reply button, and type or paste your auto-reply text into the Edit Reply window.

To use Emailer's mail actions as an auto-forwarding tool, just use the Auto forward message box, which operates under the same principle as the Auto reply to message box.

A Few Tips for Mailing List Administrators

Once you've got a list server up and running, the worst isn't over. After you've wrestled your Mac into submission and finally have your list server processing subscription requests and sending out messages and digests regularly, you'll have to start dealing with a much more complex and finicky problem: human beings.

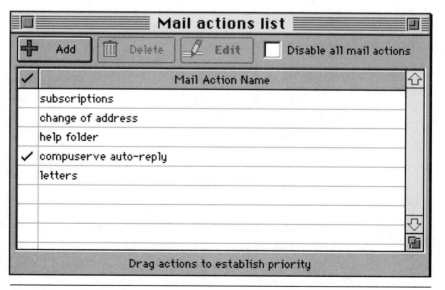

FIGURE 5.23 Emailer's Mail Action Entry Window

Those who extoll online communication as a utopia where people can meet unencumbered by issues such as geography, gender, age, race, and appearance probably haven't been online. While many of the issues that cause barriers to be built in "real-life" society don't exist online, there are plenty of new ones to be dealt with—no matter what hardware or software your list server is run on. As a list administrator, it's your job to keep the mailing lists you control a pleasant, reasoned environment. With that in mind, here are some suggestions to make sure the virtual communities you create don't get out of hand.

Prepare for the Time Commitment

Mailing list administrators have to spend some time dealing with list administrivia, including removing bad e-mail addresses from your mailing list, fixing incorrect addresses for users who can't figure out how to unsubscribe themselves, and the like. For any medium-sized mailing list, you should expect to spend around an hour a week administering the list. This can vary widely depending on the volume of your list, the number of participants, and so on, but it's good to keep the commitment in mind before volunteering to host any new mailing lists.

Write a FAQ for Your Lists

A FAQ, or Frequently Asked Questions file, is a document that attempts to head off common questions at the pass. If you've ever been on a mailing list or Usenet newsgroup for any length of time, you've seen some common questions get asked again and again by newcomers who don't realize that the questions have been hashed out for the better part of a decade.

If you create a FAQ, you can both set the ground rules for your list (see next subsection) and plant a foundation so that fundamental issues are explained in private rather than in public.

Your FAQ doesn't need to be a long and complex document, and it doesn't even need to differ substantially from list to list. Even if your FAQ contains nothing but a few fundamental rules of list conduct and how to subscribe and unsubscribe from a given list, it's worth creating.

Once you've created a FAQ, set up your list processing software to send it out automatically once a user has subscribed to a mailing list. That way, every new user will see the FAQ first, before he or she gets a chance to ask any of those questions veteran users dread.

As time goes on and your lists age, be sure to send out copies of your FAQ to the mailing list periodically. It's a good way to remind users of the ground rules, and keep them current with any changes in the FAQ that may have happened since they subscribed to your list.

Set Ground Rules

You should always set ground rules for your lists, and state them clearly in the FAQ. Define what is appropriate behavior for your list, and define the topics that are allowed to be discussed on a list. If your list is small and contains only a few friends, this probably isn't necessary. But if your list is larger and open to the public, you should be vigilant.

Most people turn to mailing lists for focused discussion on a given topic. If a discussion strays from that topic, it should probably be taken to private e-mail, or if the new topic is popular enough, to a new mailing list for people interested in discussing that topic.

As of this writing, there was still some measure of freedom of speech on the Internet, but just because people are free to say what they want doesn't mean they can do it on your mailing list. As list administrator, you're the only person with the power to protect your list from people who attack other users, either in public or in private. If a list administrator makes it known that anyone not being civil to other list members will be warned and then removed from the mailing list, people will be less inclined to "flame" one another. But if a list administrator acts as nothing more than a technician who keeps the list up and running, mailing lists can get ugly in a hurry.

Private Nudges

If the time comes to suggest to a list member that he or she should be a bit more polite or should stop discussing an off-topic subject on the public mailing list and take the discussion to private e-mail, the politic thing to do is to send a polite message to his or her private mailbox. Behaving like a vigilant "list mom" in public is a powerful tool, but publicly chastising a user may make you seem oppressive and could lead to a stifling of conversation. Of course, if people persist in making the same mistakes constantly, a public reminder of the list's ground rules is probably necessary.

Publicize Your Lists

Once your mailing list is up and running, you might want to announce it to the public if it's the kind of list that would benefit from a wide audience. Here are a few places to consider.

List of Publicly Accessible Mailing Lists

The List of Publicly Accessible Mailing Lists (PAML) is a clearinghouse for mailing list information. You can find it on the Web at <http://www.neosoft.com/internet/paml/>. Check out the site and see how list entires are formatted, and then send information about your list to *arielle@taronga.com*.

Net-Happenings

The Usenet newsgroup comp.internet.net-happenings is a good place to publicize new resources on the Internet, including mailing lists. Net-Happenings is also a mailing list; you can subscribe to it by mailing *majordomo@is.internic.net* with "subscribe net-happenings-digest" in the body of your message. To submit an entry to Net-Happenings, post your message to *comp.internet.net-happenings* or mail Gleason Sackman at *sackman@plains.nodak.edu*.

New-List

You can send a message describing your list to *NEWLIST @VM1.NODAK.EDU*, a mailing list designed for the announcement of new mailing lists.

Don't Spam

You can also post messages to relevant Usenet newsgroups announcing your mailing list, but don't "spam," or flood newsgroups with irrelevant posts. Post once, and post only on highly relevant newsgroups. For example, if you were posting about a new mailing list covering aspects of a Mac-based HTTP server, you might post an announcement to *comp.infosystems.www.announce* (a moderated newsgroup), *comp.sys.mac.announce* (also moderated), and perhaps *comp.infosystems.www.servers.mac* and *comp.sys.mac.comm*. Whatever you do, don't post to all the *comp.sys.mac.** and *comp.infosystems.www.** groups—that's a major offense to most Net citizens.

## CHAPTER 6

Serving Files via FTP

An Internet File Server

When friends are exchanging small files among themselves via the Internet, the most common approach is to send those files as e-mail enclosures. But if you want to distribute large files or make files of any size publicly available to just about anyone who wants them, you'll want to use FTP, the File Transfer Protocol.

As anyone who's been on the Net for any length of time knows, an FTP server is a file server, just as if it were a Mac with System 7 file sharing turned on, or an AppleShare server, or even a Novell NetWare file server. The difference is that while those servers are available only on your local network, FTP servers are file servers whose potential audience is made up of everyone on the Internet.

As the Macintosh has grown, it's become an increasingly capable file server. The advent of System 7 brought built-in file sharing that allowed any Mac to be a file server. As the Mac has become more and more Internet-savvy, several tools have appeared that take that file-sharing capability and transform it into an easy way to serve files to anyone on the Net.

The File Transfer Protocol

FTP has been around a long time. In fact, more than a decade before the first Macintosh 128 rolled off the Apple assembly line, machines were transferring files using FTP.

FTP is a standard that was designed to ensure that any machine, whether it's a client or a server, a UNIX machine or some other strange computer not even invented yet (like the Mac), would be able to transfer files back and forth with ease. Any FTP client or server speaks the same language. Thay all share the same set of commands that lets users log in, navigate through a file structure, and send or receive files.

 ## Stairways Software's FTPd

Australian Peter N Lewis, author of more than a dozen Mac applications (most of them Internet-oriented), is the creator of the first full-featured and most popular MacOS-based FTP server, known as FTPd. (FTPd stands for File Transfer Protocol daemon, daemon being a UNIX term for a program that provides services while running in the background.) FTPd—called "NetPresenz" as of version 4.0—is published as shareware by Stairways Software.

FTPd works in coordination with the Mac's built-in file sharing system, including the user lists found in the Users and Groups Control Panel. As a result, a Mac running local file sharing and FTPd will have the same users, passwords, and access privileges whether the user is logged on via AppleShare in your local network or via FTP from an Internet site in Tasmania.

FTPd works as an FTP, Gopher, and Web server. For more information about FTPd's Gopher and Web capabilities, see Chapters 7 and 8.

The Two-Headed App

FTPd is actually made up of two different applications. FTPd Setup is the application you use to set and change your preferences. FTPd is the server itself. In previous versions, there were two versions of the FTPd server app—one that ran in the foreground, and one that ran silently in the background, not even appearing in the Finder's list of open applications.

With version 3.0, the FTPd application can run either in the background or foreground. To select which one you'd prefer (if you're running FTPd by itself on a server, foreground is probably better; if you're running it on a Mac that someone will be using for other things, background might be preferable), pull down FTPd Background Mode from the File menu in FTPd Setup. Check the Background only box if you'd like FTPd to run only in the background.

If you place FTPd file in the Startup Items folder within your System Folder and have the Background only option checked, you'll be able to run an FTPd server on a Mac in almost complete silence. It will launch at startup and then run in the background, as if it weren't there at all. (Of course, if a dozen users connect to your Mac and begin downloading files all at once, you'll still notice it, just as you'd notice if people were copying files using File Sharing.)

Users & Groups: Creating Accounts

For FTPd to work, you must first have file sharing turned on and have run Internet Config, the universal Internet configuration application cowritten by FTPd's author, Peter Lewis. Then you can go about creating users and setting access privileges for your FTP server using file sharing. To create a new user, open Users & Groups and select New User from the File menu. Give the user a name in the Finder, and then double-click on the user's icon to define its password. You can do this for each unique user you expect to log in to your FTP server.

To enable anonymous FTP, double-click on the Guest icon and make sure that the Allow Guests to Connect box is checked. Allowing anonymous logins can be very dangerous, since you have no real way of knowing who is logging in to your file system. Be sure to carefully configure your file-sharing access before allowing anonymous logins, to make sure no files or folders that you'd prefer to keep safe and private are available to guests. If you don't want to allow anonymous logins to your server, make sure the Allow Guests to Connect box is unchecked.

Since FTPd uses System 7 File Sharing, you need to configure which files and folders will be available to your FTPd users by selecting files or folders and using the Sharing . . . command, located in the File menu. (For specifics on this, read the example setup provided later in this chapter.)

FTPd Setup: Configuring the Server

Now you'll need to launch the FTPd Setup application. Once it launches, you'll be provided with a window containing six buttons (see Figure 6.1). Since we're concerned only with FTP issues in this chapter, we'll be looking only at the four buttons that cover FTP issues.

FTP Setup

Clicking on the FTP Setup button brings up a window that lets you control fundamental access options for your FTPd server (see Figure 6.2). Within the box marked Privileges you'll find entries for Owner, Users, and Guests. The Owner is you—the name and password you entered into your Sharing Setup control panel. Users are any individuals for whom you've entered specific names and passwords in the Users & Groups control panel. Guests are users logging in anonymously as anonymous or ftp.

File Access options in this window are None, Read Only, Upload, and Full. Users with access privileges set to None will not be allowed

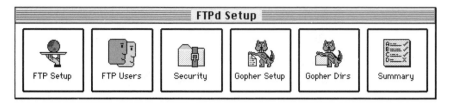

FIGURE 6.1 The FTPd Setup application lets you configure how your FTPd server will function.

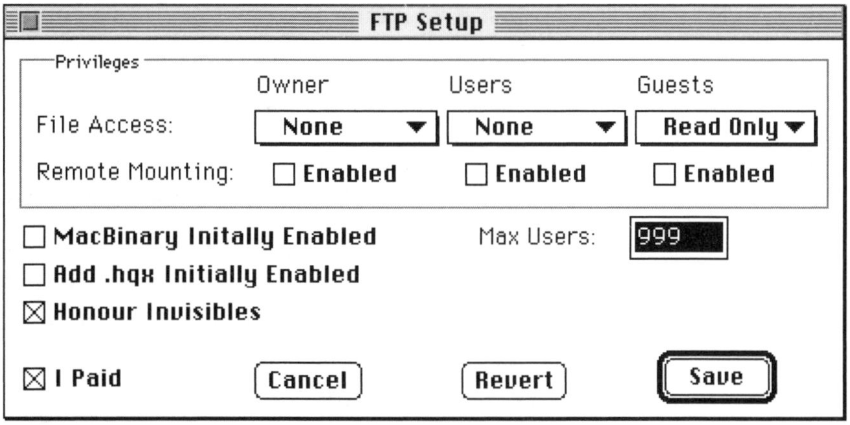

FIGURE 6.2 The FTP Setup window allows you to set basic access privileges for FTPd user types.

to log in to your server. Read Only privileges means that a user can download files, but can't upload or delete any files. Upload means that a user can download files and upload new files, but can't delete files or alter the file system in any other way. Users with privileges set to Full can upload, download, and delete files or folders at will—Full access gives a user total control over the file system.

It should go without saying, but the ramifications of allowing anyone Full access to your file system are so great that we must emphasize: Don't allow Full access to your file system to any user—even your own account—unless your files are backed up regularly, your passwords are carefully chosen, and you've carefully selected which files and directories are available to users on the outside.

Remote Mounting

Below the row of File Access pop-ups is a row of Remote Mounting check boxes. These allow users to log in to volumes on other machines on the FTPd server's local network. This can be a big security risk, since it exposes *other* machines running System 7 File Sharing on your local network to outside users, even though they're not running FTPd. As a result, you shouldn't check these boxes (especially not for Guests) unless absolutely necessary.

The command FTPd needs to receive from a connected FTP client in order to mount remote volumes is:

```
quote smnt [volume]:[server]@[zone]:[username]:[password] *
```

Volume is the name of the volume you'll be mounting; *server* is the server's name as it appears in the Chooser when AppleShare is selected. The entries that follow are optional: the zone the server is in, if it's not in the same zone as the FTPd server, and the user name and password required to log in to that server. So, to log in to a volume named Stuff on a machine named File Server on your server's local zone, you'd enter the command:

```
quote smnt Stuff:File Server
```

Whereas a more complicated login might look something like this:

```
quote smnt goodies:Network Admin@Admin:frank:xyzzy
```

meaning to log into the goodies volume on the machine named Network Admin located in the Admin zone, with a user name of frank and a password of xyzzy.

Setup Check Boxes

There are four check boxes in the bottom half of the FTP Setup window. The first, MacBinary Initially Enabled, will assume that every user logging in is using a Macintosh and wants to transfer files in the native MacBinary format if the box is checked. Since the two major

---

* Some FTP clients add "quote" to all such commands; if using a command like this with "quote" doesn't work, try it without.

Macintosh FTP clients, Peter Lewis' Anarchie and Dartmouth College's Fetch, both enable MacBinary when they log in to a server, you should probably leave this box unchecked.

The Add .hqx Initially Enabled check box will, when checked, cause FTPd to pretend that every binary file on your server is an encoded BinHex text file. BinHex is a standard method of binary file transfers on the Internet, especially among Mac users who must FTP using a UNIX system and then download what they've transferred via FTP back to their Mac using some other means. This box should probably remain unchecked unless your server is serving all Mac users and most of your users have to use a non-Mac system to FTP.*

The third check box, Honour Invisibles, tells FTPd whether it should display files that are considered invisible by the Mac's file system. Many programs create invisible files—ones that exist, but don't appear anywhere in the Finder. Unless you have invisible files you want your users to have access to, you'll want to keep this box checked.

The final box is marked I Paid. Since FTPd is shareware, you should check this box only if you've paid for the software. Users can pay for FTPd by using the Register program included with the FTPd distribution. If the I Paid flag is not checked, FTPd notes in its log in screen that your copy of FTPd is unregistered.

Maximum FTPd Users

The Max Users box is where you can specify how many users can be logged in to FTPd at one time.

FTP Users

The FTP Users window (see Figure 6.3) allows you to do two things: set a default directory for your users, and set commands that will be automatically issued when a user first logs in.

---

* FTPd will automatically convert a file into BinHex format for anyone who wants it, simply by appending .hqx to the end of any filename. For example, if you wanted to download the file test.sit as a BinHex file, you'd simply try to download test.sit.hqx instead.

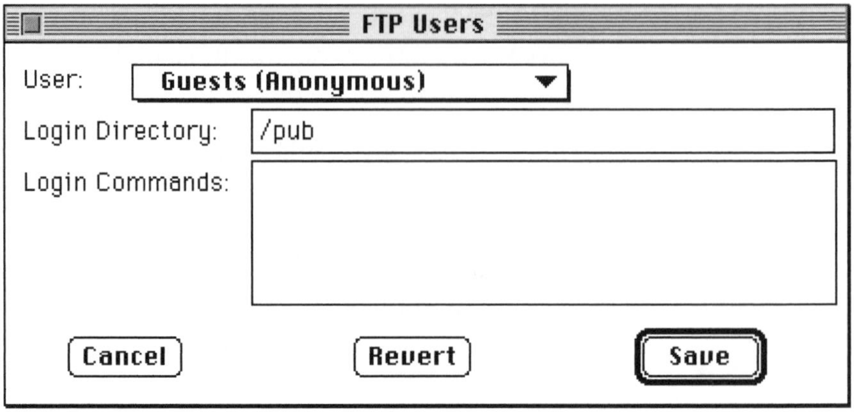

FIGURE 6.3 The FTP Users window lets you set default directories and commands for users.

You use the User pop-up to choose which user you'll be setting up preferences for. In the Login Directory field, you enter the folder you want to appear by default when a user logs in, in path format. Path format is an Internet standard for FTP that can seem a little weird for Macintosh users. Essentially, every path begins with a slash, which represents the top of your file hierarchy. You specify folders within folders by entering folder names followed by slashes until you've worked your way down from the top of the hierarchy to the folder you want to specify.

As far as FTPd and File Sharing are concerned, however, the top of your file hierarchy is a flexible concept. The top can vary from user to user, depending on which areas the user has access to. For example, a user with access to three different folders would find his or her top level containing those folders. But the owner of a Macintosh, with access to the entire hard drive, would find his or her top level containing the hard drives mounted on the server. So while a default directory of /user would point a user to a certain directory, a path to that same directory from the owner's standpoint might be something like /Hard Drive/FTP files/FTP/user.

The Login Commands box lets you specify commands you'd like automatically executed when a user logs in. For example, if you'd like to give a certain access to a certain remote file server automatically, you might enter something like:

```
smnt Stuff:File Server
```

in the Login Commands box. Another user might be automatically logged in to another server, or to none at all. If you had a user who could receive only binary files in BinHex form, you might enter:

```
site h e
```

in the box. This command tells FTPd to enable .hqx encoding of all binary files for a particular session.[*]

Security

The Security window (see Figure 6.4), which is split up into four sections, is where you can limit what FTPd can do even further, as well as control log and server notification options.

General Security

There are three options available in the General Security window: Log Actions to File, Hide Log in Background, and Allow Clear Text Passwords.

Log Actions to File. If this box is checked, everything that happens on your server will be listed in a text file. If you're interesting in knowing who is using your server and what they're doing while connected, you should check this option.

Hide Log in Background. If this box is checked, the FTPd Log window—which shows what's going on on your FTPd server while FTPd is up and running—will appear only when the FTPd application is active. If the box is checked, the log will automatically disappear when you change out of FTPd into the Finder or some other application, just as if you had chosen Hide FTPd from your applications menu. This is useful if you want to run other programs while

---

[*] For more information about these extended FTP commands, see Peter Lewis' FTPd documentation, located on this book's companion CD-ROM.

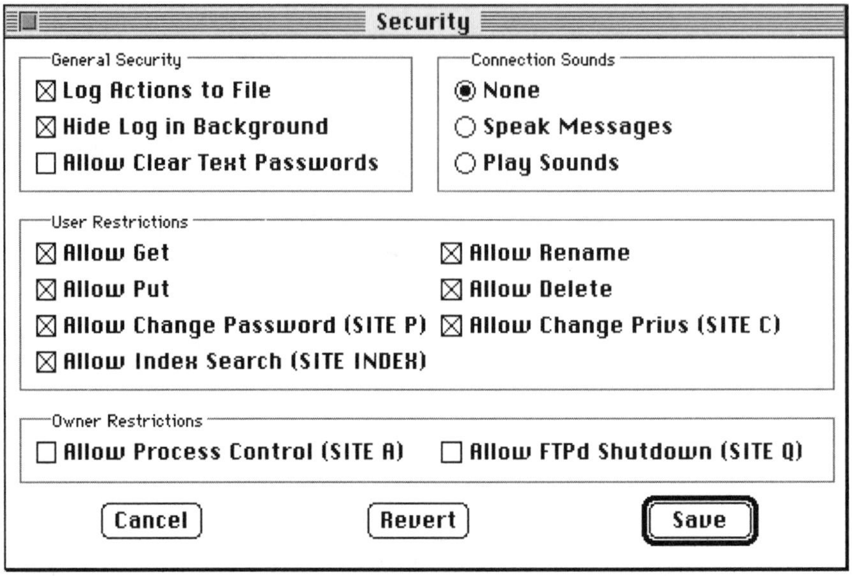

FIGURE 6.4 The FTP Security window is split into four sections.

running FTPd, but don't want to be bothered by FTPd's Log window. Leaving the box unchecked will mean the Log window will be visible no matter which application you switch to, unless you select Hide FTPd from the applications menu.

Allow Clear Text Passwords. Passwords are often scrambled when sent over AppleShare, but CAP servers and NetWare Macintosh servers (if you've got such servers on your network, you probably know) require that passwords be sent unscrambled. This is a security risk, but since the passwords have to be sent unscrambled via FTP in the first place, it's a minor one. Unless you expect to have your users log on remotely to CAP or NetWare servers, you should probably leave this box unchecked.

Connection Sounds

This set of radio buttons determines how (or if) FTPd will alert you about what someone's doing while connected via FTPd. If None is selected, FTPd will remain silent. If Speak Messages is selected, FTPd will play digitized voice samples to announce logins and other events on your server. If Play Sounds is selected, FTPd will play various sound effects to announce logins, logouts, and other events.

User Restrictions

The set of seven check boxes in the User Restrictions section of the Security window control which commands FTPd will recognize from any user—regardless of whether they're guests, users, or even owners.

Allow Get. Unchecking this box prevents all users from downloading files.

Allow Rename. Unchecking this box prevents users with appropriate access privileges from renaming files.

Allow Put. Unchecking this box prevents all users from uploading files.

Allow Delete. Unchecking this box prevents all users from deleting files.

Allow Change Password. Unchecking this box prevents all users from changing their passwords remotely via FTP. Of course, passwords can still be changed from within the Users & Groups control panel on the FTPd host machine.

Allow Change Privs. Unchecking this box prevents users with appropriate access privileges from changing the privileges on individual files and folders. When this box is checked, users with full access to a file can specify if they want to be downloadable or changeable, either by themselves or by others.

Allow Index Search. When this box is checked, any user can enter the command SITE INDEX followed by an expression, and search every folder he or she has access to for files that match that expression. For example, the command:

```
SITE INDEX .hqx
```

would return a list of every BinHex file located on the system. There's no security risk involved in allowing index searches; the only issue is one of processing power. Index searches can noticeably slow down a Mac if you're using it for other purposes. If you're using your FTPd server and are experiencing unacceptable slowdowns, you might consider disabling this command.

Owner Restrictions

The two check boxes in the Owner Restrictions section cover commands that can be issued only by the owner when he or she is logged in via FTP.

Allow Process Control. If this box is checked, the Owner can launch and quit other applications on the FTPd server remotely via FTP. For example, if you wanted to launch Microsoft Word on the FTPd server remotely, you would enter the command:

```
SITE A OAPP MSWD
```

The four-letter code is the creator signature for a given application. Every application has a unique creator signature.

To quit out of Microsoft Word, you'd enter:

```
SITE A QUIT MSWD
```

Since this option opens up the potential for abuse by someone who surreptitiously obtains the owner's name and password, you should check this box only if you plan on using this feature.

Allow FTPd Shutdown. If this box is checked, the owner can remotely shut down FTPd by issuing the command:

```
SITE Q
```

As with the Allow Process Control option, you should check this box only if you're planning on using this feature.

Summary

When you click on the Summary button in the FTPd Setup toolbar, you'll be given an easy-to-understand text listing of your FTPd server's status. If File Sharing is on, you'll see which privileges have been set in the Users & Groups control panel, which FTP privileges have been set in FTPd Setup, and whether Gopher users can connect.

Step by Step: Creating a Simple FTPd Server

Now let's walk through the creation of a simple FTP server structure using FTPd.

Creating New Users

First, make sure that you've set your preferences using Internet Config and turned on File Sharing in the Sharing Setup control panel. Then open the Users & Groups control panel. Within the Users & Groups window, you'll want to create users named dave and paul by selecting New User from the File menu, and then assign them passwords by double-clicking on their respective icons and entering passwords in the Password window.

Creating Folders and Setting Permissions

Now you'll want to create a main FTP folder, which we'll call FTP. Within it, you should create folders for individual users to do with as they wish, a "dropbox" that users can write to but not read from, and an anonymous folder that any guest can see.[*] We'll say the folders inside the FTP folder are called dave, paul, dropbox, and pub (our public folder that anyone, including anonymous users, can see).

The Dropbox

First, select the dropbox folder and choose Sharing . . . (see Figure 6.5). Then check Share this item and its contents, which makes the folder available via File Sharing. Next, turn off three check boxes in

---

[*]For more information about the logic of FTP folder hierarchies and structure, see the end of this chapter.

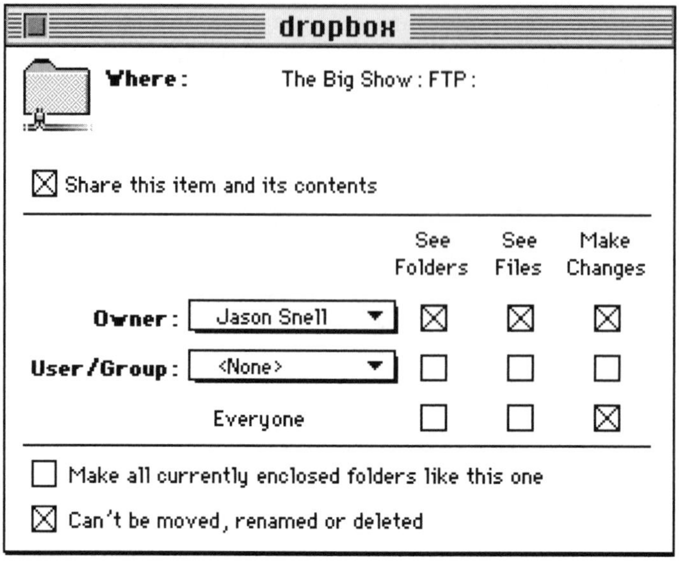

FIGURE 6.5 Set access privileges for your dropbox folder.

the User/Group row—these let you specify access for specific users, and your dropbox is going to offer the same access for every user. On the row marked Everyone, you'll need to make sure the See Folders and See Files boxes are not checked, while the Make Changes box is. This means that users can place files within the Dropbox folder, but they can't see anything inside it. Now people logging in to your server can leave files for you, but they can't see any private files other people might have already left behind.[*] Once you've closed the Dropbox window and saved your preferences, the folder is ready to be used by File Sharing and FTPd.

User Folders

Now select the dave folder and choose Sharing . . . (see Figure 6.6). Check Share this item and its contents. This time, make sure all boxes are unchecked in the Everyone row—this will be a personal folder that only the user dave will have access to. Select dave in the

---

[*] One problem with allowing a dropbox is that it allows users to fill up your hard drive with whatever they see fit to upload. If you're concerned about disk space and don't see the need for a dropbox, don't create a dropbox.

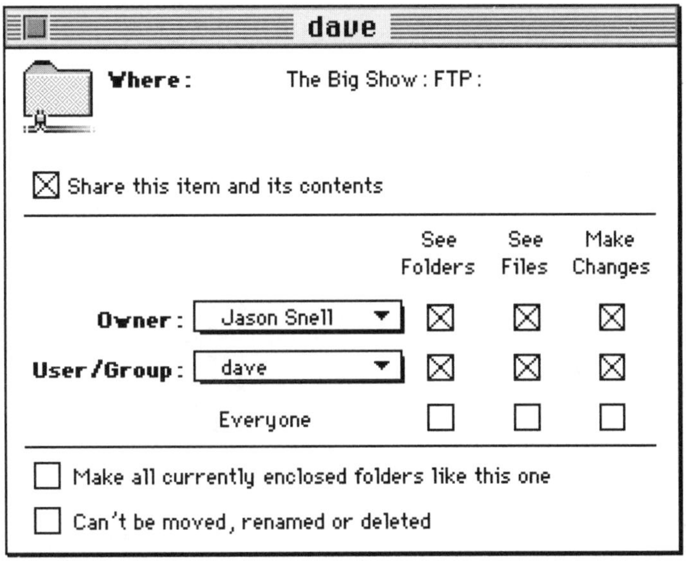

FIGURE 6.6 Set access privileges for your user folders.

pop-up list in the User/Group row, and make sure all three boxes are checked in that row. Now Dave will have control over adding and removing files from his personal folder. Repeat this step for the paul folder and for as many other different folders and users as you like.

A Public Directory

Now open the Sharing window for the Pub folder (see Figure 6.7). Check the Share this item and its contents box and uncheck all the boxes in the User/Group row. In the Everyone row, check See Folders and See Files, but be sure that Make Changes is unchecked. This way all users will be able to see anything in the Pub folder structure, but won't be able to change anything. This is how most anonymous FTP sites are structured.

Setting FTPd Permissions

Now launch FTPd Setup and click on the FTP Setup button. In the FTP Setup window, you'll probably want to set the Owner's File Access privileges to None, since you can administer your site directly

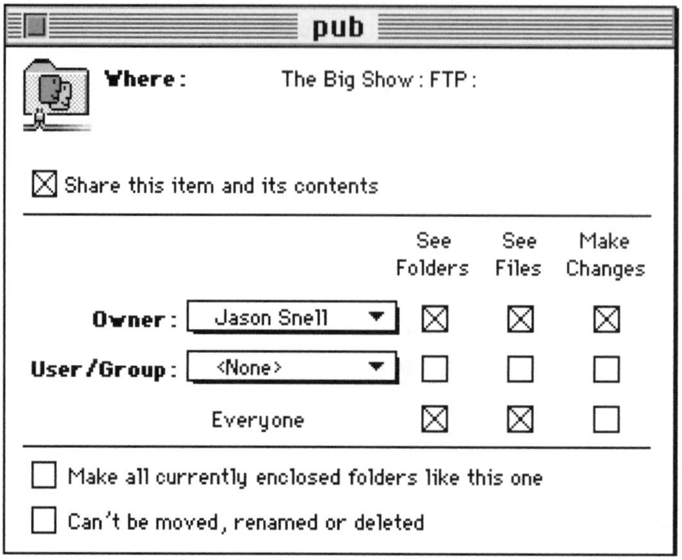

FIGURE 6.7 Set access privileges for your public folder.

from the Mac it's running on, or via File Sharing from another Mac on your local network. If you are planning on administering the site remotely via FTP, you can set File Access to Full—but if you do this, be very sure that your user name and password are secure, so that someone can't log in as you and trash your file system.[*]

Set the Users File Access privileges to Full. This allows them to upload and delete files from within their personal directories. But since you set up the pub folder without any write access (by leaving the Make Changes box unchecked in the Sharing . . . dialog for that folder), these users will still be restricted to downloading from that folder.

Set the Guests File Access privileges to Upload. Because of the privileges you set up in the Sharing . . . dialogs for all your folders, how-

---

[*] There is a way to allow full owner access while limiting access only to shared folders. To do this, go into the Users & Groups control panel and double-click on the icon representing the owner account (the "face" icon will be surrounded by a thick black border). Uncheck the Allow user to see entire disk box. This will limit the owner to shared folders, but it also means you'll no longer be able to control other parts of your FTP server's hard drive via File Sharing.

ever, anonymous users will only be able to upload files into the dropbox folder. If you don't want to have a dropbox folder available to guests, just set this pop-up to Read Only instead.

Setting Default Directories

Next, open FTPd Setup's FTP Users window. In the User pop-up, select dave. In the Login Directory window, enter:

    /dave

This means that every time Dave logs in, he'll automatically be placed in his home directory. You can do the same with Paul or any other user, putting a slash (indicating that you'll be pointing to a folder located at the top level of your file hierarchy) followed by the name of the user's folder.*

Now select Guests (Anonymous) from the User pop-up. In the Login Directory window, enter:

    /pub

Now users who log in anonymously will automatically be placed in the /pub directory by default. While they can back up to the top level and see the dropbox directory, most users will probably want to view only the files in your public directory and won't be interested in dropping off files.

Create Startup Messages

FTPd ships with generic "startup messages"—text files that are sent automatically when a user logs in (see Figure 6.8). They're located in the Startup Messages folder within your FTPd folder. If you'd like to

---

* If you've got a lot of users you'll be giving personal folders to, you might want to consider simplifying your folder situation by placing all the personal folders within a folder named something like "users." Set the permissions of that folder so that anyone can see folders within it. Then set the permissions of the individual folders within as outlined in our example. Now when you're setting default directories for these users, you'd specify something like "/users/dave" instead of just "/dave."

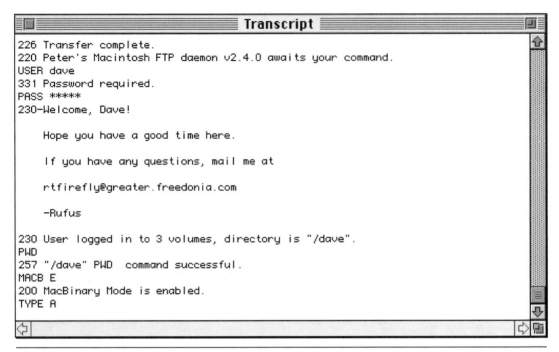

FIGURE 6.8 A welcome message sent by FTPd.

create personalized messages for your individual users, you'd place those messages in files named [username] startup. Any user without a startup file will receive the text found in Default Startup. Any anonymous user will receive the text in Anonymous Startup. Personalize these messages as you see fit, but keep them short—FTPd won't accept startup messages containing more than 5 K of text.

Ready to Go

Now FTPd is ready to use. Feel free to populate your pub directory with as many folders and files as you'd like to make available for downloading. If you'd like more information about FTPd, check out Peter Lewis' voluminous FTPd documentation, which appears on the CD-ROM accompanying this book.

White Pine Software's FTPShare

Unlike FTPd, which can run as a background application or a regular application, White Pine Software's FTPShare runs on a Macintosh as a system extension, loading at startup. Like FTPd, you configure FTPShare from a regular application; but, unlike FTPd, FTPShare does not use the System 7 Users & Groups control panel, and therefore can run on System 6.0.4 or later.

How FTPShare Works

FTPShare goes in the Extensions folder inside your System Folder, and loads when you boot the Macintosh. FTPShare also comes with three other applications, which roughly approximate the System 7 File Sharing system: FTPShare Setup, FTPShare Monitor, and FTPShare Users.

FTPShare Setup

At first glance, FTPShare Setup looks a lot like the Sharing Setup control panel (see Figure 6.9). In it, you define the name of your owner

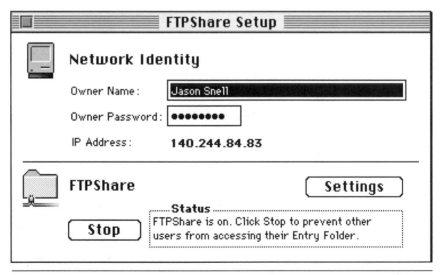

FIGURE 6.9 You enter owner information and turn FTPShare on and off in the FTPShare Setup application.

account and the password that will go with that account. A button at the bottom of the FTPShare Setup window lets you toggle FTPShare on and off. Another button, labeled Settings, takes you to a more complex settings dialog (see Figure 6.10) offering several options.

Sessions. This pop-up lets you choose the maximum number of users who can be connected to your FTPShare server at once.

Timeout. This pop-up lets you specify how long FTPShare will allow a user to remain logged in while doing nothing before that connection is terminated.

Block Size. This pop-up lets you specify how large the blocks are that FTPShare sends as part of its FTP session. For the most part, you'll want to keep this at its default.

Default Binary. This pop-up lets you specify what the default binary type will be for your server. You'll probably want to leave this as Binary, though if you're exclusively serving Macintosh clients, you could change this to MacBinary.

Transmit. Here you specify whether to transmit just carriage returns (Mac format) or carriage returns and linefeeds (UNIX and

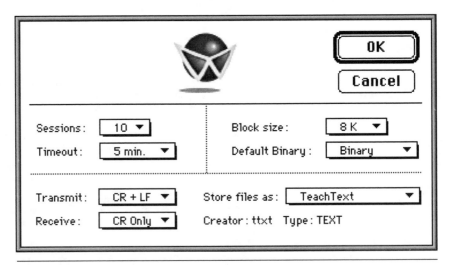

FIGURE 6.10 FTPShare Setup's Settings dialog lets you fine-tune access preferences.

PC format) at the end of every line of a text file. If you cater to Mac users, you might want to set this to CR + LF.

Receive. This is where you specify whether to save uploaded text files with just carriage returns or with carriage returns and linefeeds. Since your server is a Mac and you may want to view those files locally, you'll probably want to set this to CR only.

Store Files as. Here you can choose to which application FTPShare will point all uploaded text files. Choose your favorite text editor—SimpleText, BBEdit, Alpha, or even a word processor like Microsoft Word or WordPerfect.

FTPShare Monitor

Analagous to the File Sharing Monitor control panel, FTPShare Monitor (see Figure 6.11) lets you see which users are connected and how active they are; it also lets you also disconnect users if you see fit. In addition, FTPShare Monitor allows you to see which IP address the user is connecting from.

Clicking on the Log check box displays a log window that lets you view specific logins and logouts on your server. Clicking on the Trace button shows you which commands a given user is entering during his or her session.

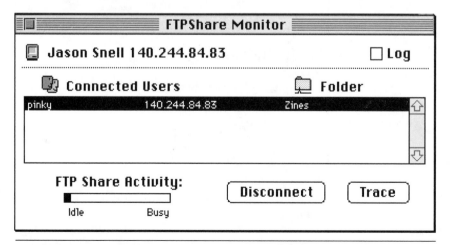

FIGURE 6.11 The FTPShare Monitor window lets you see information about connected users.

FTPShare Users

The FTPShare Users application parallels the Users & Groups control panel—in FTPShare Users, you can create new users and set their access privileges, as well as decide how anonymous logins will be handled.

If you select New User from the FTPShare window, a user preferences window will appear (see Figure 6.12). You can enter the password you'd like to assign to this new user, and click a radio button to set if he or she will have Read Only access, Write Only (dropbox) access, or Read and Write access. You also need to set an entry folder for your user—the folder he or she will be placed in by default when loging on to your server. When you're done, you can save this user by selecting Save as . . . and saving the user (the filename will be the user's login name) in the FTPShare folder.

If you select New Guest from the FTPShare window, you'll see a different window, this one allowing you to set access for your guest users (see Figure 6.13). As in the Users window, here you can set Read Only, Write Only, or Read and Write access, and can select an

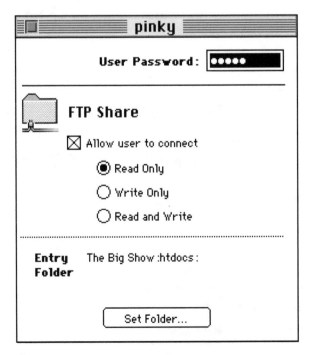

FIGURE 6.12
Creating a new user in FTPShare Users.

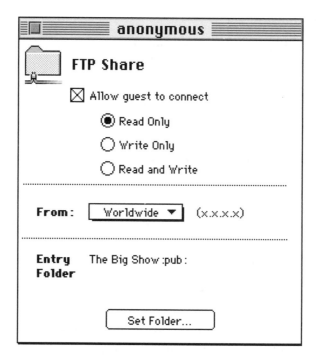

FIGURE 6.13
Setting guest access
in FTPShare Users.

entry folder. However, in the anonymous user window there's also a From pop-up that lets you restrict access somewhat. If you select Local, the window will allow access only for users whose first three IP numbers match your server's. These will in all likelihood be people on your local network. If you select Site, users logging in will have to match the first two IP numbers of your server—most likely users from your company or your service provider. If you select Country, users logging in will only have to match the first IP number of your server. A selection of Worldwide offers no IP address restrictions whatsoever.

File Access in FTPShare

FTPShare requires you to designate one folder on your FTPShare server as an entry folder for a given user or users. To give users access to other folders or volumes, you'll need to create aliases to those folders or volumes and place them inside the entry folder. This is how FTPShare controls access to files: only items located within the entry folder, including aliases, are accessible.

So, if you wanted to create a public folder that everyone could access, you'd need to place an alias to that folder in the entry folder of every user on your server. (In the case of guests, you might want to make the public folder the guest's entry folder, since anonymous users probably wouldn't need to access any other folders.)

InterCon's InterServer Publisher

InterCon Systems' InterServer Publisher is a commercial package that acts as an FTP, Gopher, and Web server. (For more information about InterServer Publisher's Gopher features, see Chapter 7; for more information about its Web features, see Chapter 8.)

You configure InterServer Publisher from the InterServer Publisher Setup application. Once you've launched it, the InterServer Publisher Configuration window will appear. To the left will be a series of icons that lets you set various server preferences.

Minimal Setup

The Minimal button (which should be selected automatically when you launch InterServer Publisher Setup) displays a window providing you with the ability to enable or disable Web, Gopher, and FTP access in InterServer Publisher (see Figure 6.14). Before you start using InterServer Publisher as an FTP server, be sure the box next to Enable FTP Server is checked. Click on the Set button directly below it to set the top level of your FTP file structure.

More FTP

Click on the More FTP button to set more preferences for Inter-Server Publisher's FTP server (see Figure 6.15). From here, you can limit the number of users who can connect to your server at once and set how long the Gopher server will wait before it disconnects an idle connection.

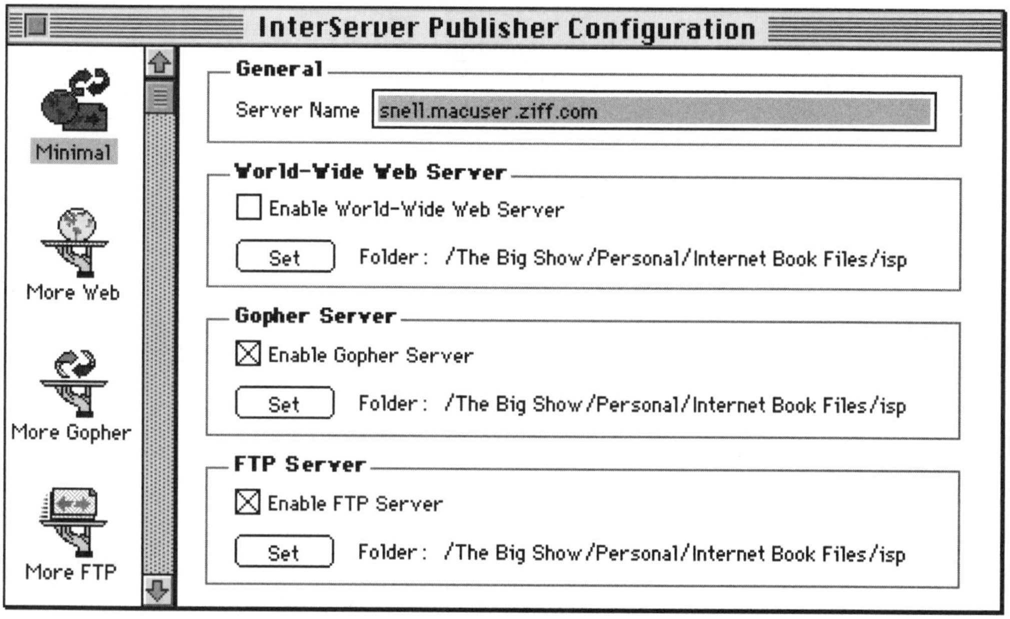

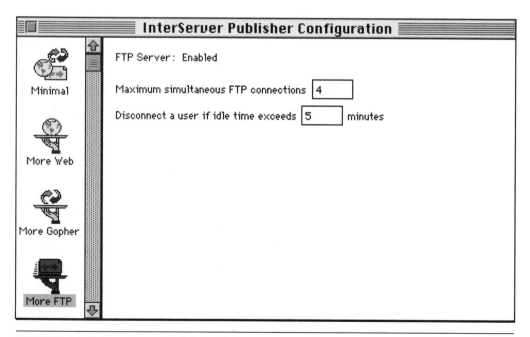

FIGURE 6.14 InterServer Publisher's Minimal Window

FIGURE 6.15 InterServer Publisher's More FTP Window

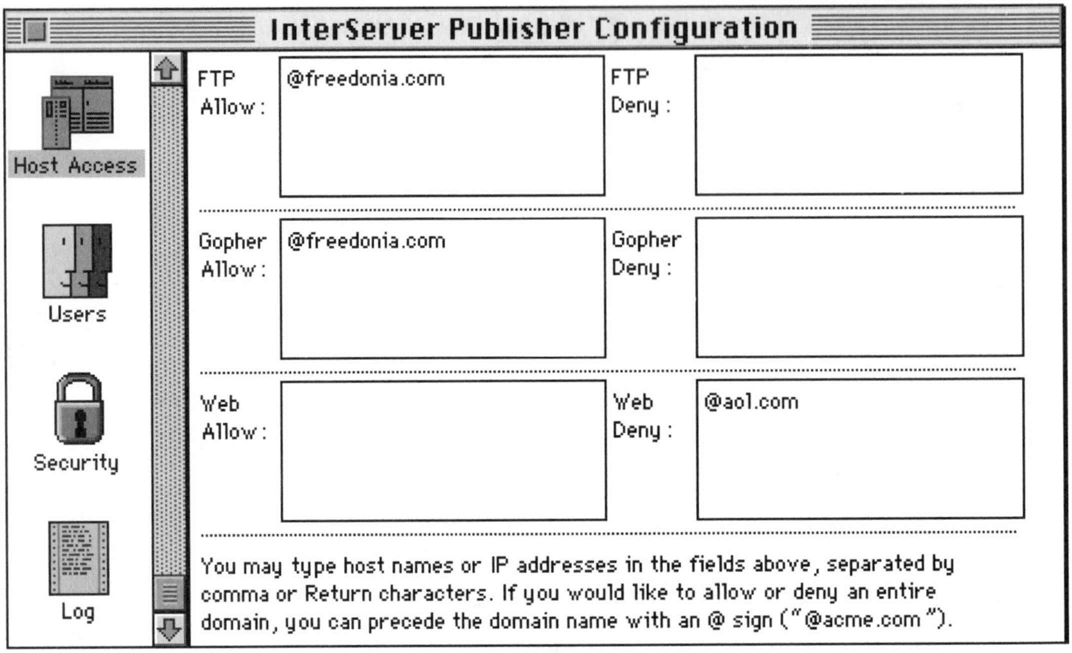

FIGURE 6.16 InterServer Publisher's Host Access Window

Host Access

InterServer Publisher allows you to control exactly which users can access your server through settings entered via the Host Access window. Click on the Host Access button to get to this window (see Figure 6.16). From here, you can enter specific addresses to which your server will allow or deny access. You can control access from either specific machines or entire Internet domains.

Users

You define which users will be able to log in to your FTP server by entering user information in the Users window, which appears when you click on the Users button (see Figure 6.17). Click on the New . . . button to enter information for a new user.

Password

Enter the password you're assigning to your user in this box.

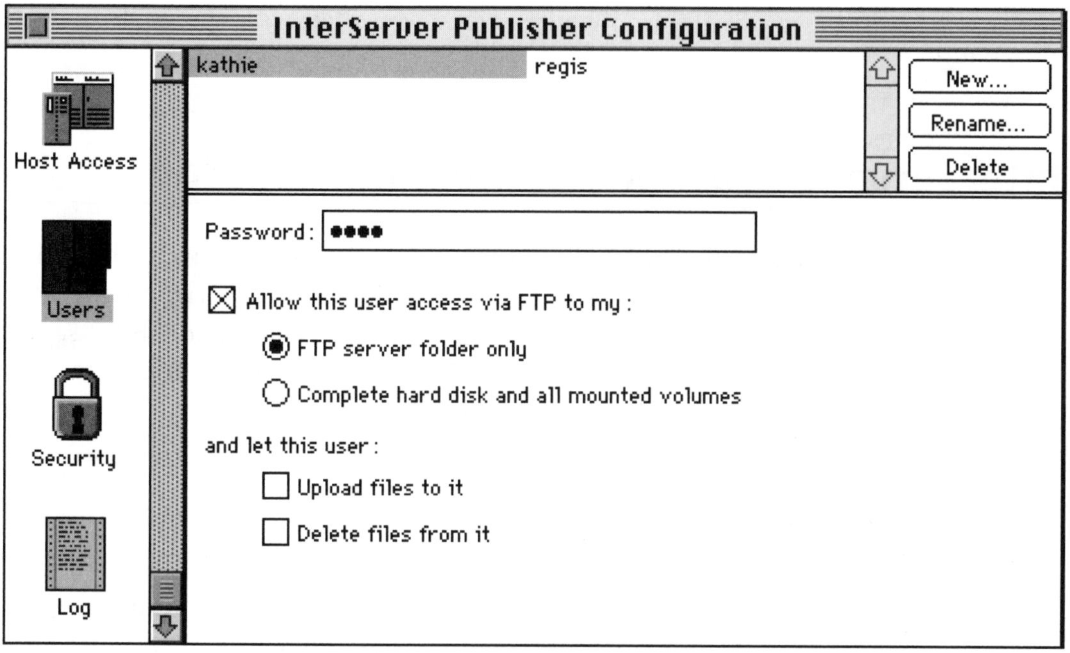

FIGURE 6.17 InterServer Publisher's Users Window.

Allow This User Access via FTP

Check the Allow this user access via FTP box if you want to activate this user. If this box is not checked, the user's logins will be denied.

Following that check box are two radio buttons. If you select FTP server folder only, the user will be restricted only to files and folders that are enclosed by your root FTP folder. If you select Complete hard disk and all mounted volumes, the user will be able to see *everything*—akin to someone logging in to your Mac via File Sharing as the owner account. Be careful not to select this button unless you know exactly what you're doing.

Upload and Delete

Beneath those options are two more check boxes, which let you define just what privileges your user will have on the server. If the Upload files to it box is checked, the user will be able to place files on your server. If Delete files from it is checked, the user will be able to remove files from your server. If you'd like your user to do both, both boxes must be checked.

InterServer Publisher: For More Information

A demonstration version of InterServer Publisher is available on the CD-ROM that comes with this book. It requires a serial number to activate the product for a limited demonstration period. For a serial number, send e-mail to *demo@intercon.com*. Be sure to mention you'd like a serial number for InterServer Publisher.

InterCon's TCP/Connect II

InterCon Systems' TCP/Connect II is a commercially available integrated package that functions as an e-mail, Web, Gopher, FTP, and news client, which also includes a basic FTP server.

FTP Server Preferences

To configure TCP/Connect II's FTP server, select Configure . . . from the Edit menu. Click on FTP Server, and you'll be prompted with a preferences window for the FTP Server (see Figure 6.18). In this window, you can set just how open your server will be, what the default directory will be, and more.

Bakckground FTP Server Mode

This series of radio buttons lets you scale how open TCP/Connect II will be to outsiders. Off, of course, means no FTP connections will be accepted. Secure means that only users identified in the Users preference window (discussed shortly) will be allowed to log in. Secure + Anonymous means that, in addition to logins from regular users, anonymous logins will be permitted. Promiscuous means that anybody can log in—a dangerous option that should be used only if you're on a small network that's protected from the rest of the Internet.

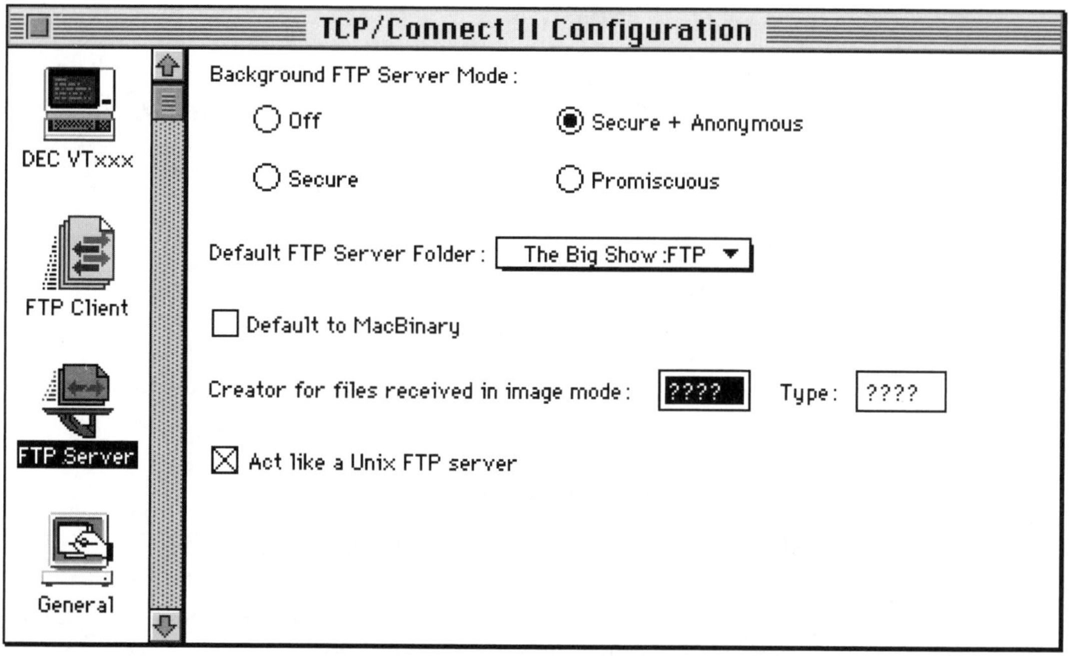

FIGURE 6.18 TCP/Connect II's FTP Server Preferences Window

Default FTP Server Folder

Click on this pop-up to select the folder on your system that users
will be placed into upon logging in. Users with their own names and
passwords can later be assigned different default directories in the
Users preferences window.

Default to MacBinary

If this box is checked, files will be transferred with the MacBinary
protocol automatically. Since most Mac FTP clients turn on
MacBinary mode when they log in, you probably don't need to
check this box.

Creator for Files Received in Image Mode

This pair of boxes lets you enter the four-letter type and creator
codes for files received by the FTP server when it's in "image mode."

Act Like a Unix FTP Server

When this box is checked, the TCP/Connect II server will look exactly like a UNIX-based FTP server to the outside world. Since most FTP clients are written to expect UNIX-based FTP servers, you should probably leave this box checked at all times.

Users Preferences

In the Users preferences window (see Figure 6.19), you can add user names, assign them passwords, and select what their default folder will be, among other options.

Adding, Renaming, Deleting

Creating users in TCP/Connect II is fairly straightforward: click on the New . . . button to add a new user. If you select a user already listed, clicking Rename . . . will let you change the user ID for that user. Clicking Delete will delete a selected user.

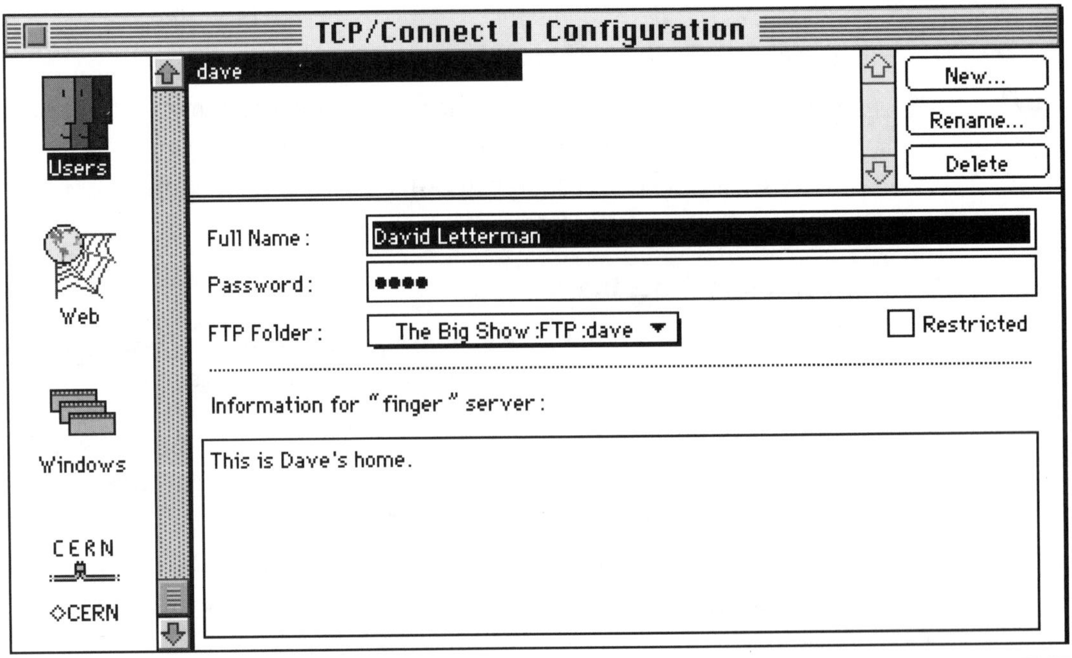

FIGURE 6.19 TCP/Connect II's Users Preferences Window

Assign a Name and Password

In the Full Name box, enter the complete name of your users. In the Password box, assign them a login password. When you click on an existing user in the user list, his or her information appears in these boxes.

Select an FTP Folder

The FTP Folder pop-up lets you select a start-up folder for your user. By default, this pop-up is set to the folder you set in the FTP Server preferences window.

Add Security Restrictions

If you check the Restricted box, users won't be able to move anywhere outside of their default folder and the folders inside it. If you leave this box unchecked, users will still *start* in the default folder, but will be able to move out of that folder and have the run of your file system.

A Bonus: Finger Information

TCP/Connect II can also act as a basic Finger server. (For more information on Finger, see Chapter 10.) If you'd like to have some user-specific information displayed when someone makes a Finger request for that user name, enter it in the box below the Information for "finger" server heading.

NCSA Telnet: No Frills

NCSA Telnet, a program created by the National Center for Supercomputing Applications (the same folks who brought you Mosaic), is designed to make connections using the Telnet protocol. You use Telnet to log in to UNIX systems and other character-based systems via the Internet. You can also use Telnet with Mac programs like ScriptDaemon (see Chapter 11).

But NCSA Telnet also includes a rudimentary FTP server that can be useful if you need to provide only the simplest FTP access. From the Edit menu in NCSA Telnet, select Preferences, then FTP Server. You'll see the FTP Server Prefs dialog (see Figure 6.20).

In this dialog, you can choose whether your server is Off, On with access allowed to everyone, or On with a user name and password required. Avoid setting the On, No passwords needed option, since this makes your entire file system vulnerable to login from anywhere on the Internet without any security measures.

Check boxes in the FTP Server Prefs dialog allow you to control other FTP options, including the ability to show Telnet's FTP log when you launch the application, and to transfer files with MacBinary rather than generic Binary mode as a default.

To control access to your NCSA Telnet server, go to the FTP Users dialog, located by selecting Preferences and then FTP Users from the Edit menu (see Figure 6.21). From this window, you can add new

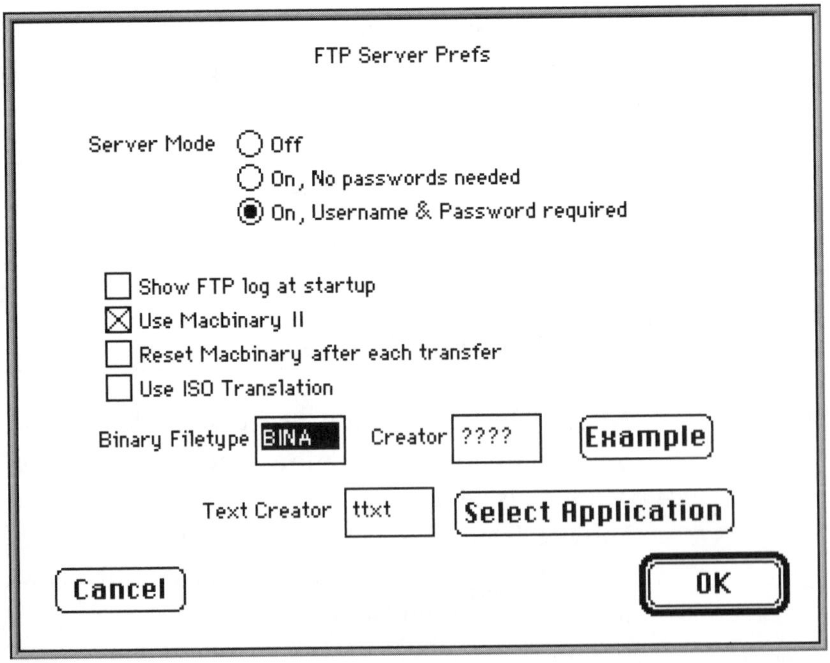

FIGURE 6.20 NCSA Telnet's FTP Server Prefs Dialog

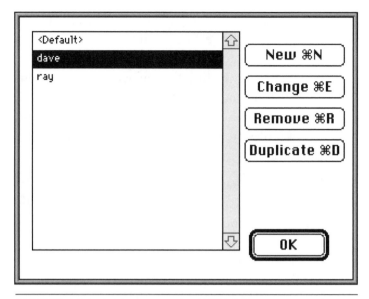

FIGURE 6.21 Add users to the NCSA Telnet server using the FTP Users Dialog.

account names, assign them passwords, and set which folder they use as a default.)

However, it's important to note that the default folder is simply there for convenience. Once users have logged in to an NCSA Telnet FTP server, there are no access restrictions: they can change to any folder in your file system and add and remove files with impunity.

In addition, there's another drawback to the NCSA Telnet FTP server: its output doesn't work very well with Stairways Software's Anarchie. As a result, it is usually preferable to use FTPd instead of NCSA Telnet for anything beyond temporary, small-scale file transfer sessions.

Designing an FTP Archive

No matter which server software you use, you should spend more time thinking about how you'll organize your site. Adding folders here and there, renaming them when they need to be renamed, and moving files from one place to another may work fine on your personal hard drive, but it can wreak havoc on an FTP site. Often, people catalog locations of files on an FTP server and then expect to be able to find the files there when they need them. If the server's administrator has moved everything around, users will have to go through a time-consuming process in order to find where the relevant files are located—or just to confirm the files aren't there anymore.

So, plan ahead and design your organizational structure before you even get your FTP site up and running. If you'll be serving lots of files to anonymous users, create a public folder and organize subfolders within it based on content—that way, people won't have to scroll slowly through a long list of files, trying to find the proverbial needle in the haystack.

Try to put a text file named README or .message in every folder. This file should contain information about what's in a particular folder, so that users can get an idea about what files they're looking at *before* they spend time downloading them.

If your folders still end up containing lots of files, consider dividing them further by some subcategory. For example, the info-mac Macintosh archives on the Internet have a directory called comm for all communications-related files. But within that directory is a subdirectory called tcp, which is specifically for files related to TCP/IP networking. Not only are both directories a lot less crowded and much easier to navigate, but users who are interested only in TCP/IP networking don't have to wade through modem-based telecom programs, and users without TCP connections likewise don't have to see files they have no use for.

If you're in doubt about how to organize a file structure, see what other administrators have done. FTP clients like Anarchie and Fetch come with a large number of "bookmarks" that point to popular FTP sites. Check them out and get a feel for how sites are designed, both good and bad. If you're a veteran Internet user, chances are that you've spent a good deal of time using FTP. Search your own memory about which archives were easy to use, and which were so impenetrable that you had to spend hours trying to track down the files you need, and then try to emulate the easy-to-use ones.

FTP Clients

There are two popular Mac-based FTP clients: Dartmouth College's Fetch and Peter Lewis' Anarchie. Both offer similar functionality with slightly different interfaces. Since each is shareware, you can try them both out and stick with the one you like better. Veteran file transferers often keep copies of both around, since each is better-suited for some tasks than for others.

 **Fetch**

The older of the two programs, Dartmouth College's Fetch offers a single window through which you can see a particular directory or folder of an FTP site. In many ways, Fetch is a little like a giant open or save dialog box (see Figure 6.22). In version 3.0, however, Fetch has become much more like Anarchie, allowing you to drag and

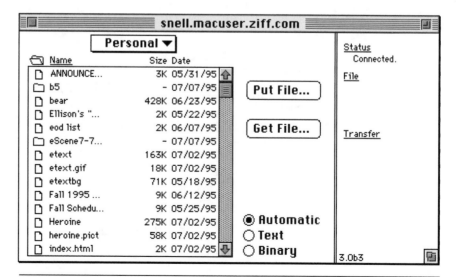

FIGURE 6.22 Fetch looks a bit like a giant open or save dialog box.

drop files into and out of Fetch windows. Fetch allows you to specify whether you want to transfer files in binary or ASCII mode, and lets you queue a large number of files to be transferred in a batch.

 ## Anarchie

Though Fetch had a big head start, Stairways Software's Anarchie became an extremely popular FTP client by emulating the Finder. All the items in a directory or folder on an FTP site appear in a window in Anarchie, similar to the Finder's list view (see Figure 6.23). As in the Finder, you can navigate up a level by command-clicking on the title bar. If you drag files out of an Anarchie window and into a folder in the Finder, the files will be downloaded into that folder by Anarchie.

Name	Size	Date	Zone	Ma
ANNOUNCE Mara...pPak volume 3	3k	5/31/95	1	
b5	-	7/7/95	1	
bear	428k	6/23/95	1	
Ellison's "City on the Edge...	2k	5/22/95	1	
eod list	2k	6/7/95	1	
eScene7-7 folder	-	7/7/95	1	
etext	163k	7/2/95	1	
etext.gif	18k	7/2/95	1	
etextbg	71k	5/18/95	1	
Fall 1995 Prime Time Schedule	9k	6/12/95	1	
Fall Schedule Grid for ABC,...	9k	5/25/95	1	
Heroine	275k	7/2/95	1	
heroine.pict	58k	7/2/95	1	
index.html	2k	7/2/95	1	

Window title: **Personal**

FIGURE 6.23 Anarchie windows bear a striking resemblance to Finder windows.

## CHAPTER 7

Gopher

Gopher: Hierarchical Net Surfing

With all the hype in the Internet world about the World Wide Web, the hypertextual and graphical means of accessing Net-based information (see Chapter 8), the little burrowing cyberspace animal known as Gopher doesn't get much attention. But before there was the Web, there was Gopher, invented by a team at the University of Minnesota.[*] Gopher is a menu-based, user-friendly system of accessing information. Unlike its predecessor FTP, Gopher menus can include links to other servers elsewhere on the Net. But unlike the Web, Gopher doesn't offer the sexy graphics and hot hypertext links. Gopher is much simpler than the Web. It's a lot like a Macintosh Open File dialog box that leads to every server in the world.

Gopher can be an easy way to hunt down information you want to see, especially since it dovetails well with text search engines like AppleSearch. And while Gopher's not nearly as popular as the Web, most Web browsers will also connect to Gopher servers, making your information available to both Gopher users and die-hard Webaholics.

Gopher servers listen to TCP/IP port 70, waiting for connections from Gopher clients. When the server transfers a menu to a client, it sends both menu entries and special codes that indicate what kind of item any particular menu choice might be (see Table 7.1). That way, when a user double-clicks on a Gopher item, they'll know if

---

[*]The University of Minnesota's mascot? The Golden Gophers. Hence the name.

TABLE 7.1 Gopher Item Types

Code	File type
0	File
1	Folder
2	Link to CSO search engine
4	BinHex file
5	DOS binary file
6	UUencoded data file
7	AppleSearch server
9	UNIX binary file
T	TN3270 terminal session
I	Image (PICT, JPEG, GIF)
s	Sound (ULAW format)
P	Adobe Acrobat PDF
h	HTML (World Wide Web) files or link to Web server
;	Movie (either QuickTime or MPEG)

they're going to be receiving a sound file, a graphic, plain text, or even a BinHex file attachment.

There are two different Gopher protocols in existence: Gopher and Gopher+. Gopher+ was carefully designed to work with Gopher, so there are rarely compatibility problems in the Gopher world.

 **Gopher Surfer**

From the University of Minnesota comes the Gopher Surfer server application. Unlike other Gopher server implementations discussed later, GopherServer has been designed specifically to act as a Gopher server. As a result, it also offers the most robust implementation of the Gopher+ protocol.

Step by Step: Setting Up Gopher Surfer

Before you launch Gopher Surfer, you should create a folder that will contain all the documents you plan on serving via Gopher. (You can point to other parts of your file hierarchy by including aliases within your Gopher folder).

At this point, you should probably place some or all of the files you're planning to serve via Gopher into this folder. Be sure to organize the files if you've got a lot of them—since Gopher's strength is that it's easy to navigate, putting 100 files all in one folder would be a tremendous waste.

Unlike with FTP, where users can see only the names of your files, filenames in Gopher aren't important, since you can give each file a custom title within Gopher. (This is true of all Gopher servers, not just Gopher Surfer).

Getting Gopher Surfer Started

Once you've launched Gopher Surfer, it's time to set your server preferences. To bring up Gopher Surfer's Configuration window (see Figure 7.1), select Configure from the Gopher menu. The top half of the window will list the most important server preferences. The bottom half, topped by a pop-up menu, is used to set various other application preferences.

Host Name

First, enter the name of the machine on which you'll be running Gopher Surfer in the Host Name box. While it's true that Gopher Surfer can get this information itself, it's often also true that servers will have *several* different names assigned to them; for example, our server's IP address might be mapped to the names stale.freedonia.com and gopher.freedonia.com.[*] Since we always want users of our server to know it as gopher.freedonia.com, we

---

[*]This double-naming system often occurs so that server machines can change transparently to users. For example, a company might start running a Gopher server on a UNIX machine, only to move it to a Macintosh later. Rather than changing the names of those machines, or just moving the IP address of your server (which can cause references from other sites to stop working), the standard practice is to allocate second, generic names to servers and allocate those names to whatever machine is acting as the server at that time. For more information on domain name services, see Chapter 9.

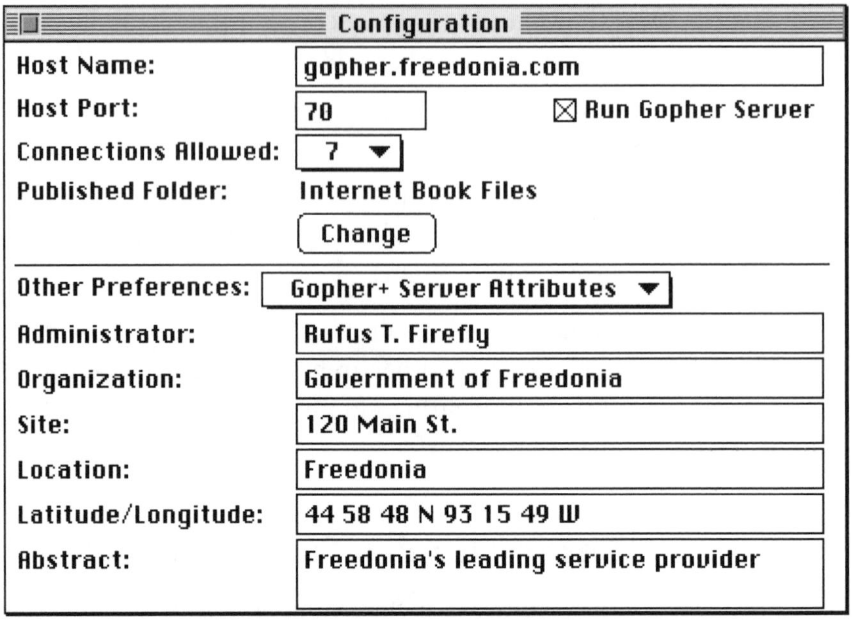

FIGURE 7.1 Gopher Surfer's Configuration window, displaying the Server Attributes preferences.

enter that in the Host Name box. If your server has only one name, just enter it here.

Host Port

This box is automatically set to 70, which is the standard port Gopher uses to conduct its business. Unless you've got a specific reason why you want to run off of a nonstandard Gopher port, leave this item set to 70.

Run Gopher Server

When this box is checked, the Gopher Surfer server is up and running, accepting connections from the outside world. Check this box only when you're ready to let others connect to your server.

Connections Allowed

The first time you launch Gopher Surfer, it may warn you that you're limited to a certain number of connections—this limitation is based on how much RAM is allocated to the Gopher Surfer application. To increase the number of simultaneous Gopher connections your server will allow, quit out of Gopher Surfer, select the application in the Finder, choose Get Info from the File menu, and increase the amount of RAM you've allocated in the Preferred size box.

You can scale this pop-up menu to allow as many or as few connections as you like (remembering the upper limit of 64 connections if you're using MacTCP). If users complain that they can't connect to your server, you may want to increase the number. If they complain that your server is too slow and unresponsive, you may want to decrease this number.

Published Folder

Click on the Select button to choose what the top-level folder for your Gopher hierarchy will be. Select the folder you created before launching Gopher Surfer.

Other Preferences

The bottom half of the window changes depending on what item has been chosen in the Other Preferences pop-up menu. Your options are Gopher+ Server Attributes, AppleSearch Configuration, Character Set Filters, Limiting Access, and Logging Connections.

Gopher+ Server Attributes

The Gopher+ protocol allows clients to find out information about the server that's providing them with information. The information you enter into this series of boxes will be what's transmitted when that information is requested of your server.

Administrator

This should be the name of the person or group responsible for administering your Gopher Surfer server.

Organization

This should be the name of the organization running the server.

Site

This is usually a street address or other contact address of where the server is located.

Location

This is usually a city and state where the server is located.

Latitude/Longitude

If you know where your server is located geographically, enter that information here.

Abstract

This box contains a short summary of what purpose your organization or server provides.

Limiting Access

Selecting the Limiting Access pop-up provides you with two options to allow you to limit access to your Gopher server (see Figure 7.2). Right out of the box, Gopher Surfer allows anybody to connect and retrieve information located in your Published folder. These two items allow you to alter those preferences.

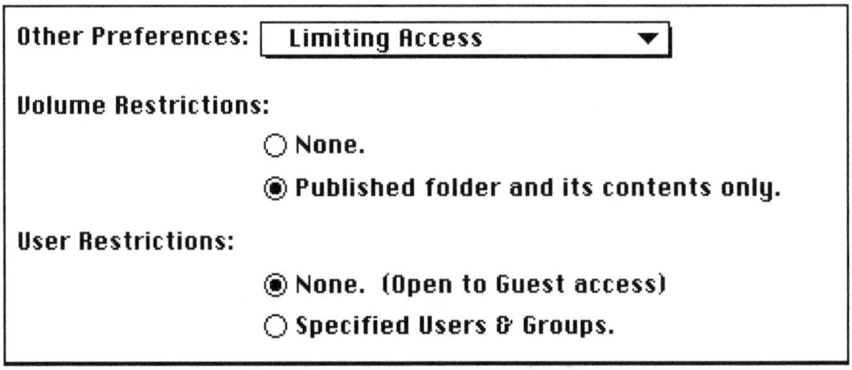

FIGURE 7.2 Gopher Surfer's Limiting Access Panel

Volume Restrictions

Users are prevented from moving out of the files and folders contained within your Published folder unless File Sharing is on. If File Sharing is on and Published folder and its contents only is selected, users will also be able to access only your Published folder and items within it. But, if File Sharing is on and you select None here, all shared items in your file system can be accessed from your server, depending on your sharing preferences (discussed shortly).

User Restrictions

This preference defaults to None. But, if you'd like to limit access to some or all of your server based on the location from which outside users are connecting, you can select Specified Users & Groups.

Limiting Access with Users & Groups

To limit access using Users & Groups, you'll have to turn on File Sharing in the Sharing Setup control panel. Be sure about the sharing preferences you may have already set in the Finder, as your server will still work as a System 7 file-sharing server even as it's working as a Gopher server, so any volumes you make publicly available via sharing will be accessible by anyone on your local AppleTalk network.

You can limit access to folders and files with Gopher Surfer just as you would with normal file sharing. The only difference? Since Gopher doesn't allow people to log in with user names and passwords, all access must be based on which IP address they're connecting from. As a result, you've got to create some specialized user names in the Users & Groups control panel that reflect which IP addresses will have access to your Gopher files.

Let's say we've got three different folders inside our Published folder, and that we want to allow different forms of access to those folders. One of them, called public, will be open to anyone who connects. Another, company, will be just for people in your company. A third, bob, is information that we want only one person to access.

Setting access for public is easy: just select the folder, choose Sharing . . . from the File menu, and allow everyone to see files and folders. It's just like creating a public folder on your AppleShare network using System 7 file sharing.

Setting access for company is a little harder, but you know all the IP addresses in your company begin with 86.25. So you open the Users & Groups control panel and create a new user called 86.25. Then open Sharing preferences for company, turn off read privileges for everyone, and give read privileges only to user 86.25. Now anyone with an IP address that begins with 86.25—in other words, only people from your company—will be able to see that folder.

Since Bob's computer is at 86.25.40.80, we can restrict access to the bob directory just to him by creating a new user called 86.25.40.80, and giving read privileges to that folder only to that user.

If we wanted to create a group of IP addresses that could access that folder, we could create multiple users, join them in a group just as you would in System 7 file sharing, and then give read access to that folder to the group.

IP Ranges. You can also give access to ranges of IP addresses. Say your company controls IP addresses 86.25, 86.26, 86.27, 86.28, and 86.29. Rather than creating five users and joining them as a group, you can create a user called 86.25-29. Gopher Surfer is smart enough to recognize that you want to allow access for any user with a range from 86.25 through 86.29.

Denying Access. You can also deny access to particular IP addresses, by creating users with exclamation points preceding their IP addresses. If you wanted to eliminate all access from IP address 86.25.40.80, all you'd have to do is create a user named !86.25.40.80. That IP address would then be prevented from connecting to your server. Likewise, a user of !86.25 would disallow anyone whose IP address began with 86.25 from connecting.

AppleSearch Configuration

You can use the AppleSearch Configuration section of the Configuration window (see Figure 7.3) to link your Gopher server to

```
┌──────────────────────────────────────────────────────────┐
│ ▫▪    ═══════════════════ Configuration ═══════════════    │
│  Host Name:      ┌──────────────────────────────────────┐ │
│                  │ gopher.freedonia.com                 │ │
│                  └──────────────────────────────────────┘ │
│  Host Port:      ┌────────┐          ⊠ Run Gopher Server  │
│                  │ 70     │                                │
│                  └────────┘                                │
│  Connections Allowed:  ┌─────┐                             │
│                        │ 7 ▼ │                             │
│                        └─────┘                             │
│  Published Folder:    Internet Book Files                  │
│                  ┌──────────────┐                          │
│                  │    Change    │                          │
│                  └──────────────┘                          │
│ ────────────────────────────────────────────────────────  │
│  Other Preferences: ┌──────────────────────────────────┐  │
│                     │ AppleSearch Configuration   ▼     │  │
│                     └──────────────────────────────────┘  │
│  AppleSearch Server:   (None selected)                     │
│                  ┌──────────────┐                          │
│                  │    Select    │                          │
│                  └──────────────┘                          │
│                     □ Auto Connect on startup              │
│                                                            │
│                                                            │
└──────────────────────────────────────────────────────────┘
```

FIGURE 7.3 Gopher Surfer's AppleSearch Configuration Panel

AppleSearch servers. AppleSearch is a program written by Apple Computer that lets you perform full-text searches on a group of text files or word processor documents.

If you click on Select, you'll be prompted with a Chooser-style window that will let you find an AppleSearch server on your local network. Once you've selected this server, you can let the users of your Gopher server start AppleSearch searches and retrieve found documents.

Once you've selected an AppleSearch server, click on Auto Connect on Startup to make sure that AppleSearch is always available to your Gopher users. We'll discuss how to add an AppleSearch item into your Gopher listings a little later on.

Character Set Filters

Unlike many other computer systems, the Macintosh standard character set includes *extended,* or 8-bit characters, such as curly quotes, ellipses, and accented letters. Since other computers can't readily interpret these characters, we need to filter outgoing text to convert them into something other computer systems can read. That's what we accomplish in the Character Set Filters section of the Configuration window (see Figure 7.4).

If None is checked, then any 8-bit characters that appear in your files will be sent out unchanged. If all your users are Mac users, this will probably go unnoticed.

If you select ISO Latin 1, Gopher Surfer will use the ISO character-translation standard to encode special charactrs so that Mac, PC, and UNIX Gopher clients will be able to see special characters in your documents.

Another option, for Japanese encoding, isn't yet available as part of Gopher Surfer.

Language

The Language pop-up in the Character Set Filters window simply lets you set what the default language will be for files on your server. Chances are, this will be the language you use every day—if you're serving files in Turkish, you'll want to select Turkish/Turkey. But most North American Gopher administrators will select English/United States.

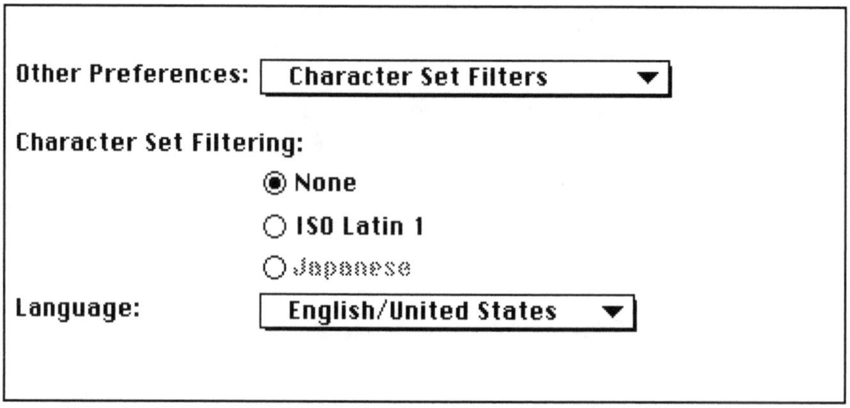

FIGURE 7.4 Gopher Surfer's Character Set Filters Panel

Logging Connections

The Logging Connections pop-up (see Figure 7.5) lets you choose how Gopher Surfer monitors actions on your server. If you choose the IP Address radio button, Gopher Surfer will log users by the IP address they connect from. If you choose Domain Name, Gopher Surfer will look up their domain name based on their IP address. Since it takes time to look up the domain name, choosing Domain Name will slow down your server somewhat. However, domain names are a lot easier to recognize on first glance than IP addresses, so the performance trade-off might be worth it if you run a low-volume server.

You can view the log (including watching connections appear as they're made) by selecting Connections Log from the Gopher menu. If you'd like to make sure the log is saved to a text file, check the Log Connections to box. Click on the Change box to create a log file.

Customizing Your File Structure

Now it's time to give the files you've placed in your Published folder some personality, since filenames can often be pretty dull by themselves. To edit what users will see when they connect via Gopher, hit Command-T or select Preview Gopher Tree from the Gopher menu. (You must have the Configure window open to use this command.)

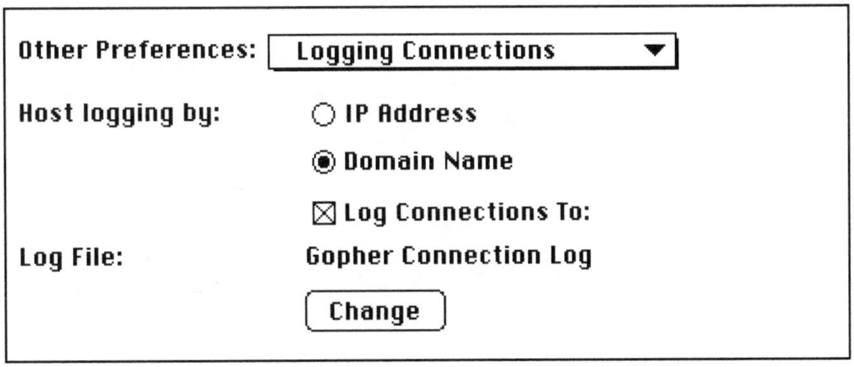

FIGURE 7.5 Gopher Surfer's Logging Connections Panel

You'll suddenly see the top level of your Published folder appear as it would via Gopher. Click on a file to select it, and then hit Command-E or select Edit Gopher Descriptor from the Gopher menu. Gopher Surfer will then present you with a dialog box containing six fields of information about the file or folder you selected (see Figure 7.6).

Domain Name

For all files on your server, this should be the name assigned to your server. This box is here because you can also create links to files and folders on other Gopher servers.

Port

This is the port users can find this file on; again, this item is here in case you're linking to a file or folder elsewhere, and need to specify a particular port for your users to attach to when looking for that referenced item.

Title

This box contains the title of the file you've selected; it can be a lot more descriptive than the filename. For record-keeping purposes, you might name your file something like ITv5n5pm-js3, but you can

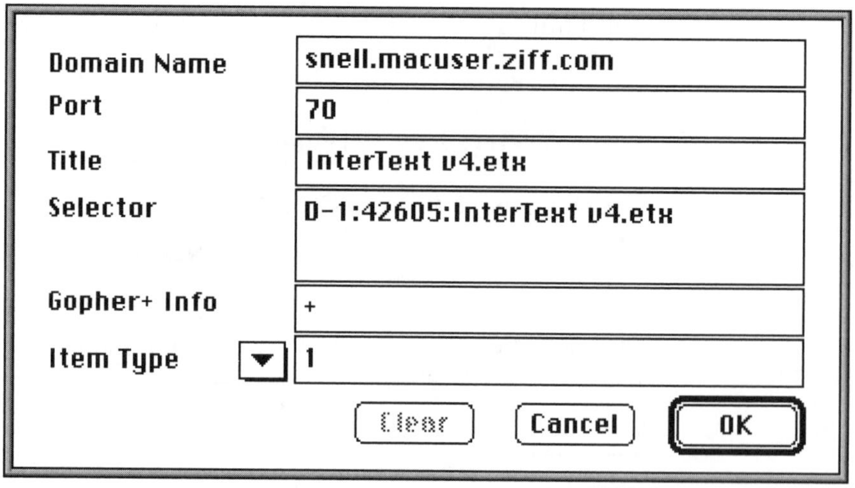

Domain Name	snell.macuser.ziff.com
Port	70
Title	InterText v4.etx
Selector	D-1:42605:InterText v4.etx
Gopher+ Info	+
Item Type	▼ 1

[Clear] [Cancel] [OK]

FIGURE 7.6 Editing file information using Gopher Surfer.

change what your Gopher users see by replacing it with something more meaningful, like September-October 1995 issue.

Selector

Like Domain Name and Port, this window is one you'll usually leave alone unless you're referring people to a document or file on another site. In that case, you'd enter in the selector information that points a user to that file. For example, a selector might be:

```
0/Zines/eScene
```

In this case, you're pointing people at a directory (hence the 0—see Table 7.1) named eScene within a top-level directory named Zines.

Gopher+ Info

This field is used when you're serving extended files, like fill-in forms, discussed shortly.

Item Type

In this box, you can enter (or select via a pop-up) the file type that is assigned to a given file (see Table 7.1). That way, you can differentiate between an HTML file and a plain text file, or between a raw binary file and a BinHex file.

Adding Links to Elsewhere

There are two ways to add links to Gopher servers elsewhere in the world. The first, and easiest, method is to do your Gopher surfing with the TurboGopher application (discussed later). Once you've found a location you like, save it as a bookmark. Then just copy the bookmark file to the appropriate folder in your Gopher Surfer file hierarchy. Gopher Surfer will automatically parse the bookmark.

You can also use the Preview Gopher Tree window to add links to other Gopher servers. To do this, make sure that no items are selected in the folder that you're previewing. (Click at the bottom of the list, beneath the last entry, to do this.) Then hit Command-E or select Edit Gopher Descriptor from the Gopher menu.

Because you don't have any items selected, Gopher Surfer will assume that you're creating a new item. Now you'll just need to enter the link information for the file or (more likely) directory you'll be pointing to. Enter the name of the machine next to Domain Name, the port the Gopher server is running on next to Port, a descriptive name for the link under Title, and the link information next to Selector.

Getting Link Information out of URLs

You can figure out what information you need to enter by viewing a Gopher site with a Web browser that displays the URLs of the places you're viewing. For example, let's say you go to a Gopher directory via the Web and want to link to it from your Gopher Surfer server. Say the URL is this:

```
gopher://gopher.etext.org/11/Zines/InterText/
```

In this case, the text between the double-slashes and the first single-slash in the machine name. It would go next to Domain Name in your window. The first digit after the first slash, a 1, indicates the item is a folder, so you'd enter a 1 next to Item Type. The balance of the URL is the path to the directory you want, so you'd enter 1/Zines/InterText/ into the Selector box.[*]

Adding AppleSearch Links

To add a link to an AppleSearch database, be sure you're in Preview Gopher Tree mode and select Place AppleSearch Database from the Gopher menu. You'll be prompted with a dialog box that includes a pop-up menu for all the databases available on the AppleSearch server you selected when you configured Gopher Surfer. Select the database you want to let your users search, and then enter the title you'd like to give to this search link.

---

[*]This is also a good rule of thumb to use when making links from Web sites to Gopher sites. Your URL would be gopher://[machine name]/[gopher type][gopher type again]/[pathname]. Or just connect to your Gopher server using a Web browser and copy the URL out of the browser and into your HTML documents.

Creating Alternate Views

One of Gopher's little-known features is its ability to serve multiple copies of the same document, through a function called *alternate views.* There are two different kinds of alternate documents: copies of the same document in different languages, and copies of the same document in different file formats.

Let's say you've got three different versions of a document: plain text, a Microsoft Word document featuring some nice fonts and formatting, and an Adobe Acrobat PDF file created from your Microsoft Word file.

First, you'd place the plain text version of the document in whatever folder in your Gopher hierarchy it belongs. Then you'll need to create a folder in that same folder. This new folder will contain the exact filename of your original text document, along with the ◊ character (created by holding down the Option and Shift keys and hitting the v key).

Copy your Word and PDF files to this folder. Then you'll need to rename them to whatever MIME filetype corresponds to their file format. In this case, you'll rename the Word files as Application/MSWord and the PDF file as Application/PDF. (For a list of MIME types supported by Gopher Surfer, see Table 7.2.)

If you're adding different language versions of a file, you'll still create a folder that corresponds to the name of your file plus a diamond character. But instead of renaming your files, you'll want to give them the name of your original file, plus a code indicating which language and country the file represents. For example, for a file named Welcome, you might create a folder named Welcome◊ containing files named WelcomeIt/IT and WelcomeFr/FR—Italian and French versions of the file, respectively. (For a list of language types supported by Gopher Surfer, see Table 7.3.)

TABLE 7.2 MIME Types Supported by Gopher Surfer

MIME Type	Type of File
Application/MacWriteII	MacWrite II file
Application/MSWord	Microsoft Word file
Application/PDF	Adobe Acrobat PDF file
Application/Post	MacWrite II file
Application/RTF	Microsoft Word file
Audio/Basic	Ulaw sound file
Image	Generic image file
Image/GIF	GIF image
Image/JFIF	JFIF image
Image/JPEG	JPEG image
Image/PICT	PICT image
Image/TIFF	TIFF image
Text/tab-separated values	Tab-delimited text
Video/MPEG	MPEG movie
Video/QuickTime	QuickTime movie

TABLE 7.3 Language Types Supported by Gopher Surfer

Language Type	Language	Country
Da_DK	Danish	Denmark
Nl_BE	Dutch	Belgium
Nl_NL	Dutch	Netherlands
En_GB	English	United Kingdom
En_US	English	USA
Fi_FI	Finnish	Finland
Fr_BE	French	Belgium
Fr_CA	French	Canada
Fr_CH	French	Switzerland
Fr_FR	French	France
De_CH	German	Switzerland
De_DE	German	Germany
El_GR	Greek	Greece
Is_IS	Icelandic	Iceland
It_IT	Italian	Italy
Jp_JP	Japanese	Japan
No_NO	Norwegian	Norway
Pt_PT	Portugese	Portugal
Es_ES	Spanish	Spain
Sv_SE	Swedish	Sweden
Tr_TR	Turkish	Turkey

FTPd: Your Basic Gopher

In addition to being an FTP server (see Chapter 6) and Web server (see Chapter 8), Stairways Software's FTPd, written by Peter Lewis, also functions as a simple Gopher server. While it allows you to name and order your files and link to other Gopher servers, it doesn't offer all the functionality of Gopher Surfer. Still, if you're looking only to run a simple Gopher surfer—especially if you also want to use FTPd as your FTP server—FTPd can be an excellent option.

Setting Up FTPd as a Gopher Server

As we described in Chapter 6, all configuration of FTPd is done via the FTPd Setup application. But before you launch FTPd Setup, be sure that File Sharing is turned on and that the folders you're going to be using for Gopher are readable by everyone—Gopher doesn't use user names in passswords, so that Gopher logins are treated by FTPd the same way as anonymous FTP sessions.

Next, launch FTPd and click on the Gopher Setup button. You'll be prompted with a window that gives you several options regarding your Gopher server (see Figure 7.7). As the text in the window says, you can safely leave the three fields in this window blank. We'll discuss them briefly, so you know what they mean and what will happen if you enter information in them.

Gopher Enabled

Check this box if you want to use FTPd as a Gopher server. When this box isn't checked, people trying to connect to your machine via Gopher won't be able to, even if you're running a live FTP server with FTPd.

Gopher Host

This is the name of the machine you're running FTPd on.

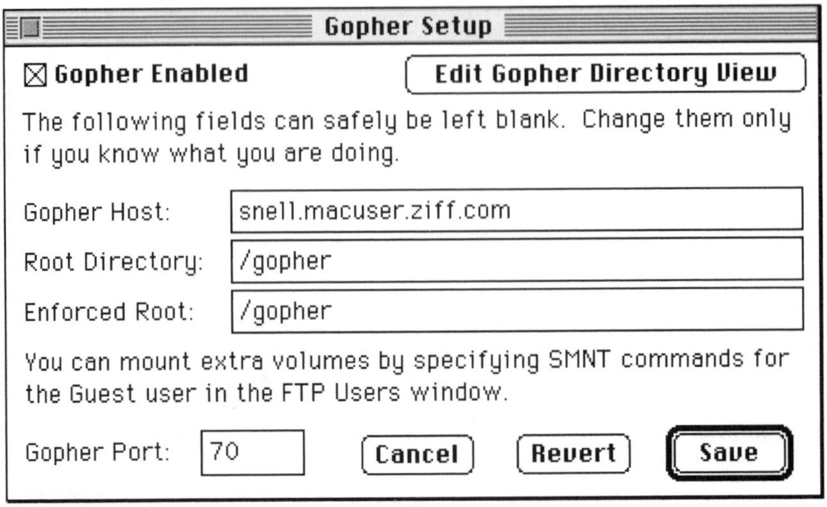

FIGURE 7.7 FTPd's Gopher Setup Window

Root Directory

This is the folder that's sent by default if a user connects to your site without specifying a particular pathname.

Enforced Root

This is the folder that's the top level of your file hierarchy. By listing a folder as the Enforced Root, you're preventing Gopher users from accessing any folders above it in the hierarchy. This is a way of walling off your Gopher users from areas accessible via FTP.

Gopher Port

This is the TCP port at which Gopher listens for incoming connections; 70 is the standard port number, and normally won't be changed.

Editing the Gopher Directory View

Also present in the Gopher Setup window is a button marked Edit Gopher Directory View. If you click on this button, you'll be prompted with a dialog box and asked to select a folder in your Gopher hierarchy (see Figure 7.8). Once you've selected a folder, FTPd will display how it would look in a Gopher window, similar to the way Gopher Surfer displays items in its Preview Gopher Tree window.

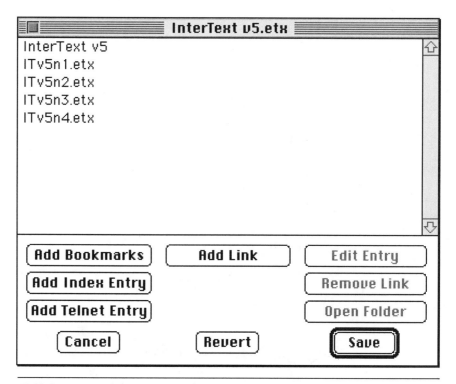

FIGURE 7.8 FTPd's preview of the Gopher Hierarchy

To edit the entry for a file, select it from the list and then click on the Edit Entry button. You'll then see a window for that particular item (Figure 7.9). You can give the item a name that's more descriptive than its filename, and you can also define its type (see the list of Gopher filetypes in Table 7.1). When you're finished editing the item, click on OK. If you make a mistake, you can hit the Revert button to change the window back to its original information.

 # InterServer Publisher

InterCon Systems' InterServer Publisher is a commercial package that acts as an FTP, Gopher, and Web server. (For more information about InterServer Publisher's FTP features, see Chapter 6; for more information about its Web features, see Chapter 8.)

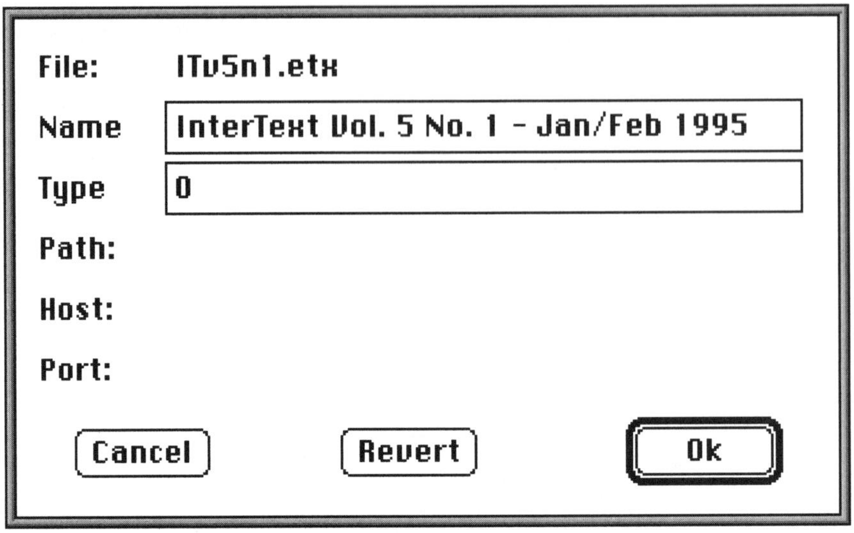

File: **ITv5n1.etx**

Name   **InterText Vol. 5 No. 1 - Jan/Feb 1995**

Type   **0**

Path:

Host:

Port:

Cancel   Revert   Ok

FIGURE 7.9 Editing a Gopher item in FTPd.

You configure InterServer Publisher from the InterServer Publisher Setup application. Once you've launched it, the InterServer Publisher Configuration window will appear. To the left will be a series of icons that let you set various server preferences.

Minimal Setup

The Minimal button (which should be selected automatically when you launch InterServer Publisher Setup) displays a window providing you with the ability to enable or disable Web, Gopher, and FTP access in InterServer Publisher (see Figure 7.10). Before you start using InterServer Publisher as a Gopher server, be sure the box next to Enable Gopher Server is checked. Click on the Set button directly below it to set the top level of your Gopher file structure.

More Gopher

Click on the More Gopher button to set more preferences for Inter-Server Publisher's Gopher server (see Figure 7.11). From here, you can limit the number of users who can connect to your server at once,

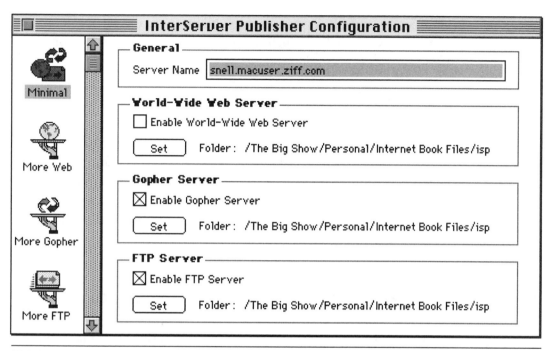

FIGURE 7.10 InterServer Publisher's Minimal Window

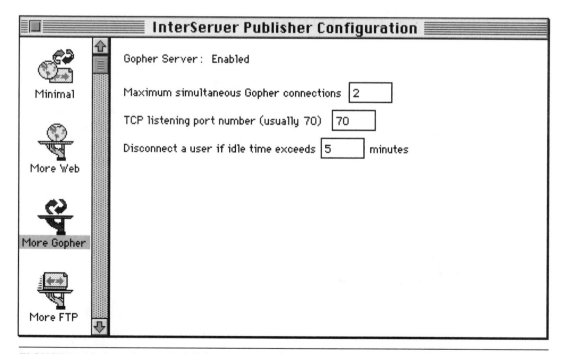

FIGURE 7.11 InterServer Publisher's More Gopher Window

select which TCP port your server will listen to, and set how long the Gopher server will wait before it disconnects an idle connection.

Host Access

InterServer Publisher allows you to control exactly which users can access your server through settings entered via the Host Access window (see Figure 7.12). Click on the Host Access button to get to this window. From here, you can enter specific addresses to which your server will allow or deny access. You can control access from either specific machines or entire Internet domains—depending upon your needs.

InterServer Publisher: For More Information

A demonstration version of InterServer Publisher is available on the CD-ROM that comes with this book. It requires a serial number to activate the product for a limited demonstration period. For a serial number, send e-mail to *demo@intercon.com*. Be sure to mention that you'd like a serial number for InterServer Publisher.

Gopher Clients

There are many different means by which you can access information on Gopher servers. As we've mentioned before, most Web client applications can connect to Gopher servers. (For more information on Web clients, see Chapter 8.) There are also several Gopher-specific clients available for machines running the Mac OS.

 TurboGopher

The most popular Gopher client for the Mac OS is probably TurboGopher, written by the Gopher team at the University of Minnesota. TurboGopher displays Gopher information in a series of

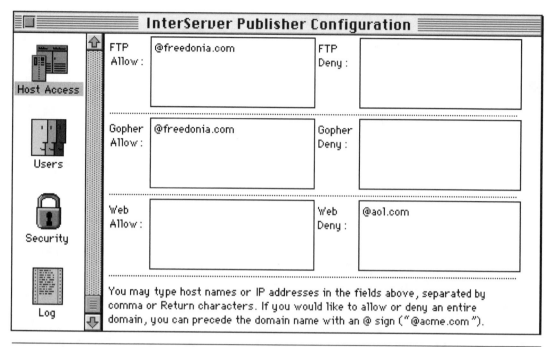

FIGURE 7.12 InterServer Publisher's Host Access Window

windows (see Figure 7.13). When you double-click on a list item, TurboGopher brings it up in a new window.

TurboGopher VR

An offshoot of TurboGopher is TurboGopher VR. TurboGopher VR intercepts Gopher menu information and generates a 3-D landscape featuring a series of tiles (resembling cemetary headstones) out of that menu (see Figure 7.14). While visually interesting, it's hard to navigate through the TurboGopher VR landscape. It actually takes much longer to wander through the 3-D world of TurboGopher VR than it does to glance at a simple Gopher menu. But it's an interesting technology demonstration, proving that while Gopher may have been passed in popularity by the Web, there's still a lot of innovation going on in Gopherspace.

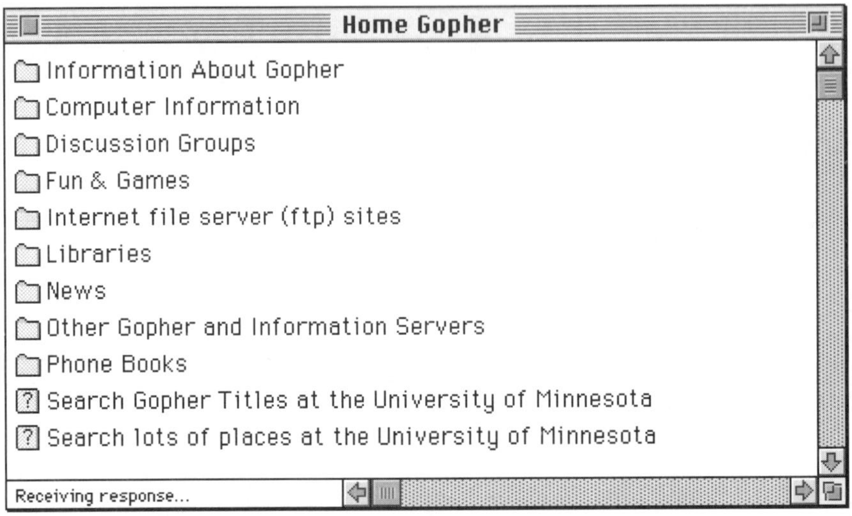

FIGURE 7.13 TurboGopher, a Macintosh Gopher Client

FIGURE 7.14 A Virtual Reality "Menu" in TurboGopher VR

## CHAPTER 8

The Web

The World Wide Web generates more traffic than any other Internet service, largely based on the easy availability of graphical clients, or *browsers*. Web sites service all types of readerships, from digital magazines devoted to culture or food to corporate sites providing product information to personal "home pages."

One distinction between serving content via the Web versus other methods is that Web clients are numerous and varied—not only are there a plethora of Web browsers, but a number of Web proxy gateways, Web-crawling robots, and user agents:

- Web browsers present information retrieved from your server to a user in an immediate fashion. Usually, this means displaying hypertext documents directly on a user's screen, but it might mean converting text to speech on the fly, or summarizing the data downloaded in some way.

- Web proxy gateways sit between the user's browser and your server, and often cache, and sometimes modify, content for the proxy's users. For example, the America Online (AOL) Web browser connects to an AOL proxy server, which then connects to your Web server. The proxy server then caches, or stores, the information the client requested via the proxy gateway from your server, so that, for the next AOL user requesting the same content, the proxy gateway can return the cached information, instead of retrieving it again from your server. The AOL proxy gateway also converts all images stored in the CompuServe GIF format to the ART format, which, because of differences in the formats, can change the appearances of your images. Proxy gateways can also be used to screen content or log requests; some gateways, for example, are configured to prevent users from connecting to sites that are deemed inappropriate by the person or organization running the proxy gateway.

■ Web-crawling robots follow links across the Web and index the content they find. Some Web-crawling robots perform indexing of the full text of documents. Others only index title and header information. Lycos <http://www.lycos.com/> and InfoSeek <http://www.infoseek.com/> are two services that rely upon databases built by Web-crawling robots.

■ User agents search resources on the Web for user-specified information and return results in some summary fashion to the user. Agents that go through a list of Web sites and check which ones have been updated since a user's last visit are becoming increasingly popular, for example.

From a Web server's and Web server administrator's viewpoints, of course, all of these clients look the same—they're simply requesting data from your server. From a content creator's vantage point, however, it's important to keep in mind that very different types of clients might be retrieving the information you make available—for that reason, it makes sense to stick to standards as much as possible. See the upcoming HTML QuickStart section for more details.

HTTP

Web servers and clients exchange information using the Hypertext Transfer Protocol, or HTTP. HTTP is a simple, stateless protocol for exchanging information between servers and clients. It's simple in that HTTP uses a straightforward request/response sequence: a client will open a connection to a server and send its request; the server responds to the request and closes the connection.

HTTP is stateless in that a client initiates a new connection for each request, and information about connections isn't used by the protocol from one connection to the next. Although statelessness makes HTTP very efficient for some applications, like serving up pages of text, it's less than ideal for scenarios in which you'd like to remember user information from connnection to connection—if, for example, you'd like to track a user's movement or remember a user's selections as he or she moves through your Web.

HTTP Ports

Web servers normally listen for HTTP requests on port 80. Most Web servers will let you specify a different port to listen for requests, which can be then be accessed from a client by specifying the optional port value in a URL. For example, to access a Web server running on www.pism.com which listens on port 8080, you would use the URL <http://www.pism.com:8080/>. (See Appendix A, Uniform Resource Locators, for more information on URLs.) Ports other than 80 are usually chosen to implement a "security through obscurity" policy—although there are better ways to secure a server (described later), using an uncommon port number is an easy way to make your Web service that much more difficult for strangers to stumble upon. If you do choose to run your Web server on a port other than 80, select one numbered above 1024 so that it doesn't conflict with a standard Internet service. Ports numbered 1024 and below are reserved for well-known services.

A Typical HTTP Transaction

Although it's not necessary for you to know anything about HTTP in order to run a Web server, it is helpful to have a basic understanding of the protocol, especially as you choose to offer dynamic documents—information resources that can change based upon context—through the use of common gateway interfaces, or CGI, scripts. See CGI Scripting, later, for more information on programming CGIs.

A typical HTTP transaction proceeds something like this: The client connects to the server and sends a *request method,* or the type of action it would like the server to perform, a *URI,*[*] or the location of the requested resource, and the version of HTTP that the client speaks, followed by information about the client, including its name and the type of data it prefers. For example, a client may send to a server:

```
GET /index.html HTTP/1.0
User-Agent: Mozilla/2.0a1 (Macintosh; I; 68K)
Accept: */*
Accept: image/gif
Accept: image/x-xbitmap
Accept: image/jpeg
```

Here, the client is requesting a file index.html in the topmost folder of your Web hierarchy. Each Web server application allows you to choose some folder on your hard drive as the topmost folder for your Web server, so that a folder several levels down on your hard drive can appear to be the topmost folder to people typing in Uniform Resource Locators, or URLs (see About URLs, later). The client is also telling the server that it understands HTTP/1.0, so that if the server speaks a later version of HTTP, it will adjust accordingly.

In our example, the client identifies itself as Mozilla/2.0a1, or version 2.0a1 of Netscape Navigator, which was named Mozilla in development versions, and has kept that name in its User-Agent field.

It's also telling the server that it will accept any kind of media type with Accept: */*; the client then goes on to say it will accept gif, x-xbitmap, and jpeg files, although this was already explicit in Accept: */*.

---

* URI stands for Uniform Resource Indicator, which is like a Uniform Resource Locator, or URL, only different. URLs are a subset of URIs; someday, there may be such things as Uniform Resource Names, or URNs, which, in a way similar to how the Domain Name System resolves names into IP addresses (see Chapter 9), will resolve into URLs. A URI would then mean either a URL or a URN. Until URNs are widely supported, though, a URI is a URL.

The server then responds with

```
HTTP/1.0 200 OK
Date: Mon, 11 Sep 1995 05:25:43 GMT
Server: InterServer_Publisher/1.0d75
Content-Type: text/html
Content-Length: 2318
Last-Modified: Tue, 12 Sep 1995 01:37:46 -0500
```

The server has identified itself as speaking HTTP/1.0 and returned a status code of 200, or OK. Status codes that you may commonly come across are:

```
200 OK
301 Moved Permanently
302 Moved Temporarily
401 Unauthorized
403 Forbidden
404 Not Found
500 Internal Server Error
```

In general, the first digit of a Status Code defines its broad purpose. 2xx indicates a successful action; 3xx indicates a redirection; 4xx indicates an error originating from the client; and 5xx indicates an error originating at the server.

The server—in this case, Intercon's InterServer—then identifies itself. The next header is the content type of the data represented in the body of the response; here, it's text/html for a standard HTML document. See Content Types, upcoming, for more information. InterServer then returns a Content-Length header, which is the size in bytes of the response body. InterServer then sends a Last-Modified date, or the last time the HTML file it's returning in the body was modified. Most servers return a Date header as well, giving the date and time of the response in Greenwich mean time. Finally, the server sends a carriage return and linefeed followed by the requested data, called the *entity body*.

Once again, in most cases, you can remain blissfully ignorant of these request and response formats. However, when creating dynamic documents or sending redirects—which we'll cover in the section on CGI scripting—your scripts will usually return data directly to clients without any intervention by the server, and, as a result, you'll need to generate your own headers. In most cases, this is a relatively simple task, since a header is just comprised of a few lines of text, and most headers, like Date and Last-Modified, are optional.

Content Types

Your server needs to be able to serve files with appropriate Content-type headers, so that Web clients can properly interpret and display the data they receive. To do so, it's necessary to associate the filename extensions you use in your local Web to content types, which are based upon Multipart Internet Mail Extension, or MIME, types. When a server retrieves a file from your file system, it looks at the file extension, and then consults its table of content types to label the data with the appropriate Content-Type: header when it returns the data to the client. In almost all cases, your server will come preconfigued to return the proper content types for the appropriate file extensions; if you're returning data via CGI scripts, however (see CGI Scripting), you're responsible for returning your own Content-Type header. See Table 8.1, Common Content Types, for content types that are common in a Web environment.

Root Directories and Paths

When configuring any Web server, you will be asked to specify the "root directory," or topmost folder, for the server. When a client requests a file from the server, the client requests a file in relation to the root directory; for example, if a client asks for the URL <http://www.pism.com/index.html>, and the root directory for your Web server is a folder www on your boot drive Macintosh HD, the server will return the file index.html in the www folder on Macintosh HD, or Macintosh HD:www:index.html—even though the client

TABLE 8.1 Common Content Types

Content-Type	Description File	Extension
application/excel	Microsoft Excel	.xl
application/mac-binhex40	BinHex	.hqx
application/msword	Microsoft Word	.word, .doc
application/octet-stream	Uninterpreted binary	.bin, .exe
application/pdf	Adobe Acrobat	.pdf
application/postscript	Adobe PostScript	.ps, .eps, .ai
application/x-compressed	UNIX compress	.z, .gz, .tgz
application/x-gtar	GNU tar	.gtar
application/x-rtf	RTF	.rtf
application/x-stuffit	Aladdin Stuffit	.sit
application/x-tar	UNIX tar	.tar
application/zip	ZIP	.zip
audio/basic	μ-law	.au, .snd
audio/x-aiff	AIFF	.aiff, .aif
audio/x-pn-realaudio	RealAudio	.ra, .ram
audio/x-wav	Windows WAVE	.wav
image/gif	GIF	.gif
image/jpeg	JPEG	.jpeg, .jpg, .jpe
image/pict	Macintosh PICT	.pict, .pic
image/tiff	TIFF	.tiff, .tif
image/x-xbitmap	X Bitmap	.xbm
text/html	HTML	.html, .htm
text/plain	Text	.txt, .text
video/mpeg	MPEG	.mpeg, .mpg, .mpe
video/quicktime	QuickTime	.mov, .qt
video/x-msvideo	Video for Windows	.avi
application/x-httpd-cgi	Common Gateway Interface	.cgi

only asked for index.html, and is unaware of where index.html actually lives on your Mac's hard drive. In the same way, if a client were to request the URL <http://www.pism.com/dns/dns.html>, the file Macintosh HD:www:dns:dns.html would be returned.

You'll have noticed that the paths in the URLs given here use slashes to separate directories, or folders, while the Mac file system uses colons. There are other differences between URLs and paths within the Mac OS: URLs reserve a number of characters for special use, which must be escaped using a percent sign and its hexadecimal code. Of special note is the space character, which needs to be coded as %20. For example, if you wanted a URL to refer to a file my file.html, it would need to be coded as my%20file.html. Appendix A gives a complete list of reserved characters, but you'll make your URLs easier to use if you restrict your filenames to numbers, lowercase letters, and the underscore (_), hypthen (-), and period (.).

Why the recommendation to restrict your filenames to lowercase letters? Because although the filenames debord.html and Debord.html are equivalent under the Mac OS, these would be two different files under UNIX. Because people don't know if they're accessing a Web server running the Mac OS or UNIX when they're typing in a URL, they've learned that capitalization does matter. If you keep everything lowercase, it's easier for people to type in your URLs—and if, for whatever reason, you someday need to move your Web structure to another platform, you've saved yourself a bit of trouble by giving all your files lowercase names.

Security Basics

You might want to restrict your Web to only certain people—if you're running an internal Web server that contains information that should be accessible only within your organization, for example. All Web servers tend to handle security in the same basic ways: restricting access to certain machines using the machines' domain names or IP numbers, and restricting access to users and groups, using an account name and password.

Restricting access based upon the client's domain name or IP address is an easy-to-set-up basic security measure. The server will allow you to list domain names or IPs, or portions of domain names or IPs, and put them in an allow or deny category. For example, you might specifically allow any client from freedonia.com to your Web server, so that hosts with the name of hail.freedonia.com and nail.freedonia.com can retrieve information from your server, and then deny access to all other machines. Or, you might specifically deny access from any host that has an IP address that begins with 204.62.130, so that a machine with an IP of 204.62.130.118 would be denied access to your server. This security method is site-wide: it restricts access to every document available from your server.

User authentication allows you to restrict access based on a user or group name and a password. When a client requests a document in a restricted directory, the server instructs the client to prompt the user for an account name and password. This security method is usually directory- or file-based, although you can use this method to protect your entire Web, by adding authentication to the root directory (see Root Directories and Paths, previously).

Naming Your Web Server

Most Web servers are named in the form www.companyname.com. Chapter 9 describes how to create a name-to-address record (an A record), which will resolve a name like www.freedonia.com into its IP address, or to set up an alias name (a CNAME record) for an existing machine, so that a computer known as hail.freedonia.com, for example, can also be known as www.freedonia.com. That's convenient if hail.freedonia.com provides both Web and FTP service, and you later want to make www.freedonia.com a dedicated machine. You can just change the CNAME record to point to another machine, and people can go on using www.freedonia.com without necessarily realizing they're now accessing a different host.

Via CNAME records, you can give one machine any number of names. You might assign a machine with an IP address of 192.0.0.1 both the name www.cats.com and the name www.dogs.com, for example. The URL <http://www.cats.com/cats/> could then contain information about cats, and the URL <http://www.dogs.com/dogs/> could contain information about dogs. The two URLs, of course, really point to the same machine with two folders—one named cats,

and one named dogs. You could just as well use the URL
<http://www.cats.com/dogs/> and get information about dogs.

For those who choose to use a single machine to serve multiple
domains, a common request is for the root directory to be depen-
dent upon the machine name used in the URL, so that
<http://www.cats.com/> has the cats folder defined as its root direc-
tory, and <http://www.dogs.com/> has the dogs folder defined as its
root directory. Otherwise, both of these URLs point to the same file,
which would need to contain information on both cats and dogs,
and provide appropriate links to the information contained in the
cats and dogs folders.

Unfortunately, if you recall our walk-through earlier of an HTTP
session (A Typical HTTP Transaction), the client doesn't send
to the server the server name within its request. For the URL
<http://www.cats.com/>, for example, the client first resolves the
domain name www.cats.com into the IP address 192.0.0.1, connects
to port 80 of that machine, and sends the HTTP request GET /
HTTP/1.0. The server has no way of knowing if the client was
requesting a URL for www.cats.com or www.dogs.com. Also, there's
no way to map a domain name to a port number; you can't, for
example, have www.cats.com map through DNS to port 80, and
www.dogs.com map through DNS to port 8080. It's just not possible.

OS's that support multiple IP addresses on the same physical
Ethernet interface can assign each domain name a separate IP
address, so that a Web server can distinguish between requests for
different domains. This is called *virtual hosting,* and if it sounds a
little obscure, it is. And the current Mac OS won't support multiple
IP addresses on the same Ethernet interface, so that option isn't
available to Mac Web servers. However, Open Door Networks has
released a product called HomeDoor that can interpret client
requests for a given domain name and redirect the client to the
proper subdirectory. For example, requests for <http://www.cats.
com/> can be redirected to <http://www.pets.com/cats/>.
HomeDoor provides this redirection before the request reaches your
Web server.

The HTTP 1.1 specification includes a new mandatory header, Host:, which will contain the host name of the server the client is requesting data from. Once HTTP 1.1 is in wide use, servers running atop the Mac OS updated for HTTP 1.1. will be able to distinguish between requests for different domains and serve the appropriate content.

FTPd 3.0

Peter Lewis's shareware FTPd (now called NetPresenz) added a simple Web server in version 3.0. FTPd can serve up HTML documents and related files, including any image, sound, or other media format. FTPd 3.0 doesn't support any server-side scripting: you won't be able to dish up dynamic documents, process forms, or use server-side image maps with version 3.0, although NetPresenz does support such applications. FTPd 3.0 has also removed the limit of 10 guest users that was present in previous versions, so that FTPd should be able to handle the traffic of anyone needing a basic Web server for personal use.

Setting Up FTPd

For FTPd to serve files with appropriate Content-Type headers, so that Web clients can properly interpret and display the data they receive (discussed in Content Types, previously), you need to associate the filename extensions you use in your local Web to media (MIME) types using Internet Config. (For example, mapping a file that ends in .gif to the media type image/gif.)

For most media types, Internet Config's default mappings should be fine. To view or edit Internet Config's mappings, launch Internet Config, and, from the Internet Preferences window, select the File Mappings window, shown in Figure 8.1. From here, you can add, delete, or change mappings; the only mapping information that FTPd needs in order to serve up documents is the extension and MIME type. We'd give an example of adding a media type to Internet Config, but, as we've said, the default list is more than complete.

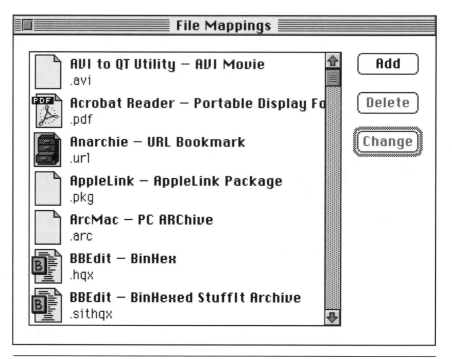

FIGURE 8.1 The File Mappings Window

Make sure to enter your e-mail address using the e-mail window before quitting Internet Config, since FTPd won't use Internet Config unless at least your e-mail address is filled in.

Since FTPd relies on System 7 Personal File Sharing to make files available to the outside world, you'll then need to give read-only access to guests for your Web documents.

To do so, enable file sharing by clicking on the Start File Sharing button in the Sharing Setup control panel, as shown in Figure 8.2. You'll also want to define an owner name and password if you haven't already done so.

To enable guest access, select the Users & Groups control panel and double-click on the <Guest> icon. In the File Sharing portion of the <Guest> icon window, make sure the Allow guests to connect box is checked, as shown in Figure 8.3.

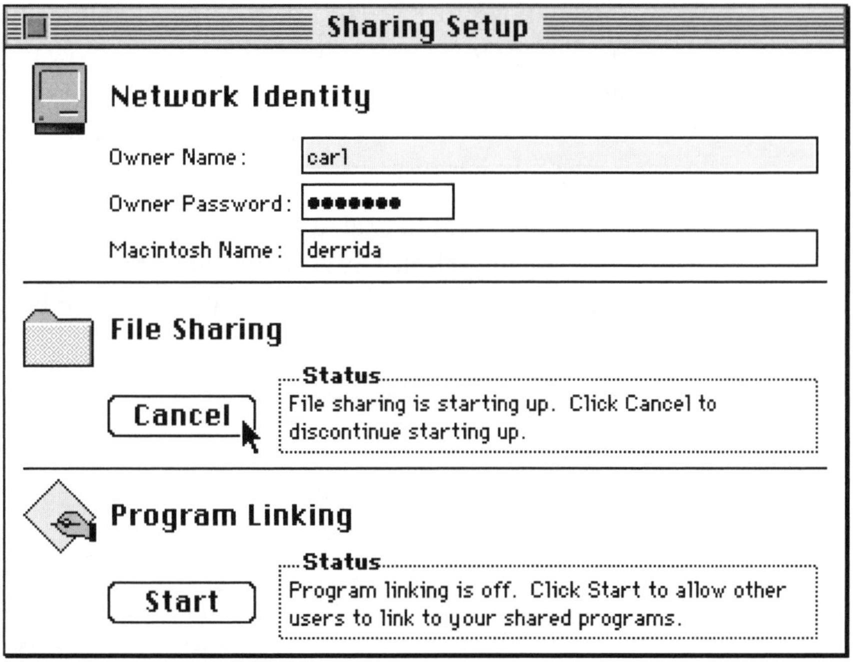

FIGURE 8.2 The Sharing Setup Control Panel

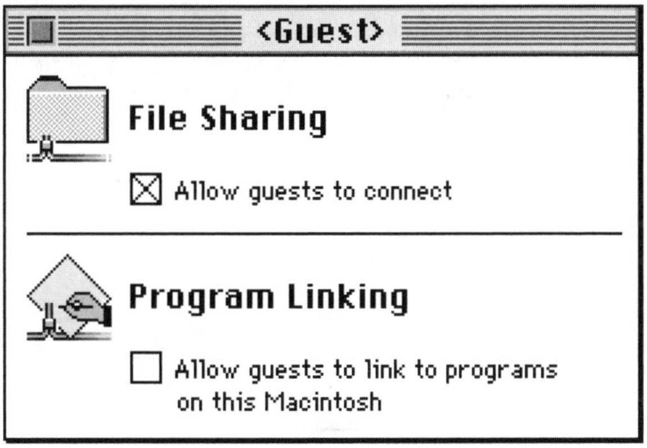

FIGURE 8.3
Allowing Guest
Access

Finally, create the topmost, or root, folder for your Web structure, if one doesn't yet exist. Highlight it, and, from the Finder's File menu, choose Sharing. . . . From the sharing privileges window for this folder, you'll want to make sure the Share this item and its contents box is checked, and to enable everyone to see folders and files, as shown in Figure 8.4. The other settings don't really matter, although you'll want to be restrictive as to who you allow to make changes, since this also allows access via AppleShare via the Chooser, and you may have other services running, such as FTP, which will use the same set of permissions.

You'll then want to enable Web services from FTPd. From the FTPd Setup menu, select WWW Setup; from the WWW Setup window, shown in Figure 8.5, check the WWW Enabled box, and specify the

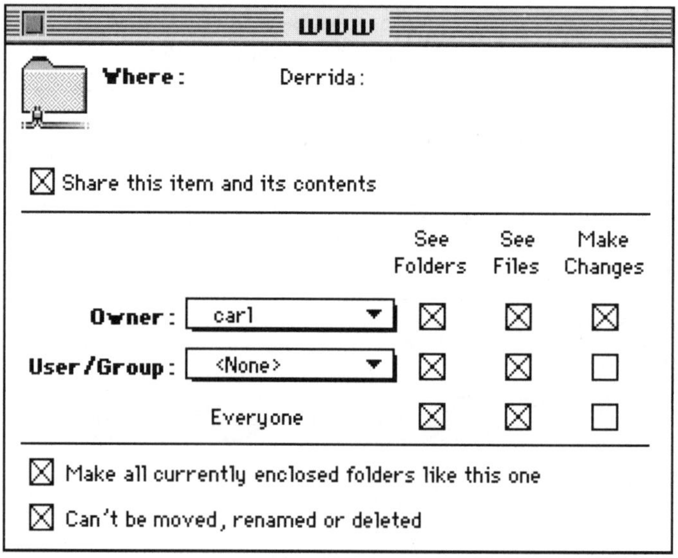

FIGURE 8.4 The Sharing Privileges Window

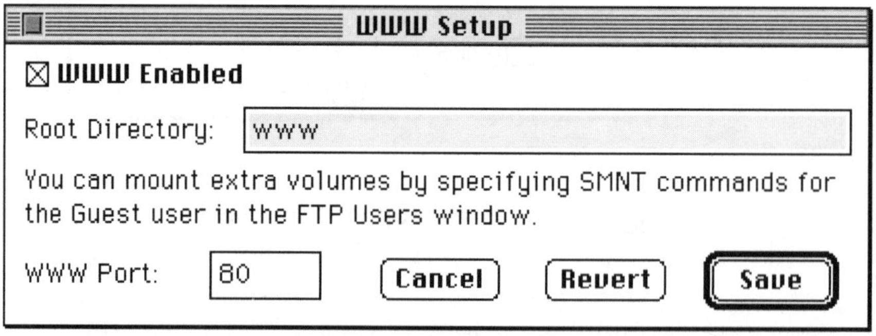

FIGURE 8.5 The FTPd WWW Setup Window

root directory for your Web server. If, for example, you want to store all your Web files in a folder called www on your local hard drive, simply specify www in the Root Directory: box. You can also tell FTPd to use a TCP port other than 80 for Web services, but 80 is the standard port for Web services and the one to which clients default. See HTTP Ports, discussed previously, for more information on ports for Web servers. (Note: FTPd must be quit and relaunched in order for a port change to take effect.)

Monitoring FTPd

You can monitor FTPd by viewing the FTPd log, available from the FTPd Log Window, shown in Figure 8.6. This log window should be fairly self-explanatory; FTPd logs the time and date of the request, the client's IP, the transfer type (HTTP for Web requests) and the

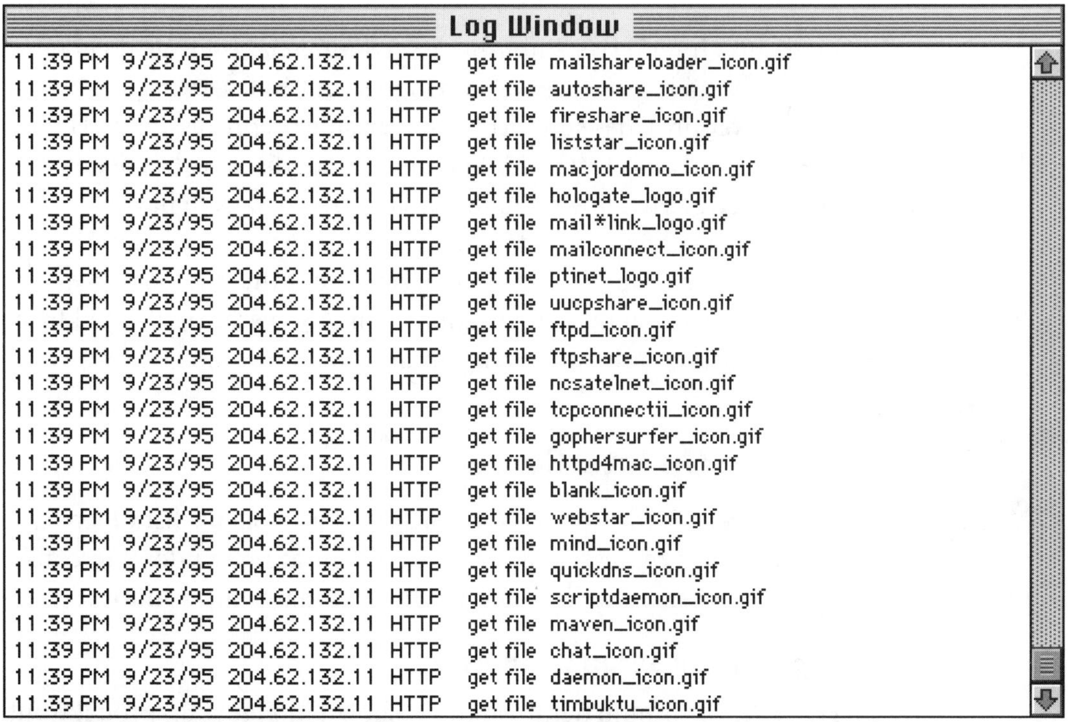

11:39 PM	9/23/95	204.62.132.11	HTTP	get file	mailshareloader_icon.gif
11:39 PM	9/23/95	204.62.132.11	HTTP	get file	autoshare_icon.gif
11:39 PM	9/23/95	204.62.132.11	HTTP	get file	fireshare_icon.gif
11:39 PM	9/23/95	204.62.132.11	HTTP	get file	liststar_icon.gif
11:39 PM	9/23/95	204.62.132.11	HTTP	get file	macjordomo_icon.gif
11:39 PM	9/23/95	204.62.132.11	HTTP	get file	hologate_logo.gif
11:39 PM	9/23/95	204.62.132.11	HTTP	get file	mail*link_logo.gif
11:39 PM	9/23/95	204.62.132.11	HTTP	get file	mailconnect_icon.gif
11:39 PM	9/23/95	204.62.132.11	HTTP	get file	ptinet_logo.gif
11:39 PM	9/23/95	204.62.132.11	HTTP	get file	uucpshare_icon.gif
11:39 PM	9/23/95	204.62.132.11	HTTP	get file	ftpd_icon.gif
11:39 PM	9/23/95	204.62.132.11	HTTP	get file	ftpshare_icon.gif
11:39 PM	9/23/95	204.62.132.11	HTTP	get file	ncsatelnet_icon.gif
11:39 PM	9/23/95	204.62.132.11	HTTP	get file	tcpconnectii_icon.gif
11:39 PM	9/23/95	204.62.132.11	HTTP	get file	gophersurfer_icon.gif
11:39 PM	9/23/95	204.62.132.11	HTTP	get file	httpd4mac_icon.gif
11:39 PM	9/23/95	204.62.132.11	HTTP	get file	blank_icon.gif
11:39 PM	9/23/95	204.62.132.11	HTTP	get file	webstar_icon.gif
11:39 PM	9/23/95	204.62.132.11	HTTP	get file	mind_icon.gif
11:39 PM	9/23/95	204.62.132.11	HTTP	get file	quickdns_icon.gif
11:39 PM	9/23/95	204.62.132.11	HTTP	get file	scriptdaemon_icon.gif
11:39 PM	9/23/95	204.62.132.11	HTTP	get file	maven_icon.gif
11:39 PM	9/23/95	204.62.132.11	HTTP	get file	chat_icon.gif
11:39 PM	9/23/95	204.62.132.11	HTTP	get file	daemon_icon.gif
11:39 PM	9/23/95	204.62.132.11	HTTP	get file	timbuktu_icon.gif

Log Window

FIGURE 8.6 The FTPd Log Window

request method, and the file requested for each transaction. Common errors you might catch in the log are "HTTP local connect failed/File sharing is disabled," which means you need to enable file sharing, as described earlier, and "HTTP local connect failed/No accessible volumes," which means file sharing is enabled, but you've forgotten to enable guest access. For both of these errors, the client will return "Error: 500—Server is not accepting connections."

Another common configuration error is not enabling Internet Config before running FTPd. If you just see raw text instead of rendered HTML in your client when accessing HTML documents, FTPd isn't able to use Internet Config to properly associate media types with file extensions. Launch Internet Config and supply your e-mail address to enable it.

 # InterServer Publisher

InterCon's InterServer Publisher is a commercial package that includes a Web server, as well as Gopher and FTP servers. InterServer provides support for server-side preprocessing of HTML files, which it calls InterXTML; although not discussed in detail here, InterXTML allows you to use HTML-like tags to have the server insert objects into documents such as an access counter or file listings. InterServer provides its services from the InterServer Publisher Extension; configuration of InterServer is performed from the InterServer Publisher Setup application.

Setting Up InterServer

InterServer's Setup application consists of a scrollable list of icons, each of which represents a separate configuration window. To configure InterServer, we'll begin the the Minimal Setup window.

The Minimal Setup Window

From the Minimum Setup window, shown in Figure 8.7, you'll want to do three things: specify the name of your server, in the Server

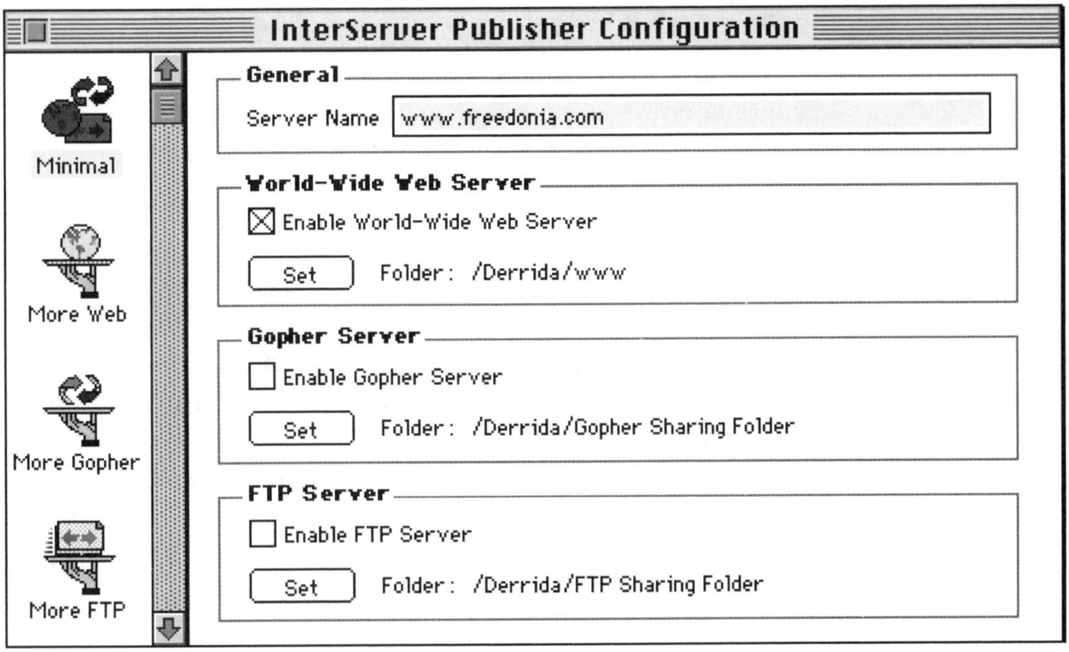

FIGURE 8.7 The Minimal Setup Window

Name box (for example, www.pism.com); check the Enable World-Wide Web Server box; and set the root directory for your Web server.

The default value for your server name is the name returned by your DNS server (see Chapter 9 for more information on DNS); if this isn't the name the server should be running as (if, for example, you have an alias name for the server; see Naming Your Web Server, discussed previously), you'll want to specify the server's name manually.

The root directory for your Web server is chosen by clicking the Set button and using a standard file dialog box to select the topmost folder for this service. See Root Directories and Paths, discussed earlier, for more information on the root directory.

That's all that's needed to begin serving Web documents with InterServer, although you'll probably want to go on to learn about the other configuration options available to you.

The More Web Window

From the More Web window, shown in Figure 8.8, you can set the maximum number of simultaneous connections, the port the Web server runs on, and the timeout value for client connections:

- ■ **Maximum simultaneous Web connections** is the number of client connections that your server will accept at the same time. Note that the number of simultaneous client connections isn't the number of simulataneous users; the Netscape Navigator browser, for example, defaults to opening up to four connections at the same time. InterServer's default value is eight simultaneous connections; if you run a busy server, you'll want to increase this value. If you're using MacTCP, however, remember that the maximum number of simultaneous TCP connections for the entire machine is 64 (Open Transport doesn't have this limit).

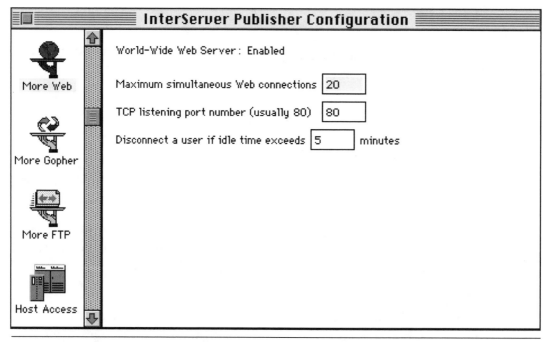

FIGURE 8.8 The More Web Window

■ **TCP listening port number** is the port number for your Web service. Normally, you'll want this number to be the default value of 80. See HTTP Ports, earlier, for more information on ports for Web servers.

■ **Disconnect a user if idle time exceeds ____ minutes** is the amount of time InterServer should leave a TCP port open for an idle connection. Five minutes is a good value for clients over (extremely) slow links. You want to avoid setting this value too high so that InterServer doesn't use up its maximum simultaneous Web connections waiting for clients that have improperly terminated their sessions.

Monitoring InterServer

You can set options to monitor InterServer from the Log window in the InterServer Publisher Setup application, shown in Figure 8.9.

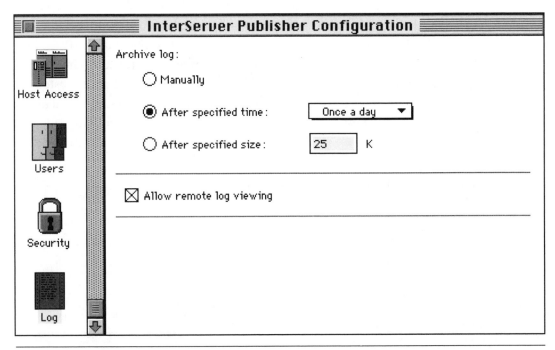

FIGURE 8.9 The InterServer Log Window

The Log window allows you to set automatic log rotation and to make your logs remotely available to Web clients.

You can choose to rotate your logs manually, automatically after a specified time, or automatically after a specified size by using the appropriate radio buttons for the archive log options. InterServer maintains its logs in your System's Preferences folder, in a folder called InterServer Publisher Logs. The current log file is named Current Log; automatically archived logs are named Log-001, Log-002, and so on.

If you've checked the Allow Remote Log Viewing option, you can view your logs with a Web browser by requesting an object ".log" at the root level of your server, as shown in Figure 8.10; that is, if your server were named www.pism.com, you would use the URL <http://www.pism.com/.log>.

InterServer also allows you to view the current log file from either the Log window in the InterServer Publisher Setup application or from the InterServer Log Viewer utility. Both display the same fields as the Remote Log report: date and time, the type of connection (FTP, Gopher, or Web), the transaction status, the client's IP address, the client's host name, the number of bytes sent, the connection time, the user name (if authenticated), and the requested file. The Log Viewer runs in less memory than the Setup application, but, beyond that, there's little difference in viewing logs in either one.

```
                                          Log
09/13/1995  00:47:38  Web  OK  204.62.132.14  mo.hotwired.com  332   00:00:01.2   /ism/server_icons/tcpconnectii_icon.gif
09/13/1995  00:47:38  Web  OK  204.62.132.14  mo.hotwired.com  1232  00:00:01.2   /ism/server_icons/ncsatelnet_icon.gif
09/13/1995  00:47:39  Web  OK  204.62.132.14  mo.hotwired.com  1204  00:00:01.3   /ism/server_icons/gophersurfer_icon.gif
09/13/1995  00:47:39  Web  OK  204.62.132.14  mo.hotwired.com  1280  00:00:01.3   /ism/server_icons/httpd4mac_icon.gif
09/13/1995  00:47:40  Web  OK  204.62.132.14  mo.hotwired.com  1004  00:00:01.0   /ism/server_icons/blank_icon.gif
09/13/1995  00:47:40  Web  OK  204.62.132.14  mo.hotwired.com  1309  00:00:01.0   /ism/server_icons/webstar_icon.gif
09/13/1995  00:47:41  Web  OK  204.62.132.14  mo.hotwired.com  1270  00:00:01.1   /ism/server_icons/mind_icon.gif
09/13/1995  00:47:41  Web  OK  204.62.132.14  mo.hotwired.com  435   00:00:01.1   /ism/server_icons/quickdns_icon.gif
09/13/1995  00:47:42  Web  OK  204.62.132.14  mo.hotwired.com  1278  00:00:02.2   /ism/server_icons/scriptdaemon_icon.gif
09/13/1995  00:47:43  Web  OK  204.62.132.14  mo.hotwired.com  1260  00:00:02.3   /ism/server_icons/maven_icon.gif
09/13/1995  00:47:43  Web  OK  204.62.132.14  mo.hotwired.com  1371  00:00:02.3   /ism/server_icons/daemon_icon.gif
09/13/1995  00:47:43  Web  OK  204.62.132.14  mo.hotwired.com  1199  00:00:02.3   /ism/server_icons/chat_icon.gif
```

FIGURE 8.10 Remote Viewing of the InterServer Log

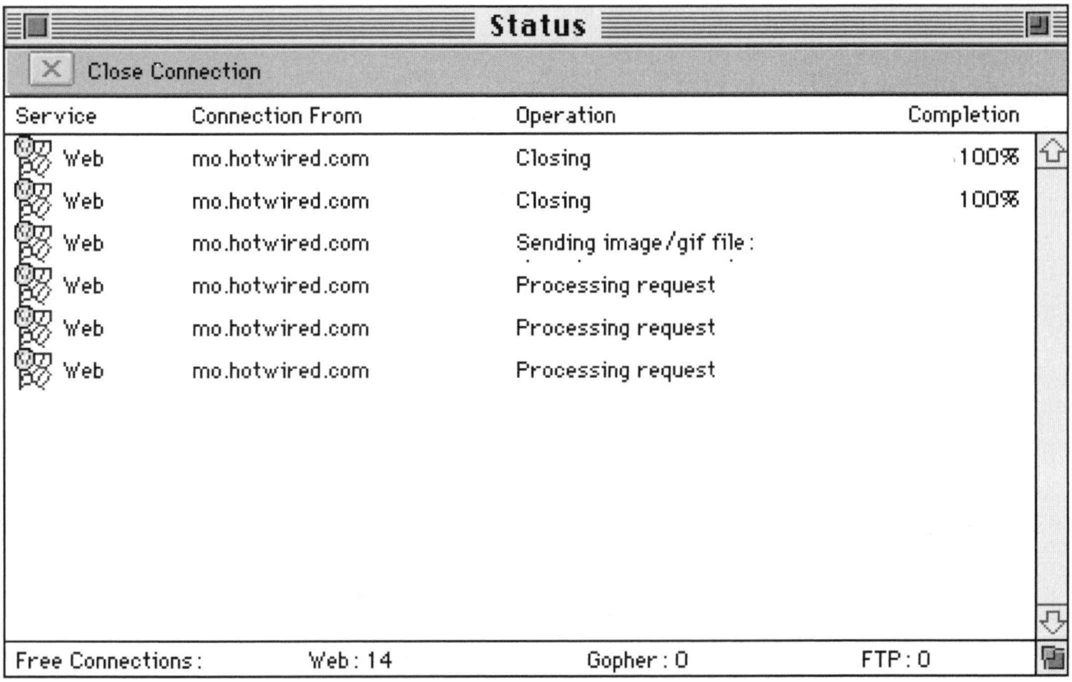

FIGURE 8.11 The InterServer Configure/Show Status Window

The Status window, shown in Figure 8.11, shows currently connected clients, displaying the connection type (FTP, Gopher, or Web) in the Service field, the client's IP address or host name in the Connection From field, the connection status in the Operation field, and the percentage completion in the Completion field. From the Status window, you can disconnect clients by highlighting a transaction and clicking the Close Connection box, which will ask you to verify that you do want to disconnect that client.

Security

You may need to restrict access to your site to only those people authorized by you. There are two ways of doing this: through restricting host access and through authenticating directories so that they require a user name and password for access. See Security Basics, discussed earlier, for more information.

Host Access

The Host Access configuration panel, available from the Host Access icon in the Configuration window and shown in Figure 8.12, allows you to restrict access based on the client's domain name or IP address.

To deny specific hosts, type the IP addresses or domain names to which you wish to deny access in the Web Deny: box. Adding entries to the Deny box doesn't change the default behavior of InterServer, which is to allow any hosts not explicitly denied.

To allow specific hosts, type the IP addresses or domain names of the hosts that you wish to allow in the Web Allow: box. The default behavior of InterServer is to allow all hosts and deny none; by specifying host names here, the default behavior is to deny any hosts not explicitly allowed. Adding entries to both columns has the same effect: InterServer will still deny all hosts not explicitly allowed, making the deny information redundant.

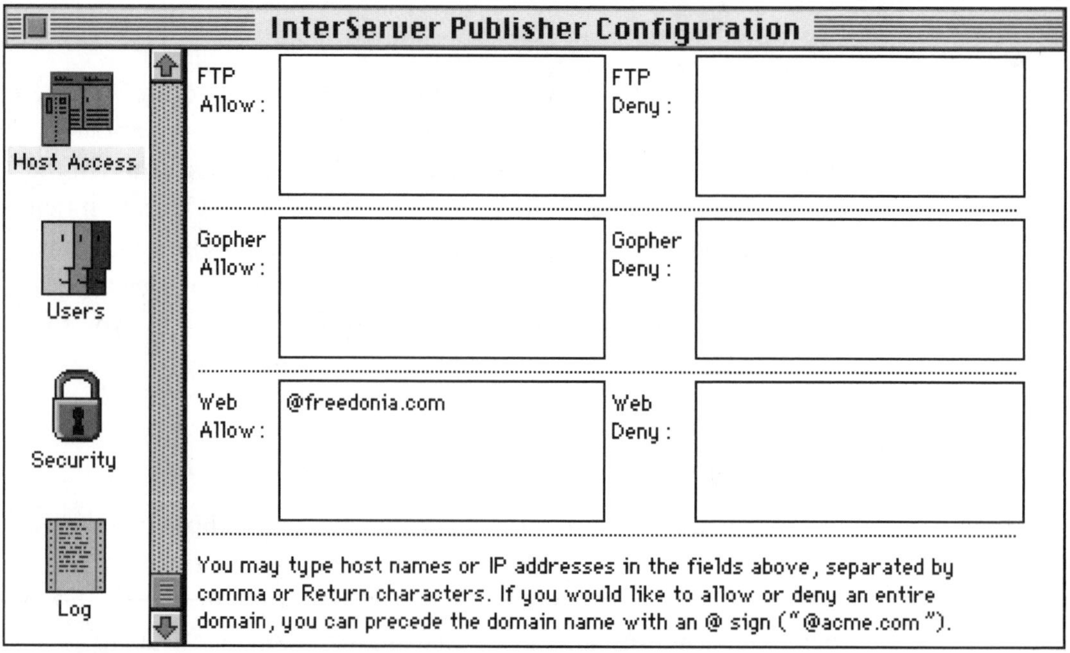

FIGURE 8.12 The InterServer Host Access Configuration Panel

Host names you supply here should always be in standard form (nail.freedonia.com, for example). Domain names that would match multiple hosts should be preceded by a commercial at symbol (@) to perform a wildcard match; for example, @freedonia.com would match both the host names nail.freedonia.com and hail.freedonia.com. IP addresses can be full or partial: 192.31.25.8 would allow or deny that specific host, while 192.31.25 would allow or deny the hosts 192.31.25.1, 192.31.23.2, and so on.

User Authentication

User authentication requires two steps: creating users with passwords, and then creating authenticated realms in which to place those users.

Creating User Accounts. From the InterServer Publisher Configuration window, select the Users icon for the Users window, shown in Figure 8.13. To create a new user, click New . . . and enter the

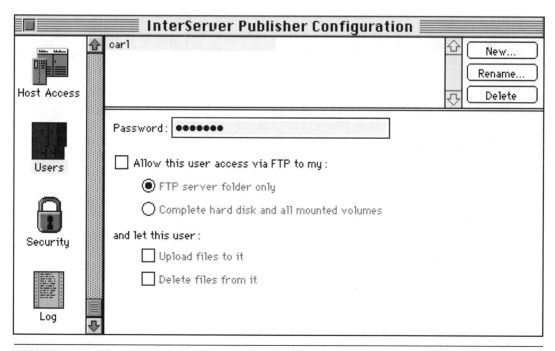

FIGURE 8.13 The InterServer Users Window

name of the user. Then, with the user name highlighted, enter a password in the Password field.

You can rename or delete existing user accounts by using the Rename... or Delete buttons, respectively; you can edit existing user accounts by highlighting a user and supplying a new password.

Creating Realms. Each realm you create has a keyword associated with it; when the keyword matches a portion of a requested URL, InterServer asks the client for a user name and password. For example, a keyword of "reports" would match the URLs <http://www. freedonia.com/reports/> and <http://www.freedonia.com/ magazines/conreports.html>. You'll need to select your keywords carefully to make sure they match only the URLs you want them to.

To create a realm, select the Security icon from the InterServer Publisher Configuration window for the Security window, shown in Figure 8.14. To create a new realm, click New . . ., enter the name of the realm, and click OK. Then, with the name of the realm high-

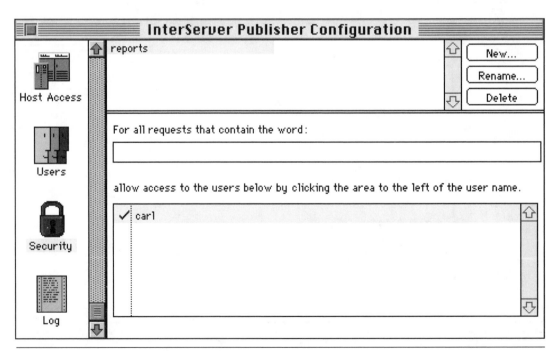

FIGURE 8.14 The InterServer Security Window

lighted, supply a keyword in the For all requests that contain the word: box, and check each user that should be able to access that realm.

You can rename or delete existing realms by using the Rename . . . or Delete buttons, respectively; you can edit existing realms by high-lighting a realm and supplying new information.

InterXTML

InterXTML, supported by the InterServer Publisher package, relies on server-side preprocessing to allow you to insert some predefined objects within your HTML documents; because InterXTML is pre-processed, clients see only the resulting HTML from InterXTML tags, and don't need to be able to understand InterXTML in any way. InterXTML is convenient if you want one of the InterXTML features; the downside of using InterXTML is that the HTML docu-ments you create using InterXTML will no longer be portable to other servers or platforms.

To use an InterXTML command, you need to place an <interxtml> tag at the top of your document; this instructs InterServer to pre-process your document before sending the data to the client, and prevents the server from having to preprocess the full contents of all HTML files, which should result in better performance. The three basic InterXTML tag sets are a group of <ix-file-counter> tags, which display the number of times a file has been accessed; a group of <ix-filelisting> and <ix-file> tags, for generating on-the-fly file listings for your folders; and an <ix-file-date> tag and its options, which allow you to display the last modified date and time for your document. Full documentation for the InterXTML tags is included with InterServer Publisher.

WebSTAR

WebSTAR, commercial software by StarNine Technologies, is a full-featured Web server based on MacHTTP, the first Web server package available for the Macintosh. While InterServer offers

InterXTML, WebSTAR has support for pre- and postprocessing of URLs, and support for secure transactions, including Secure Sockets Layer support, via its Security and Commerce Toolkits.

WebSTAR is made up of two applications: the WebSTAR server and WebSTAR Admin. While there is some overlap between the two, the WebSTAR server is used primarily to serve content, while WebSTAR Admin is used primarily to administer the server (as you might expect based on their respective names).

Setting Up WebSTAR

WebSTAR sets its root directory to the folder in which you choose to place the WebSTAR application. (See Root Directories and Paths, discussed previously, for an explanation of the root directory.) WebSTAR also stores all its preferences files within this same folder, allowing you to run multiple copies of WebSTAR listening on different ports on the same machine (see HTTP ports, discussed earlier).

Once you've placed the WebSTAR application within the folder that you want to make your server's root directory, you can simply launch WebSTAR to begin serving Web documents. Most other settings for WebSTAR are configured via the WebSTAR Admin application.

The WebSTAR Admin application can be used to control the WebSTAR server application from the same machine or from another machine via System 7 Personal File Sharing. If you'd like to adminster your WebSTAR server remotely via an AppleTalk network (including Apple Remote Access), you need to enable Program Linking from the Sharing Setup control panel, as shown in Figure 8.15. After switching on Program Linking, a Chooser-like dialog box allows you to select your WebSTAR server.

After launching the WebSTAR Admin application, either locally or remotely, there are a number of configurable options available from the Configure menu. Some of the more basic settings are available from the Miscellaneous Settings window, shown in Figure 8.16.

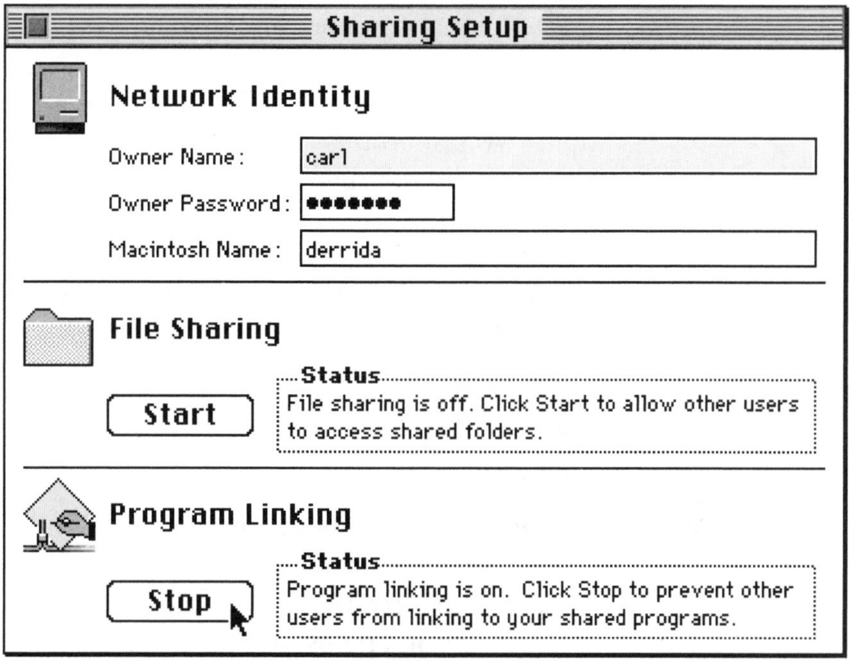

FIGURE 8.15 Enabling Program Linking

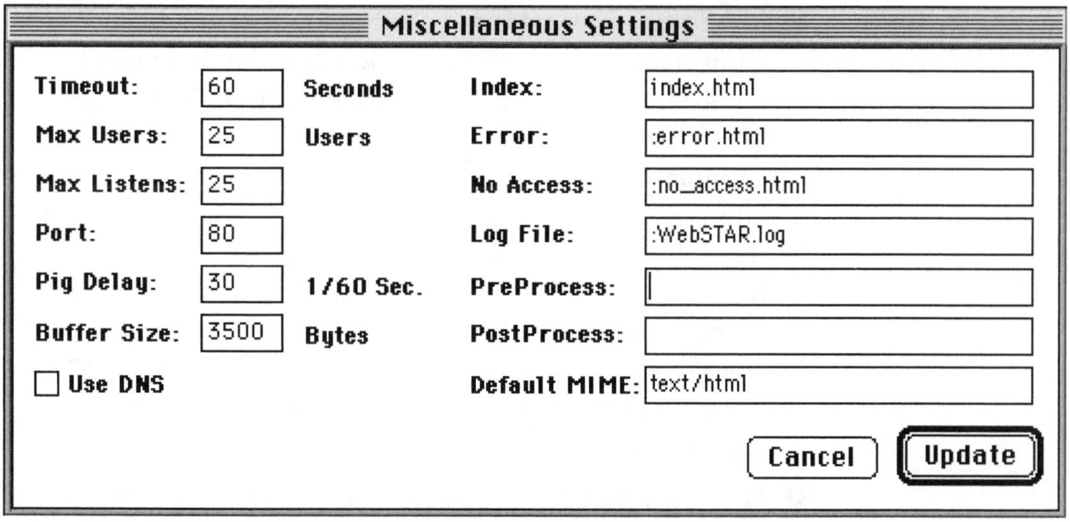

FIGURE 8.16 The WebSTAR Miscellaneous Settings Window

Of greatest initial importance is probably the Index option, which is the name of the default file returned when a client requests a directory rather than an actual file. For example, if a client requests <http://www.pism.com/>, the server will actually return the file found at the URL <http://www.pism.com/default.html> given WebSTAR's default setting. However, almost all other Web servers use the default name index.html; although default.html might make more sense for a default file, those interested in portability will use index.html instead. Of course, you can specify any filename you wish.

The other options available from the Miscellaneous Settings window are:

- **Timeout** is the amount of time WebSTAR should leave a TCP port open for an idle connection. This is also the amount of time that WebSTAR will wait for a reply in response to an AppleEvent it sends to another application, as it does with CGIs (see CGIs, discussed later); setting this value too low can cause your CGI scripts to time out, but a script that keeps the user waiting too long is probably too slow to begin with.

- **MaxUsers** and **MaxListens** are the number of simultaneous client connections that WebSTAR will accept. Note that the number of simultaneous client connections isn't the number of simultaneous users; the Netscape Navigator browser, for example, defaults to opening up to four connections at the same time. WebSTAR's default value is 12 connections, with three of those connections reserved to report that the server is busy when the other available connections are in use. You'll want to increase MaxUsers and MaxListens if you find that WebSTAR is refusing connections (see Monitoring WebSTAR, discussed later). WebSTAR limits the maximum MaxUsers value to 50.

- **Port** is the port number of your Web service. Normally, you'll want this number to be the default value of 80. See HTTP Ports, discussed earlier, for more information on ports for Web servers.

- **Pig Delay** is no longer a valid parameter in the threaded version of WebSTAR—and if you're running WebSTAR under System 7.5, as you should, WebSTAR is running as a threaded application.

- **Buffer Size** is the size, in bytes, of the TCP packet that is sent to the client; a smaller value is better for clients on slow connections, while larger values are better for clients on fast connections. This value can be anywhere between 256 and 10,240 bytes. The default vlaue of 4096 bytes is appropriate for most situations.

- **Use DNS** tells WebSTAR to perform DNS lookups of client IP addresses. Logs are generally easier to read if you resolve IP addresses into domain names; if you have a slow connection to your DNS server, however, you may want to uncheck this box to turn DNS lookups off, since the server will wait until a lookup is complete (or times out) before further processing the client's request.

- **Error** is the path for the file that WebSTAR returns when it encounters an error, usually of the 401 File Not Found variety. Your error file should provide some guidance to the user, such as providing a link to an index for the resources you make available via the server.

- **No Access** is returned when a client fails to authenticate when asked in order to retrieve a particular file. See Security, discussed later, for information on requiring authentication for files with WebSTAR.

- **Log File** is the path of the file to which WebSTAR writes its log file. See Monitoring WebSTAR for information on customizing the log file.

- **Preprocess** allows you to intercept client requests before being fulfilled by the server for preprocessing by a program or script. If your preprocessing application returns the null string to WebSTAR, WebSTAR will continue to fulfill the client's request in the usual fashion; if, on the other hand, your preprocessing application returns data to WebSTAR,

WebSTAR will return the data it receives from the preprocessor to the client instead. You might use preprocessing to return files based on browser type or a preferred language, or to pull data out of a database. The path of your preprocessor is specified here.

- **Postprocess** allows you to specify a program or script that will run after the client request has been completely fulfilled. In postprocessing, WebSTAR sends the requested data to the client, closes the connection, and then sends the same data to the postprocessor.

- **Default MIME type.** If a file doesn't use a file extension (such as .html or .gif) that WebSTAR recognizes (see Suffix Mapping, next), the file is returned with the Content Type supplied here (see Content Types, discussed previously). Typically, you'll set this value to either text/html or text/plain. It's a good idea always to use file extensions on your filenames, regardless of this value.

Suffix Mapping

The Suffix Mapping window, shown in Figure 8.17 and available from the Configure menu in WebSTAR Admin, allows you to associate MIME, or content, types with their filename suffixes, or extensions. This allows WebSTAR to serve files with appropriate Content-Type headers, so that Web clients can properly interpret and display the data they receive. See Content Types, discussed earlier, for more information.

For most media types, Internet Config's default mappings should be fine. To edit a mapping, highlight it and click on the Edit button, which places that mapping's information in the text fields below the scrolling mappings window. To add a mapping, click the Add button. Edit the fields, then click the Replace button to accept your changes. Finally, click Update when you're done editing mappings.

Actions

The Actions window, shown in Figure 8.18 and available from the Configure menu in WebSTAR Admin, allows you to run a script

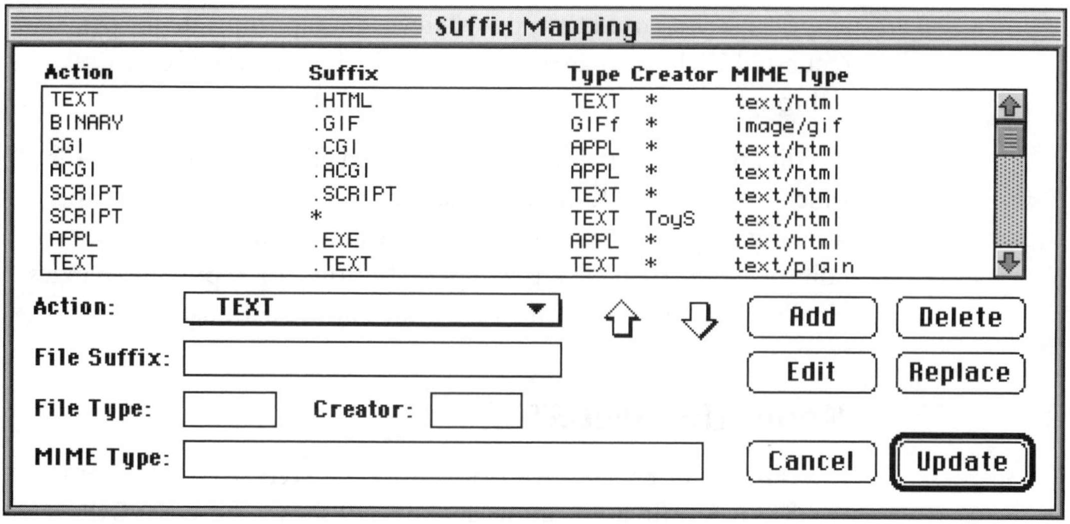

FIGURE 8.17 The WebSTAR Suffix Mapping Window

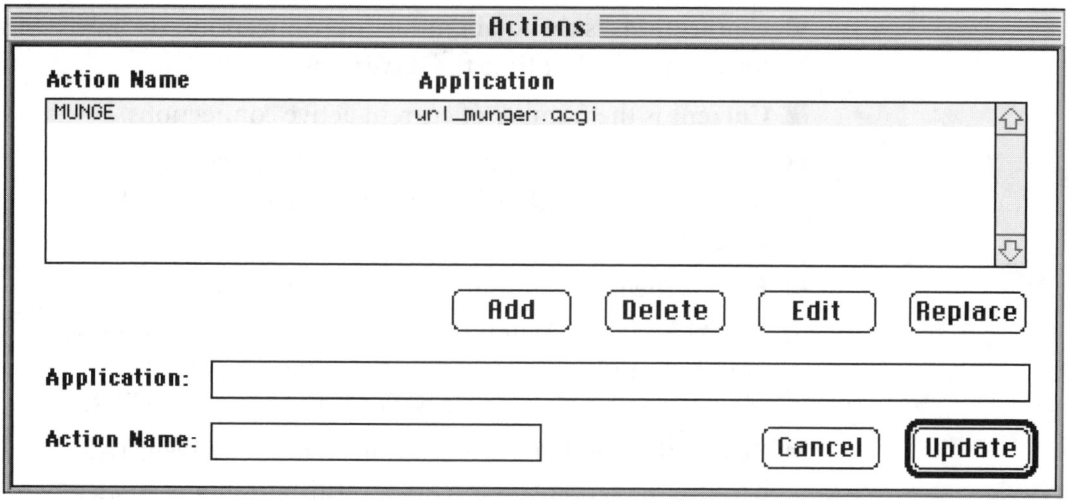

FIGURE 8.18 The WebSTAR Admin Actions Window

based on the *suffix* of a file path reference, versus the complete URL. For example, for a defined action zippy that was associated to the CGI zippy.cgi, a client could specify the URL <http://www.pism. com/reviews/reviews.zippy>; WebSTAR would pass off the request to zippy.cgi instead of referring to the file reviews.zippy. The zippy.cgi script could then do whatever was appropriate for the requested URL, such as returning the file reviews.txt after processing it through a Zippy filter.

To edit an existing action, highlight it and click on the Edit button, which places that action's information in the text fields below the scrolling mappings window. To add an action, click the Add button. Edit the fields, then click the Replace button to accept your changes. Finally, click Update when you're done editing actions.

Monitoring WebSTAR

You can monitor WebSTAR from either the WebSTAR server or the WebSTAR Admin application. Figure 8.19 shows the WebSTAR Admin monitor window. Both applications provide the same basic information:

- **Connections** is the total number of connections, or "raw hits," since the last time the server was restarted.

- **Current** is the number of current active connections.

- Listens/Max is the number of simultaneous client connections that WebSTAR will accept. See Setting Up WebSTAR (page 214).

- **High** is the highest number of simultaneous connections WebSTAR has served. If this number is equal to the number of Listens, preceding, you may need to increase the MaxListens/MaxUsers values. See Setting Up WebSTAR.

- **Busy** is the number of connections refused by WebSTAR because the server was too busy. If this number is greater than 0, you may need to increase the MaxListens/MaxUsers values. See Setting Up WebSTAR.

- **Denied** is the number of client requests that were denied based upon failure to authenticate. See WebSTAR Security (page 223).

- **Timeout** is the number of client requests that sat idle long enough to time out. See Setting Up WebSTAR.

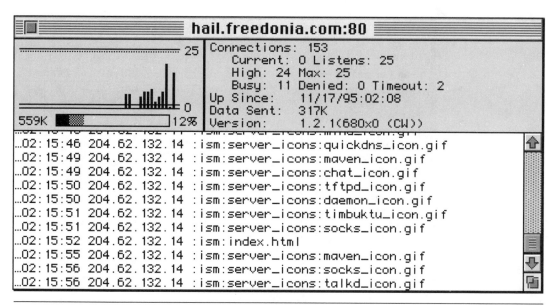

FIGURE 8.19 The WebSTAR Admin Monitor Window

- **Up Since** is the date and time the server was last restarted.
- **Data Sent** is the total amount of data, in kilobytes, that the server has delivered.
- **Version** is the version number of the WebSTAR application.

Logging

WebSTAR allows you to select which transaction data is logged through the Log Format item available in the Configure window of WebSTAR Admin, shown in Figure 8.20. The following fields are available:

- **DATE** is the date of the logged request.
- **TIME** is the time of the logged request.
- **HOSTNAME** is the domain name or the IP address of the client host making the request, depending upon whether Use DNS is checked in WebSTAR Admin's Miscellaneous options. See Setting Up WebSTAR.

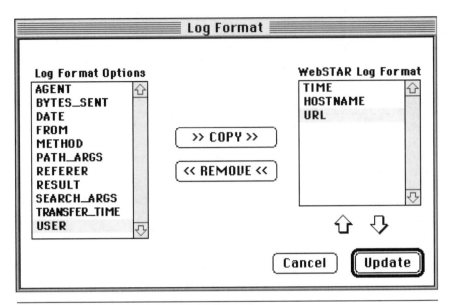

FIGURE 8.20 The WebSTAR Admin Configure Window

- **URL** is the path of the requested data.
- **PATH_ARGS** is the path arguments of the requested data. Path arguments are passed in by the client after the URL, separated by a dollar sign ($).
- **SEARCH_ARGS** is the search, or query, arguments of the requested data. Query arguments are passed in by the client after the URL, separated by a question mark (?).
- **METHOD** is the HTTP method, normally GET, HEAD, or POST.
- **RESULT** is the status of the request, which can return OK, ERR!, or PRIV.
- **BYTES_SENT** is the number of bytes, or the content length, of the data sent to the client.
- **TRANSFER_TIME** is the number of "ticks," or sixtieths of a second, that WebSTAR requires to field the client request.
- **AGENT** is the string with which the client identifies itself; for example, Netscape 2.0b1 identifies itself as "Mozilla/2.0b1 (Macintosh; I; 68K)."

■ **REFERER** is the URL of the document that referred to, or linked, to this one.

■ **USER** is the name of the authenticating user if authentication is needed to access the requested URL.

■ **FROM** is the e-mail address of the person requesting data via the client. This field is not required in recent versions of the HTTP specification, and will usually not be returned by the client.

To enable or disable any of these logging options, highlight the option in either the Log Format column (the disabled logging options) or the WebSTAR log column (the enabled logging options), and use the Copy and Remove buttons to move the option to the appropriate column. To change the order in which WebSTAR logs data, highlight an option in the WebSTAR Log column, and use the up and down arrows. Click on Update to accept your changes.

Logged information is written to the Log file specified in the Miscellaneous Settings window of the WebSTAR application. See Setting Up WebSTAR.

WebSTAR Security

You may need to restrict access to your site to only those people authorized by you. There are two ways of doing this: through restricting host access, and through authenticating directories so that they require a user name and password for access. See Security Basics, page 196, for more information.

IP Address or Domain Name-Based Security

The WebSTAR Allow and Deny window is available from the Allow/Deny item in the Configure menu from the WebSTAR server application, shown in Figure 8.21.

Allow and Deny statements allow you to specifically deny or allow access to a domain or subdomain or to an IP range. For example, if you want machines only in the domain freedonia.com to be able to access your Web server, you can explicitly allow freedonia.com and

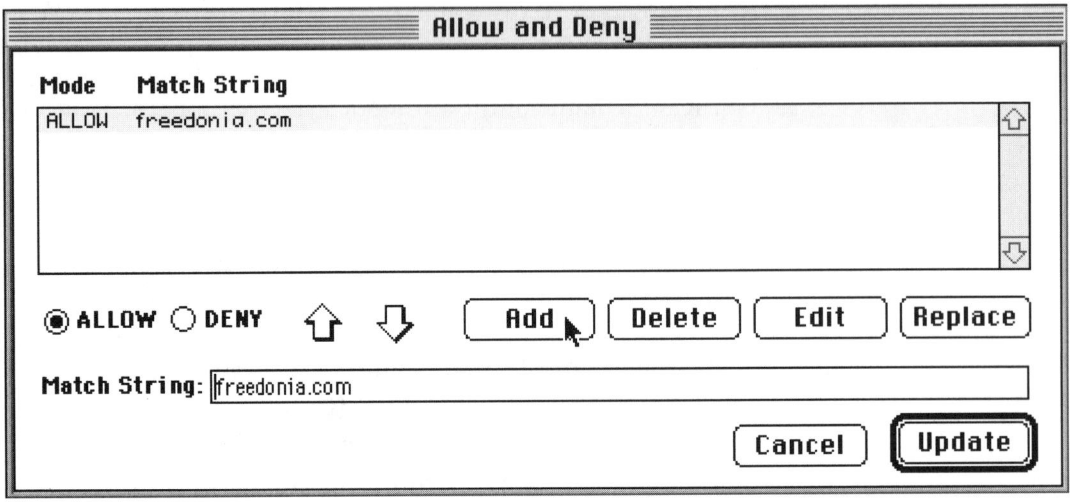

FIGURE 8.21 The WebSTAR Allow and Deny Window

deny access to all other machines. To do so, you would create an Allow for freedonia.com. WebSTAR's standard default behavior is to allow access from all hosts, but, by creating an Allow or Deny statement, WebSTAR's default behavior is to deny access to all hosts not explicitly allowed, so a wildcard Deny statement after the Allow isn't needed (it's implied, and WebSTAR's allows and denies don't support wildcards).

To allow access to an IP address range, you simply create an Allow for it in the same way; for example, Allow 204.62.130. To allow access to a single host by IP address, trail the IP number with a dot, as in Allow 204.62.130.1., which will allow access to the IP 204.62.130.1, but prevent WebSTAR from matching another IP address, such as 204.62.130.10.

To edit an existing Allow or Deny, highlight it and click on the Edit button, which places the information for that allow or deny in the fields below the scrolling Allow and Deny windows. Edit the fields, then click the Replace button to accept your changes. To add an Allow or Deny, edit the fields, and click the Add button. Finally, click Update when you're done editing.

User Authentication

The Realms window, available from the Configure menu in the WebSTAR Admin application and shown in Figure 8.22, allows you to specify strings that will match partial pathnames, which will then require the user requesting the URL containing the path to supply a valid user name and password.

From the Realms window, you can specify a Realm Name and a Match String. The Realm Name is the name that you give to the realm, which you'll then use when assigning user name and passwords to the realm (see next section); the Match String is the string that WebSTAR will attempt to match against each URL. For example, a match string of reports would match the URLs <http://www.freedonia.com/reports/> and <http://www.freedonia.com/magazines/conreports.html>. You'll need to select your match string carefully to make sure it matches only the URLs you want it to.

To edit an existing realm, highlight it and click on the Edit button, which places that action's information in the text fields below the scrolling mappings window. To add a realm, click the Add button.

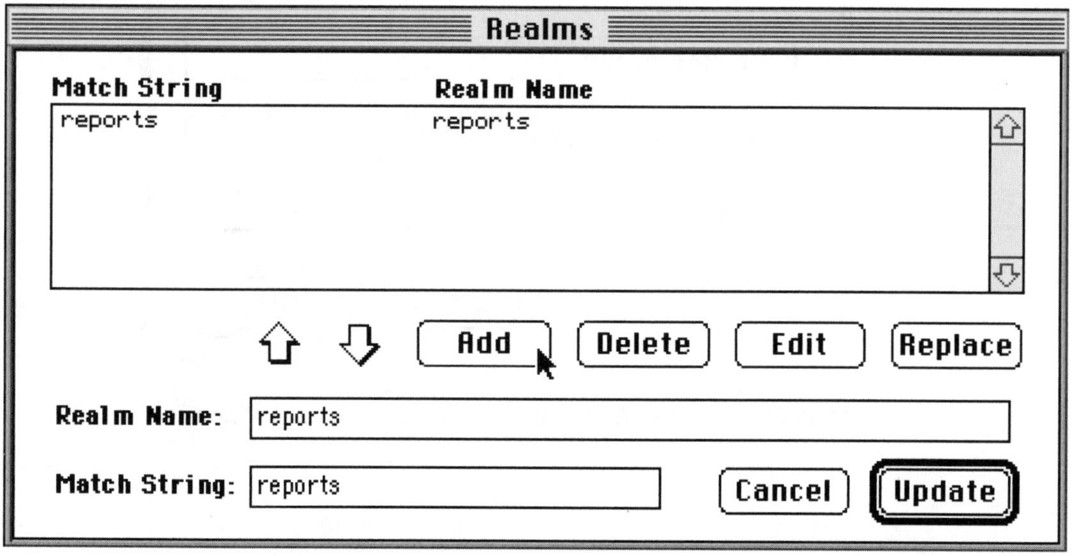

FIGURE 8.22 The WebSTAR Admin Realms Window

Edit the fields, then click the Replace button to accept your changes. Finally, click Update when you're done editing.

WebSTAR matches realms from order of first to last; for example, if you had two realms, cat and cats, and a client was requesting the URL <http://www.cats.com/catsrus.html>, the URL would be matched to whichever of the realms—cat or cats—appeared first in the list of realms. To change the matching order, highlight a realm, and use the Up and Down arrows; click Update when the order is correct.

You'll then need to define a user name and password for each realm. This is done in the WebSTAR Admin application, from the Passwords item in the Configure menu, as shown in Figure 8.23.

Select the corresponding realm in the Realm pop-up field, and supply a user name and password for the realm. Click Add to save your addition. You can create as many user names and passwords for the realm as you like.

```
╔═══════════════ Add Password ═══════════════╗
║                                            ║
║   User Name: │carl                      │  ║
║                                            ║
║   Password: │w5hgu!x                    │  ║
║                                            ║
║      Realm: │  REPORTS              ▼  │   ║
║                                            ║
║              ( Cancel )  (( Add ))         ║
║                                            ║
╚════════════════════════════════════════════╝
```

FIGURE 8.23 The WebSTAR Admin Add Password Window

HTML QuickStart

Most Web documents are created using HTML, or Hypertext Markup Language. We've provided a quick introduction to HTML to help you get started producing Web pages; although this is by no means a comprehensive tutorial, it should be complete enough to give you a good start.

We've found the best way to learn HTML is to view the source of existing documents, so that we can learn by example. We're mimicking that in our tutuorial: on one side of the page, we show the HTML document source, while on the other side, we show the rendered document, so that the whole tutorial on HTML is itself written in HTML.

After you've moved beyond the tutorial, the best way to teach yourself, as we've said, is to view source of other documents, in order to learn by example. Every Web browser should have a View Source or Save As Source option, although you may need to consult your browser's documentation to find the exact command.

```
</body>
</html>


<html>
<head>
<title>PISM: HTML Tutorial Introduction</title>
</head>

<body>
<p>Q: What is HTML?

<p>A: HTML, or Hypertext Markup Language, is used to describe the structural charactistics of
documents. With HTML, you can label, or mark up, the different elements of your text as such -
titles, headings, paragraphs, lists, and the like. You can also create links to other documents: you
can label words or images in your HTML documents as pointing to other objects (words, images, or
what have you) on the Web.

<p>The most important feature of HTML is that it's widely accepted and available across many
platforms. Graphical browsers running on desktop platforms, such as Netscape Navigator running under
the Mac OS, are common, but Web clients also exist for text-only computer terminals, as well as for
platforms that aren't as common as the Mac OS, Microsoft Windows, or the X Window System - the
Amiga, for example.

<p>The way HTML achieves this cross-platform compatibility is to describe the structure of
documents, not their presentation. With HTML, you can only label a paragraph as being a paragraph,
not to, say, indent each paragraph half an inch. (In theory, the reader, instead of the writer,
should be able to tell a Web browser how to display paragraphs - whether to indent them or to flush
them left, for instance - although few browsers give users this sort of control.) Different Web
browsers can choose to display the same structural elements in different ways. While it can be a
little disappointing to those used to the page layout capabilities of PageMaker or Quark XPress (or
even Word or WordPerfect), the simplicity of HTML makes a cross-platform, "World Wide" Web possible.

<p>HTML documents are just plain text files. As such, they can be produced with any text editor or
word processor. Although a good HTML editor or HTML converter may give you a production environment
that might address your needs better than a generic text editor, you certainly don't require
anything beyond the most basic of editors in order to produce HTML. A small, memory-resident editor
in one window and a Web browser in another to preview your work in progress will usually suffice. In
your text editor, you edit your HTML document, and save the document without quitting the editor
when you'd like to preview your work; with your Web browser, you begin by opening the file using
Open Local, or Open File, or the equivalent, and then reload after you've saved a new version from
your text editor using the Reload command. HTML is so simple and straightforward, in fact, that this
may be your preferred work environment.

<p>HTML comes in several flavors, the most recent being HTML 3. HTML 2, the last version, is still
most common, and a browser that only understands HTML 2 elements might get confused when given an
HTML 3 element; when we talk about a feature that's only available in HTML 3, we'll label it as such.

</body>
</html>
```

Q: What is HTML?

A: HTML, or Hypertext Markup Language, is used to describe the structural charactistics of documents. With HTML, you can label, or mark up, the different elements of your text as such - titles, headings, paragraphs, lists, and the like. You can also create links to other documents: you can label words or images in your HTML documents as pointing to other objects (words, images, or what have you) on the Web.

The most important feature of HTML is that it's widely accepted and available across many platforms. Graphical browsers running on desktop platforms, such as Netscape Navigator running under the Mac OS, are common, but Web clients also exist for text-only computer terminals, as well as for platforms that aren't as common as the Mac OS, Microsoft Windows, or the X Window System - the Amiga, for example.

The way HTML achieves this cross-platform compatibility is to describe the structure of documents, not their presentation. With HTML, you can only label a paragraph as being a paragraph, not to, say, indent each paragraph half an inch. (In theory, the reader, instead of the writer, should be able to tell a Web browser how to display paragraphs - whether to indent them or to flush them left, for instance - although few browsers give users this sort of control.) Different Web browsers can choose to display the same structural elements in different ways. While it can be a little disappointing to those used to the page layout capabilities of PageMaker or Quark XPress (or even Word or WordPerfect), the simplicity of HTML makes a cross-platform, "World Wide" Web possible.

HTML documents are just plain text files. As such, they can be produced with any text editor or word processor. Although a good HTML editor or HTML converter may give you a production environment that might address your needs better than a generic text editor, you certainly don't require anything beyond the most basic of editors in order to produce HTML. A small, memory-resident editor in one window and a Web browser in another to preview your work in progress will usually suffice. In your text editor, you edit your HTML document, and save the document without quitting the editor when you'd like to preview your work; with your Web browser, you begin by opening the file using Open Local, or Open File, or the equivalent, and then reload after you've saved a new version from your text editor using the Reload command. HTML is so simple and straightforward, in fact, that this may be your preferred work environment.

HTML comes in several flavors, the most recent being HTML 3. HTML 2, the last version, is still most common, and a browser that only understands HTML 2 elements might get confused when given an HTML 3 element; when we talk about a feature that's only available in HTML 3, we'll label it as such.

```
<html>
<head>
<title>PISM: HTML Tutorial Continued</title>
</head>

<body>
<p>Q: What does a bare-bones HTML document look like?

<p>A: Why, something like this.

<p>HTML uses <i>elements</i> to tag sections of text. Elements are set off by angle brackets.
In HTML, you'll see an opening angle bracket (&lt;), followed by the element name, followed by
a closing angle bracket (&gt;).

<p>All HTML elements are <i>containers</i>. That means elements usually come in pairs, which
you can see in the previous sentence, where we used the italic element (i) to tag the word
"containers"; there's an opening tag, followed by the text, followed by a closing tag. The
entire document is enclosed by the html element, which in turn contains a head element and a
body element. The head element contains elements that describe the document as a whole; it
requires a title element. Think of elements as Tupperware: you can put containers inside of
containers (nesting elements), but you can't overlap containers (physically impossible with
Tupperware, and a big no-no with HTML).

<p>The closing tags of some elements, like the paragraph element, can be assumed. It's like
when your mom would later put the tops on the Tupperware containers you put in the fridge
without the lids (or Saran Wrap on those plates of an uneaten hotdish you left sitting out).
It's like that, except html doesn't yell at you.

<p>The great thing about using the Tupperware metaphor is that you can think of all your
content as Jell-O.

</body>
</html>
```

Q: What does a bare-bones HTML document look like?

A: Why, something like this.

HTML uses *elements* to tag sections of text. Elements are set off
by angle brackets. In HTML, you'll see an opening angle bracket
(<), followed by the element name, followed by a closing angle bracket (>).

All HTML elements are *containers*. That means elements usually come in pairs, which you can see in the previous sentence, where we used the italic element (i) to tag the word "containers"; there's an opening tag, followed by the text, followed by a closing tag. The entire document is enclosed by the html element, which in turn contains a head element and a body element. The head element contains elements that describe the document as a whole; it requires a title element. Think of elements as Tupperware: you can put containers inside of containers (nesting elements), but you can't overlap containers (physically impossible with Tupperware, and a big no-no with HTML).

The closing tags of some elements, like the paragraph element, can be assumed. It's like when your mom would later put the tops on the Tupperware containers you put in the fridge without the lids (or Saran Wrap on those plates of an uneaten hotdish you left sitting out). It's like that, except HTML doesn't yell at you.

The great thing about using the Tupperware metaphor is that you can think of all your content as Jell-O.

```
<html>
<head>
<title>PISM: HTML Tutorial Continued</title>
</head>

<body>
<p><b>Q:</b> How do I add boldface, italic, and other formatting to HTML documents?

<p><b>A:</b> Well, we're already doing it.

<p>You can specify <b>boldfaced text</b> by using the bold element, b.

<p><i>Italicized text</i> is as easy as using the italic element, i.

<blockquote>
<p>If you have a longer quotation that you don't want to put into quotes, you can use the
blockquote element, blockquote.
</blockquote>

<pre>
You can use the preformatted element, pre, to tag preformatted text - text that should be
rewrapped or otherwise formatted within the browser. Preformatted text is usually put into a
nonproportional font, so you can
      line
      things
      up
from one line of text to the next, and white space - multiple spaces or carriage returns -
isn't collapsed in preformatted text as it is in normal HTML.
</pre>
```

Q: How do I add boldface, italic, and other formatting to HTML documents?

A: Well, we're already doing it.

You can specify **boldfaced** text by using the bold element, b.

Italicized text is as easy as using the italic element, i.

> If you have a longer quotation that you don't want to put into quotes, you can use the blockquote element, blockquote.

```
You can use the preformatted element, pre, to tag preformatted text - text that should be
rewrapped or otherwise formatted within the browser. Preformatted text is usually put into a
nonproportional font, so you can
     line
     things
     up
from one line of text to the next, and white space - multiple spaces or carriage returns -
isn't collapsed in preformatted text as it is in normal HTML.
```

<p>There are also lists:

<ul>
<lh>A short list about lists.</lh>
<li>There are ordered lists (ol) and unordered lists (ul).
<li>Ordered lists are numbered - the list element is labeled as 1, the second as 2, and so on.
<li>Unordered lists aren't numbered. They're usually just indented and bulleted. This is an unordered list.
<li>Each list item is preceded with the tag for a list item, <li>. (The closing tag is assumed when the browser encounters the next opening list item tag, but you can put it in, if you like.)
<li>HTML 3 allows you to have a list header (lh), if you want one. When present, it should come before the first list item.
</ul>

<p>And, if you need a line break without any added white space,
there is one. It's the break element (br).

<p>You might also like to know about character entities. Character entities are used to encode reserved characters in HTML. The two most important ones, which we've already used, are for the left angle bracket (<) and the right angle bracket (>). Character entities begin with an ampersand (&), and end in a semicolon (;). You can find a full chart of character entities in Appendix B.

There are also lists:

A short list about lists.

- There are *ordered* lists (ol) and *unordered* lists (ul).
- Ordered lists are numbered - the list element is labeled as 1, the second as 2, and so on.
- Unordered lists aren't numbered. They're usually just indented and bulleted. This is an unordered list.
- Each list item is preceded with the tag for a list item, <li>. (The closing tag is assumed when the browser encounters the next opening list item tag, but you can put it in, if you like.)
- HTML 3 allows you to have a list header (lh), if you want one. When present, it should come before the first list item.

And, if you need a line break without any added white space,
there is one. It's the break element (br).

You might also like to know about character entities. Character entities are used to encode reserved characters in HTML. The two most important ones, which we've already used, are for the left angle bracket (<) and the right angle bracket (>). Character entities begin with an ampersand (&), and end in a semicolon (;). You can find a full chart of character entities in Appendix B.

```
<html>
<head>
<title>PISM: HTML Tutorial Continued</title>
</head>

<body>
<h1>HTML Tutorial Continued</h1>

<h2>Headers</h2>
<p><b>Q:</b>How do I add headings to my document?

<p><b>A:</b>There are six levels of headers, the elements h1 through h6. Because headers are
meant to describe the structure of a document, headers should be used in order, so that, for
example, a second-level header (h2) is always subordinate to a first-level header (h1).
You're using headers correctly if you can imagine your document collapsed so that you could
see only the headers; it would provide a good, outline view of your document.

<p>Most people don't use headers "correctly," though; instead, they use the heading level
that gives them the font size they want for that heading. Although that doesn't really work as
well as most people think - they end up choosing a header that looks best in their browser of
choice, and a different browser may very well render the same heading level in a different
font size and in italic, for example - it is one of the few tools that people who want to
"design" HTML documents have to control the look of things. And we suppose it's better than
making the entire document one large image, as some particularly clueless companies and
individuals are doing.


<h2>Images</h2>

<p><b>Q:</b>How do I add images to my documents?

<p><b>A:</b>Well, first, let's define two types of images: <i>inline</i> images and
<i>linked</i> images. Inline images are images that appear directly within the HTML document
that includes them; linked images are images to which a document uses a hypertext link to
refer (we'll cover hypertext links in the next section).
```

PISM: HTML Tutorial Continued

Headers

Q: How do I add headings to my document?

A: There are six levels of headers, the elements h1 through h6. Because headers are meant to describe the structure of a document, headers should be used in order, so that, for example, a second-level header (h2) is always subordinate to a first-level header (h1). You're using headers correctly if you can imagine your document collapsed so that you could see only the headers; it would provide a good outline view of your document.

Most people don't use headers "correctly," though; instead, they use the heading level that gives them the font size they want for that heading. Although that doesn't really work as well as most people think - they end up choosing a header that looks best in their browser of choice, and a different browser may very well render the same heading level in a different font size and in italic, for example - it is one of the few tools that people who want to "design" HTML documents have to control the look of things. And we suppose it's better than making the entire document one large image, as some particularly clueless companies and individuals are doing.

Images

Q: How do I add images to my documents?

A: Well, first, let's define two types of images: *inline* images and *linked* images. Inline images are images that appear directly within the HTML document that includes them; linked images are images to which a document uses a hypertext link to refer (we'll cover hypertext links in the next section).

<p>Linked images have two advantages: the first is that the reader doesn't need to download the image unless he or she wants to view it, which is especially considerate of those using slow modem connections to access the Web; and the second is that a browser can rely on a helper application to display the image; so that even if the browser doesn't know how to display a particular image format, it can send the image to an application that does.

<p>The advantage of inline images, of course, is that they make your documents look good (well, at least in theory; there's no accounting for taste). Most browsers are able to inline GIF and JPEG images, and most browsers should support the upcoming PNG standard, as well.

<p>GIF images use a compression algorithm which is good at compressing solid blocks of color. GIFs can have a transparency index, a color which will appear transparent when placed on a browser's background. GIFs can also be interlaced, which creates that venetian blind or blurry-to-sharp effect you're probably familiar with. JPEGs don't have a transparency index, but the JPEG compression code is very good at compressing photographic images, and the JPEG format is 24-bit, or contains millions of colors, while the GIF format is 8-bit, or 256 colors.

<p>PNG is being developed as a new cross-platform image standard. It's a 24-bit format that has a transparency index and can be interlaced. Unfortunately, PNG compression isn't as good as JPEG compression, so PNG doesn't appear to the one "true" graphics format we've been waiting for.

<p>Since HTML documents are text documents, images are saved as separate files, and inlined using the image element (img) in conjunction with the image source attribute (src), so that if we have a file, logo.gif, the tag <img src="logo.gif"> would include it:

<p><img src="logo.gif">

Linked images have two advantages: the first is that the reader doesn't need to download the image unless he or she wants to view it, which is especially considerate of those using slow modem connections to access the Web; and the second is that a browser can rely on a *helper application* to display the image; so that even if the browser doesn't know how to display a particular image format, it can send the image to an application that does.

The advantage of inline images, of course, is that they make your documents look good (well, at least in theory; there's no accounting for taste). Most browsers are able to display inline GIF and JPEG images, and most browsers should support the upcoming PNG standard, as well.

GIF images use a compression algorithm which is good at compressing solid blocks of color. GIFs can have a transparency index, or a color that will appear transparent when placed on a browser's background. GIFs can also be interlaced, which creates that venetian blind or blurry-to-sharp effect you're probably familiar with. JPEGs don't have a transparency index, but the JPEG compression code is very good at compressing photographic images, and the JPEG format is 24-bit, or contains millions of colors, while the GIF format is 8-bit, or 256 colors.

PNG is being developed as a new cross-platform image standard. It's a 24-bit format that has a transparency index and can be interlaced. Unfortunately, PNG compression isn't as good as JPEG compression, so PNG doesn't appear to the one "true" graphics format we've been waiting for.

Since HTML documents are text documents, images are saved as separate files, and inlined using the image element (img) in conjunction with the image source attribute (src), so that if we have a file, logo.gif, the tag <img src="logo.gif"> would include it:

<p>Other attributes to the image element include alternative text (alt), which displays alternative text to a graphic for text-only browsers or for graphical browsers with automatic image loading turned off, and the height and width attributes (height and width) that tell the browser the dimensions of an image, in pixels, before it downloads it: that allows the browser to display all the text for an HTML document before it downloads all the images, since it knows how much white space to leave for the image. The height and width attributes were added in the HTML 3 specification, but browsers that only understand HTML 2 will safely ignore them.

<p>If we add in those image attributes, the preceding tag becomes "&lt;img src="logo.gif" alt="Project Name" height=60 width=125&gt;", or:

<p><img src="logo.gif" alt="Project Name" height=125 width=60>

<h2>Links</h2>

<p><b>Q:</b>How do I link to other objects?

<p><b>A:</b>If HTML were a powerful hypertext language - allowing for multiple links, so that one link could point to more than one place, and two-way links - so that the objects you link to would know about those links and be able to link back if the creator of the linked-to object so chose, it might take a considerable amount of time to learn how to link from one document to another. For better or for worse, however, HTML was kept very simple, and linking from a document to other objects is fairly straightforward.

<p>You link to other objects using the anchor element (a) in conjunction with its hypertext reference element (href). Between the opening and closing anchor tags, you provide text or an inlined image, which then becomes the hypertext link. For example, if you wanted to link to an HTML document about zebras called zebras.html, the HTML would look something like &lt;a href="zebras.html"&gt;zebras&lt;/a&gt;, or <a href="zebras.html">zebras</a>. If you were linking to a JPEG image of zebras, you might specify &lt;a href="zebras.jpeg" &gt;zebras&lt;/a&gt;, or <a href="zebras.jpeg">zebras</a>.

Other attributes to the image element include alternative text (alt), which displays alternative text to a graphic for text-only browsers, or for graphical browsers with automatic image loading turned off, and the height and width attributes (height and width) that tell the browser the dimensions of an image, in pixels, before it downloads it: that allows the browser to display all the text for an HTML document before it downloads all the images, since it knows how much white space to leave for the image. The height and width attributes were added in the HTML 3 specification, but browsers that only understand HTML 2 will safely ignore them.

If we add in those image attributes, the preceding tag above becomes <img src="logo.gif" alt="Project Name" height=60 width=125>, or:

Links

Q: How do I link to other objects?

A: If HTML were a powerful hypertext language - allowing for multiple links, so that one link could point to more than one place, and two-way links - so that the objects you link to would know about those links and be able to link back if the creator of the linked-to object so chose, it might take a considerable amount of time to learn how to link from one document to another. For better or for worse, however, HTML was kept very simple, and linking from a document to other objects is fairly straightforward.

You link to other objects using the anchor element (a) in conjunction with its hypertext reference element (href). Between the opening and closing anchor tags, you provide text or an inlined image, which then becomes the hypertext link. For example, if you wanted to link to an HTML document about zebras called zebras.html, the HTML would look something like <a href="zebras.html">zebras</a>, or zebras. If you were linking to a JPEG image of zebras, you might specify <a href="zebras.jpeg">zebras</a>, or zebras.

<p>The two preceding examples use relative links. Give us a moment to explain the difference between relative and absolute links:

<p>Relative links refer to documents in relation to the current folder or directory. Usually, relative links are just a filename - like zebras.html - but you can also use relative links to refer to files in folders relative to the current one; for example, ../tigers.html would refer to the file tigers.html in the folder that contains the current folder - the .. moves us one level up. What's good about relative links is that they allow you to move whole portions of your file system within your overall file structure without disturbing any of the (relative) links.

<p>Absolute links provide the full URL for a link.

<p>Well, most absolute links provide the full URL. There are also links that are absolute to the server root, which begin with a slash. They're called absolute links, too, and they're about the same as an absolute link, except that they're missing the "http://www.myservername.com" part - they begin with a leading slash.

<p>Now, there's no particular magic in using a relative links; the client simply looks at the current URL - called the "base" URL - and prepends it to the relative URL. You'll want to remember that if you're aliasing files from one folder to another; a client won't know where a file really is within your file system, only which URL it retrieved it from. It would really go beyond this guide's role as a quick introduction to HTML to tell you about the base element (base), which uses the hypertext reference attribute just like the anchor element (for instance, <base href="http://www. pism.com/dns/index.html">), and can be placed within the head (versus the body) of a document. See Appendix A, Uniform Resource Locators, for more discussion on relative and absolute paths and the base element.

<h2>Backgrounds and Other Layout Tricks</h2>

<p>Q: How do I load in backgrounds for my pages?

The two preceding examples use *relative* links. Give us a moment to explain the difference between relative and *absolute* links:

Relative links refer to documents in relation to the current folder or directory. Usually, relative links are just a filename - like zebras.html - but you can also use relative links to refer to files in folders relative to the current one: for example, ../tigers.html would refer to the file tigers.html in the folder that contains the current folder - the .. moves us one level up. What's good about relative links is that they allow you to move whole portions of your file system within your overall file structure without disturbing any of the (relative) links.

Absolute links provide the full URL for a link.

Well, most absolute links provide the full URL. There are also links that are absolute to the server root, which begin with a slash. They're called absolute links, too, and they're about the same as an absolute link, except that they're missing the "http://www.myservername. com" part - they begin with a leading slash.

Now, there's no particular magic in using a relative links; the client simply looks at the current URL - called the "base" URL - and prepends it to the relative URL. You'll want to remember that if you're aliasing files from one folder to another; a client won't know where a file *really* is within your file system, only which URL it retrieved it from. It would really go beyond this guide's role as a *quick* introduction to HTML to tell you about the base element (base), which uses the hypertext reference attribute just like the anchor element (for instance, <base href="http://www.pism.com/ dns/index.html">), and can be placed within the head (versus the body) of a document. See Appendix A, Uniform Resource Locators, for more discussion on relative and absolute paths and the base element.

Backgrounds and Other Layout Tricks

Q: How do I load in backgrounds for my pages?

<p>A: Backgrounds can be specified as an attribute to the body element (background), and should specify an image file for the browser to load in and tile as the background. So <body background="blue.gif"> will load in "blue.gif" as the background.

<p>Netscape Navigator introduced a background color attribute (bgcolor), which allows you to specify the hexadecimal RGB value for a background. You know, the hexadecimal RGB value. Some other browsers, such as Microsoft's Internet Explorer, support the bgcolor attribute. Using bgcolor, <body bgcolor="#ffffff"> would produce a white background; <body bgcolor="#6970E5"> would produce the shade of Carl's eyes.

<p>Now, all browsers don't support the background and bgcolor attributes, so don't rely upon them in your page design. And we probably don't have to tell you to choose a background on which your text is still readable.

<p>Speaking of readable text, Netscape Navigator also allows you to change the color of text and the color of links, both traversed ("visited"), and nontraversed. We'd rather you didn't use these attributes, but they're text, vlink, and link, respectively.

<p>Q: How do I center text on my pages?

<p align="center">A: The paragraph element and the header elements have an align attribute defined in HTML 3, which you can give a value of center, right, or left. You can use the align attribute with images, as well.

<p>Netscape Navigator introduced a center element (center), which centers anything you put between the open center tag and the closing center tag. Lots of other browsers support the center element, as well; in fact, more than support the align attribute, which is in the official specification. Go figure.

A: Backgrounds can be specified as an attribute to the body element (background), and should specify an image file for the browser to load in and tile as the background. So <body background="blue. gif"> will load in "blue.gif" as the background.

Netscape Navigator introduced a background color attribute (bgcolor), which allows you to specify the hexadecimal RGB value for a background. You know, the hexadecimal RGB value. Some other browsers, such as Microsoft's Internet Explorer, support the bgcolor attribute. Using bgcolor, <body bgcolor="#ffffff"> would produce a white background; <body bgcolor="#6970E5"> would produce the shade of Carl's eyes.

Now, all browsers don't support the background and bgcolor attributes, so don't rely upon them in your page design. And we probably don't have to tell you to choose a background on which your text is still readable.

Speaking of readable text, Netscape Navigator also allows you to change the color of text and the color of links, both traversed ("visited"), and nontraversed. We'd rather you didn't use these attributes, but they're text, vlink, and link, respectively.

Q: How do I center text on my pages?

A: The paragraph element and the header elements have an align attribute defined in HTML 3, which you can give a value of center, right, or left. You can use the align attribute with images, as well.

Netscape Navigator introduced a center element (center), which centers anything you put between the open center tag and the closing center tag. Lots of other browsers support the center element, as well; in fact, more than support the align attribute, which is in the official specification. Go figure.

```
<h2>Tables</h2>
```

```
<table border>
<tr><td><b>Q:</b>      <td>How do I create a table?
<tr><td><b>A:</b>      <td>Why, like this.
<tr><td colspan=2>Tables are beautiful, orderly things. But when you create the HTML for a
```
table (and this is HTML 3, mind you), your source may look far from beautiful or orderly. With
tables, outward appearance is everything. This is a simple example of a table. We started it
by using the table element (table) with the border attribute (border) to produce reassuring
lines around our tables, so our words don't run off somewhere. We then defined each table row
using the table row element (tr), and label each cell within that row with the table data
element (td). In this, our third row, we've used the column span attribute (colspan), and
given it a value of 2, telling the browser that this cell should span two columns. There's
also a row span element (rowspan) that works as you expect it might, and you can use the align
attribute you learned about in a previous Q/A session in tables, as well. Tables!
```
</table>
```

```
<p>At the time of this writing, many browsers still don't support tables. When a browser that
```
doesn't support tables comes across a table, it just places all the table's text on the
screen, without formatting it as a table - with predictably unreadable results. We recommend
using tables sparingly until they're broadly supported - probably about the time this book
sees print.

```
<h2>Image Maps</h2>
```

```
<p><b>Q:</b> What's an image map?
```

```
<p><b>A:</b> An image map is an image for which certain "hot" areas have been defined: when a
```
user clicks on one, the click coordinates are mapped to a URL, which the user is then sent to.
There are two types of image maps: server-side and client-side. In a server-side image map,
the coordinates of the mouse click are sent to the server, which then consults a map file for
the image, and returns the URL that the click would indicate to the client, which the client

Tables

Q:	How do I create a table?
A:	Why, like this.

Tables are beautiful, orderly things. But when you create the HTML for a table (and this is HTML 3, mind you), your source may look far from beautiful or orderly. With tables, outward appearance is everything. This is a simple example of a table. We started it by using the table element (table) with the border attribute (border) to produce reassuring lines around our tables, so our words don't run off somewhere. We then defined each table row using the table row element (tr), and label each cell within that row with the table data element (td). In this, our third row, we've used the column span attribute (colspan), and given it a value of 2, telling the browser that this cell should span two columns. There's also a row span element (rowspan) that works as you expect it might, and you can use the align attribute you learned about in a previous Q/A session in tables, as well. Tables!

At the time of this writing, many browsers still don't support tables. When a browser that doesn't support tables comes across a table, it just places all the table's text on the screen, without formatting it as a table - with predictably unreadable results. We recommend using tables sparingly until they're broadly supported - probably about the time this book sees print.

Image Maps

Q: What's an image map?

A: An image map is an image for which certain "hot" areas have been defined: when a user clicks on one, the click coordinates are mapped to a URL, which the user is then sent to. There are two types of image maps: server-side and client-side. In a server-side image map, the coordinates of the mouse click are sent to the server, which then consults a map file for the image, and returns the URL that the click would indicate to the client, which the client then proceeds to download. In a client-side image map, the coordinates and corresponding URLs are embedded within the HTML, so that all the processing can occur directly within the client.

<p>We'll only describe server-side image maps here, because, at the time of this writing, client-side image maps aren't yet very well supported, and Netscape introduced its own client-side image map scheme, which diverges from the one in the HTML 3 specification; it's too early to say which method will be more widely adopted.

<p>A server-side image map, then, requires three things: an image that is displayed on the user's screen, which he or she can click on; a map file, which contains the coordinates of "hot" areas for the image, and the corresponding URLs; and a CGI application to process the coordinates passed by the client to the server, using the map file. Given an image, leftright.gif, which contains two clickable regions, we might produce a map file like this:

```
<pre>
default index.html
rect left.html 0,0 50,25
rect right.html 51,0 100,25
</pre>
```

<p>Different map processing CGIs recognize different map file formats; the preceding is NCSA-compatible, which is the most popular of map formats. We tend to just create our map files by hand, given the x and y coordinates of the hot areas for our areas, but most people use a mapping utility to make the process transparent: WebMap is one popular piece of software for creating image maps.

<p>We can now put together a bit of HTML that tells the client that our image has an image map associated with it, and to which CGI program to send the coordinates of a mouse click. To do so, you use an image element, img, as you might expect, with the addition of an ismap attribute, which tells the client that this is a clickable image map. You then place the image tag within an anchor element, which tells the client the URL of the map processing CGI. It's also necessary to pass the location of the map file for the image to the mapping CGI,

then proceeds to download. In a client-side image map, the coordinates and corresponding URLs are embedded within the HTML, so that all the processing can occur directly within the client.

We'll only describe server-side image maps here, because, at the time of this writing, client-side image maps aren't yet very well supported, and Netscape introduced its own client-side image map scheme, which diverges from the one in the HTML 3 specification; it's too early to say which method will be more widely adopted.

A server-side image map, then, requires three things: an image that is displayed on the user's screen, which he or she can click on; a map file, which contains the coordinates of "hot" areas for the image, and the corresponding URLs; and a CGI application to process the coordinates passed by the client to the server, using the map file. Given an image, leftright.gif, which contains two clickable regions, we might produce a map file like this:

```
default index.html
rect left.html 0,0 50,25
rect right.html 51,0 100,25
```

Different map processing CGIs recognize different map file formats; the preceding is NCSA-compatible, which is the most popular of map formats. We tend to just create our map files by hand, given the x and y coordinates of the hot areas for our areas, but most people use a mapping utility to make the process transparent: WebMap is one popular piece of software for creating image maps.

We can now put together a bit of HTML that tells the client that our image has an image map associated with it, and to which CGI program to send the coordinates of a mouse click. To do so, you use an image element, img, as you might expect, with the addition of an ismap attribute, which tells the client that this is a clickable image map. You then place the image tag within an anchor element, which tells the client the URL of the map processing CGI. It's also necessary to pass the location of the map file for the image to the mapping CGI, so that the URL is usually a combination of the location of the mapping application, followed by the location of the map file for the image in question. If we were using MapServe to process our map file, the necessary HTML to make our image map work might look like this:

<p><a href="/map/mapserve.acgi$/leftright.map"><img ismap
src="leftright.gif"></a>, or

<p><a href="/map/mapserve.acgi$/leftright.map"><img ismap src="leftright.gif"></a>

<p>That is, the client is told to display the image leftright.gif, and to pass any mouse-click coordinates to the application to the CGI (in this case, the ACGI, but the difference between a CGI and an ACGI doesn't enter this discussion), which is given the location of the map file we created earlier.

<p>If image maps seem a bit complicated, they can be, the first few times around. Like a lot of things on the Web, they were an afterthought, and far from an ideal solution; when client-side image maps become common, things should become considerably easier.

<h2>Forms</h2>

<p>Q: How do I create a fill-in form?

<p>A: Ah, the fill-in form: the online marketer's dream, allowing one to create questionnaires nobody wants to fill out and provide online order forms for products that nobody wants to buy. Forms are great if you're providing a unique, customized service, but it's always best to keep your fill-in forms as simple and straightforward as possible.

<p>A form begins with a form element, form, which specifies a method with the method attribute and an action with the action element. A method tells the browser how to send the data the user supplies to the server. There are two common form methods: get and post. The get method appends the form data to the URL the data is submitted to; the post method sends the data in a more transparent fashion. Our example will be of the post method.

so that the URL is usually a combination of the location of the mapping application, followed by the location of the map file for the image in question. If we were using MapServe to process our map file, the necessary HTML to make our image map work might look like this:

<a href="/map/mapserve.acgi$/leftright.map"><img ismap src="leftright.gif"></a>, or

L | **R**

That is, the client is told to display the image leftright.gif, and to pass any mouse-click coordinates to the application to the CGI (in this case, the ACGI, but the difference between a CGI and an ACGI doesn't enter this discussion), which is given the location of the map file we created earlier.

If image maps seem a bit complicated, they can be, the first few times around. Like a lot of things on the Web, they were an afterthought, and far from an ideal solution; when client-side image maps become common, things should become considerably easier.

Forms

Q: How do I create a fill-in form?

A: Ah, the fill-in form: the online marketer's dream, allowing one to create questionnaires nobody wants to fill out and provide online order forms for products that nobody wants to buy. Forms are great if you're providing a unique, customized service, but it's always best to keep your fill-in forms as simple and straightforward as possible.

A form begins with a form element, form, which specifies a method with the method attribute and an action with the action element. A method tells the browser how to send the data the user supplies to the server. There are two common form methods: get and post. The get method appends the form data to the URL the data is submitted to; the post method sends the data in a more transparent fashion. Our example will be of the post method.

<p>The action attribute for the form element tells the client the URL of the program or script that will process the data the user will submit. Here, we've specified a script called form_process.cgi, which we'll talk about more in the section on CGI Scripting, next. The whole tag, then, becomes <form method=post action="form_process.cgi">

<form method=post action="form_process.cgi">

<p>Next, we'll ask for an e-mail address in a text input box, using the input element, input. We're giving this piece of information the name of email using the name attribute, which we'll use to identify the data when processing the form. We've specified a type attribute of text, which is a single-line text field. Other types include password, which is the same as text, except that the client prints a bullet or asterisk instead of the character typed; textarea, for multiline text fields; checkbox, for check boxes; radio, for radio buttons; submit, for a button to submit the supplied data using the action supplied in the form element; and reset, for clearing the form. In this example, we're only using the text, radio, and submit types.

<p>We're also supplying a size attribute for our e-mail submission box. The size value tells the browser how many characters to make the input box, so that the HTML for our e-mail submission box becomes <input type="text" name="email" size=24>.

<p>Your e-mail address:

<input type="text" name="email" size=24>

<p>Now that we have an e-mail address that will uniquely identify each user, let's ask the user a question. Here, we're conducting a poll on whether or not people like spam. We'll use two radio buttons with the same name, spam, which will let the user choose between the values yes and no. Since we assume that most people do like spam, we've made yes the default value, by giving it the checked attribute.

<p>Would you say that you like spam?

<input type="radio" name="spam" value="yes" checked> Yes
<input type="radio" name="spam" value="no"> No

The action attribute for the form element tells the client the URL of the program or script that will process the data the user will submit. Here, we've specified a script called form_process.cgi, which we'll talk about more in the section on CGI scripting, next. The whole tag, then, becomes <form method=post action="form_ process.cgi">

Next, we'll ask for an e-mail address in a text input box, using the input element, input. We're giving this piece of information the name of email using the name attribute, which we'll use to identify the data when processing the form. We've specified a type attribute of text, which is a single-line text field. Other types include password, which is the same as text, except that the client prints a bullet or asterisk instead of the character typed; textarea, for multi-line text fields; checkbox, for check boxes; radio, for radio buttons; submit, for a button to submit the supplied data using the action supplied in the form element; and reset, for clearing the form. In this example, we're only using the text, radio, and submit types.

We're also supplying a size attribute for our e-mail submission box. The size value tells the browser how many characters to make the input box, so that the HTML for our e-mail submission box becomes <input type="text" name="email" size=24>.

Your e-mail address: [   ]

Now that we have an e-mail address that will uniquely identify each user, let's ask the user a question. Here, we're conducting a poll on whether or not people like spam. We'll use two radio buttons with the same name, spam, which will let the user choose between the values yes and no. Since we assume that most people do like spam, we've made the yes value the default value, by giving it the checked attribute.

Would you say that you like spam?

 Yes

○ No

<p>Finally, we'll let our user submit the data. The value attribute we supply here, "spam!", becomes the text for the submit button:

<p><input type=submit value="spam!">

<p>And we need to close the form by supplying the closing </form> tag.

</form>

<p>That's the HTML side of a form; for the form to be useful, though, it still needs to be processed by the CGI script we specified in the action attribute to the form element. We cover that in our processing form data example in the CGI Scripting section, next.

<h2>And...</h2>

<p>Q: Anything else I should know?

<p>A: Well, we've covered most of the basics of HTML, and then some - document structure, text formatting, headings, images, links, backgrounds, aligning text, tables, image maps, and forms. That should cover what you need to know to get you started. You'll undoubtedly find that the best way to learn is to do. Just keep in mind that browsers other than your preferred browser are out there, and be careful to look at the HTML pages you put together in one of those other browsers once in a while to make sure you're creating pages that appeal to as wide an audience as possible. Beyond that, learn by example: if you see a page that does something you'd like to do, view the source and see how it's done. It's that simple.

</body>
</html>

Finally, we'll let our user submit the data. The value attribute we supply here, spam!, becomes the text for the submit button:

> [spam!]

And we need to close the form by supplying the closing </form> tag.

That's the HTML side of a form; for the form to be useful, though, it still needs to be processed by the CGI script we specified in the action attribute to the form element. We cover that in our processing form data example in the CGI Scripting section, next.

And...

Q: Anything else I should know?

A: Well, we've covered most of the basics of HTML, and then some - document structure, text formatting, headings, images, links, backgrounds, aligning text, tables, image maps, and forms. That should cover what you need to know to get you started. You'll undoubtedly find that the best way to learn is to do. Just keep in mind that browsers other than your preferred browser are out there, and be careful to look at the HTML pages you put together in one of those other browsers once in a while to make sure you're creating pages that appeal to as wide an audience as possible. Beyond that, learn by example: if you see a page that does something you'd like to do, view the source and see how it's done. It's that simple.

CGI Scripting

The Common Gateway Interface, or CGI, was defined as a way to allow scripts and programs,* to add functionality that isn't built directly into the server. CGIs are commonly used to produce interactive, or dynamic, documents, from processing image map data to providing an access counter to storing forms data to giving Web access to a specialized database.

A typical CGI transaction between a client and server goes something like this:

- The client requests the CGI, either by requesting a file defined by the server as a CGI program or script—usually, a filename ending in .cgi—or by clicking on an image map or submitting form data.
- The server launches the appropriate CGI script or program, passing it information about the request, such as the form data posted, by setting global, or environmental variables. See our second example CGI script, Printing the Global Variables, for a listing of all the variables passed to the CGI script.
- The CGI then performs whatever actions it was programmed to perform, and returns its output to the client.

Sometimes, instead of returning output directly to the client in the last step, a CGI will return its output to the server, for further processing. If the CGI is returning output directly to the client, as is most commonly the case with Mac OS-based Web servers, it's the CGI's responsibility to generate proper HTTP headers, as previously discussed in HTTP Headers.

Some CGI programs will be ready-to-use: for example, you don't need to write a program to process image map coordinates; you can use one that someone else has already written. However, if you wish

---

* Scripts are usually interpreted, or translated, into machine code each time the script is run. Programs are usually compiled, or translated, into machine code once, with the resulting compiled code run each time—which results in better execution speeds.

to do any custom processing of client data, you'll need to write your own scripts or programs in an appropriate language.

Of the popular scripting and programming languages available under the Mac OS—including AppleScript, MacPerl, Frontier, and C—we've chosen to put our CGI scripting examples in MacPerl.

The advantages of scripting in MacPerl are that it's reasonably quick and full-featured and it's cross-platform. Since the Web itself is cross-platform, we put a lot of credence in a cross-platform scripting language; a MacPerl script usually ports easily enough to a UNIX box running Perl and vice versa, and the skills you pick up with MacPerl are applicable to other environments. Perl also makes it easier to manipulate text than just about any other language you'll ever come across, which is important, since most of the scripting related to the Web has to do with manipulating text. MacPerl and Perl are also free.

That said, other languages may be better suited to your tasks: AppleScript is probably the easiest language to learn of the ones discussed here, with its natural-language syntax, and it's included with every copy of System 7.5 or later. AppleScript is slow, however, and you can't do much from within AppleScript itself—building AppleScript CGIs will often require you to assemble multiple Open Scripting Architecture components (OSAXen), and each OSAX will have its own documentation and perhaps its own license. Although AppleScript itself is very simple, each extension you need to add to your AppleScript environment makes it that much more complex, and sometimes it's more trouble than it's worth.

Properly built Frontier scripts or C programs can be run multi-threaded, or asynchronously, meaning the script or program can process more than one request at a time; with both MacPerl 4 (the most current version as of this writing; MacPerl 5 will be multithreaded) and Applescript, multiple requests wait in a queue, since only one request can be processed at a time. Frontier has a small but active user community behind it. It can run Applescripts in its own environment asynchronously, and it's available free; C is ubiquitous as a programming language and has the steepest learning curve of the languages discussed here, but will give the best results in terms of speed.

We have four MacPerl CGI examples: a simple redirect; printing the global variables that the server passes to the script; returning different HTML based on the browser requesting the data; and forms processing.

Installing MacPerl

If you've never used MacPerl before, it comes in two flavors: the MPW, or Macintosh Programmer's Workshop, version, and a stand-alone version. Unless you're familiar with MPW, you'll want to create your scripts using the standalone version.

After you unpack the MacPerl package, you'll end up with a folder called MacPerl ƒ. This contains the MacPerl application and its supporting files. To create a MacPerl script, launch the MacPerl application and select New from the File menu; enter your script into the Untitled window or paste from your favorite text editor. You can run your script from the Script menu and save it from the File menu; consult the MacPerl documentation for more information.

Creating CGI Scripts with MacPerl

To set up MacPerl to create scripts that can run as CGIs, you'll need to install the MacPerl PCGI extension. To do so, unpack the PCGI package, and drag the MacHTTP CGI Script MacPerl Extension from the PCGI folder to the MacPerl Extensions folder within your MacPerl folder. This will add an additional option when you save a script using the Save As . . . item from the File menu. From the Type pull-down menu in the standard file dialog, you can choose MacHTTP CGI Script.

Finally, you'll want to make sure your Web server recognizes the .cgi extension, if that's the extension you're giving to your scripts, as indicating a CGI script. See Content Types, earlier.

A Word on CGI Security

A Web server is only as secure as the CGI scripts it runs. It's possible for you to create scripts that do things as obvious as deleting files from the file system, or things slightly more subtle such as returning data from outside your Web directory, potentially allowing others access to information you don't intend to give access to. Scripts should parse user input so that you don't create a script that allows people to, say, read your Eudora mailbox, and they should be able to deal with errors gracefully, so they don't hang or crash your server. When creating scripts, keep security in mind.

1. A Simple Redirect

A redirect simply points a client requesting one URL to another URL. This would be quite useful, except that, most times, you'd want to provide a redirect when a client requests an HTML file (for example, from pigs.html to pork.html), and, in order for your script to execute to perform the redirect, it needs to end in an extension that would type it as a CGI file (for example, you could create a redirect from pigs.cgi to pork.html).

Despite that, we're using a redirect as our first example, since it's simple and demonstrates a little about HTTP headers. Normally, your CGI scripts will return the HTTP headers "HTTP/1.0 200 OK" and Content-Type: text/html, which identify the output from the CGI as standard HTML (see HTTP headers, discussed peviously). In this case, however, we're returning a status of "302 Redirect" ("HTTP/1.0 302 Redirect") and a Location header, that supplies to the client a URL that presumably contains the information it's seeking.

Here's the script:

```perl
#!perl
#
# simple redirect script
# pism
#
```

```
# define the variable $target_url with a URL to redirect to
$target_url = "http://www.pism.com/pork.html";

# print the HTTP header with a status of 302 Redirect
print "HTTP/1.0 302 Redirect\r\n";

# print the URL that the client should get instead
print "Location: $target_url\r\n\r\n";
```

We can test the script by running it straight from MacPerl. It won't simulate the CGI environment (none of the global variables will be set, but we're not using them here, anyway), but it will compile our script to catch any syntax errors, and display the output that we would send to the client in the MacPerl window. So we get:

```
HTTP/1.0 302 Redirect
Location: http://www.pism.com/pork.html
```

which looks right. A client requesting the URL for our script will be told that the URL has moved, and that the new location is <http://www.pism.com/pork.html>.

We can install the script by saving it as a CGI script, by selecting MacHTTP CGI Script from the Save As . . . item from the File menu in the MacPerl application, and moving it into our Web structure. When we access the script from a Web client, it should work as advertised.

2. Printing the Global Variables

Your Web server (either WebSTAR or InterServer) passes a number of variables to the CGI environment via AppleEvents. These include query or post arguments sent by a user submitting a search request or forms data, and the domain name or IP address of the host that the client is running on, among others. These variables are called the *environmental,* or *global,* variables.

The following is a simple script that returns all the environmental variables it receives. It allows you to see what information is being passed to your CGI environment.

MacPerl places its environmental variables in an associate array, %ENV, so that, for example, the value of an environmental variable called USER_AGENT would be referred to as $ENV{'USER_AGENT'}. It just so happens that that's the way you would access these variables from a Perl script under UNIX; even though the underlying methodology is different, MacPerl takes pains to keep the environment as cross-platform as possible.

Here's the script:

```perl
#!perl
#
# print the environmental variables
# pism
#

# return an HTTP header with a status of 200 OK
print "HTTP/1.0 200 OK\r\n";

# return an HTTP header with the content-type
print "Content-type: text/html\r\n\r\n\";

#
# print the environmental variables

# place each sorted key for the associative array %ENV into
# the variable $key

foreach $key (sort keys(%ENV)) {

   # skip the MacPerl-specific variables
   next if $key =~ /PERL/;

   # print the key and the value of the key
   print "<p>$key = $ENV{$key} \n";
}
```

If we save this script and access it from a browser, we get:

```
GATEWAY_INTERFACE = CGI/1.1

HTTP_USER_AGENT = Mozilla/2.0b1 (Macintosh; I; 68K)
```

```
REMOTE_ADDR = 204.62.132.28

REQUEST_METHOD = GET

SCRIPT_NAME = /test.cgi

SERVER_NAME = hail.freedonia.com

SERVER_PORT = 80

SERVER_PROTOCOL = HTTP/1.0

SERVER_SOFTWARE = MacHTTP/2.0
```

Useful? Perhaps, depending upon what you might do with the information. See our next example, Delivering Content Based on Browser Type.

3. Delivering Content Based on Browser Type

By checking the browser type (the HTTP_USER_AGENT global variable), you can assemble different HTML pages for different browsers. Instead of saying "Enhanced for" a particular browser, for example, you can just deliver your "enhanced" page for that browser and another design for other browsers.

It may be unwise to produce enhanced pages either way—what you're either explicitly (by providing a single page that necessitates a particular browser) or implicitly (by providing any enhanced content) doing is encouraging divergent, proprietary HTML "standards" by the companies that produce Web browsers. Insofar as a "world wide" Web is important, enhancing pages for particular browsers makes that goal more difficult to attain. And besides, it's more work for you. But here's the script:

```perl
#!perl
#
# delivering content based on browser type
# pism
#

# define the variable $browser to contain the user agent
# global variable
```

```
$browser = $ENV{"HTTP_USER_AGENT"} ;

# print the HTTP header with a status of 200 OK
print "HTTP/1.0 200 OK\r\n";

# print the Content-type header to identify the script's
output as HTML
print "Content-type: text/html\r\n\r\n";

# print some HTML
print <<EOM;

<html>
<head>
<title>Delivering Content Based On Browser Type</title>
</head>

<body>
<p>A comparison of apples to oranges:

EOM

# pattern match for "Mozilla" (Netscape Navigator) or
# "MSIE" (Microsoft Internet Explorer)
# both of which support tables. if it matches, return a
# table otherwise, print out some preformatted text

if ($browser =~ /Mozilla|MSIE/) {
    print "<table>\n";
    print "<tr><td>       <th>Apples <th>Oranges\n";
    print "<tr><th>Jan. 1 <td>$1.09  <td>$1.18\n";
    print "<tr><th>Feb. 1 <td>$2.01  <td>$1.29\n";
    print "</table>\n";
 } else {
    print "<pre>\n";
    print "              Apples    Oranges";
    print "              ----      ---\n";
    print "Jan. 1        $1.09     $1.18\n";
    print "Feb. 1        $2.01     $1.29\n";
    print "</pre>\n";
 }
```

```
# print some more HTML

print <<EOM;

<p>As you can see, the prices of apples and oranges vary.

</body>
</html>

EOM
```

If we view this document using Netscape 1.1, we get the results shown in Figure 8.24. If, however, we view the document in a version of Mosaic that does not have table support, we instead get what's shown in Figure 8.25.

4. Processing Form Data

In our HTML Tutorial, we went through a form example that collected an e-mail address and whether that user liked spam. This script, our last example, is the back end to that form: it takes the form data that the client passes to the script and processes it.

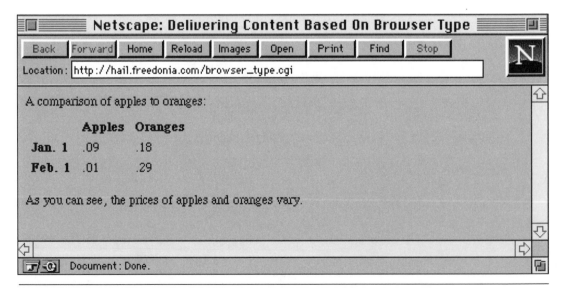

FIGURE 8.24 Our Dynamic Document in Netscape

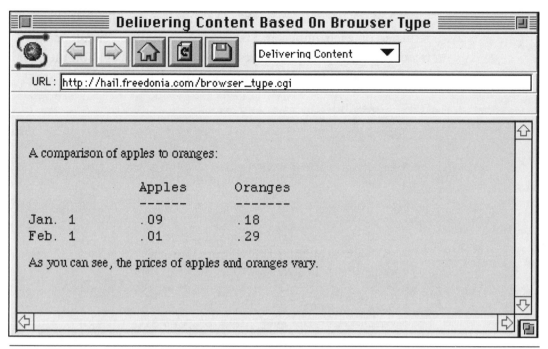

FIGURE 8.25 Our Dynamic Document in Mosaic

In the tutorial example, we began our form with the tag <form method=post action="form_process.cgi">; that action is this script. So, if you're using this script with the form example, you'll want to save this script under the name form_process.cgi, and save it in the same folder as the form example.

This script doesn't really do much with the form data it receives; it just processes the data into key/value pairs, and displays them to the client. In a real-world situation, you'd probably do some nice formatting for the user, and store the data you collect in a file or database; by keeping things simple in our example, though, we hope to focus on how you would access the form data from the CGI environment, rather than on what you might do with that data.

A lot of the script has to do with processing the data it receives from the client into key/value pairs that are easy for the person writing the script to use. For example, a client might return the forms data "email=carl@freedonia.com&spam=yes" to the script. We want the

script to first separate each piece of form data by splitting the string
returned on each ampersand (so that we would get "email=carl@
freedonia.com" and "spam=yes"); we then want to split on the equal
sign (=) to get simple key/value pairs stored in an associative array.

Here's the script:

```perl
#!perl
#
# processing form data
# pism
#

# read the input from standard input
# without exceeding the content length
read(STDIN,$in,$ENV{'CONTENT_LENGTH'} );

# split on every ampersand
# which separates each piece of form data
@in = split(/&/,$in);

foreach $i (0 .. $#in) {

    # convert pluses to spaces
    # (spaces are coded as pluses)
    $in[$i] =~ s/\+/ /g;

    # split on the first "="
    # to separate the data into key and value pairs
    ($key, $value) = split(/=/,$in[$i],2);

    $in{$key}  = $value;

}


# display the processed data to the client

# print the HTTP header with a status of 200 OK
print "HTTP/1.0 200 OK\r\n";
```

```
# print the Content-type header to identify the script's
# output as HTML
print "Content-type: text/html\r\n\r\n";

# print each key/value pair
foreach $key (sort(keys(%in))) {
    print "<p>$key = $in{$key}\n ";
}
```

If we save this script and access it by submitting our previous forms example, we get:

```
email = carl@freedonia.com

spam = yes
```

Those are our four examples. They should give you a good idea of how the common gateway interface works, and some of the things that are possible using CGI. CGI scripts and programs can be very simple, as on the preceding, or get very complex; you might, for example, dynamically serve all the information you present via your Web via a CGI program that bridges your Web server to a back-end database that stores all your data. The most important thing to keep in mind while you're building dynamic documents, however, is the user's needs: you should always try to create documents, whether static or dynamic, that give users the information they seek with the least amount of effort. However complex the back end, remember to keep the front end as clean and simple as possible.

## CHAPTER 9

Domain Name Services

The Domain Name System, or DNS, is a naming scheme for dotted decimal Internet Protocol, or IP, addresses. Every computer, or "host," on the Internet has an IP address assigned to it; every host name refers to an IP address.

Host names were put into place to benefit people; computers are perfectly content to call each other by number. Even if you've been on the Internet for some time, you may know relatively few of the 32-bit long IP addresses, but even a relative newcomer knows several host names, from his or her e-mail address, which probably uses a host name, to favorite FTP sites. And the Web has us guessing host names, as we use the form *www.companyname.com* with wild abandon.

In fact, it's considered bad form to go around using IP addresses, since IP addresses can change. Because of the Domain Name System's higher level of abstraction, it's a more reliable way to name a service—when an IP address changes, a domain name server can be updated, so that the old name can be resolved into the new address. DNS makes the Internet seem a much friendlier, more stable place.

Who makes this all happen? In many cases, your Internet Service Provider can provide domain name service for your computers, and will even help you register your own domain name (explained later), as part of a package of services it offers. You may choose to run your own DNS if your ISP doesn't offer those services or doesn't meet your needs in terms of cost or turnaround time—or if your local network is more than a few machines, in which case you may find the ability to offer domain name resolution for the local network, and to make changes to the domain name database when needed, quite useful. Whether or not you choose to run your own domain name server, however, it is helpful to be aware of the domain name architecture to at least some extent, and a quick read over the first part of this chapter, covering the general concepts behind DNS, can give you a useful, basic understanding of the domain name system.

Domain Name Architecture

The Domain Name Database

The Domain Name System uses a client/server mechanism, with domain name resolvers as the clients and domain name servers as the servers. For most TCP/IP applications under the Mac OS, the resolver built into MacTCP or Open Transport is used, although some applications, like Apple Internet Mail Server, use their own domain name resolver.

The Domain Name System is implemented as a distributed database, existing in something called a domain name space. The key features of such an implementation are that it allows local control of domain names, and doesn't put too much load or responsibility on one, centralized authority. The domain name space is organized hierarchically, with the root domain at the top, and the rest of the structure branching from this root domain. Conceptually, the domain name space is a large, inverted tree. Figure 9.1, shows a portion of that name space.

Key here is that there is no master domain name database; because the domain name system is a distributed one, each domain generally keeps records only of its next-level subdomains. However, all domain name resolvers have a pointer to the root domain (served by multiple servers), which in turn has pointers to all the top-level domains (those one level below the root domain—com, edu, org, and so on), which in turn have pointers to their subdomains, and so

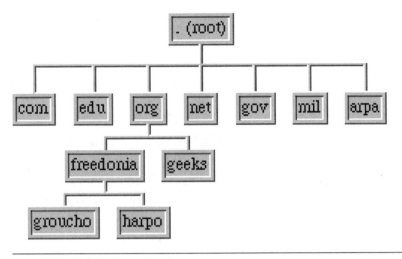

FIGURE 9.1 The Domain Space

on, so that any name within the name space can be queried and resolved.

Resolvers and Servers

Domain name queries are sent by domain name resolvers to domain name servers, which return a result. That's straightforward enough. However, due to the distributed nature of DNS, name servers act as both name servers and resolvers: they answer queries for which they are *authoritative,* and they attempt to resolve, or query, other name servers about information regarding domains for which they are not authoritative.

For example, a name server may know that it is authoritative for any host in the domain freedonia.org. If any resolver asks it for information about a host in freedonia.org—say, for example, for the IP address for www.freedonia.org—the name server can respond with an answer to its query. But if the same name server were asked for information about a host for which it is not authoritative—say, the IP address for abs.apple.com—it in turn queries a *root* name server, which then refers it to a name server in the next-level domain—in this case, com—which would then refer it to a server authoritative for the Apple domain, and so on, until the query is resolved. The name server would then return the result to the client that requested the information.

You might ask, why would a name server be asked for information about which it is not an authority in the first place? If MacTCP and Open Transport contain their own resolvers, why would a name server need to act in this role? Indeed, name servers normally act as resolvers only for their local network—the root name servers always refer queries to only authoritative name servers. However, it's usually the case that on a local network only the name server knows about the root servers, so that resolvers like MacTCP or Open Transport don't need to keep track of this info—if they did, it could easily make configuring each host a nightmare. Also, on machines that don't run the Mac OS, resolvers associated with TCP/IP stacks may not have the smarts to follow referrals to other name servers, as the name server did in our preceding example.

Recursion and Iteration

The previous example was an illustration of recursion. The name server followed successive referrals until it found an answer. The local host's resolver is said to have issued a *recursive* query.

Resolvers can also issue *iterative* queries, in which the queried name server must return the requested information or the name of a name server that can in turn be queried for the requested information. In the example just given, in which the local host's resolver issued a recursive query, the name server (acting as a resolver) issued a succession of iterative queries; it was referred by name servers to other name servers, which it then queried, and so on, until it found the information it was looking for.

Caching

To reduce network traffic and answer queries more quickly, most resolvers and name servers store the answers they receive to queries in a *cache*. If a resolver or name server then receives a successive query for the same information, it can simply return the requested data from its cache. Even if a resolver or name server hasn't cached the exact answers to the query, it can still use its cached data to speed up queries; for example, if the name server from our previous example is asked to resolve www.apple.com after resolving solutions.apple.com, it can do so by directly querying the name server for apple.com, and avoid querying name servers authoritative for the root and com domains.

Of course, when information about other domains change, cached data becomes outdated and useless. Because of this, all information records have associated with them a time to live: the amount of time for which that information should be assumed valid. After the time to live for a record expires, that information is flushed from the cache, and the authoritative name server for the flushed data is again consulted.

Hosts, Domains, and Zones

Hosts are computers with a network connection. Although the term "host" could be interpreted to mean a computer that provides infor-mation to clients—a server—it's come to mean any machine on the network, whether or not its primary purpose is to provide resources via the network.

Domain names usually refer to specific hosts—for example, a domain name north.freedonia.org might refer to a computer, north, in the domain freedonia.org—but don't always do so: north might simply be a subdomain of freedonia.org, with the hosts wintry and cold within it, which would have the domain names wintry.north.freedonia.org and cold.north.freedonia.org, respec-tively; wintry.north.freedonia.org, then, would be a subdomain of north.freedonia.org, but also a domain in its own right; similarily, there might be a host north.freedonia.org or there might not—in either case, north.freedonia.org is still a domain name (whether it refers to a specific computer or not).

A zone is an administrative division of the domain name space. Name servers are said to be authoritative for any portion of the domain name space for which they contain complete data; a zone consists of the name space for which a server is authoritative.

Zones are not always congruous with domains. For example, a name server hail.freedonia.org for the domain freedonia.org might delegate the authority over some of its subdomains to others—perhaps north.freedonia.org and east.freedonia.org—while retaining control of other subdomains—south.freedonia.org and west.freedonia.org. In this case, the domain would include all its subdomains—north, south, east, and west—but the zone would include only those subdomains over which the name server maintained authority—south.freedonia.org and west.freedonia.org, as well as freedonia.org.

If the domain for which you're responsible contains no subdomains, it's likely your domain and your zone are one and the same.

Primary and Secondary Servers

Every domain connected to the Internet needs to be served by at least two servers, so that if one server becomes unavailable, name service can still be provided. In most cases, one of the servers serving your domain will be a secondary server, although you can run two primary servers, as well.

A primary server gets its domain name information from an administrator-configured database or from administrator-configured files. Under the Mac OS, these might be plain text files or information stored in the server application's preferences file (or elsewhere), depending upon the server application. A secondary server gets its data instead from another server on the network, performing what is called a *zone transfer*.

Using a secondary server means domain name information needs to be maintained in only one place—on the primary server. Information is kept current on the secondary server by the secondary server periodically checking the primary server for changes, and updating its database if a change has been made.

Registering Your Domain Name

To become part of the domain name space, you need to become a subdomain of an existing domain. This means you'll need to determine where you fit within the existing name space, and contact the administrator of the appropriate domain. Most domains are registered in the "com" top-level domain, although a subdomain to a geographical or other domain may be more appropriate to your situation. The following overview of the domain structure should give you enough context that you'll be able to determine where your network would fit within the domain name system.

Top-Level Domains

Top-level domains are organized along two lines: organizationally (the com, edu, and gov domains, among others), and geographically (us, nz, and au, among others).

Organizational Domains

In the United States, most domain names in use are split along organizational lines; there's a total of seven recognized top-level organizational domains by the Internic, a central registry for top-level domains supported in part by the National Science Foundation. These top-level organizational domains are:

com: For use by commercial organizations.

edu: For use by four-year colleges and universities. Other schools are registered under geographical domains.

gov: For use by agencies of the U.S. federal government.

int: For use by international organizations, those established by international treaty.

mil: For use by the U.S. military.

net: For use by network providers.

org: For use by miscellaneous organizations that don't fit in the other top-level domains.

Geographical Domains

Geographical domains are based upon the two-letter country codes listed in Table 9.1 (see pages 298–300). Each geographical domain can be organized however the administrative organization for the domain sees fit; not all adhere to the U.S. model, described next.

The U.S. Top-Level Domain. The hierarchy of the U.S. top-level domain is based on political geography. The general format is a host name, followed by an organization name, followed by a locality, followed by a two-letter postal abbreviation for the state, followed by us, although actual domain names can and do differ.

Beyond the Top Level: states, fed, and dni. Two-letter postal abbreviation for a state: Most second levels in the us top-level domain use the two-letter postal abbreviation for a state—for example, ca.us or mn.us.

> **fed:** For use by federal agencies.
>
> **dni:** For use by distributed national institutes, organizations that go across state or regional boundaries and that have facilities in multiple regions.

Levels Beyond State.

> **locality:** cities, counties, parishes, and townships. For example, berkeley.ca.us. Berkeley might also have been set up as a subdomain under Alameda county, in which case it would have been berkeley.alameda.ca.us.
>
> **cc:** For use by community colleges. For example, elcamino.cc.ca.us.
>
> **ci:** For use by city agencies. For example, ci.berkeley.ca.us.
>
> **co:** For use by county agencies. For example, co.hennepin.mn.us.
>
> **gen:** For use by miscellaneous organizations that don't fit in the other domains defined under the state level. For example, rfo.gen.mn.us.
>
> **k12:** For use by primary and secondary schools. Subdomains are usually the school district, then the school name. For example, happy-valley.hvsd.k12.ca.us.

pvt: For use by private K-12 schools as a subdomain to the k12 domain. For example, nueva.pvt.k12.ca.us.

lib: For use by libraries. For example, hennepin.lib.mn.us.

state: For use by state agencies. For example, northstar.state.mn.us.

tec: For use by technical and vocational schools. For example, washburn.tec.ca.us.

Searching the Domain Space

Once you have an idea of the domain name your service or organization might belong in, you'll want to search the domain space to find contact information or to see that no one else already has authority over the domain you seek. One way to do this is to use the Whois service, available from many UNIX hosts, including rs.internic.net, which you can access using a telnet client (<telnet://rs.internic.net/>). This is a sample Whois session:

```
SunOS UNIX 4.1 (rs) (ttyp5)
[...]
[vt220] InterNIC > whois domain mcdonalds
Connecting to the rs Database . . . . . .
Connected to the rs Database
McDonald's Corporation (MCDONALDS-DOM)
    Network Computing
    Facilities and Systems
    McDonald's Plaza
    Oak Brook, IL 60521

    Domain Name: MCDONALDS.COM

    Administrative Contact, Technical Contact, Zone Contact:
        Rush, Chuck  (CR21)  crush@BIGMAC.MCD.COM
        (708) 575-6512

    Record last updated on 04-Jan-95.
```

```
Domain servers in listed order:

PJL53PK.I-P.MAIL.ATT.NET    198.152.3.8
PJL53IG.I-P.MAIL.ATT.NET    198.152.2.8
PJL53WO.I-P.MAIL.ATT.NET    198.152.4.8
```

Here, we searched for all domains that contain "mcdonalds" using the domain command, and found that mcdonalds.com is indeed registered. We were then given contact info for the domain, and the domain name servers that are authoritative for the domain. No match would have indicated that the domain name may be available for registration. (Of course, someone else may have submitted a registration that is in process; the domain registry usually has a turnaround time of several days.)

However, Whois contains information only for second-level organizational domains and top-level geographical domains. Usually, Whois is sufficient to find an appropriate contact if you wish to register a subdomain to a geographical or second-level organizational domain.

For additional commands you can use with Whois, type **help** from the Whois prompt, or **whois help** from a UNIX prompt.

Domain Registry

The Internic domain registration template, found at the end of this chapter (see page 301), is appropriate for registering second-level domains in the com, edu, gov, net, and org domains. In the fall of 1995 the Internic began charging a hundred dollars per domain registration in the com, org, and net domains, with an annual maintenance fee of fifty dollars starting in the third year. For other domain registrations, you should contact the domain's administrative contact—see Searching the Domain Space, discussed earlier.

Naming Hosts

When setting up a domain name server, you'll need to name the hosts within your domain. Some general guidelines follow.

- **Don't use non-alphanumeric characters.** Some software doesn't deal well with nonalphanumeric characters in host names. Avoid the use of these characters, such as underscores.

- **Don't name machines after projects or people.** Projects are expanded, completed, and abandoned; people get new computers, leave, and move to other departments within the organization.

- **Use short, easy-to-remember, easy-to-spell, speakable names.** Domain names were put into use so that people wouldn't have to remember IP addresses; don't make things difficult by naming a machine something that's hard to spell, or will always have to be clarified. For example, a machine named "whether" might often be taken for a host called "weather."

- **Use names along a common theme.** Naming your computers along a common theme, such as names of characters in Shakespeare's plays, makes naming machines easier, and names easier to remember.

Don't worry about using common names. Names can only conflict with other names within your particular subdomain; for example, there can be a host called indigo.freedonia.org, and another called indigo.geeks.org, with no conflict.

Resource Records

When configuring your name server, you'll largely be dealing with resource records, or RRs. Resource records are returned to a domain name resolver when it queries a domain name server. There are several record types that hold different kinds of information for your domain and the hosts in your domain, detailed next.

Record Types

There are fewer than a dozen common resource record types, and several that are "experimental" or obsolete; we cover the six most important record types here, which, in almost all situations, will be the only record types you'll need to be aware of. These are:

SOA: Start of Authority

NS: A Name Server, listing a name server for this domain

MX: A Mail Exchanger, providing routing information for mail

A: An Address, providing name-to-address mapping

CNAME: A Canonical Name for an alias, providing alias-to-name mapping

PTR: A Pointer, providing address-to-name mapping

Start of Authority (SOA)

A Start of Authority (SOA) record indicates that the records held by a server for the named domain are *authoritative;* that is, the name server knows the best answers to questions regarding this domain.

A Start of Authority record contains the following information:

- **Domain Name:** The domain name for which this SOA record applies.
- **MName:** The name of the primary name server for the zone.
- **RName:** The e-mail address of the person responsible for the zone.
- **Serial:** The unique serial number for the current version of the Hosts file. The serial is used by secondary name servers to check if the data in the primary Hosts file has been updated; this number should be incremented whenever you make changes to any data for which the SOA record is authoritative.
- **Refresh:** This is the time interval that should elapse before a secondary server checks the primary server to see if any changes have taken place in the Hosts file, based on the Serial value; if changes have occurred, a zone transfer takes place; 10 hours, or 36000 seconds, is a common value.
- **Retry:** If a secondary server can't reach a primary server after the Refresh value is reached, this is the next time interval

before the next attempt should be made; 2 hours, or 7200 seconds, is a common value.

- **Expire:** If a secondary server can't perform a Refresh from a primary server in this amount of time, information for the zone stored on the secondary server is no longer considered authoritative; 1 week, or 604800 seconds, is a common value.

- **Minimum TTL:** The Minimum Time To Live is the amount of time that a resource record should be cached before the name server is asked for the same information again. The Minimum TTL applies to all resource records for the data in this zone, unless a particular resource record is given its own TTL to override this value; 1 day, or 86400 seconds, is a common value.

Name Server (NS)

Name Server (NS) records list the name servers for a domain. A Name Server record contains the following information:

- **Domain Name:** The domain name for which this NS record applies.

- **Name Server Name:** A name server which is authoritative for the domain name.

Mail Exchanger (MX)

Mail Exchanger (MX) records point to hosts that can accept mail for a domain. For example, an MX record could exist for freedonia.org which would point to hail.freedonia.org; when mail is then sent to an account carl@freedonia.org, it would be routed to the machine hail.freedonia.org.

A Mail Exchanger record contains the following information:

- **Domain Name:** The domain name for which this MX record applies.

- **Preference:** A preference number for this record. There may be multiple MX records for the same domain; the preference number indicates the priority of records, with lower numbers having higher priority. When a mail server attempts to deliver mail to this domain, the record with the lowest number is tried first, and then the next lowest, and so on, until a host is found that is able to accept mail. A common value for a single record is 10; this allows MX records with higher priority (a lower number) to be added at a later time.

- **Mail Exchange:** A mail server that can accept mail for the domain name.

Address (A): Name-to-Address Mapping

Address (A) records convert domain names to dotted decimal IP addresses, and are the *raison d'être* of a domain name server. An Address record contains the following information:

- **Domain Name:** The domain name for the host for which this A record applies.
- **Host Address:** The IP address of a host that is referred to by the given name.

Canonical Name (CNAME): Aliases

Canonical Name (CNAME) records define an alias for the official (canonical) host name, stored in an A record in your Hosts file. This can be useful when providing Internet services in which there is a common naming scheme (such as host names providing WWW and FTP service beginning with www and ftp, respectively), and you don't plan on solely dedicating a host to the named service. A Canonical Name record contains the following information:

- **Domain Name:** The domain name for the host for which this CNAME record applies (the alias name).
- **Canonical Name:** The actual name of the machine that can be referred to by the alias name.

Pointer (PTR): Address-to-Name Mapping

Pointer (PTR) records are used for reverse domain name mapping—when someone has an IP address, and would like to find its host's name. This is commonly done for storing addresses in log files, and sometimes used for simple authentication. For example, ftp.apple.com will reject your connection unless your machine's IP address reverse maps into a host name.

Pointer records map host names to their IP numbers using a special domain, in-addr.arpa. The domain in-addr.arpa exists so that all IP numbers can be recorded in a separate, hierarchical space; hence it isn't necessary to search the entire domain name space to find a host with a given IP address.

The in-addr.arpa address of a host that has an IP address of 192.0.1.1 would be 1.1.0.192.in-addr.arpa. You'll notice the IP address is reversed. This is because host names are ordered from the most specific domain, on the left, to the least specific domain (closest to root) on the right, while the order of IP addresses is the opposite—from the least specific number, on the left, to the most specific number, on the right.

A Pointer record contains the following information:

- **Pointer Name:** The in-addr.arpa domain name for which this PTR record applies.
- **Domain Name:** The domain name for the host for which this PTR record applies.

 **MIND**

MIND (Macintosh Internet Name Daemon) is a freeware domain name server for the Macintosh made available by ACME Technologies.

Configuring MIND

MIND is configured through a text file in virtually the same format as UNIX BIND, or Berkeley Internet Name Domain, the standard software package for providing domain name services on UNIX boxes. To configure MIND, you'll need to edit the Hosts file, found in the same folder as MIND, with a text editor, such as SimpleText or BBEdit. This is a sample Hosts file, which we'll walk through step by step:

```
; a sample hosts file
;
; origin
;   the origin is appended to all domain names not ending in a "." (period)
;   "@" refers to a name which is the origin
;
$ORIGIN freedonia.org.
;
; start of authority information
;   here, "@" can be read as "freedonia.org."
;   "IN" stands for the Internet data class
;   "hostmaster.freedonia.org." translates into
;   the mail address "hostmaster@freedonia.org"
;
@               IN  SOA hail.freedonia.org. hostmaster.freedonia.org.  (
                    9503231     ; serial (yymmddn)
                    36000       ; refresh (every 10 hours)
                    7200        ; retry (after 2 hours)
                    604800      ; expire (after 1 week)
                    86400 )     ; minimum time to live (1 day)
;
; name servers
;   the "@" is now implied
;
                IN  NS      hail.freedonia.org.
                IN  NS      ns.geeks.org.
;
; mail exchangers
;
                IN  MX      10 mail.freedonia.org.
;
; host addresses
;
hail            IN  A       192.0.1.1
mail            IN  A       192.0.1.2
nail            IN  A       192.0.1.3
;
; aliases
;
www             IN  CNAME   nail.freedonia.org.
;
```

```
; files to include
;    ReverseZones holds reverse information for inverse queries
;    RootServers holds top level domain information
$INCLUDE ReverseZones
$INCLUDE RootServers
```

Hosts File Formatting

The Hosts file is formatted using a number of conventions from UNIX BIND configuration files. Generally:

- Entries are made one record to a line. The exception to this is the Start of Authority record (shown later), which spans multiple lines through the use of parentheses.

- Any combination of spaces and tabs is considered a single delimitor.

- If a value isn't supplied for a particular field, the data for the previous corresponding field is used. For example, if a domain name hail.freedonia.org. is supplied for one record, and the domain name for the next record is left blank, the value hail.freedonia.org. will be used for the second record.

- Domains will have the origin appended to them (shown later) if not fully qualified. A fully qualified domain name ends in a dot. For example, if a MIND configuration file specifies the origin as being freedonia.org., and a record has as its domain name entry north, the origin will be appended to the domain name to form north.freedonia.org.

- Comments begin with a semicolon (;).

Fields in records are separated by any amount of white space, and usually organized in columns for readability; the order of these fields is:

1. **Domain Name:** The domain for which this record applies.

2. **Class:** The class of data for this record. "IN" stands for the Internet class of data, and it is the only class most administrators need to be aware of.

3. **Record Type:** The type of this record.

4. **Record-specific Data:** The data for this record. This is usually another domain name or an IP address, depending upon the record type.

A MIND Hosts file begins with a $ORIGIN command, which sets the origin for relative domains. In the sample Hosts file, the origin is set to "freedonia.org"; any relative domain—any domain not ending in a dot (.)—will have "freedonia.org" appended to it. *Any domain name in the Hosts file which does not end with a dot (.) is expanded with the origin.* Domain names ending with a dot are called *absolute,* or *fully qualified,* domains, and are not expanded with the origin.

The at symbol (@) is used to denote the current origin, and we use it in our Start of Authority record, below. The @ symbol can't be used to append the origin to a domain; instead, use relative domains, as described. You could also use a relative or fully qualified domain name in place of the at symbol; its use is in no way required in any particular context.

The $INCLUDE command inserts the named file into the current file. We include two files in our Hosts file example, ReverseZones and RootServers. It wasn't necessary to include these files: we could have just placed the same information into the Hosts file directly, but administration and maintainance of the Hosts file can be made slightly easier by using the $INCLUDE command. ReverseZones holds the Pointer records for the zone; RootServers contains Address records for the name servers for the root domain.

```
@        IN   SOA hail.freedonia.org.  hostmaster.freedonia.org.  (
                    9503231    ; serial (yymmddn)
                    36000      ; refresh (every 10 hours)
                    7200       ; retry (after 2 hours)
                    604800     ; expire (after 1 week)
                    86400 )    ; minimum time to live (1 day)
```

The origin in the preceding Start Of Authority record, then, is expanded into "freedonia.org." IN is supplied for the Internet data class—since MIND uses the same file format as BIND and BIND allows data class types other than Internet, it's included here, although the other data classes aren't supported by MIND (and needn't be). Next is given the record type, followed by the name of the primary name server, followed by the e-mail address of the technical contact for this domain. For historical reasons, the first dot (.) of this field is replaced with an at sign (@) to form the e-mail address; in the case of an account that includes a dot—for example, *carl.steadman@ freedonia.org*—this dot can be escaped with a backslash (\ character, so that the field would read *carl\.steadman.freedonia. org*. Following that are the serial, refresh, retry, expire, and minimum time to live fields. The serial number should be incremented every time the file is edited, and it is given in yymmddn format, where yy=year, mm=month, dd=day, and n=a per-day revision number, although any format that works for you can be used. The refresh, retry, expire, and minimum time to live values are given in seconds.

The Name Server records in the sample MIND configuration file read:

```
                IN    NS    hail.freedonia.org.
                IN    NS    ns.geeks.org.
```

Here, the Domain Name field is implied from the SOA entry, so it doesn't need to be supplied again. If we had, the NS records would have looked like this:

```
@               IN    NS    hail.freedonia.org.
@               IN    NS    ns.geeks.org.
```

which would have been equivalent to:

```
freedonia.org.  IN    NS    hail.freedonia.org.
freedonia.org.  IN    NS    ns.geeks.org.
```

We could have also taken three more shortcuts in specifying the data in these records: we could have allowed the Class field, which holds the value IN, to be implied as well; we could have omitted the second NS, for the same reason; and we could have typed hail for the name of the first name server, in which case freedonia.org. would have been appended to hail. For the sake of readability and maintainability, however, we're taking shortcuts only in the first field, the domain name field. This is standard practice among many BIND maintainers.

The next record in the sample file is a Mail Exchanger record.

```
                        IN   MX     10 mail.freedonia.org.
```

As with the Name Server record, the domain name for which the service is being offered is implied—we can read it as "freedonia.org." IN we can safely ignore, knowing it stands for the Internet data class and that we needn't worry about other data classes, and MX is the designation for a mail exchanger record. The next value is the preference number for this record—see the explanation of MX records, discussed earlier, for more details. Following that, and delimited by a single space—for conformance with standard BIND formatting—is the domain name of the mail server, mail.freedonia.org. which can accept mail for the domain name in the first field, freedonia.org., so that all mail sent to user@freedonia.org gets routed to mail.freedonia.org.

The next three lines in our sample file are Address records.

```
hail            IN   A      192.0.1.1
mail            IN   A      192.0.1.2
nail            IN   A      192.0.1.3
```

Since these follow the same format as the previous two record types, these should be fairly self-explanatory. In our first Address record, hail, which isn't fully qualified—it doesn't end in a dot—has the origin appended to it, and it is expanded to hail.freedonia.org. It's then of the Internet data class, is an Address, or A, record type, and has the Address data 192.0.1.1, which is the IP address for the host hail. The hosts mail and nail are then assigned IP addresses, as well.

We then list a canonical name for the alias www:

```
www                     IN   CNAME  nail.freedonia.org.
```

Here, www is expanded into www.freedonia.org., the data class is of type Internet, and the record type is CNAME, or canonical name. We then give the canonical domain name for the www.freedonia. org. alias: nail.freedonia.org. (Once again, we could have simply typed nail and let the name expand with the origin, but, for the sake of readability and maintainability, we didn't.) This CNAME record allows us to refer to the same machine under two different names: in our example, nail may be a machine that does more than just serve Web pages, but should be known as www to the outside world for the sake of consistency with other Web sites.

Finally, two files are included with the $INCLUDE command (see the discussion of $INCLUDE, earlier)—ReverseZones and RootServers.

```
$INCLUDE ReverseZones
$INCLUDE RootServers
```

ReverseZones has the same formatting as the sample Hosts file; it begins with its own origin and SOA record, since it uses the special in-addr.arpa. domain discussed in the section on pointer records in our description of record types. Our sample ReverseZones file looks like this:

```
; a sample reverse zones file
;
; origin
;   the origin is appended to all domain names not ending in a "." (period)
;   "@" refers to a name which is the origin
;
$ORIGIN 1.0.192.in-addr.arpa.
;
; start of authority information
;   here, "@" can be read as "freedonia.org."
;   "IN" stands for the Internet data class
;   "hostmaster.freedonia.org." translates into
;   the mail address "hostmaster@freedonia.org"
;
@           IN  SOA hail.freedonia.org.  hostmaster.freedonia.org.  (
                        9503231     ; serial (yymmddn)
                        36000       ; refresh (every 10 hours)
                        7200        ; retry (after 2 hours)
                        604800      ; expire (after 1 week)
                        86400 )     ; minimum time to live (1 day)
;
; pointer records
;
1           IN  PTR                 hail.freedonia.org.
2           IN  PTR                 mail.freedonia.org.
3           IN  PTR                 nail.freedonia.org.
```

As with our previous records, the 1 for the first Pointer record, not being fully qualified (not ending in a dot), is expanded by the origin into 1.1.0.192.in-addr.arpa.; IN stands for the Internet data class, PTR signifies the Pointer record type, and "hail.freedonia.org." is the name of the host to which this pointer record refers. The Pointer records for mail.freedonia.org. and nail.freedonia.org. follow the same format.

Finally, our sample RootServers file contains the following:

```
;       This file holds the information on root name servers needed to
;       initialize cache of Internet domain name servers
;       (e.g. reference this file in the "cache  .  <file>"
;       configuration file of BIND domain name servers).
;
;       This file is made available by InterNIC registration services
;       under anonymous FTP as
;           file                /domain/named.root
;           on server           FTP.RS.INTERNIC.NET
;       -OR- under Gopher at    RS.INTERNIC.NET
;           under menu          InterNIC Registration Services (NSI)
;             submenu           InterNIC Registration Archives
;           file                named.root
;
;       last update:   Nov 8, 1995
;       related version of root zone:   1995110800
;
;
; formerly NS.INTERNIC.NET
;
.                           3600000  IN  NS   A.ROOT-SERVERS.NET.
A.ROOT-SERVERS.NET.         3600000      A    198.41.0.4
;
; formerly NS1.ISI.EDU
;
.                           3600000      NS   B.ROOT-SERVERS.NET.
B.ROOT-SERVERS.NET.         3600000      A    128.9.0.107
;
; formerly C.PSI.NET
;
.                           3600000      NS   C.ROOT-SERVERS.NET.
C.ROOT-SERVERS.NET.         3600000      A    192.33.4.12
;
```

```
; formerly TERP.UMD.EDU
;
.                               3600000      NS    D.ROOT-SERVERS.NET.
D.ROOT-SERVERS.NET.             3600000      A     128.8.10.90
;
; formerly NS.NASA.GOV
;
.                               3600000      NS    E.ROOT-SERVERS.NET.
E.ROOT-SERVERS.NET.             3600000      A     192.203.230.10
;
; formerly NS.ISC.ORG
;
.                               3600000      NS    F.ROOT-SERVERS.NET.
F.ROOT-SERVERS.NET.             3600000      A     192.5.5.241
;
; formerly NS.NIC.DDN.MIL
;
.                               3600000      NS    G.ROOT-SERVERS.NET.
G.ROOT-SERVERS.NET.             3600000      A     192.112.36.4
;
; formerly AOS.ARL.ARMY.MIL
;
.                               3600000      NS    H.ROOT-SERVERS.NET.
H.ROOT-SERVERS.NET.             3600000      A     128.63.2.53
;
; formerly NIC.NORDU.NET
;
.                               3600000      NS    I.ROOT-SERVERS.NET.
I.ROOT-SERVERS.NET.             3600000      A     192.36.148.17
; End of File
```

This is from the file available from <ftp://rs.internic.net/domain/named.root>. The RootServers file allows MIND to find answers to any query it might need to answer, by giving it the addresses of root servers, which can then point to subdomains of the root-level domain, which can then point to subdomains of those domains, and so on, until an answer is found—see Domain Name Architecture, discussed previously.

You'll note a second column we haven't been using in our MIND configuration files—the time to live value we mentioned in our discussion of the Start of Authority record type. These time to live values override any values found in the SOA record; you'll want this list of root servers never to expire, since they're needed to find any other domain, and 3600000 seconds, or three years, is comfortably considered to be forever on the Internet. You'll also note that IN is only used once, and then assumed for the rest of the records—once again, we could have done that in our sample files, but we think that the files are easier to read and maintain if the IN is explicit for each record.

 QuickDNS

Men and Mice offer two DNS products for the Mac OS: QuickDNS Lite, which is covered here, and QuickDNS Pro, a full-featured DNS server that should be available by the time you read this.

QuickDNS Lite is a caching-only name server. This means it can provide only name services for entries that already exist in the domain name database; you won't be able to enter any domain name records or otherwise provide primary or secondary name services for a domain. If, however, you have a network of computers connected to the outside world through a slow link, and no name server already in place on your side of the Net connection, you can point all the local machines at a single Mac OS machine running QuickDNS Lite to take advantage of caching—storing requested records in memory of the machine running QuickDNS Lite—for the local network, instead of using only the cache for each local networked machine's MacTCP, Open Transport, or the TCP/IP stack running on non-Mac OS platforms. Although MIND will cache DNS records as well, QuickDNS Lite allows you to provide a caching name service with absolutely no configuration.

To run QuickDNS Lite, you simply need to double-click on its icon. You'll then see the QuickDNS Lite status screen, shown in Figure 9.2. Free memory is the amount of memory, in bytes, that QuickDNS Lite has available to it; when this number drops below 40000, entries are purged from the cache. Packets in and Packets out list the number of UDP packets sent in and out of QuickDNS Lite

```
╔═══════════════════════ QuickDNS ═══════════════════════╗

          QuickDNS - Caching only. Version 1.0b
          © 1995 Men & Mice      Free memory : 145780
     ─────────────────────────────────────────────────

     Packets in :  116         Packets out :  122

     Requests in :  43         Requests out : 79

     Replies in :   67         Replies out :   43
     ─────────────────────────────────────────────────

     Replies from cache : 12

     Entries in cache :    198        purged : 0

     Records in cache :    69         purged : 0

╚═════════════════════════════════════════════════════════╝
```

FIGURE 9.2 QuickDNS Status Screen

(UDP is a transport layer, like TCP, that sits atop the IP network layer). Requests in and Requests out log the number of times QuickDNS Lite talks to domain name resolvers (clients), and Replies in and Replies out record the number of times QuickDNS Lite talks to domain name servers. Replies from cache tells you how effective the caching of QuickDNS Lite is for your environment.

Testing Your DNS

After setting up a domain name server, you'll normally want to ensure that it's answering queries with the proper data. We'll cover two utilities that allow you to do that: MacTCP Watcher, which runs under the Mac OS, and nslookup, available on most UNIX systems.

A utility we're not covering here is Query It!, which runs under the Mac OS and handles record types beyond Address and Pointer—the extent of the record types that MacTCP Watcher will return. Because Query It! relies on MacTCP to provide domain name resolution, however, and because MacTCP doesn't appropriately handle some record types, such as Mail Exchanger, the situations in which Query It! provides truly useful output is limited.

Additionally, other utilities, such as DIG, are available under UNIX, but aren't as widely available as nslookup. And covering more than two UNIX utilities (Whois and nslookup), however briefly, in the same chapter in a book about providing Internet services via the Mac OS—even if it is the chapter on DNS—is probably bad luck.

MacTCP Watcher

MacTCP Watcher, freeware by Peter N Lewis, provides a lot of data from the MacTCP control panel. As its name would indicate, it wasn't designed to be used under Open Transport. The MacTCP Info screen is shown in Figure 9.3. The function of interest here is MacTCP Watcher's ability to perform DNS lookups, available from the DNS button or from Test DNS . . . from the File menu.

When you select the DNS option, you're prompted for a domain name or IP address. If you provide a domain name, MacTCP

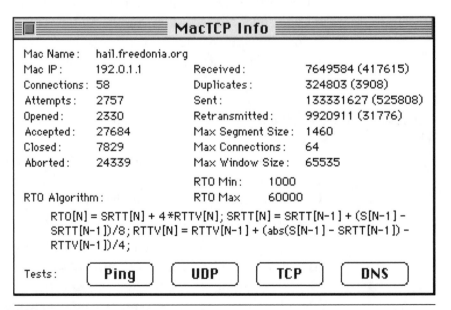

FIGURE 9.3 MacTCP Watcher Info Screen

Watcher will return the corresponding IP address; if you provide the IP address, MacTCP Watcher will return the corresponding domain name.

Some useful data, however, isn't returned, such as where MacTCP Watcher received its data from. Depending upon your situtation, this may or may not make a difference—MacTCP Watcher will query whatever name server(s) are specified in the MacTCP Control Panel (see Chapter 2 for configuration information), although you don't know whether MacTCP has gotten its answer from one of the servers listed in its Domain Name Server Information or if the query was answered by another server through a recursive query. If you're testing a single primary name server, and if the MacTCP control panel is configured to refer first to your primary name server, that usually isn't a problem, but if you need further information than Address or Pointer records, or need to know which server is producing the results returned to you, you'll want to take a look at nslookup.

nslookup

nslookup is a utility found on most UNIX machines for doing name server queries. Being a UNIX utility, you'll need to access it through Telnet using a UNIX account you have access to. If using a command-line utility for debugging purposes puts you off, you can rest assured that, in time, an nslookup-like utility will exist under the Mac OS. Until that time, however, nslookup will remain a valuable tool in the domain name administrator's toolbox, and it's very likely that others you need to work with to get your DNS up and running—the administrator of the name server providing secondary services for your domain, or your Internet Service Provider—will be using nslookup to test your configuration. Having an understanding of the utility can help you communicate with this person more effectively, and come to a resolution of any problems that may be occurring that much more quickly.

```
% nslookup
Default Server: ns.geeks.org
Address: 199.199.123.1
```

The default server is the server being queried. In most cases, you'll want to set the default server to the name server you're testing. You can do this in nslookup using the **server** command.

```
> server hail.freedonia.org.
Default Server: hail.freedonia.org
Address: 192.0.1.1
```

You'll note that we appended a dot to the end of the server name, using the fully qualified domain name; you'll get in the habit of using fully qualified domain names with nslookup, to ensure it's not appending a default domain name to your queries. Although there's a command, **nodefname**, that you can issue to nslookup to turn this default behavior off, it's usually just easier to append the dot yourself.

You can test name-to-address resolution with nslookup simply by typing the domain name in question and examining the output:

```
> nail.freedonia.org.
Server: hail.freedonia.org
Address: 192.0.1.1

Name:  nail.freedonia.org
Address: 192.0.1.3


> www.freedonia.org.
Server: hail.freedonia.org
Address: 192.0.1.1

Name:  nail.freedonia.org
Address: 192.0.1.3
Aliases: www.freedonia.org
```

In our first example of name-to-address resolution, the name nail.freedonia.org resolves into the IP address 192.0.1.3. The next query is for www.freedonia.org; here, we discover that it is an alias for the host nail.freedonia.org with the IP address 192.0.1.3. To test address-to-name resolution, simply provide the address:

```
> 192.0.1.2
Server: hail.freedonia.org
Address: 192.0.1.1

Name:   mail.freedonia.org
Address:  192.0.1.2
```

You can also use nslookup to look up only certain types of records, using the **set type=recordtype** command. For example, to find all the mail exchanger records for freedonia.org, we can type:

```
> set type=mx
> freedonia.org.
Server:  hail.freedonia.org
Address:  192.0.1.1

freedonia.org   preference = 10, mail exchanger = mail.freedonia.org
mail.freedonia.org      internet address = 192.0.1.2
```

In the same vein, we can query for any record type, using **set type=any**:

```
> set type=any
> freedonia.org.
Server:  hail.freedonia.org
Address:  192.0.1.1

freedonia.org
        origin = hail.freedonia.org
        mail addr = hostmaster.freedonia.org
        serial = 9503231
        refresh = 36000 (10 hours)
        retry  = 7200 (2 hours)
        expire  = 604800 (7 days)
        minimum ttl = 86400 (1 day)
freedonia.org   nameserver = hail.freedonia.org
freedonia.org   nameserver = ns.geeks.org
freedonia.org   preference = 10, mail exchanger = mail.freedonia.org
hail.freedonia.org      internet address = 192.0.1.1
mail.freedonia.org      internet address = 192.0.1.2
```

Finally, we can also use the LIST command in nslookup, **ls**, to list all the records for a given domain. The **ls** command performs a zone transfer and displays the results. To do so, we'll want to use the -**d** option to list all record types, so that our command becomes **ls -d domainname:**

```
> ls -d freedonia.org.
[hail.freedonia.org]
freedonia.org.              SOA   hail.freedonia.org
  hostmaster.freedonia.org. (9503231 36000 7200 604800 86400)
hail                        A     192.0.1.1
mail                        A     192.0.1.2
nail                        A     192.0.1.3
www                         CNAME nail.freedonia.org
freedonia.org.              NS    hail.freedonia.org
freedonia.org.              NS    ns.geeks.org
freedonia.org.              MX    10 mail.freedonia.org
freedonia.org.              SOA   hail.freedonia.org
hostmaster.freedonia.org. (9503231 36000 7200 604800 86400)
```

You can type help at an nslookup prompt to learn additional commands and parameters for nslookup.

TABLE 9.1 Two-Letter Country Codes from ISO 3166

Afghanistan	af	Bahamas	bs	British Indian Ocean	
Albania	al	Bahrain	bh	Territory	io
Algeria	dz	Bangladesh	bd	Brunei Darussalam	bn
American Samoa	as	Barbados	bb	Bulgaria	bg
Andorra	ad	Belarus	by	Burkina Faso	bf
Angola	ao	Belgium	be	Burundi	bi
Anguilla	ai	Belize	bz	Cambodia	kh
Antarctica	aq	Benin	bj	Cameroon	cm
Antigua and Barbuda	ag	Bermuda	bm	Canada	ca
Argentina	ar	Bhutan	bt	Cape Verde	cv
Armenia	am	Bolivia	bo	Cayman Islands	ky
Aruba	aw	Bosnia and Herzegovina	ba	Central African Republic	cf
Australia	au	Botswana	bw	Chad	td
Austria	at	Bouvet Island	bv	Chile	cl
Azerbaijan	az	Brazil	br	China	cn

TABLE 9.1 (Continued)

Christmas Island	cx	Germany	de	Latvia	lv
Cocos (Keeling) Islands	cc	Ghana	gh	Lebanon	lb
Colombia	co	Gibraltar	gi	Lesotho	ls
Comoros	km	Greece	gr	Liberia	lr
Congo	cg	Greenland	gl	Libyan Arab Jamahiriya	ly
Cook Islands	ck	Grenada	gd	Liechtenstein	li
Costa Rica	cr	Guadeloupe	gp	Lithuania	lt
Côte d'Ivoire	ci	Guam	gu	Luxembourg	lu
Croatia (local name:		Guatemala	gt	Macau	mo
Hrvatska)	hr	Guinea	gn	Macedonia, the Former	
Cuba	cu	Guinea-Bissau	gw	Yugoslav Republic of	mk
Cyprus	cy	Guyana	gy	Madagascar	mg
Czech Republic	cz	Haiti	ht	Malawi	mw
Denmark	dk	Heard and McDonald		Malaysia	my
Djibouti	dj	Islands	hm	Maldives	mv
Dominica	dm	Honduras	hn	Mali	ml
Dominican Republic	do	Hong Kong	hk	Malta	mt
East Timor	tp	Hungary	hu	Marshall Islands	mh
Ecuador	ec	Iceland	is	Martinique	mq
Egypt	eg	India	in	Mauritania	mr
El Salvador	sv	Indonesia	id	Mauritius	mu
Equatorial Guinea	gq	Iran (Islamic Republic of)	ir	Mayotte	yt
Eritrea	er	Iraq	iq	Mexico	mx
Estonia	ee	Ireland	ie	Micronesia, Federated	
Ethiopia	et	Israel	il	States of	fm
Falkland Islands		Italy	it	Moldova, Republic of	md
(Malvinas)	fk	Jamaica	jm	Monaco	mc
Faroe Islands	fo	Japan	jp	Mongolia	mn
Fiji	fj	Jordan	jo	Montserrat	ms
Finland	fi	Kazakhstan	kz	Morocco	ma
France	fr	Kenya	ke	Mozambique	mz
France, Metropolitan	fx	Kiribati	ki	Myanmar	mm
French Guiana	gf	Korea, Democratic		Namibia	na
French Polynesia	pf	People's Republic of	kp	Nauru	nr
French Southern		Korea, Republic of	kr	Nepal	np
Territories	tf	Kuwait	kw	Netherlands	nl
Gabon	ga	Kyrgyzstan	kg	Netherlands Antilles	an
Gambia	gm	Lao People's Democratic		New Caledonia	nc
Georgia	ge	Republic	la	New Zealand	nz

TABLE 9.1 (Continued)

Nicaragua	ni	Saudi Arabia	sa	Tonga	to
Niger	ne	Senegal	sn	Trinidad and Tobago	tt
Nigeria	ng	Seychelles	sc	Tunisia	tn
Niue	nu	Sierra Leone	sl	Turkey	tr
Norfolk Esland	nf	Singapore	sg	Turkmenistan	tm
Northern Mariana Islands	mp	Slovakia (Slovak Republic)	sk	Turks and Caicos Islands	tc
Norway	no	Slovenia	si	Tuvalu	tv
Oman	om	Solomon Islands	sb	Uganda	ug
Pakistan	pk	Somalia	so	Ukraine	ua
Palau	pw	South Africa	za	United Arab Emirates	ae
Panama	pa	South Georgia and		United Kingdom	gb
Papua New Guinea	pg	the South Sandwich		United States	us
Paraguay	py	Islands	gs	United States Minor	
Peru	pe	Spain	es	Outlying Islands	um
Philippines	ph	Sri Lanka	lk	Uruguay	uy
Pitcairn Island	pn	St. Helena	sh	Uzbekistan	uz
Poland	pl	St. Pierre and Miquelon	pm	Vanuatu	vu
Portugal	pt	Sudan	sd	Vatican City State	
Puerto Rico	pr	Suriname	sr	(Holy See)	va
Qatar	qa	Svalbard and Jan Mayen		Venezuela	ve
Reunion	re	Islands	sj	Vietnam	vn
Romania	ro	Swaziland	sz	Virgin Islands (British)	vg
Russian Federation	ru	Sweden	se	Virgin Islands (U.S.)	vi
Rwanda	rw	Switzerland	ch	Wallis and Futuna Islands	wf
Saint Kitts and Nevis	kn	Syrian Arab Republic	sy	Western Sahara	eh
Saint Lucia	lc	Taiwan, Province of China	tw	Yemen	ye
Saint Vincent and the		Tajikistan	tj	Yugoslavia	yu
Grenadines	vc	Tanzania, United		Zaire	zr
Samoa	ws	Republic of	tz	Zambia	zm
San Marino	sm	Thailand	th	Zimbabwe	zw
São Tome and Principe		Togo	tg		
Islands	st	Tokelau	tk		

Domain Registration Template

```
[ URL ftp://rs.internic.net/templates/domain-template.txt ]        [ 09/95 ]

******************** Please DO NOT REMOVE Version Number ********************

Domain Version Number: 2.0

**************** Please see attached detailed instructions ******************

******** Only for registrations under ROOT, COM, ORG, NET, EDU, GOV ********

0.    (N)ew (M)odify (D)elete....:

1.    Purpose/Description........:

2.    Complete Domain Name.......:

Organization Using Domain Name
3a.   Organization Name..........:
3b.   Street Address.............:
3c.   City.......................:
3d.   State......................:
3e.   Postal Code................:
3f.   Country....................:

Administrative Contact
4a.   NIC Handle (if known)......:
4b.   Name (Last, First).........:
4c.   Organization Name..........:
4d.   Street Address.............:
4e.   City.......................:
4f.   State......................:
4g.   Postal Code................:
4h.   Country....................:
4i.   Phone Number...............:
4j.   E-Mailbox..................:

Technical Contact
5a.   NIC Handle (if known)......:
5b.   Name (Last, First).........:
5c.   Organization Name..........:
5d.   Street Address.............:
```

```
5e.  City.....................:
5f.  State....................:
5g.  Postal Code..............:
5h.  Country..................:
5i.  Phone Number.............:
5j.  E-Mailbox................:

Billing Contact
6a.  NIC Handle (if known)......:
6b.  Name (Last, First).........:
6c.  Organization Name..........:
6d.  Street Address.............:
6e.  City.......................:
6f.  State......................:
6g.  Postal Code................:
6h.  Country....................:
6i.  Phone Number...............:
6j.  E-Mailbox..................:

Primary Name Server
7a.  Primary Server Hostname....:
7b.  Primary Server Netaddress..:

Secondary Name Server(s)
8a.  Secondary Server Hostname..:
8b.  Secondary Server Netaddress:

Invoice Delivery
9.   (E)mail (P)ostal...........:
```

A domain name registration fee of $100.00 US is applicable.
This charge will cover the $50.00 maintenance fee for two (2)
years. After the two year period, an invoice will be sent on
an annual basis.

The party requesting registration of this name certifies that,
to her/his knowledge, the use of this name does not violate
trademark or other statutes.

Registering a domain name does not confer any legal rights to
that name and any disputes between parties over the rights to
use a particular name are to be settled between the contending
parties using normal legal methods (see RFC 1591).

By applying for the domain name and through the use or continued use of the domain name, the applicant agrees to be bound by the terms of NSI's then current domain name policy (the 'Policy Statement') which is available at ftp://rs.internic.net/policy/internic/internic-domain-1.txt. (If this application is made through an agent, such as an Internet Service Provider, that agent accepts the responsibility to notify the applicant of the conditions on the registration of the domain name and to provide the applicant a copy of the current version of the Policy Statement, if so requested by the applicant.) The applicant acknowledges and agrees that NSI may change the terms and conditions of the Policy Statement from time to time as provided in the Policy Statement.

The applicant agrees that if the use of the domain name is challenged by any third party, or if any dispute arises under this Registration Agreement, as amended, the applicant will abide by the procedures specified in the Policy Statement.

This Registration Agreement shall be governed in all respects by and construed in accordance with the laws of the United States of America and of the State of California, without respect to its conflict of law rules. This Registration Agreement is the complete and exclusive agreement of the applicant and NSI ("parties") regarding domain names. It supersedes, and its terms govern, all prior proposals, agreements, or other communications between the parties. This Registration Agreement may be amended only as provided in the Policy Statement.

------------------------- cut here -------------------------

GENERAL INSTRUCTIONS

Use the form above for registering new domain names, for making changes to existing domain name records and for removing a domain name from the Internic database and root servers. The form, and only the form, should be sent via e-mail to HOSTMASTER@INTERNIC.NET Please do not send hardcopy registrations to the InterNIC. Your provider will be able to send e-mail applications if you are not connected.

In the Subject of the message, use the words, "NEW DOMAIN", "MODIFY DOMAIN", or "REMOVE DOMAIN" as appropriate, followed by the name of the domain to assist in sorting and locating incoming registration requests.

In response to the submission of a form, you should receive an auto-reply with a tracking number. Use the number in the Subject of any messages you send regarding that registration action. When the registration is completed you will receive a notification via e-mail.

If you regularly submit domain applications, you will note three changes in the registration form. Section 4 has been removed. We assume that the domain will essentially be operational when the template is submitted and have found the "operational date" to be of little use. Removal of Section 4 moves the Administrative and Technical Contact sections to Section 4 and 5 respectively. A Billing Contact section was added as Section 6, so that invoices and other billing information can be sent to the Billing Contact. Finally, additional fields have been added to the parts of the form that deal with addresses. Street Address, City, State, Postal Code and Country MUST be placed in separate fields.

Please do not modify the form nor remove the version number. The computer program that scans and parses the form is looking for section numbers, followed by a period, followed by a colon. Information following the colon is compared with and inserted into the database as appropriate. Please send only one form per message.

When completing the form, make use of "whois" at rs.internic.net to check to see if the domain name, organization name, people, and name servers have been registered. Use the information in the database where appropriate. This will minimize the number of registrations that are returned for incomplete or inaccurate information.

The instructions for completing each field are in the following three sections - one each for NEW, MODIFY and DELETE. The interpretation of missing or blank fields can vary between the New and Modify registration actions. Please read the instructions carefully and make sure the form is properly completed to accomplish the action you desire.

The information on billing of domains and invoices is available at ftp://rs.internic.net/billing/README

REGISTERING A NEW DOMAIN NAME

Section 0 — Registration Action Type

Following the colon, place the character "N" or the word "NEW" to indicate a NEW domain registration. Changing a name from DOMAINAME1to DOMAINAME2 is treated as a New registration. The transfer of a name from one organization to another is also treated as a New registration. If the intent is to effect a transfer from one organization to another, clearly indicate this in Section 1 and include a statement from the current holder of the name that it is being transferred.

Section 1 — Purpose of Registration

Briefly describe the organization and/or the purpose for which this domain name is being registered. The description should support the choice of top-level domain in Section 2. If the domain name is for an organization that already has a domain name registered, describe the purpose of this domain and why the additional name is needed. Indicate why existing names cannot be used or why the proposed second-level name cannot be used as a third-level name under a domain name that is already registered.

Section 2 — Complete Domain Name

Top-level country domains may be registered by inserting the two-letter country code in this section. See RFC1591 for the duties and responsibilities of top-level domain administrators.

For second-level domain names under COM, ORG, NET, EDU, GOV insert the two-part name of the domain you wish to register, for example, ABC.COM. The total length of the two-part name may be up to 24 characters. The only characters allowed in a domain name are letters, digits and the dash (-). A domain name cannot begin or end with a

dash (see RFC952). Consult RFC1591 to determine the most
appropriate top-level domain to join. Briefly:

> COM is for commercial, for-profit organizations
> ORG is for miscellaneous usually non-profit
>   organizations
> NET is for network infrastructure machines and
>   organizations
> EDU is for 4-year, degree granting institutions
> GOV is for United States federal government agencies

US state and local government agencies, schools,
libraries, museums, and individuals should register under
the US domain. See RFC1480 for a complete description of
the US domain and registration procedures.

GOV registrations are limited to top-level US Federal
Government agencies (see RFC1816).

Section 3 — Organization using the Domain Name

The domain name is considered to be registered to an
organization, even if the "organization" is an individual.
It is important in this section to list the name and
address of the end-user organization, not the provider
organization.

If the organization has the same name as one that is
already registered, explain this in Section 1 above. Item
3b may be copied as many times as necessary to reflect
different lines of the Street Address. If item 3c, 3d or 3e
is not applicable for your country, leave that item blank.

Section 4 — Administrative Contact

The administrative contact is the person who can speak on
behalf of the organization listed in Section 3.This person
should be able to answer non-technical questions about the
organization's plans for the name, and procedures for
establishing sub-domains, and should be able to represent
the organization regarding use of the name. See RFC1032
for more detail on administrative contacts.

Each person in the InterNIC database is assigned a "handle" - a unique tag consisting of the person's initials and a serial number. This tag is used on records in the database to indicate a point of contact for a domain name, network, name server or other entity. Each person should have only one handle.

If the person's handle is known, insert just the handle in item 4a and leave the rest of Section 4 blank.

If a person's handle is unknown or the person has never been registered, leave item 4a blank. The registration software will check for an existing user record. If a matching user record is found, the record will be updated with any new information contained in the template.

All contacts MUST include information in items 4i and 4j. Templates that do not have this information will be returned.

Section 5 — Technical Contact

The technical contact is the person who tends to the technical aspects of maintaining the domain's name server, resolver software, and database files. This person keeps the name server running, and interacts with technical people in other domains to solve problems that affect the domain. The Internet Service Provider often performs this role.

The procedures for completing Section 5 are the same as those for Section 4. If Section 5 is left blank, the information from Section 4 will be assumed and vice-versa.

Section 6 — Billing Contact

The billing contact will be sent invoices for new domain registrations and re-registrations.

The procedures for completing Section 6 are the same as those for Section 4. If Section 6 is left blank, the information from Section 4 will be assumed.

Section 7 — Primary Name Server

Domains MUST provide at least two independent servers for
translating names to addresses for hosts in the domain.
The servers should be in physically separate locations and
on different networks if possible. The servers should be
active and responsive to DNS queries BEFORE this
application is submitted. Incomplete information in
Sections 7 and 8 or inactive servers will result in delay
of the registration.

The registration software makes a cross check between the
host name given and the IP addresses given to see if there
are matches with either in the database. If a match with an
IP number in the database is found, the name in the
database will be assumed. Neither the name nor number of a
registered name server will be changed as a result of a new
domain registration. A Modify registration request MUST be
sent to change either of these values.

Please provide the fully-qualified name of the machine
that is to be the name server; for example:
"machine.domainame.com" not just "machine"

Section 8 — Secondary Name Server(s)

The procedures for completing Section 8 are the same as for
Section 7. At least one secondary name server is required.
If several secondary servers are desired, copy Section 8
as many times as needed. Please do not renumber or change
the copied section.

Section 9 — Invoice Delivery

If you wish to receive your invoice electronically, place
the character "E" or the word "EMAIL" in item 9. If you
wish to receive your invoice by postal mail, place the
character "P" or the word "POSTAL" in item 9.

MODIFYING A DOMAIN NAME RECORD

Changing an existing record is done by replacement. That is, the contents of various fields in the database are replaced with new information from the form. If the modification involves first registering a person or name server that is not in the database, the instructions for completing Sections 4-8 "REGISTERING A NEW DOMAIN NAME" apply. Use "whois" if you are unsure about the current information for a domain, name server, or individual.

Changes will be made if it appears that the modification request has come from a "reasonable" source. This source may be from a listed contact for the domain, others in the same organization, the current provider, or a new provider that is about to provide support for the domain.

Notification of the change and the approximate time the change will take effect will be sent to:

— the requester
— if contacts are changing, both old and new contacts
— if name servers are changing, the technical contacts for the domains in which the old and new primary name servers reside

This dissemination of change information is to ensure that all parties involved are aware and concur with the change.

Transfer of a name from one organization to another is considered a new registration. See, "REGISTERING A NEW DOMAIN NAME."

Section 0 — Registration Action Type

   Following the colon, place the character "M" or the word "MODIFY" to indicate a modification to an existing domain registration. Transfer of a name from one organization to another is considered a new registration. See, "REGISTERING A NEW DOMAIN NAME."

Section 1 — Purpose of Registration

Briefly describe the purpose of the modification. If the intent is to change either the name or the IP address of name servers, make this very clear, otherwise changes to name servers will not be made.

If you wish to change the name of the domain itself, file a separate NEW registration and a DELETE registration when you are ready to have the old name removed. Make it clear in this section that you are changing from one domain name to another and estimate how long you will need the old domain name.

Section 2 — Complete Domain Name

Insert the two-part name of the domain name you wish to modify, for example, ABC.COM. This section MUST be completed, even if you are making minor changes, like the phone number of a point of contact, for example.

Section 3 — Organization Using the Domain Name

The domain name is considered to be registered to an organization, even if the "organization" is an individual. Therefore, a change in the organization name should be explained in Section 1. Transfer of a domain name from one organization to another is considered a new domain registration. See, "REGISTERING A NEW DOMAIN NAME."

Section 4 — Administrative Contact

If a handle is given in item 4a, the database will be updated with any information on the form in items 4b through 4j. If any item is missing or blank, the corresponding information in the database will not be altered.

If no handle is given, the database will be searched to see if the person is already registered. If so, the person's record will be updated with any new information on the form. If not registered, the person will be entered into the database and assigned a handle. The handle will be attached to the domain name record, thus replacing the old contact with the new one. Both old and new contacts will be notified of the change.

Section 5 — Technical Contact

The procedures for modifying information in Section 5 are the same as those for Section 4.

Section 6 — Billing Contact

The procedures for modifying information in Section 6 are the same as those for Section 4.

Section 7 — Primary Name Server

If any changes in name servers are being made, provide a complete list of name servers (both primary and secondary). The list in the application will replace the list in the database.

If the intention is to change the name or IP address of a name server, clearly state that in Section 1 above. The default is to NOT change either of these values unless so instructed in Section 1 and the requester is authorized to do so.

Section 8 — Secondary Name Server(s)

If any changes in name servers are being made, provide a complete list of name servers (both primary and secondary). The list in the application will replace the list in the database.

Section 9 — Invoice Delivery

Leave this section blank.

DELETING A DOMAIN NAME RECORD

A request to remove a registered domain name from the database may come from the administrative or technical contact for the domain or from a provider who is no longer supporting the name. A third party who believes that a domain is inactive and wants to become the holder of the name should NOT submit a Delete form. Instead, a New form should be submitted with a description in Section 1 of attempts to contact the listed domain name holder.

When the name is removed, it will no longer be visible via whois, wais, gopher, or Web browsers that query the InterNIC database. It will also be removed from the root name servers on the subsequent update.

Notification of the deletion and the approximate time it will take effect will be sent to:

- the requester
- the contacts currently listed
- the technical contact for the domain in which the primary name server resides

When a name is transferred from one organization to another, the InterNIC will first delete the existing record and then process a new registration.

If an invoice is not paid within the specified time period, the domain name will be automatically deleted.

If the domain name has been placed on hold for more than 90 days because of lack of name service, the domain name may be deleted.

Section 0 — Registration Action Type

Following the colon, place the character "D" or the word "DELETE" to indicate a deletion of an existing domain registration.

Section 1 — Purpose of Registration

Briefly state the reason for removing the name.

If additional records, such as the point(s) of contact or name servers should also be deleted, state that in this section. These will not be automatically removed. The InterNIC will check further to see if they are used on other domain, network, or autonomous system number records before removing them.

Section 2 — Complete Domain Name

Insert the two-part name of the domain name you wish to have deleted.

Section 3 — Organization Using the Domain Name

This section MUST be filled completely.

Section 4 — Section 9

These sections should be left blank.

CHAPTER 10

Other Services

Other Mac OS-Based Internet Server Applications

We've now covered the mainstays, but we haven't finished discussing all the Mac OS-based server applications out there. There are many less-popular or less-used services that can be hosted by Mac-based servers. In this chapter, we'll give you more information about these services and the programs that host them.

 ## The Swiss Army Knife: Daemon

Peter Lewis (author of FTPd and Anarchie, among other programs) has written an application named Daemon that acts as a server for five different services common on various UNIX systems: Finger, Whois, Ident, Daytime, and Time.

Daemon is a background-only application, meaning you can place it in your Startup Items folder and forget about it—it will launch when you start up your Macintosh and will run invisibly in the background, not appearing among the applications listed in your applications menu. Most of Daemon requires no special configuration. The parts of Daemon that do need configuration can be done via editing a text file.

Finger

Finger lets Internet users find out more information about a specific user on a given machine. Since many UNIX servers act as hosts to many different users at one time, Finger has become a standard service to use when you want to see who is logged in to a given machine, and to see more information about any user on that machine. Users can add personal information to their Finger response, by editing a "plan" file that can contain items such as their office location, employer, occupation or job, and even favorite quotations.

Users of Daemon specify what will be returned when someone contacts your server via Finger by editing a text file called Plan located in your Preferences folder, within the System Folder (see Figure 10.1). This text file can contain plain text, as well as references to text in other files, and special strings that translate into variable information. For example, a Plan file could include a statement like:

```
Today is %%CURRENT-LONG. The time is %CURRENT-TIME.
```

The items beginning with two percent signs are variable tokens (see Table 10.1), which will be sent out with current information when a Finger request is received. For example, the preceding text would end up being returned via Finger as something like:

```
Today is Saturday, 16 September 1995. The time is 12:30.
```

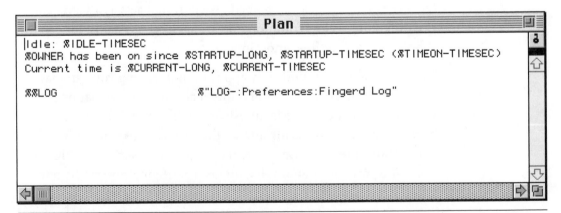

FIGURE 10.1 A Sample Plan File for Daemon

TABLE 10.1 Daemon Plan/Whois Tokens

Token Name	What it Does	Sample Result
%STARTUP-LONG	Day and Date Mac last started up	Thursday, 11 February 1993
%STARTUP-SHORT	Date Mac last started up	11/2/93
%STARTUP-ABBREV	Day and Date Mac last started up	Thu, 11 Feb 1993
%STARTUP-TIME	Time Mac last started up	4:59
%STARTUP-TIMESEC	Time Mac last started up	4:59:56
%CURRENT-LONG	Current Day and Date	Thursday, 11 February 1993
%CURRENT-SHORT	Current Date	11/2/93
%CURRENT-ABBREV	Current Day and Date	Thu, 11 Feb 1993
%CURRENT-TIME	Current Time	16:50
%CURRENT-TIMESEC	Current Time	16:50:30
%IDLE-TIME	Length of time with no action	0:03
%IDLE-TIMESEC	Length of time with no action	0:03:15
%IDLEINWORDS	Length of time with no action	3 minutes 15 seconds
%TIMEON-TIME	Length of time since last start-up	11:50
%TIMEON-TIMESEC	Length of time since last start-up	11:50:34
%MACHINE	Name of Machine	Internet Server
%OWNER	Name of Owner	Administrator
%ICBM	Location in Map Control Panel	N=-31.55' E=115.49'
%GMT	Current Greenwich Mean Time	8:00
%MACENVY-APPLETALK	Version of AppleTalk being run	56
%MACENVY-FPU	Version of FPU present	unknown
%MACENVY-KEYBOARD	Kind of Keyboard being userd	Extended ADB Keyboard
%MACENVY-LOWMEMORY	Location of low memory	8192
%MACENVY-RAMSIZE	Amount of RAM	16M (010B7890)
%MACENVY-LOGICALRAMSIZE	Amount of logical RAM	16M (010B7890)
%MACENVY-REALRAMSIZE	Amount of real RAM	17M (01100000)
%MACENVY-PHYSICALRAMSIZE	Amount of physical RAM	17M (01100000)
%MACENVY-MACHINE	Kind of machine	Macintosh IIsi
%MACENVY-ICON	ASCII version of the icon in your "About this Macintosh" window	
%MACENVY-MMU	Kind of MMU present	68030 MMU
%MACENVY-PAGESIZE	Memory page size	32768
%MACENVY-CPU	CPU type	68030
%MACENVY-QUICKDRAW	QuickDraw version	2.3.0
%MACENVY-ROMSIZE	Size of ROM	512K (00080000)
%MACENVY-ROM	ROM type	067C
%MACENVY-SLOTS	Number of slots	0
%MACENVY-SOUND	Sound type	Stereo sound with sound input
%MACENVY-SYSTEM	Version of OS being used	7.0.1
%MACENVY-TEXTEDIT	TextEdit version	5
%MACENVY-GESTALT	Gestalt code	1

TABLE 10.1 (Continued)

Token Name	What it Does
%FILE-:[filename]	Returns the file you specify
%FILES-:[folder]	Returns the file in the folder you specify that matches the name of the I.D. fingered
%LOOKUP-:[file]	Returns any line in the specified file containing the name of the I.D. fingered
%FORTUNE-:[folder]	Returns a randomly selected fortune from the specified folder. Fortunes are specified with lines separated by a line containing only a pound sign (#)

By including the %%FILES token, your Plan text file can include text from other text files depending on which user was requested by Finger. For example, if someone on a remote site sent a Finger request for jason@yoursite.edu, a result containing personal information for that user could be returned. A Finger request for carl@yoursite.edu could return completely different information.

Perhaps the most common Mac-based Finger client is the e-mail program Eudora. Hitting Command-U in both Eudora Pro 2.x and Eudora Light 1.x will open a Finger client window.

Whois

The Whois protocol is quite similar to Finger, but is more commonly used to look up information about entire sites, not individual users. Daemon uses the same tokens it uses for Finger to send out variable information for Whois. All Whois information should go in a text file named Whois in the Preferences folder located inside the System Folder.

Ident

Ident is a protocol designed to register who is using a particular connection on a multiuser machine such as a UNIX server. Implementing this protocol on the Macintosh, a single-user machine, is fairly straightfoward: Daemon will simply return the owner name found in the Sharing Setup control panel of the server Macintosh.

Daytime

This protocol returns the local time. It's a useful system for far-flung users who might not know what time it is where they are.

Time

Time is a time protocol that lets other machines on the network query your machine for the current time. Be sure your position is set correctly in your server's Map control panel if you're planning to use this feature, so that your information can be plotted in the correct time zone.

Telnet to AppleScript: Script Daemon

Yet another Internet application written by Peter Lewis is Script Daemon, which lets the owner of a Mac log in via Telnet (using his or her user name and password) and issue AppleScript commands (see Figure 10.2).

To use Script Daemon, place it (or an alias of it) in your Startup Items folder within the System Folder. Drop the included Users & Groups scripting addition into the Scripting Additions folder, located within the Extensions Folder within the System Folder. Once you've restarted, Script Daemon will be up and running.

Of course, if you run Script Daemon, you'll need to make sure that your owner password is well guarded; if people can issue AppleScript commands, they can potentially use your server almost as easily as if they were sitting right in front of it, mouse in hand.

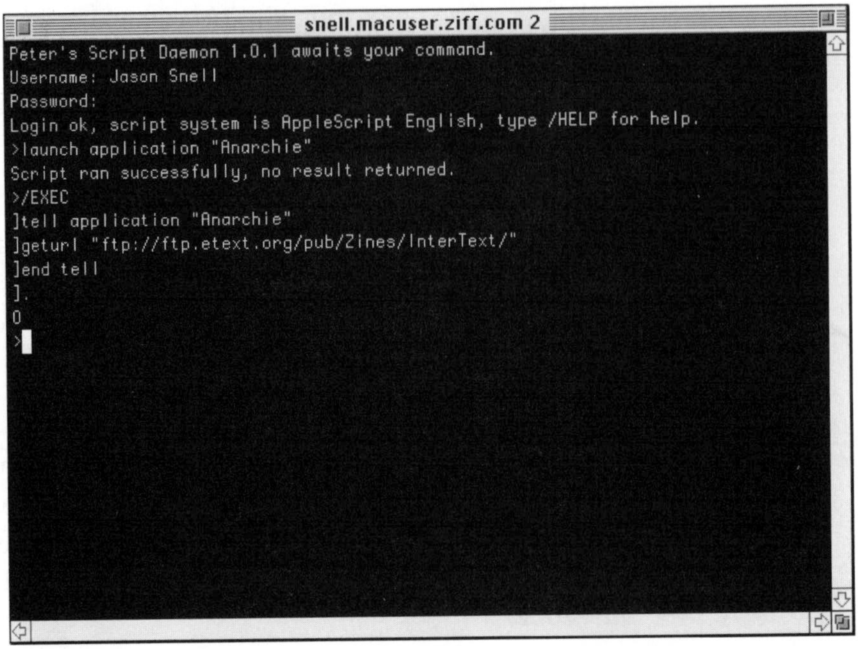

```
╔═══════════════ snell.macuser.ziff.com 2 ═══════════════╗
Peter's Script Daemon 1.0.1 awaits your command.
Username: Jason Snell
Password:
Login ok, script system is AppleScript English, type /HELP for help.
>launch application "Anarchie"
Script ran successfully, no result returned.
>/EXEC
]tell application "Anarchie"
]geturl "ftp://ftp.etext.org/pub/Zines/InterText/"
]end tell
].
0
>▮
```

FIGURE 10.2 Logging in to a Script Daemon session via Telnet.

In addition to AppleScript, Script Daemon supports a few internal commands: /HELP, which lists all available commands; /EXEC, which lets you enter a multiline AppleScript that ends when you type a period on a line by itself; and /QUIT, which logs out the user and closes the connection.

Person-to-Person: Talk

Talk is an Internet protocol that enables live person-to-person text chats. Quite common on UNIX machines, it's also supported on the Macintosh by the Talk program. If we told you that Talk was written by the prolific Peter Lewis, would you be surprised? We didn't think so.

Since Talk is a peer-to-peer system, it might seem a bit strange to include it in a book about Internet servers. However, since Talk sessions work like telephone connections—somebody's got to place the call and the other person has to be on the other end to pick it up—Talk does include a server component, a program that detects when a Talk request is coming in and responds appropriately to that request.

Talk comes in two forms: the Talk application allows you to listen for incoming Talk requests, place "calls" to other machines, and conduct the actual chat session once you're connected. The Talkd application is a background-only application that senses an incoming Talk request and warns the user to launch Talk and answer the call.

Talk Preferences

In the Talk Preferences window (see Figure 10.3) you can configure how Talk responds to Talk requests. A series of radio buttons underneath On request: allows you to configure how Talkd will notify the

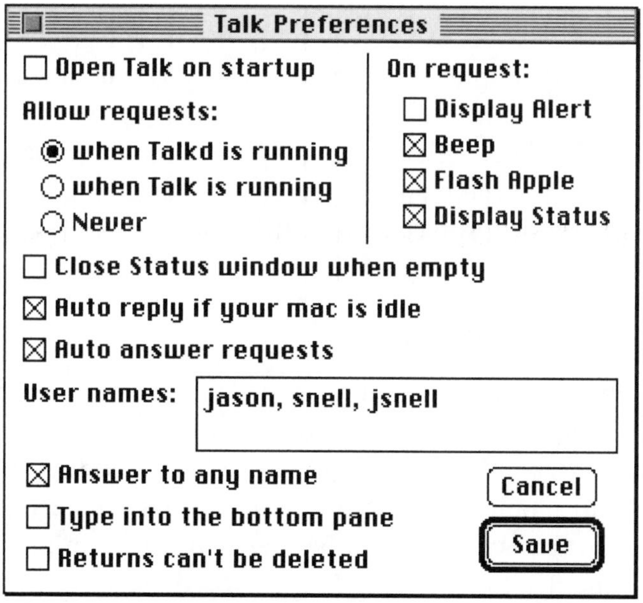

FIGURE 10.3 Talk's Preferences Window

user of a Macintosh that a Talk request has been received. You can choose to have Talkd display an alert, sound a beep, flash an icon in the Apple menu, or display Talk's status window. Checking the Open Talk on startup box instructs Talkd to launch Talk automatically.

A series of three radio buttons below Allow requests: lets you choose when Talk will accept incoming Talk requests. If when Talkd is running is selected, Talk requests will be accepted whenever either Talkd or Talk is running. If when Talk is running is selected, Talk requests will not be accepted unless the Talk application itself is running. If Never is selected, Talk requests will never be accepted.

Talk requests must be made in the form of user@host. In the User names box, you can enter acceptable user names for your machine, or check Answer to any name to allow anyone to connect, no matter which user name was requested. This makes sense for the Macintosh, since it's not a multiuser system like many UNIX-based systems.

If Auto reply if your Mac is idle is selected, Talk will automatically respond to an incoming connection if the server Macintosh has been left idle.

The other options in the Preferences window affect Talk's user interface—whether Talk's status window is automatically closed when it's empty, whether users can type into the bottom pane of the Talk window, and whether if returns can be deleted (an option that can cause formatting problems on UNIX systems).

Placing a Call

To initiate a Talk session, select Talk from the File menu. You'll be prompted with a Talk window (see Figure 10.4). Enter the name of the user and machine you'll be trying to reach. If the user is logged in to a multi-user system multiple times, you can specify which session you want to talk to by specifying the terminal to use (which you can often find by using Finger). To set this user and machine as the user and machine you'll connect to by default, click Set Default. To initiate a talk request, click Talk.

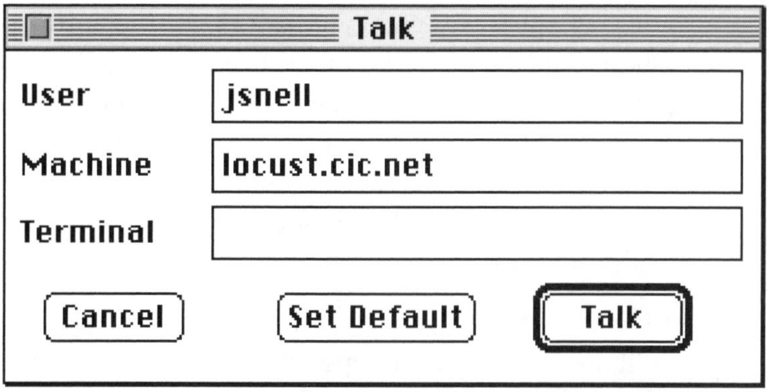

Talk
User
jsnell
Machine
locust.cic.net
Terminal
Cancel
Set Default
Talk

FIGURE 10.4 Initiate Talk connections in the Talk window.

Answering a Call

To answer a call, you need to use the Status window (see Figure 10.5), which appears when you select Show Status from the File Menu. In this window you'll see a list of past and present Talk connections. You can remove sessions from the list by selecting the session and clicking on the Remove button. If a request has come in from the outside world, the first icon in the window will be a globe.

Status
Abort
Connect
To Front
? 11:43 AM jsnell@locust.cic.net

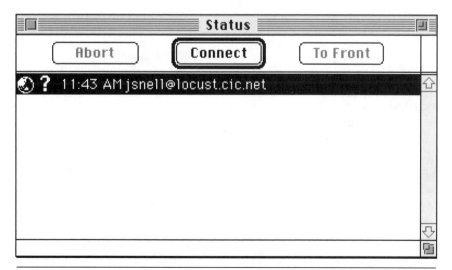

FIGURE 10.5 Answering a Talk request in the Status window.

If the request was going out from your Macintosh, the first icon will be a Mac. If a Talk session has been requested but hasn't yet been initiated, the second icon will be a question mark. If the session is inactive, the icon will be a two-paned window with no text in it. If the session is active, the icon will be a two-paned window with text inside. To answer a Talk request, select the incoming request and click on the Connect button.

Once you've connected, a window with two panes will appear (see Figure 10.6). You can type into the top window, and what you type is relayed across the network to the screen of the person you're conversing with. What they type will appear in your lower pane.

When you're done with your conversation, click on the close box in the upper left corner of the window. Your connection will automatically be terminated.

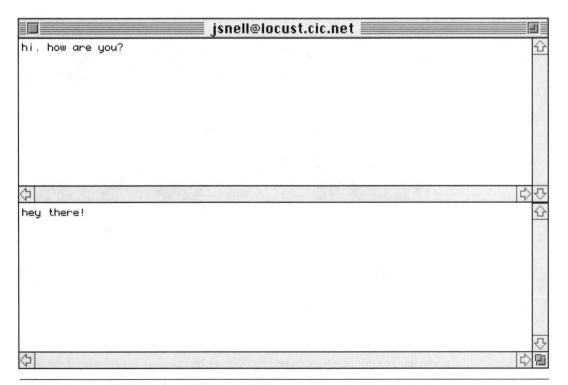

FIGURE 10.6 A Talk Conversation in Progress

Live Chat: Chat

While Talk allows two users to converse by typing back and forth, Chat is a program that lets multiple users connect to a Macintosh via Telnet and converse among themselves. Like all the other programs we've dealt with so far in this chapter, Chat was created by Peter Lewis. However, Peter stopped developing Chat after the release of version 1.1, and the current version of Chat is developed by Nathan Neulinger.

Since Chat allows clients to log in via Telnet, any person using a machine on the Internet with a Telnet client (which means just about every machine out there) can connect to and use Chat. Chat can be a source of nothing but entertainment, or it can be a good way to do cheap "teleconferencing" among people who are scattered around the world.

Chat Preferences

The Chat application's interface is fairly rudimentary. Most server preferences are set by checking or unchecking items in the Preferences menu (see Figure 10.7).

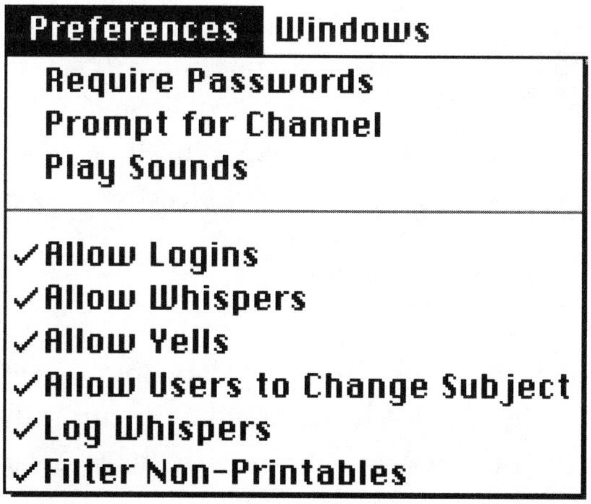

Preferences Windows
Require Passwords
Prompt for Channel
Play Sounds
✓ **Allow Logins**
✓ **Allow Whispers**
✓ **Allow Yells**
✓ **Allow Users to Change Subject**
✓ **Log Whispers**
✓ **Filter Non-Printables**

FIGURE 10.7
Chat's Preferences Menu

Require Passwords

If this item is checked, users will need to know a master password (it's the same for all users) before they can enter the chat server. This password is set by using Apple's ResEdit utility (discussed shortly).

Prompt for Channel

If this item is checked, when new users log in, they will be prompted as to which "channel" of the Chat server they'd like to enter. A chat server contains 10 channels. If you're on a particular channel, you can hear only conversations going on that channel. By using different channels, several conversations can take place at once on a Chat server. If this item is not checked, users are placed in Channel 1 by default.

Play Sounds

If this item is checked, sounds will be played when users log on and off the server.

Allow Logins

If this item is checked , users can log in to the Chat server. If it's not checked, the server is closed—currently logged-in users can remain online, but nobody new can enter. This is useful if you're going to be shutting down the server soon and don't want to let anyone else on, or if everyone you wanted to be online for a Chat-based meeting has arrived and you want to refuse access to anyone else.

Allow Whispers

In Chat, a whisper is a way that one user can send a message that can be read by only one other user. With this item checked, individual users can quietly "talk among themselves" while a more public conversation goes on around them.

Allow Yells

A yell is a message that is heard by all people logged in to the Chat server, regardless of which channel they're currently tuned into. Yells can be useful, but they can also be extremely distracting, since people tend to abuse the Yell command. If this item is checked, Yells will be allowed.

Allow Users to Change Subject

Each channel of a Chat server has its own predefined subject (editable by using ResEdit). If this item is checked, individual users can change the subject of a chat as they see fit. This is another feature that can often be abused, but if you're not very serious about keeping people on-topic in various channel areas, and would rather just let people do what they want on your server, you can check this item.

Log Whispers

Whispers, private communications between two users, can be very personal in nature. As a matter of course, Talk logs all conversations on a server. If this item is checked, that log will also include whispers. If you'd prefer to preserve some privacy option on your server, leave this item unchecked and whispers will remain just between the whisperer and the whisperee.

Filter Non-Printables

If this item is checked, characters that can't be seen, such as control characters, will be stripped out rather than being passed through to other users.

Chat Windows

Chat's Windows menu (see Figure 10.8) lets you see what's happening on Chat's various channels by opening several informative windows.

If you open the Channels window (see Figure 10.9), you'll be given a list of all the channels on your Chat server, what the subject is on each channel, and how many users are currently using that channel.

If you open the Users window (see Figure 10.10), you'll see a list of all currently logged in users, which channel they're currently tuned to, and the IP address of the machine from which they're connecting.

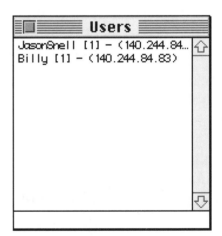

FIGURE 10.8
Chat's Windows Menu

Windows

Channels	⌘S
Users	⌘U
Room Monitor	⌘M

[1] General
[2] Hot Topics
[3] Internet
[4] Computers
[5] Work
[6] Music
[7] Games
[8] Talk
[9] Help
[10] Sports

Channels

```
1 - General    (2)
2 - Hot Topics  (0)
3 - Internet   (0)
4 - Computers  (0)
5 - Work  (0)
6 - Music  (0)
7 - Games  (0)
8 - Talk  (0)
9 - Help!  (0)
10 - Sports  (0)
```

Users

```
JasonSnell [1] - (140.244.84...
Billy [1] - (140.244.84.83)
```

FIGURE 10.9 Chat's Channels window lists all the available channels.

FIGURE 10.10 Chat's Users window lists all current users.

Opening the Room Monitor window allows you to view what's going on throughout your Chat server. You can also select individual channels and view them seperately by choosing a channel from the Windows menu.

Modifying Chat in ResEdit

To set your user and administrator passwords as well as control other settings, you'll need to launch ResEdit, open the Chat application, and double-click on the STR# resource.

When you open STR#, you'll see a list of different items, all of which pertain to different defaults in Chat. Double-click on I.D. 133 to change the user password; double-click on I.D. 134 to change the admin password; double-click on I.D. 147 to alter the default names for your channels.

If you double-click on the CPrf resource in the main Chat window in ResEdit and then double-click on the one item inside, you can pick the default settings for the Preferences menu. Click on 0 if you'd like the setting to be off by default, 1 if it should be on by default.

When you're done, be sure to save the changes you've made to the Chat application before quitting ResEdit.

User Commands from within Chat

Inside Chat, users can issue many different commands to control what they're seeing and doing. For a list, see Table 10.2. All commands begin with a slash character.

TABLE 10.2 User Commands in Chat

/?	Displays list of available commands
/HELP	Displays command help
/ABOUT	Displays information about a given chat room
/ME	Displays information about yourself
/QUIT	Exits the chat room
/LIST	Lists all users on currently selected channel
/LISTALL	Lists all users connected to the server
/DO [text]	Sends [text] as an action ("/DO waves and smiles")
/YELL [text]	Sends [text] to all users on the server
/PAGE [user]	Asks [user] to come to your current channel
/CHANNEL	Lists available channels on the server
/CHANNEL [channel]	Changes you to new channel [channel]

TABLE 10.2 (Continued)

/WHISPER [user] [text]	Sends [text] only to user [user]
/MSG	Shows messages posted to the message board
/MSG [text]	Adds [text] to the message board
/INFO	Displays general server info
/SHOW	Displays your current user settings
/CLEAR	Clears your screen
/SET	Lists available user settings
/SET [setting] [value]	Sets a particular setting to a specific value
/SET NAME [name]	Changes your name to [name]
/SET SUBJECT [text]	Changes the subject of the current channel
/SET ECHO [on or off]	Determines if you can see your own messages
/SET AWAY [on or off]	Lets people know if you've stepped away from your terminal
/SET AWAYMSG [text]	Sets message to be displayed while you're away
/SET USERINFO [text]	Sets message to be displayed when you're active
/SET IGNORE [name]	Lets you ignore all messages from a particular user
/SET ANNOUNCE [on or off]	Choose if you want to see announcements
/RECENT	Lists recent users of the Chat server
/ROLL	Rolls one twenty-sided die
/ROLL [number]d[sides]	Rolls [number] of [sides]-sided dice

Administrator Commands from within Chat

Inside Chat, administrators can also issue commands to control what they're seeing and doing. All the commands begin with a backslash character, and most require knowledge of the administrator password, set using ResEdit. For a list, see Table 10.3.

 # Internet Security: SOCKS

SOCKS is another Internet application from Peter Lewis. SOCKS implements the SOCKS protocol under the Mac OS, one part of a firewall solution. A firewall is a machine, or a number of machines, that screens all traffic between an internal, protected network and an external network; it permits only authorized traffic to pass through. When a computer "behind" the firewall needs to exchange data with

TABLE 10.3 Administrator Commands in Chat

\?	Displays list of available commands
\HELP [password]	Displays administrative command help
\KILL [password] [user]	Logs [user] off the server
\QUITNOW [password]	Quits the Chat application altogether
\RESTART [password]	Kicks every user off the server and restarts
\HIDE [password]	Hides yourself from appearing in /LIST and /LISTALL
\UNHIDE [password]	Shows yourself in /LIST and /LISTALL
\LISTALL [password]	Lists all users, including hidden ones
\GAG [passsword] [user]	Prevents a user from speaking
\UNGAG [password] [user]	Allows a gagged user to speak again
\SHOW [password]	Displays your current administrative settings
\INFO [password]	Displays Chat application information
\SET [password]	Displays administrative settings
\SET [password] LOGINS [On or Off]	Allows or denies new logins
\SET [password] YELLS [On or Off]	Allows or refuses use of /YELL
\SET [password] WHISPERS [On or Off]	Allows or refuses use of /WHISPER
\SET [password] PASSWORDS [On or Off]	Requires or doesn't require login password
\SET [password] BEEP [On or Off]	Turns beeping on or off when there's a login
\SET [password] PROMPT [On or Off]	Prompts or doesn't prompt for channel at login
\SET [password] SUBJECT [On or Off]	Sets subject of current channel
\SET [password] USERSUB [On or Off]	Allows or disallows changing of channel's subject

a machine "outside" the firewall, it connects to a gateway that allows only certain types of network traffic to traverse the firewall.

When such a system is in place, a company can drastically reduce the number of machines it needs to ensure security. For example, a person mistakenly running a wide-open FTP server behind a firewall would still leave the company as secure as the firewall it has in place because the firewall should block traffic from the Internet at large to the internal machine.

SOCKS can enable a machine to act as a proxy server, or a server that connects to another server outside the firewall on behalf of a client behind the firewall. SOCKS provides screening, authentication, and logging for application-level connections. Users need clients that are SOCKS-capable in order to make SOCKS part of their firewall solution.

Since SOCKS is only one part of a complete firewall solution and setting up a firewall is beyond the scope of this book, we'll leave the specifics of this application to the administrators experienced with the issues involved in creating a secure network.

Quick-and-Dirty File Transfer: TFTPd

Peter Lewis' TFTPd is a program that allows users to transfer files from a host system using TFTP (Trivial File Transport Protocol). Though its name might make it sound like a trivial implementation of FTP, that's not the case; TFTP isn't really related to FTP. It's a rarely used protocol that can be useful for quick-and-dirty file transfers.

When TFTPd is launched for the first time, it creates a TFTPd folder in the Preferences folder inside the System Folder. This is the only folder that is initially accessible to users logged in to the TFTPd server, though you can extend their reach by placing aliases to other folders within that folder. Just as with FTPd and other FTP servers (see Chapter 6), you have to be careful about which files and folders you allow access to.

Since TFTP has no permission or password system, there's no way to control who logs in to your server. If someone logs in to TFTPd, that person will have full access to the TFTPd folder.

## CHAPTER 11

Remote Administration and Maintenance Tools

U NIX administrators have one very real advantage over administrators of systems running the Mac OS: the ability to telnet into a UNIX box from virtually anywhere, and receive the command-line prompt with full control of the system. That said, there are good remote administration and maintenance tools available for the Mac OS: some let you connect to the remote Mac and control it from another computer, while others run quietly in the background, attempting to make the Mac OS a more reliable and server application-friendly platform than it is out of the box.

Timbuktu Pro

Timbuktu Pro is a virtual necessity for any Mac OS administrator. What Timbuktu Pro does is very simple: It allows you to control a computer running the Mac OS remotely, by placing the remote computer's display in a window, and sending all keystrokes and mouse movements to the remote machine—it's as if you just had very long keyboard and monitor cables. If you're using a modem to connect remotely to your network, however, you'll want to connect at the fastest speed possible: at 14.4 K speeds, Timbuktu is usable, but still sluggish. At 28.8 Kbps—and higher, for nonmodem links—Timbuktu is quite responsive.

Timbuktu Pro also allows you to run your Mac as a *headless server*— to use your Mac without a monitor—although a cheap monitor always seems to come in handy when problems arise; for example, when you can't connect to your server with Timbuktu Pro for some unknown reason and you need to troubleshoot the machine locally.

The Timbuktu Menu

The Timbuktu menu, shown in Figure 11.1, is available whenever the Timbuktu extension is loaded at system startup. Beyond providing a quick, convenient way to launch the Timbuktu application— which is used as the client portion of Timbuktu Pro and to configure the server portion of Timbuktu Pro—the Timbuktu menu also provides an easy way to monitor server activity. See Monitoring Timbuktu Pro, later. Timbuktu Pro can be launched from the Timbuktu menu using the Open Timbuktu Pro menu item.

Setting Up Timbuktu

Timbuktu Pro is configured from items available in the Setup menu from the Timbuktu application. Here, we'll first define the users

FIGURE 11.1
The Timbuktu Menu

whom we would like to be able to access the server remotely, using Define Users . . . ; we'll then set the password requirement for those users using Set Password Requirements; and then we'll secure those options by selecting a master password in Set Preferences. Finally, the User Access item will allow us to enable access to the server via TCP/IP and review user privileges.

Define Users

Timbuktu accounts are created using the Define Users item from the Setup menu, shown in Figure 11.2. The first two users in the Define Users dialog box are Guest and Temporary Guest. You'll want to ensure that all options for these accounts are left inactive. Guest access is a reasonable option when Timbuktu Pro is installed on a local AppleTalk network; when your Mac is available to the whole of the global Internet,* however, security becomes a larger concern, and enabling guest access, in most cases, is unwise.

Users are added by selecting the New User button and typing a user name and password. See Set Password Requirements, next, for general password guidelines.

You then have a choice of multiple privileges you can assign the user. The first column in the Define Users dialog box has a function similar to guest accounts: it allows access to Timbuktu Pro from earlier versions of Timbuktu, using only a password (no user name is required). Once again, this option isn't recommended when security is a concern. The next five columns after user name and password are:

- ■ **Control:** This allows full access to your Mac OS server. You'll want to set this option in order to perform remote administration.

- ■ **Observe:** With this option, remote users can view the Mac's screen, but not control it. This is more useful in help desktype situations than in performing remote administration.

---

* This is so unless you use Timbuktu Pro via AppleTalk using a modem link and Apple Remote Access, or via a link with the incoming SLIP or PPP connection behind a firewall, with packet filtering blocking outside connections to the Timbuktu control port (407).

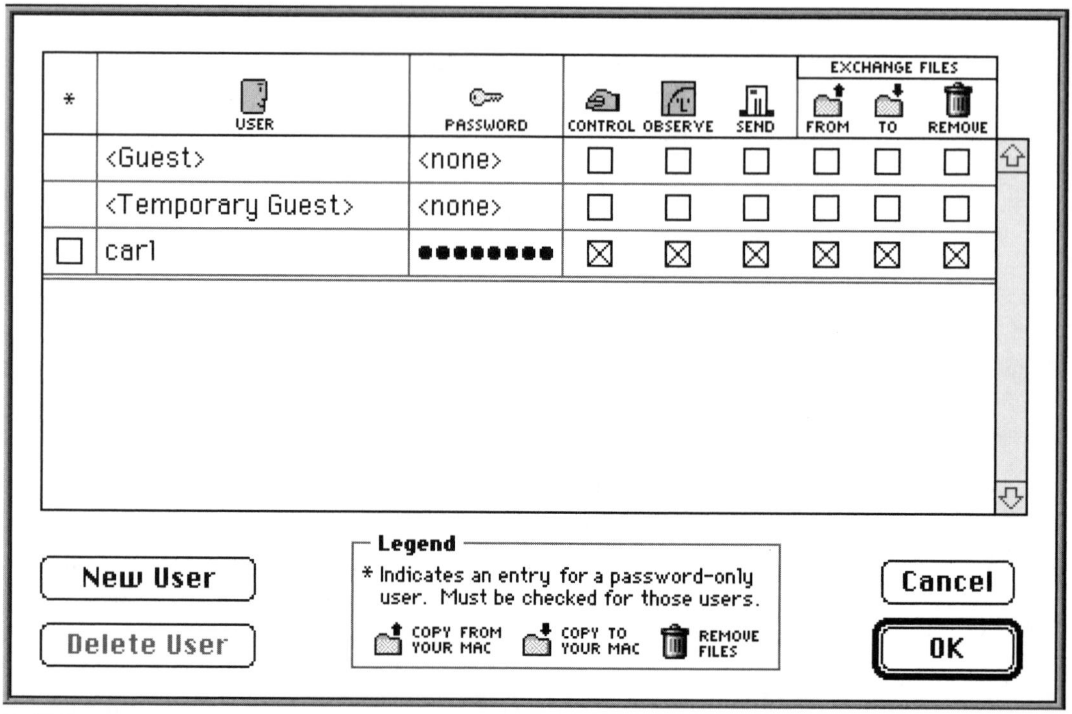

FIGURE 11.2 Timbuktu's Define Users Window

- **Send:** The remote user can drop files into a specified dropbox. Once again, this is not needed for remote administration.

- **Copy From:** The user is allowed to copy any file from this machine to a remote machine using Timbuktu Pro's Exchange Files function. Sometimes this is useful for copying log files or configuration files from the server to a local machine for quicker formatting or editing, depending upon the speed of your Timbuktu Pro link. Note, however, that it's usually faster to transfer files using FTP.

- **Copy To:** A companion to Copy From, this allows the remote user to place any file on the server.

- **Remove:** This allows the remote user to delete files from the server.

For the purposes of remote administration, you'll want to give yourself at least the Control privilege—and having the ability to copy and remove files from within Timbuktu Pro can sometimes be quite useful.

Password Requirements

The Password Requirements dialog box enforces good, general guidelines for password access if options are turned on and set to reasonable values, as shown in Figure 11.3.

It's difficult to stress how important a secure password is when running Timbuktu to remotely administer your Internet server. In our previous example, we gave the account with privileges the name carl—an account name that is easily enough guessed— to control the machine. The only thing securing your Mac OS machine from an intruder, given the user name, is your password. Choose a password wisely, using the guidelines Timbuktu provides, and change it often.

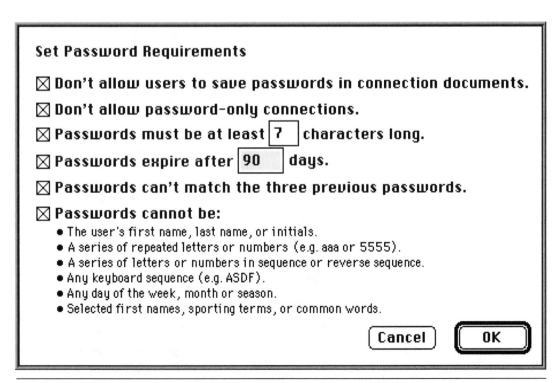

FIGURE 11.3 Timbuktu's Password Requirements Window

Set Preferences

Timbuktu Pro makes a number of preferences available from the Set Preferences dialog box, shown in Figure 11.4. Of most importance here is the ability to set a Master Password to prevent others with physical access to your server from adding user accounts or modifying privileges of existing user accounts. You'll want to set a Master Password for the additional peace of mind it can afford you. You can also set the amount of disk space you'd like Timbuktu Pro to reserve for dropbox users, although this value probably doesn't matter to you, since you'll probably choose to run FTP instead. Additionally, you can allow color connections (which can be significantly slower than black-and-white connections across modem-based links), and allow for automatic scrolling of the Timbuktu screen as you reach the edges of its window (instead of using the scroll bars), if the screen size of your server is larger than the Timbuktu window on your remote machine.

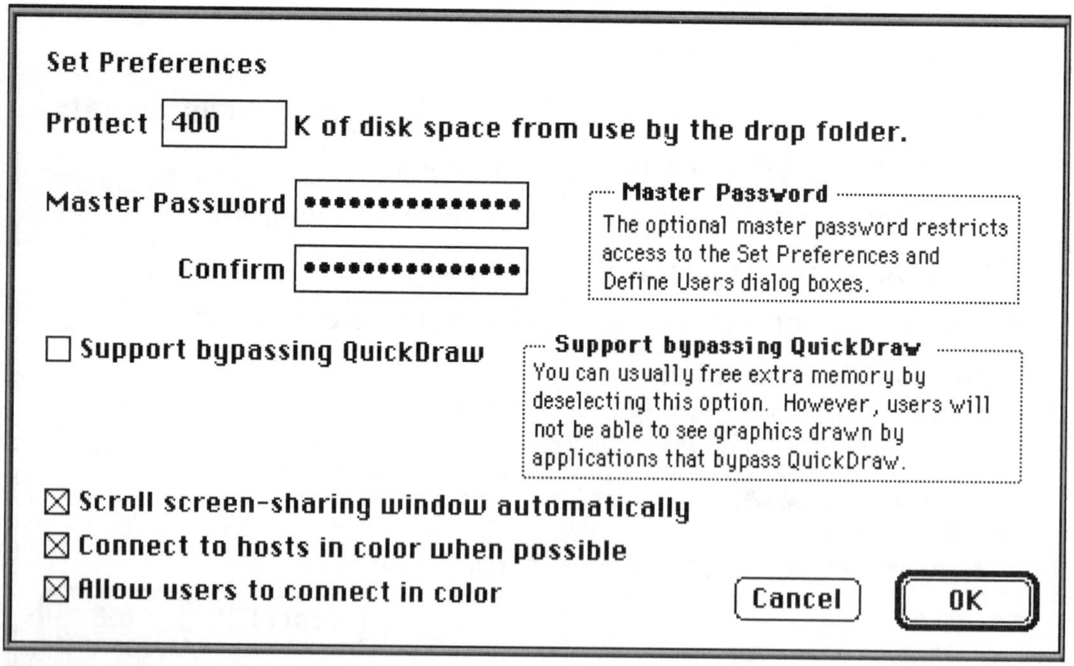

FIGURE 11.4 Timbuktu's Set Preferences Window

User Access

Finally, the User Access screen, shown in Figure 11.5, controls whether you allow AppleTalk or TCP/IP access to your machine, and summarizes the privileges you've enabled for remote users. Options that require a password for all users (e.g. guest access isn't enabled) will be marked with a key; options disabled for all users will have an X through them.

Using Timbuktu

Initiating a New Connection

The New Connection window initiates a connection from a Timbuktu client to a Timbuktu server. A pop-up menu allows you to choose between AppleTalk and TCP/IP access; for a TCP/IP connection, you can type in either the dotted decimal IP address or the domain name for the machine you wish to connect to. In the New Connection window pictured in Figure 11.6, we've specified the domain name hail.freedonia.com.

FIGURE 11.5 Timbuktu's User Access Window

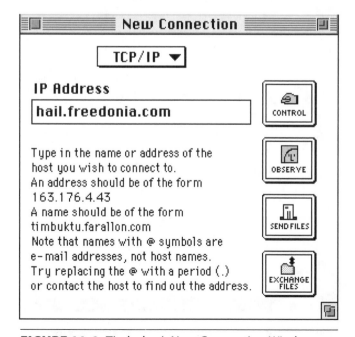

FIGURE 11.6 Timbuktu's New Connection Window

You can then choose to Control, Observe, Send Files, or Exchange Files with the remote Timbuktu Pro host. For purposes of remote administration, you'll want to select the Control icon, which gives you remote control of your Internet server. Once you choose Control, you'll be prompted for your user name and password, with the default user name taken from the Owner Name specified in the Sharing Setup control panel.

The Timbuktu screen-sharing window will then open onto your remote host. Timbuktu's screen sharing should be fairly intuitive; within the Timbuktu window, things should work as if you were sitting in front of the remote Mac. A snapshot of a window opened onto hail.freedonia.com is shown in Figure 11.7.

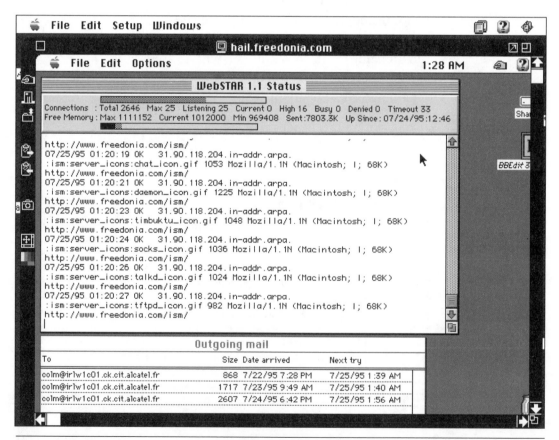

FIGURE 11.7 The Timbuktu Screen-Sharing Window

Screen-Sharing Options

Timbuktu Pro makes a row of buttons available along the left-hand border of the screen-sharing window, which are used to specify options for that Timbuktu Pro session.

Control/Observe: This button allows you to switch between controlling the server and observing it, if you initially connected using Control. This can be safely ignored for remote administration purposes.

Send Files: Allows you to send files to the host.

Exchange Files: Allows you to exchange files with the host.

Send Clipboard: Copies the contents of the clipboard from the local host to the remote host, allowing you to cut and paste between the two machines. This option is also available as Send Clipboard to Host from the Edit menu.

Get Clipboard: Copies the contents of the clipboard from the remote host to the local host. This option is also available as Get Clipboard from Host under the Edit menu.

Snapshot: Saves a screen shot of the remote host's desktop in PICT format, similar to Command-Shift-3 on the local machine.

Autoscroll: Switches between automatic and manual scrolling.

Color/Grayscale: Switches between color and grayscale if the remote host's Monitors control panel is set for a greater number of colors than the guest's. Switching to grayscale may improve the appearance of the screen, but won't affect screen drawing time—this is a separate setting from the Connect to hosts in color when possible option available from the Set Preferences item in the Setup menu, which will improve screen drawing times.

Switch Monitors (not pictured in Figure 11.7): Switches between monitors if the remote host has multiple displays.

Exchanging Files

As we stated in the Setting Up Timbuktu section, Timbuktu's Exchange Files option can at times be convenient for an administrator to use, even if you do have FTP enabled. We're not covering Send Files here, since it provides only a subset of the functionality of Exchange Files, making its usefulness in remote administration marginal—and FTP is better used as a cross-platform, nonproprietary solution for allowing users to drop files into incoming file directories.

Once you choose the Exchange Files option from either the Open Connection dialog or from the Exchange Files button in the Timbuktu screen-sharing window, you'll be prompted for a user name and password, and then be given the Exchange Files window, shown in Figure 11.8.

Exchange Files presents two standard file dialogs. You can simply select files or folders in the usual manner, and choose the Copy button to copy documents from one machine to another. Along with copying files, you can also remove files, create new folders, eject disks, and move to the desktop using the control row of icons.

Saving Connections

Finally, Timbuktu allows you to create a bookmark file to open subsequent connections to your server easily—you might place the

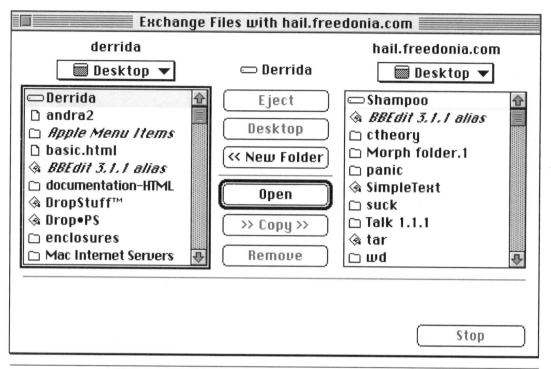

FIGURE 11.8 Timbuktu's Exchange Files Window

bookmark file on your desktop, or within the Apple menu for quick access. To save a connection, simply choose the Save Connections item from the File menu. You'll be prompted for the connection file's name, and you are given the option to save your password within the connection document, as well, although this isn't wise unless you can guarantee the physical security of your remote machine—if, say, your PowerBook is stolen, you'll probably have enough things to worry about without the added necessity of changing your Timbuktu password.

Monitoring Timbuktu Pro

Timbuktu Pro makes monitoring client connections to the server easy, by flashing the Timbuktu Pro icon after any connection, and displaying previously connected users along with the level of privilege for each connection made at the bottom of the Timbuktu Pro menu. The list of previous users can be cleared by selecting the Clear Previous Users item from the Timbuktu Pro menu.

Timbuktu Pro also maintains an activity log, available from the Show Activity Log . . . item in the Timbuktu Pro menu. Here, you can review previous connections to your Internet server, including failed login attempts and addresses of remote connections.

Okey Dokey

In the classic tradition of a utility doing one thing and doing it well, Dan Walkowski and Brent Pease's freeware Okey Dokey is a control panel that selects the default option for modal dialog boxes after a preset time limit. Modal dialog boxes are showstopping for an Mac OS-based Internet server, since they can stop other normally scheduled tasks from occurring until the dialog box is dismissed. Okey Dokey dismisses the dialog box using its default option, in the event some application throws up a modal dialog box while you're away from the machine.

Configuration of Okey Dokey, which occurs in the Okey Dokey control panel, shown in Figure 11.9, is easy: simply specify the amount of time before the default option for a dialog box should be automatically selected by Okey Dokey. You can also have Okey Dokey display the time remaining to select the default button in the lower left-hand portion of modal dialog boxes by checking the Display time remaining check box. Reboot the machine for your changes to take effect.

FIGURE 11.9 The Okey Dokey Control Panel

Keep It Up

Keep It Up, a shareware utility by Karl Pottie, will guarantee that the applications you specify—your server applications, most likely—continue to run, despite those pesky "unexpectedly quit" messages. Keep It Up monitors the processes running on your machine, and if an application that should be running isn't (that is, a user quit the program or the application crashed), Keep It Up will attempt to relaunch the program. You can also tell Keep It Up to restart the machine after a specified number of attempted relaunches by Keep It Up, to try to clean up what could be problems due to fragmented memory.

Application Surveillance

To specify the applications you'd like Keep It Up to watch, simply place aliases of the applications in the Keep It Up Items folder in the Preferences folder, created the first time you launch Keep It Up. You'll then want to place an alias of the Keep It Up application in the Startup Items folder of your System Folder, so that Keep It Up is launched each time your machine is restarted. Keep It Up will then, in turn, launch all its watched applications. Note: Keep It Up must be quit and relaunched in order for changes in the Keep It Up Items folder to take effect.

Keep It Up is configured through the dialog box available from the Preferences item in the File menu, shown in Figure 11.10. You can specify values for the following options:

- **Idle time before activation:** The amount of idle time—time without any mouse movements or keyboard strokes—Keep It Up will allow to pass before attempting to relaunch an application. If you're running your server apps on a dedicated machine, this number shouldn't matter, although you may want to set it to a low value in case an application is accidentally quit by a user.

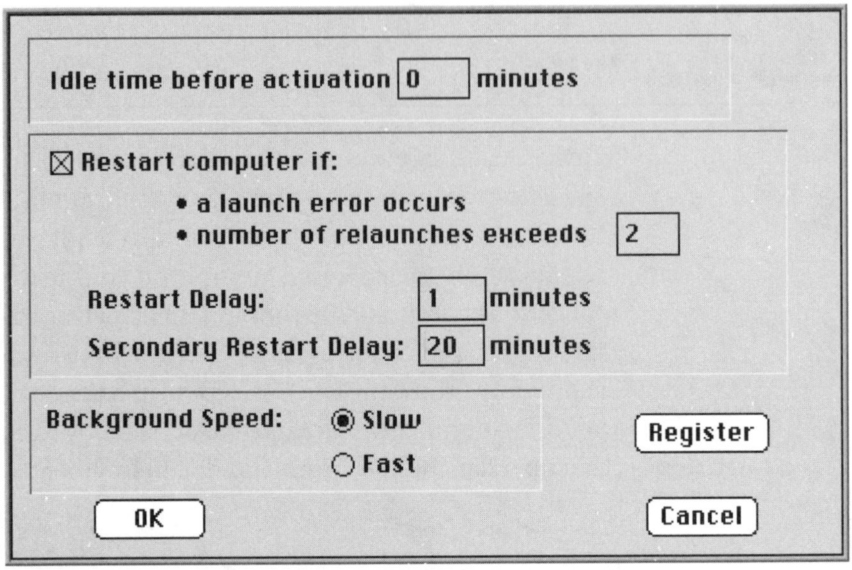

```
┌─────────────────────────────────────────────────────────────┐
│  ┌──────────────────────────────────────────────────────┐   │
│  │  Idle time before activation │0    │ minutes          │   │
│  └──────────────────────────────────────────────────────┘   │
│  ┌──────────────────────────────────────────────────────┐   │
│  │  ⊠ Restart computer if:                                │   │
│  │       • a launch error occurs                          │   │
│  │       • number of relaunches exceeds   │2    │         │   │
│  │                                                        │   │
│  │     Restart Delay:              │1 │ minutes           │   │
│  │     Secondary Restart Delay: │20│ minutes              │   │
│  └──────────────────────────────────────────────────────┘   │
│  ┌───────────────────────────────────┐                       │
│  │  Background Speed:   ◉ Slow        │      ┌──────────┐     │
│  │                      ○ Fast        │      │ Register │     │
│  │  ┌────────┐                                └──────────┘     │
│  │  │   OK   │                               ┌──────────┐     │
│  │  └────────┘                               │  Cancel  │     │
│  └───────────────────────────────────┘       └──────────┘     │
└─────────────────────────────────────────────────────────────┘
```

FIGURE 11.10 Keep It Up Preferences

■ **Restart computer if number of relaunches exceeds:** Keep It Up keeps track of how many times it relaunches an application; if the number of relaunches exceeds this number, it will attempt to restart the machine, in hopes of resolving problems stemming from fragmented memory. If the box is unchecked, Keep It Up will simply quit after this number instead of restarting the computer.

■ **Restart Delay:** The amount of time Keep It Up will wait before attempting to restart the machine, to allow for user intervention. For an unattended dedicated server, you can set this value very low.

■ **Secondary Restart Delay:** If Keep It Up finds that it isn't getting appropriate processing time—if some other application is misbehaving so that Keep It Up, and probably the other applications on your machine, can't get enough processing time to execute its instructions—Keep It Up can attempt to reboot the machine after the amount of time specified here passes. You'll want to set this to a long enough duration so that it doesn't restart the machine mistakenly, especially if you happen to run a foreground application that isn't good about giving up processing time to background applications.

- **Background Speed:** This is the amount of processor time Keep It Up uses when in the background to check for mouse movement or keyboard strokes, to prevent it from "missing" user actions and relaunching an application when you quit an application manually. On a dedicated server, you can comfortably set this to Slow.

Remember to place Keep It Up in your Startup Items folder in order for it to become active upon relaunch.

Through the Schedule item in the File menu, Keep It Up allows you to schedule times when it shouldn't be active—a feature you probably won't take advantage of if you're using your machine as a dedicated server—and periodic restarts of your computer. Periodic restarts can prevent problems related to fragmented memory, if it occurs, although there's a certain geek cred to be gained from claiming your server's been up continuously for a long period of time, which periodic rebooting doesn't allow you to partake of. Figure 11.11 shows Keep It Up configured to restart the machine daily at 3 A.M. You'll want to keep Clean Restart checked; this ensures that all applications exit cleanly before restarting the machine. Allowing Keep It Up to restart the machine without Clean Restart checked— the equivalent of pressing the Reset key on the machine—can cause more harm than good, in lost or corrupted data.

AutoBoot

AutoBoot is a companion shareware utility to Keep It Up, also by Karl Pottie. While Keep It Up tries to ensure that specific applications are kept running at all times, AutoBoot attempts to restart the computer in the case of system crashes and freezes.

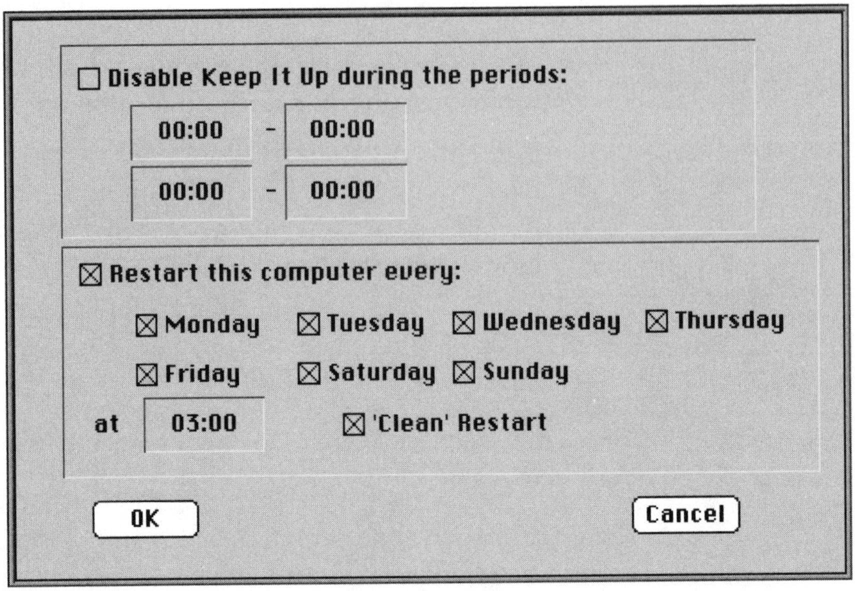

FIGURE 11.11 Keep It Up Schedule Window

Whether it's wise or necessary to run an autorebooting utility will remain up to you; if you're selective about the extensions and applications you run on your server, your system should be stable enough that an autorebooting utility is unnecessary. And, even if your machine crashes and is restarted automatically, whether that's a good thing is debatable. When a system goes down abruptly, it should really have its file systems checked and possibly repaired before futher work is done on it, to prevent compounding problems and risking data loss. However, although disk check and repair utilities exist for the Mac OS, none of them can currently be set up to run automatically at system startup time.

Still, if 24/7 service is important to you, and given the above caveats, AutoBoot can be quite useful. AutoBoot is installed by dropping the control panel onto your System Folder and restarting the machine. If you're running System 7.5.x, you'll also want to turn off (uncheck) the Shut Down Warning box in the General Controls control panel. AutoBoot can then be configured from the AutoBoot control panel, shown in Figure 11.12.

```
╔═══════════════════════════════════════╗
║ ▣▦═══ AutoBoot 1.4.1 ═══▦▦ ║
║ ┌─⊠ Restart after System Error ─┐ ║
║ │                               │ ║
║ │  Restart Delay : 0  [▲▼] minutes. │ ║
║ └───────────────────────────────┘ ║
║                                       ║
║ ┌─⊠ Restart after Freeze Up ────┐ ║
║ │                               │ ║
║ │  Inactivity Period : 10 [▲▼] minutes. │ ║
║ └───────────────────────────────┘ ║
║ ┌─ Options ─────────────────────┐ ║
║ │ ☐ Post Notification on Restart │ ║
║ │ ⊠ Maintain Log File           │ ║
║ └───────────────────────────────┘ ║
║ ┌─────────────────────────────────┐ ║
║ │                    version 1.4.1 │ ║
║ │ AutoBoot                         │ ║
║ │ Carl Steadman (one user)         │ ║
║ └─────────────────────────────────┘ ║
╚═══════════════════════════════════════╝
```

FIGURE 11.12
The AutoBoot Control Panel

From the AutoBoot control panel, you have four options:

- **Restart after System Error:** When this box is checked, AutoBoot will attempt to restart the machine after the number of minutes specified here has passed, after it detects a system error.

- **Restart after Freeze Up:** If this box is checked, AutoBoot will attempt to restart the machine after it logs a lack of normal, low-level system activity for the amount of time specified.

- **Post Notification on Restart:** This option puts up a dialog box notifying a user of a restart. The notification is dismissed after 10 minutes. Since this alert will disable all foreground processing until the dialog box is dismissed, and since your main objective in running AutoBoot is to maintain services continuously while the machine is unattended, you'll probably want to leave this box unchecked.

- **Maintain Log File:** This option will write out information on each restart to a file called AutoBoot log in the Preferences folder of your System folder, recording the date and time of all reboots, and potentially helping you locate any problems. You'll want to leave this item checked.

 Remote Process Management Using FTPd

FTPd includes process control as part of its extended feature set—with FTPd, you can quit or launch applications on a remote Mac. Although this gives you only a very limited tool set with which to control a remote Mac, FTPd can be used, for example, to transfer DNS database files from a UNIX box running BIND to a Mac running MIND, and then to quit and restart MIND for the changes to take effect.

To take advantage of FTPd's process control, you'll need to allow process control by checking the appropriate box in the Owner Restrictions area of the Security dialog of FTP Setup. You can then access the server using a text-based FTP client, or via Telnet. In Figure 11.13, NCSA Telnet is being used to connect to the machine hail.freedonia.com using the control port of FTPd—port 21—

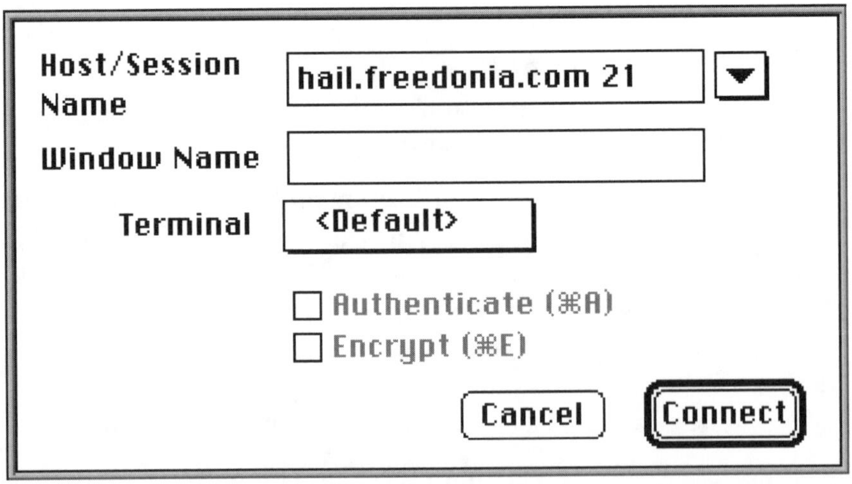

FIGURE 11.13 Connecting to FTPd via a Telnet session.

so that the user types **hail.freedonia.com 21** in the Host/Session Name box.

After the connection is made, you'll need to supply a user name and password using the FTP commands **user** and **pass**. Note that the password is sent as clear text (without any encoding or encryption) and echoed to the screen:

```
220 Peter's Macintosh FTP daemon v3.0.0 awaits your command.
user carl
331 Password required.
pass a4ubk12!
230-Hail Freedonia!
230 Owner logged in to 1 volumes, directory is "/".
```

You can then successively issue the help command to remember the syntax of the process control commands:

```
help
214-The following commands are  implemented:
    USER    PASS    HELP    QUIT    SMNT    SITE    NLST    LIST
    CWD     XCWD    PORT    CDUP    XCUP    PWD     XPWD    RETR
    STOR    NOOP    ACCT    ALLO    MODE    STRU    TYPE    MACB
    ABOR    SYST    DELE    RMD     XRMD    MKD     XMKD    PASV
    RNFR    RNTO
214 Send FTPd bug reports to peter@kagi.com
help site
214 SITE ACHILPQSUV - See "HELP SITE <letter>".
help site a
214 SITE A LIST|NLST|OAPP crea|QUIT crea—Process control
```

A **site a list** will list all the programs that are currently running; **site a quit** [*application code*] will quit the selected application; and **site a oapp** [*application code*] will quit the selected application. Here we'll quit and restart MIND:

```
site a list
200-Process list follows:
    MACS Finder
    hhgg File Sharing Extension
    MIND MIND
```

```
     MaiL Apple Internet Mail Server
     FTPd FTPd
     cron cron
     McPL MacPerl
200 7 processes.
```
site a quit MIND
```
200 Quit sent.
```
site a list
```
200-Process list follows:
     MACS Finder
     hhgg File Sharing Extension
     MaiL Apple Internet Mail Server
     FTPd FTPd
     cron cron
     McPL MacPerl
200 6 processes.
```
site a oapp MIND
```
200 Application Launched.
```
site a list
```
200-Process list follows:
     MACS Finder
     hhgg File Sharing Extension
     MaiL Apple Internet Mail Server
     FTPd FTPd
     cron cron
     McPL MacPerl
     MIND MIND
200 7 processes.
```

Note that the application codes are case-sensitive; mind would be considered a different application from MiND or MIND.

We can then close the FTP session by issuing the **quit** command, and allow Peter's Macintosh FTP daemon to exchange a final pleasantry:

```
quit
221 Nice chatting with you.
```

Uniform Resource Locators

A Uniform Resource Locator (URL) is a string that identifies the location of a resource somewhere on the Internet. There is work being done to define other standard formats to describe resources on the Internet, such as URNs and URCs; see Other URs, later in this appendix.

Syntax

General Syntax

In general, a URL is represented as:

```
scheme:scheme_specific_part
```

in which the *scheme* is the protocol used to refer to the resource (such as HTTP or Gopher), and the *scheme specific part* is a specific instance of the scheme being used. The scheme and scheme-specific part are separated by a colon. For example,

```
mailto:carl@freedonia.com
```

refers to a scheme of type `mailto`, and a scheme specific part of carl@freedonia.com, which, for a `mailto`-type resource, is interpreted as an Internet mail account.

Generic Scheme-Specific Part

In general, URLs that refer to a scheme that directly retrieves information from a server (such as Web or Gopher) use a scheme-specific part in the form:

```
//user:password@host:port/path;params?querystring#fragment
```

The values for the scheme-specific part are described as follows:

- **user (optional):** An optional user name for those schemes, such as FTP, that allow a user name.
- **password (optional):** An optional password can follow the user name, separated by a colon.
- **host:** The host name or its IP address.
- **port (optional):** A port to connect to. If no port is specified, most schemes default to the standard port for the protocol being used.
- **path (optional):** An optional pathname, using the slash (/) as a delimiter.

The slash between the host name and the path is not part of the path; don't make the assumption that paths begin from the root directory of a host's file structure. While there is a limited mapping between the paths of the file system of the machine the server is running on and the paths of the server itself, the details of that mapping will vary from server to server. See the section discussing FTP, upcoming, for details on encoding root directory access.

Generally, paths ending in a slash refer to directories, while those not ending in a slash refer to files; see the specific schemes, upcoming, for details on how paths are implemented for each scheme.

You may also use *relative paths* in the construction of URLs. Once a base URL is established (either by the client, using the first URL to access a document tree, or the document itself, using the base tag for HTML documents), you can use relative paths under some schemes (for example, HTTP):

./ refers to the same directory as the base reference

../ refers to one directory above the base reference

../../ refers to two directories above the base reference, and so on.

For example, for a base path of a/b/c/d,

./ refers to a/b/c/

../e refers to a/b/e

../../e refers to a/e

- **;params (optional):** For those schemes, such as FTP, that allow optional parameters.

- **querystring (optional):** For those objects that allow an optional query string, such as CGI scripts.

- **fragment (optional):** For those schemes, such as HTTP, that allow an optional fragment, preceded by a crosshatch (#) symbol. This is not considered part of a URL, and is the responsibility of the client, rather than the server, to interpret.

Reserved Characters

URLs use the ASCII character set, and reserve the characters ;, /, ?, :, @, =, and & for special use. The URL specification also declares the space character, the quote mark, <, >, #, %, {, } , |, \, ^, ~, [,], and ` as unsafe, because of potential conflicts with delimiters, transcribers, and gateways. Any reserved or unsafe character or character not in the ASCII character set must be escaped using a percent sign and its hexadecimal ASCII code. For example, a space is represented as %20. It's best if you can avoid the use of characters that would need to be escaped within your URLs.

Case-Sensitivity

URL scheme-specific parts may be case-sensitive; <http://www.freedonia.com/ducks.html> may refer to a different resource than <http://www.freedonia.com/Ducks.html>, although this is not necessarily the case. Because case is only sometimes significant, and since beginning users and print publications often don't realize URLs can be case-sensitive, it is recommended that you name your resources such that case doesn't become an issue; that is, name all your Web documents (and other resources you administer) in all lowercase. This gives you one less thing to worry about, as there will then be no special cases. Do the same for special characters: avoid using filenames that will result in URLs with escaped characters.

Delimiters

When run in text, URLs may be optionally preceded by the characters URL: to identify them as such, and they may be set off by the angle brackets (< and >). As a result, you might see any of these forms of the same address:

```
http://www.freedonia.com/
URL:http://www.freedonia.com/
<http://www.freedonia.com/>
<URL:http://www.freedonia.com/>
```

If a long URL needs to be broken into multiple lines, it's especially important to use angle brackets so that the URL can be easily delimited from other text. The form set off by angle brackets only—the third example, preceding—is most common; a form that includes the URL: prefix will become important only when there are other URI types in common use (see Other URs, upcoming).

Specific URL Schemes

There are eight URL schemes in common use: file, ftp, gopher, http, mailto, news, nntp, and telnet. We'll cover the specifics of each separately.

file

```
file://host/path
```

The file scheme indicates a file available from a particular machine, in which host can be either a domain name, the string "localhost," or an empty string, the latter two indicating a file on the machine on which the URL is being interpreted.

Since file doesn't specify a network protocol for files on remote hosts, its use across hosts is limited.

Examples:

```
file://zeppo/www/index.html
```

Refers to the file index.html in the directory www on the
machine zeppo.
`file:///www/index.html`
Refers to the file index.html in the directory www on the
local host.

ftp

`ftp://user:password@host:port/path;type=typecode`
default port is 69

The ftp scheme is used to refer to directories and files available via
the File Transfer Protocol (FTP), as either an anonymous or vali-
dated user. URLs referring to a resource available via anonymous
FTP are the most common, which contain no user name or password; instead, the user name anonymous and a password consisting
of the end user's e-mail address is used. FTP URLs may alternatively
contain only a user name, in which case, the end user should be
prompted for a password, or both a user name and password. If
you're using a password within an FTP URL, keep in mind there's no
attempt to hide or protect the password in any way.

Within the FTP path, each successive string followed by a slash (/) is
interpreted as a CWD (change working directory) command; a final
string not followed by a slash, if present, is interpreted as a RETR
(retrieve) command. Note that the slash character is reserved and
must be encoded if needed explicitly; if an FTP site's default directory is /pub, and you need to point to the root directory /, you must
encode a slash to go explicitly to the root directory. For example, the
URL <ftp://ftp.freedonia.com/utilities/> may or may not be relative
to the default directory—that is, it may point to the directory /utili-
ties or to the directory /public/utilities. In the latter case, you can
use an escaped slash, and form the URL <ftp://ftp.freedonia.com/
%2Futilities/>.

The ;type=typecode portion of the FTP URL is optional. If a type
isn't specified, the client attempts to deduce the type from the specified file's extension, if one is present. Typecode can be d, a, or i, in
which d refers to a directory listing, a refers to a text file (ASCII),
and i refers to a binary file (image).

You will occassionally see an HTML file served via FTP. Most Web browsers will display an HTML document retrieved via FTP directly, if it recognizes it as an HTML file either by its file extension or by its content.

Examples:

> ftp://ftp.hawaii.edu/mirrors/info-mac/
> *Connect to the FTP server of the host ftp.hawaii.edu, and retrieve the directory listing for mirrors/info-mac.*

> ftp://rtfm.mit.edu/pub/usenet-by-group/news.answers/
> xanadu-faq
> *Connect to the FTP server of the host rtfm.mit.edu, change to the directory pub/usenet-by-group/news.answers, and retrieve the file xanadu-faq.*

> ftp://ftp.freedonia.com:25713/public/games/duckshoot.bin;
> type=i
> *Connect to the FTP server of the host ftp.freedonia.com on port 25713, and change to the directory public/games. Then retrieve the file duckshoot.bin as a binary image, since it is a compressed binary executable program.*

gopher

> gopher://host[:port]/[gophertype selector[%09 search[%09
> gopher+_string]]]
> *default port is 70*

A URL specifying a Gopher resource is labeled as the scheme Gopher. The optional Gopher-type code identifies the data type of the resource for the client. The optional selector string points to the Gopher resource within the Gopher hierarchy, and the optional search and Gopher+ string further modifies the resource being referred to.

The most common Gopher types are 0, which refers to a file; 1, which refers to a directory; and 7, which refers to a searchable index database. Gopher types are sometimes "doubled" within URLs, as in the first example following; in these cases, the selector string begins with a copy of the Gopher type character.

Examples:

```
gopher://gopher.tc.umn.edu/11/Information%20About%20Gopher
```
retrieves the gopher directory "Information About Gopher"

```
gopher://mudhoney.micro.umn.edu/00/Gopher.FAQ
```
retrieves the gopher document "Gopher.FAQ"

```
gopher://mudhoney.micro.umn.edu:4326/7?nuts
```
performs a gopher search for nuts, using port 4326 of the gopher server mudhoney.micro.umn.edu

http

```
http://host:port/path?querystring#fragment
```
default port is 80

A URL of type HTTP designates a resource available via the Hypertext Transfer Protocol (HTTP). Most HTML and related files are delivered using the HTTP protocol.

Paths ending in a slash refer to a directory, and the file retrieved through the URL should be the default file for that directory. Depending upon the HTTP server being referenced, the file returned may be an on-the-fly-generated listing of the directory's contents, a file within the directory labeled as the default file (usually named index.html), or an error message indicating that no file was available. Paths not ending in a slash indicate a filename.

An optional query string may be specified using a question mark (?) followed by a string. Any spaces within the query string are encoded as the plus character (+); interpretation and processing of the query string varies according to the host machine.

An optional fragment isn't considered part of the URL, and is not passed on to the server, but instead interpreted within the client.

Examples:

```
http://www.freedonia.com:6243/
```
Connect to port 6243 of the host www.freedonia.com, and get the default document or index for the top-most directory of the server.

```
http://www.bugs.org/insects/bees.html
```
Retrieve the document bees.html from the directory insects on the server www.bugs.org.

```
http://www.hotwired.com/cgi-bin/users/search?wordquery=
crypto+clipper
```
Connect to the host www.hotwired.com, and execute a script called search, passing the values for a named key "wordquery" as "crypto" and "clipper".

mailto

```
mailto:mail_account
```

A URL of type mailto specifies an Internet e-mail account. Any percent signs (%) within the address need to be encoded as %25.

Example:

```
mailto:carl@freedonia.com
mailto:listserv%25yalevm.bitnet@cunyvm.cuny.edu
```

news

```
news:newsgroup_name
news:message_id
```

URLs of type news point to Usenet resources, and may be in one of two forms. The first type, news:newsgroup_name, refers to an entire newsgroup as a period-deliminited hierarchical name, and will cause a newsreader or news-capable browser to show a list of articles available within that newsgroup for reading. A special case of news:* indicates all newsgroups available to the client.

The second type, news:message_id, refers to a specific Usenet message by its unique message ID in the form unique_id@domain_ name. Note that Usenet messages date-expire and are sometimes canceled, so any particular message should be available for only a few weeks in a newsgroup with moderate traffic.

Unlike most other schemes, news does not specify a specific news server from which articles should be retrieved. The specific news server used is up to the client, and is often a local server provided for local use only. Despite this, news:message_id URL will point to the same article, regardless of which news server is used, since message IDs are unique for each message posted to Usenet.

Examples:

> news:comp.infosystems.www.providers
> *refers to the newsgroup "comp.infosystems.www.providers"*

> news:carl-3103952231340001@harpo.freedonia.com
> *refers to a news article with message-ID <carl-3103952231340001@harpo.freedonia.com>*

nntp

> nntp://host:port/newsgroup-name/article-number
> *Port default is 119.*

A URL of type nntp also refers to a Usenet resource, as an instance of a specific news server. Because of the nature of news (with many local servers, each loosely replicating the contents of each other), news servers are often configured to allow only local access. URLs with a wide audience should use the news scheme instead.

Example:

> nntp://news.freedonia.com/comp.infosystems.www.providers/
> carl-3103952231340001@harpo.freedonia.com

telnet

> telnet://user:password@host:port/
> *Port default is 23.*

The Telnet scheme refers to an interactive Telnet session on a remote host.

> telnet://spacebar.com:7227
> *refers to an interactive session on port 7227 of the host spacebar.com*

```
telnet://whois@rs.internic.net
refers to an interactive session on the host
rs.internic.net, logging in as the user "whois".
```

Other URs

You'll occasionally (and perhaps increasingly) see mention of three other UR types: URIs, URNs, and URCs.

Universal Resource Identifier (URI)

A Universal Resource Identifier (URI) is any address or name that refers to an object. URLs and URNs are instances of URIs.

Uniform Resource Name (URN)

A Uniform Resource Name (URN) is meant to refer to an object with greater persistance than a URL does. Unlike a URL, a URN will identify a resource, not its location—a resource referred to by a URN might have multiple instances, might move from one location to another, or might not exist at all.

URNs will probably be implemented as a distributed naming system with hierarchical naming authorities, as with the Domain Name System.

Uniform Resource Characteristics (URC)

Uniform Resource Characteristics (URC) will provide meta-level information about a resource, such as author, owner, content type, or access restrictions.

Character Entities

Character entities are used to display special and reserved characters within HTML documents. Text within HTML documents defaults to the ISO-Latin-1 character set, which is a superset of ASCII. ISO-Latin-1 (also referred to as ISO 8859/1) is made up of a functional equivalent of the 128-character ASCII character set (ISO 646), and an additional 96 special characters, which, along with each character's entity, is listed in table B.1, ISO-Latin-1 Character Entities. A character entity, which, in HTML, always begins with an ampersand and ends with a semicolon, is a way of representing these special characters (and the reserved characters <, >, and &) using the ASCII character set.

The ISO-Latin-1 character entities listed in Table B.1 are neccessarily valid only for the default ISO-Latin-1 character encoding of HTML; it is possible for servers to specify other character encodings to clients— for example, in order to provide documents in non-Western European languages.

The character entities an HTML author needs to be particularly aware of are the angle brackets (< and >) and ampersand (&), which are reserved characters in HTML and need to be escaped for proper rendering within the text of a document. It's not a requirement that you use character entities for the special characters within the ISO-Latin-1 character set, if you can enter these characters directly from your keyboard; however, because of different character set mappings, filetypes, and transfer mechanisms, it's always a good idea to use the following entities instead of the character itself, to guarantee the proper display of these characters across browsers.

TABLE B.1 ISO-Latin-1 Character Entities

Character	Named Entity	Numeric Entity	Description
		&#00; - &#08;	unused
		&#09;	horizontal tab
		&#10;	line feed
		&#11; - &#31;	unused
		&#32;	space
!		&#33;	exclamation mark
"	&quot;	&#34;	double quotation mark
#		&#35;	number sign
$		&#36;	dollar sign
%		&#37;	percent sign
&	&amp;	&#38;	ampersand
'		&#39;	apostrophe
)		&#40;	right parenthesis
(		&#41;	left parenthesis
*		&#42;	asterisk
+		&#43;	plus sign
,		&#44;	comma
-		&#45;	hyphen
.		&#46;	period
/		&#47;	slash
0 - 9		0 - 9	digits 0-9
:		&#58;	colon
;		&#59;	semicolon
<	&lt;	&#60;	less than sign
=		&#61;	equal sign
>	&gt;	&#62;	greater than sign
?		&#63;	question mark
@		&#64;	commercial at
A - Z		A - Z	uppercase letters A-Z
[		&#91;	left square bracket
\		&#92;	backslash
]		&#93;	right square bracket
^		&#94;	caret
_		&#95;	horizontal bar (underscore)
`		&#96;	grave accent

TABLE B.1 (Continued)

Character	Named Entity	Numeric Entity	Description
a - z		a-z	lowercase letters a-z
{		&#123;	left curly brace
|		|	vertical bar
}		&#125;	right curly brace
~		&#126;	tilde
		&#127; - Ÿ	unused
			nonbreaking space
¡		&#161;	inverted exclamation
¢		&#162;	cent sign
£		&#163;	pound sterling
¤		&#164;	general currency sign
¥		&#165;	yen sign
¦		&#166;	broken vertical bar
§		&#167;	section sign
¨		&#168;	umlaut (dieresis)
©	&copy;	&#169;	copyright
ª		&#170;	feminine ordinal
«		&#171;	left angle quote, guillemet left
¬		&#172;	not sign
-		&#173;	soft hyphen
®	&reg;	&#174;	registered trademark
¯		&#175;	macron accent
°		&#176;	degree sign
±		&#177;	plus or minus
2		&#178;	superscript two
3		&#179;	superscript three
´		&#180;	acute accent
µ		&#181;	micro sign
¶		&#182;	paragraph sign
•		&#183;	middle dot
¸		&#184;	cedilla
1		&#185;	superscript one
º		&#186;	masculine ordinal
»		&#187;	right angle quote, guillemet right
1/4		&#188;	one-fourth

TABLE B.1 (Continued)

Character	Named Entity	Numeric Entity	Description
1/2		&#189;	one-half
3/4		&#190;	three-fourths
¿		&#191;	inverted question mark
À	&Agrave;	&#192;	uppercase A, grave accent
Á	&Aacute;	&#193;	uppercase A, acute accent
Â	&Acirc;	&#194;	uppercase A, circumflex accent
Ã	&Atilde;	&#195;	uppercase A, tilde
Ä	&Auml;	&#196;	uppercase A, dieresis or umlaut mark
Å	&Aring;	&#197;	uppercase A, ring
Æ	&AElig;	&#198;	uppercase AE dipthong (ligature)
Ç	&Ccedil;	&#199;	uppercase C, cedilla
È	&Egrave;	&#200;	uppercase E, grave accent
É	&Eacute;	&#201;	uppercase E, acute accent
Ê	&Ecirc;	&#202;	uppercase E, circumflex accent
Ë	&Euml;	&#203;	uppercase E, dieresis or umlaut mark
Ì	&Igrave;	&#204;	uppercase I, grave accent
Í	&Iacute;	&#205;	uppercase I, acute accent
Î	&Icirc;	&#206;	uppercase I, circumflex accent
Ï	&Iuml;	&#207;	uppercase I, dieresis or umlaut mark
Ð	&ETH;	&#208;	uppercase Eth, Icelandic
Ñ	&Ntilde;	&#209;	uppercase N, tilde
Ò	&Ograve;	&#210;	uppercase O, grave accent
Ó	&Oacute;	&#211;	uppercase O, acute accent
Ô	&Ocirc;	&#212;	uppercase O, circumflex accent
Õ	&Otilde;	&#213;	uppercase O, tilde
Ö	&Ouml;	&#214;	uppercase O, dieresis or umlaut mark
×		&#215;	multiply sign
Ø	&Oslash;	&#216;	uppercase O, slash
Ù	&Ugrave;	&#217;	uppercase U, grave accent
Ú	&Uacute;	&#218;	uppercase U, acute accent
Û	&Ucirc;	&#219;	uppercase U, circumflex accent
Ü	&Uuml;	&#220;	uppercase U, dieresis or umlaut mark
Ý	&Yacute;	&#221;	uppercase Y, acute accent
Þ	&THORN;	&#222;	uppercase THORN, Icelandic
ß	&szlig;	&#223;	lowercase sharp s, German (sz ligature)

TABLE B.1 (Continued)

Character	Named Entity	Numeric Entity	Description
à	&agrave;	&#224;	lowercase a, grave accent
á	&aacute;	&#225;	lowercase a, acute accent
â	&acirc;	&#226;	lowercase a, circumflex accent
ã	&atilde;	&#227;	lowercase a, tilde
ä	&auml;	&#228;	lowercase a, dieresis or umlaut mark
å	&aring;	&#229;	lowercase a, ring
æ	&aelig;	&#230;	lowercase ae dipthong (ligature)
ç	&ccedil;	&#231;	lowercase c, cedilla
è	&egrave;	&#232;	lowercase e, grave accent
é	&eacute;	&#233;	lowercase e, acute accent
ê	&ecirc;	&#234;	lowercase e, circumflex accent
ë	&euml;	&#235;	lowercase e, dieresis or umlaut mark
ì	&igrave;	&#236;	lowercase i, grave accent
í	&iacute;	&#237;	lowercase i, acute accent
î	&icirc;	&#238;	lowercase i, circumflex accent
ï	&iuml;	&#239;	lowercase i, dieresis or umlaut mark
ð	&eth;	&#240;	lowercase eth, Icelandic
ñ	&ntilde;	&#241;	lowercase n, tilde
ò	&ograve;	&#242;	lowercase o, grave accent
ó	&oacute;	&#243;	lowercase o, acute accent
ô	&ocirc;	&#244;	lowercase o, circumflex accent
õ	&otilde;	&#245;	lowercase o, tilde
ö	&ouml;	&#246;	lowercase o, dieresis or umlaut mark
÷		&#247;	division sign
ø	&oslash;	&#248;	lowercase o, slash
ù	&ugrave;	&#249;	lowercase u, grave accent
ú	&uacute;	&#250;	lowercase u, acute accent
û	&ucirc;	&#251;	lowercase u, circumflex accent
ü	&uuml;	&#252;	lowercase u, dieresis or umlaut mark
ý	&yacute;	&#253;	lowercase y, acute accent
þ	&thorn;	&#254;	lowercase thorn, Icelandic
ÿ	&yuml;	&#255;	lowercase y, dieresis or umlaut mark

The CD-ROM

J ust about every piece of software we've written about in this book is available on the Internet, either as a complete software package or as a functional demo. But it can be time-consuming to track a lot of this software down, and, depending upon your network connection, it might be difficult to rationalize downloading a megabyte of data just to fiddle with a program in order to see if it's the tool you're looking for.

To make things a little easier, we've included a CD-ROM with *Providing Internet Services via the Mac OS,* so much of the software we've mentioned is available to you immediately. This appendix is a guide to what's on the CD-ROM.

Keep in mind that the inclusion of software on the CD-ROM doesn't mean that you own the software. A specific software package might be freeware, demoware, or shareware. If a piece of software is freeware, you're entitled to use it to your heart's content. If it's demoware, the software is time-limited or crippled in some other way; you'll need to purchase the commercial package to use it past the demo period or to make the software fully functional. If it's shareware, you're bound to pay the shareware fee if you continue to use it, according to the documentation that came with the package. Please pay your shareware fees—shareware authors can't continue to develop and support their software if you don't pay your fees, and shareware is a cool method of distribution.

For information on updates of the software on the CD-ROM and on additional software packages, point your Web client to the *Providing Internet Services via the Mac OS* Web site at <http://www.pism.com/>.

ACME Script Widgets

ACME Technologies' ACME Script Widgets is a $29 shareware collection of AppleScript Scripting Additions that provides text and list manipulation capabilities.

Acrobat Reader

Adobe Systems' Acrobat Reader is a free application that lets you view and print PDF (Portable Document Format) files.

Adobe PageMill

Adobe Systems' PageMill is a commercial HTML editing tool. Rather than editing raw HTML, PageMill lets you assemble Web pages just as if you were working on a word processor or in a page-layout program. A demonstration version has been included on the CD-ROM.

AIMS LocalTalk Bridge

Chris Owen's AIMS Localtalk Bridge is a $10 shareware LocalTalk bridge between AIMS (Apple Internet Mail Server) and Qualcomm's Eudora mail client.

AutoBoot

Karl Pottie's AutoBoot is a $20 shareware control panel that restarts your computer after it crashes or locks up, which is useful when your computer is running unattended as a server.

AutoShare

Mikael Hansen's AutoShare is a free application that works in conjunction with AIMS to provide auto-reply mailbot and mailing list services.

BBEdit Lite

Bare Bones Software's BBEdit Lite is a free text editor that's useful for editing HTML documents. Also included is a demonstration version of the commercial BBEdit.

BBEdit HTML Tools

Lindsay Davies' BBEdit HTML Tools is a free set of HTML-specific extensions to BBEdit that make editing HTML documents in BBEdit easier.

Chat

Nathan Neulinger's Chat is a $10 shareware application that lets a Macintosh serve as a simple Internet chat room, in order to host text-based discussions among two or more people.

clip2gif

Yves Piguet's clip2gif is a free utility used to convert images between PICT, GIF, TIFF, and JPEG formats. Conversions are completely scriptable, making clip2gif useful for CGI scripts.

ColorFinder

Acme Technologies' ColorFinder is a free application that allows you to generate the hex value for any color using an eyedropper tool or color wheel. Some Web browsers support specifying a hex value in order to set color attributes.

cron

Chris Johnson's cron is a free application that executes commands at specified dates and times. In conjunction with a scripting language or scriptable application it can be useful in automating various server functions.

Daemon

Stairways Software's Daemon is a free application that acts as a Finger, Whois, Ident, Daytime, and Time protocol server.

FireShare

Jerry Stratton's FireShare is a $10 liberalware (see the accompanying documentation) collection of AppleScripts that works in conjunction with AIMS in order to provide auto-reply mailbot, mailing list, and file services.

FlattenMooV

Robert Hennessy's FlattenMooV is a free application that converts QuickTime movies into documents viewable by UNIX and Windows machines, in addition to Macs.

FTPd

Stairways Software's FTPd is a $10 shareware FTP, Web, and Gopher server.

FTPShare

White Pine Software's FTPShare is a commercial FTP server. A demonstration version has been included on the CD-ROM.

Hologate

Hologate is a commercial gateway between Microsoft Mail, QuickMail, FirstClass, other mail systems, and the Internet. A demonstration version has been included on the CD-ROM.

InterServer Publisher

InterCon Systems' InterServer Publisher is a commercial Web, Gopher, FTP, and Finger server. A demonstration version has been included on the CD-ROM. You'll need to get a demonstration serial number in order to use this version for a limited time. To get that serial number, connect to <http://www.intercon.com/demokey/demokey.html> or by mailing **demo@intercon.com**.

Keep It Up

Karl Pottie's Keep It Up is a $25 shareware application that ensures certain applications are always running on your Mac. If an application quits unexpectedly, Keep It Up will attempt to relaunch it. If it fails to relaunch, Keep It Up can restart the computer.

ListSTAR

StarNine Technologies' ListSTAR is a commercial e-mail–on–demand and mailing list server. Demonstration versions of all four versions of ListSTAR—SMTP, POP, QuickMail, and Microsoft Mail—have been included on this CD-ROM.

Macintosh Internet Name Daemon (MIND)

ACME Technologies' Macintosh Internet Name Daemon (MIND) is a free domain name server.

Macjordomo

Michele Fuortes' Macjordomo is a free application that uses both POP and SMTP to act as a mailing list server. Since its only requirement is a POP account, it can work with any virtually any Internet-based mail server.

MacPerl

Matthias Neeracher's MacPerl is a free port of Larry Wall's Perl that runs under the Mac OS. Perl is a scripting language often used for creating Web server CGI scripts. The use of Perl is governed under GNU "Copyleft" or the Perl Artistic License.

MapServe

Kelly Campbell's MapServe is a $20 shareware Web server CGI that allows you to provide image maps on your Web pages.

MacTCP Watcher

Stairways Software's MacTCP Watcher is a free application that lets you check on the TCP status of your computer and perform Ping, UDP, TCP, and DNS requests. It's useful in testing the network connectivity of your host to other hosts.

MacTraceroute

Jim Browne's MacTraceroute is a free application that works in conjunction with the Traceroute Ethernet LAP to display the route an IP packet follows to an Internet host.

Negative Space Collection

Jerry Stratton's Negative Space Collection is a $10 shareware collection of AppleScript-based CGI scripts.

NetCloak

Maxxum Development's NetCloak is a commercial Web server CGI that allows you to generate dynamic HTML pages. A demonstration version has been included on the CD-ROM.

NetForms

Maxxum Development's NetForms is a commercial Web server CGI that allows information entered by users of your server to be automatically converted to formatted HTML documents, which can then be read by other Web clients. A demonstration version has been included on the CD-ROM.

NetWings

NetWings Software's NetWings is a commercial mail, list, Gopher, and Web server built atop ACI US' 4Th Dimension database program. A demonstration version has been included on the CD-ROM.

Overlord Internet Gateway

NetWings Software's Overlord Internet Gateway is a caching proxy server with a firewalled software gateway between your Internet connection and a LocalTalk LAN. A demonstration version has been included on the CD-ROM.

PhotoGIF

BoxTop Software's PhotoGIF is a $25 shareware plug-in for Adobe Photoshop that makes it easy to import and export transparent, interlaced GIF files—used on Web pages—from Photoshop.

ProJPEG

BoxTop Software's ProJPEG is a $25 shareware plug-in for Adobe Photoshop that allows you to import and export Progressive JPEG images, a format supported by some Web browsers.

QuickDNS Lite

Men and Mice's QuickDNS Lite is a $49 shareware caching-only domain name server.

Russell Owen's FileMaker CGI

Russell Owen's FileMaker CGI is a free CGI application for Web servers. It allows you to serve information from Claris FileMaker databases on the Web.

Script Daemon

Starways Software's Script Daemon is a free background application that lets you telnet to a Mac OS-based server and issue AppleScript commands via a command line.

ServerStat Lite

Kitchen Sink Software's ServerStat Lite is a $20 shareware application that analyzes GopherSurfer, MacHTTP, and WebSTAR log files and reports connection statistics. It also serves as a demonstration version of the commercial ServerStat application.

SOCKS

Starways Software's SOCKS is a $50 shareware application that implements version 4 of the SOCKS protocol, which provides screening, authentication, and logging for application-level connections. SOCKS can act as one part of a Mac OS-based firewall solution.

Talk

Starways Software's Talk is a $5 shareware implementation of the UNIX Talk protocol, which allows real-time text-based conversations between two persons.

TFTPd

Stairways Software's TFTPd is a $10 shareware application that serves files via the Trivial File Transfer Protocol (TFTP), which is distinct from the File Transfer Protocol (FTP). TFTP does not require account names or passwords.

Timbuktu Pro

Farallon's Timbuktu Pro is a commercial screen-sharing application that can be used for remote administration of Mac OS-based servers. Timbuktu Pro can also be used to facilitate a workgroup environment. A demonstration version has been included on the CD-ROM.

Transparency

Aaron Giles' Transparency is a free application that converts regular GIF images into transparent GIFs for use on Web pages.

WebMap

Rowland Smith's WebMap is a $20 shareware utility for creating image map files for use with Web servers.

WebSTAR

StarNine Technologies' WebSTAR is a commercial Web server. A demonstration version has been included on the CD-ROM.

WebStat

Phil Harvey's WebStat is a free application that provides log summaries from standard-format MacHTTP or WebSTAR logs.

Permissions

Acme Script Widgets and Mac Internet Name Daemon (MIND) are trademarks of Acme Technologies. Acme Technologies can be reached at support@acme-tech.com, <http://www.acmetech.com>, or by telephone at (203) 856-0631.

Acrobat Reader and Adobe PageMill are trademarks of Adobe Systems Incorporated, located at 1585 Charleston Road, P.O. Box 7900, Mountain View, CA 94039-7900. They can be reached at (415) 961-4400 (voice), (415) 961-3769 (fax) or online at <http://www.adobe.com/>.

AutoBoot and Keep It Up. Copyright © 1995 Karl Pottie. You may not sell this product or bundle it with any other products (commercial or otherwise) without explicit written permission from Karl Pottie. You may not modify this software or the documentation in any way or distribute this software without the documentation or the other files and applications.

BBEdit HTML Tools. Copyright © 1995, 1996 Lindsay Davies. E-mail: Lindsay.Davies@pobox.com.

BBEdit Lite and BBEdit are products of Bare Bones Software, Inc., P.O. Box 108, Bedford, MA 01730-0108. They can be reached at (508) 651-3561 (voice), (508) 651-7584 (fax), or online at bbsw@netcom.com.

clip2gif. Copyright © 1995 Yves Piguet. All rights reserved. Yves Piguet, Av. de la Chablière 35, 1004 Lausanne, Switzerland. E-mail: piguet@ia.epfl.ch.

Flatten MooV. Copyright© 1994, 1995 Robert J. Hennessy. All rights reserved.

FTPd, MacTCP Watcher, Talkd, Daemon, Script Daemon, SOCKS, and TFTPd. Copyright © 1995 Peter N Lewis. Licensed through Stairways Software Pty Ltd. Some of these programs are shareware, which means if you keep them and use them for more than a few weeks, you must pay for them.

FTPShare by White Pine Software, 40 Simon St., Ste. 201, Nashua, NH 03060-3043, (800) 241-7463 (voice).

HoloGate is a registered copyright and trademark of Information Access Technologies, Inc., 2115 Milvia Street, 4th Floor, Berkeley, CA 94704-1112. They can be reached by phone at (415) 704-1060, or online at <http://www.holonet.net/>.

InterServer Publisher. Copyright © 1995 InterCon Systems Corporation. All rights reserved. InterServer and InterServer Publisher are trademarks of InterCon Systems Corporation.

ListSTAR and WebSTAR by StarNine Technologies, a Quarterdeck company. For more information about ListSTAR and WebSTAR visit <http://www.starnine.com/>. Ordering information is available at this site, or by calling (800) 525-2580.

A serial number is required to activate ListSTAR. To obtain a ten-day evaluation serial number, please send e-mail to keys@starnine.com with the subject of the product you wish to evaluate (either "ListSTAR/SMTP<" "ListSTAR/POP," "ListSTAR/QM," or "ListSTAR/MS." The serial number you receive in the auto-reply will activate the software for ten days from the day of your request. Only one serial number will be provided for each customer. Please request the serial number once you are ready to begin the evaluation period.

Time-limited copies of WebSTAR are available for evaluation purposes. After downloading the archive, a serial number is required to activate the software. To obtain a ten-day evaluation serial number, please send e-mail to keys@starnine.com with the subject of WebSTAR. The serial number you receive in the auto-reply will activate the software for ten days from the day of your request. Only one serial number will be provided for each customer. Please request the serial number once you are ready to begin the evaluation period.

Macjordomo, written by Michele Fuortes. Copyright © 1995 by Michele Fuortes. TCP low-level routines by Peter N Lewis (used with permission).

MacTraceroute and the Traceroute Ethernet LAP. Copyright © 1994, 1995 by Jim Browne. E-mail: jbrowne@jbrowne.com.

NetCloak, a Web server add-on tool from Maxum Development Corp, gives you over forty-five new commands for use in your HTML pages. Execute commands on the fly as you send documents to the client. Customize your pages by client domain, time, date, browser, referrer, username, password, at random, or by some other variable you choose. Dynamically serve graphics, text hyperlinks, and so on. Advanced features include macros and high performance caching. Countless combinations of these commands make your site truly unique and personal. Create dynamic Web pages. No programming required. <http://www.maxum.com/>.

NetForms is an add-on application from Maxum Development that runs on your WebSTAR World Wide Web server. It allows forms entered by your users to be automatically converted to formatted HTML documents that can then be read by other Web clients. The HTML documents generated can contain any elements normally found in Web documents, including text, bullet lists, graphics, and hypertext links. Instead of simply publishing information for users to read, NetForms gives your users the ability to give feedback, add information, and contribute to your Internet server. Build interactive Web sites. No programming required. <http://www.maxum.com/>.

NetWings Internet Server Software and Overlord Internet Gateway. Copyright © 1995 NetWings, Inc. All rights reserved. NetWings and the NetWings logo are trademarks of NetWings, Inc., (510) 656-1962 (voice), (510) 656-9680 (fax), service@netwings.com. Call for current pricing. Overlord programmers: Roy Roberts and Patrick Van Zant.

Perl was written by Larry Wall and ported to the Macintosh by Matthias Neeracher, who also wrote the Perl CGI glue code.

PhotoGIF and ProJPEG by BoxTop Software, P.O. Box 2347, Starkville, MS 39760, (601) 324-7352, boxtop@aris.com, <http://www.aris.com/boxtop>, <ftp://aris.com/boxtop>.

ServerStat Lite. Copyright © 1995 J. Eric Bush. All worldwide rights reserved. Published by Kitchen Sink Software, Inc. ServerStat is a trademark of Kitchen Sink Software, Inc. For information regarding the full version of ServerStat, contact Kitchen Sink Software, Inc. at <http://www.kitchen-sink.com>, gforsyth@kitchen-sink.com, or call (800) 235-5502 (from inside the continental United States) or (614) 891-2111 (from elsewhere).

Timbuktu Pro for Networks. Copyright © 1995 Farallon Computing, Inc. Cross-platform screen sharing technology is covered by U.S. Patent Number 5,241,625. All trademarks are the property of their respective holders. All rights reserved.

WebMap. Copyright © 1995 Rowland D. Smith

Glossary

14.4K 14.4 Kilobits (Kbps) per second, or .018 Megabytes (MB) per second, the speed of v.32bis modems.

28.8K 28.8 Kilobits (Kbps) per second, or .036 Megabytes (MB) per second, the speed of v.34 modems.

56K 56 Kilobits (Kbps) per second, or .07 Megabytes (MB) per second. A common maximum transmission rate for frame relay or leased lines.

absolute path A file path that begins from the root, or topmost, level of a hard drive or server.

anonymous FTP Using FTP with a user name of anonymous and the user's e-mail address as a password. A common way of making files available to the general public on the Internet.

Apple Remote Access A protocol defined by Apple Computer for transmitting AppleTalk over serial lines; that is, using modems over telephone lines.

AppleScript A scripting language developed by Apple Computer that allows for the control and automation of Mac OS applications.

ARA See *Apple Remote Access.*

ASCII American Standard Code for Information Interchange. A standard for representing text characters in 7 bits, as the numbers 1 through 128.

bandwidth The amount of data that can be carried through a given network connection.

binary A binary file is any nontext file, made up of 8-bit data, as opposed to 7-bit ASCII.

BIND Berkeley Internet Name Domain. A common UNIX software package which provides DNS, or Domain Name Services.

browser A Web client with which a user interacts directly.

cache A collection of data stored in a location more readily accessible than the original location.

CGI Common Gateway Interface. Any program or script run on a Web server, which is triggered by a client's actions.

Chat An application that lets users communicate in real time by typing lines of text, which are then displayed to all the other users of the system. Users log in to Chat via a Telnet session.

client Computer software that requests a service from a server; for example, an FTP client can retrieve files from an FTP server.

command line A user interface that relies upon commands typed by a user rather than graphical representations of objects in the environment. See also *GUI*.

CSU/DSU Customer Service Unit/Digital Service Unit. An interface for connecting a computer or other device to a digital medium. A modem is the analog equivalent of a CSU/DSU.

daemon A background process that performs a task when some condition becomes true. Programs that provide Internet services under UNIX are usually run as daemons, and named by using the service protocol's name followed by a d, for daemon—for example, FTPd or HTTPd. Often pronounced dee-mon, but also as day-mon.

dial-up A connection between two computers or networks established via ordinary phone lines.

digest A compilation of messages sent to a mailing list periodically.

distributed service A way of providing a resource over a computer network that allows for more than one machine to deliver a service, through the use of standard protocols and conventions. The Web is an example of a distributed service with no central authority.

DNS Domain Name System. A distributed database for performing name-to-address and address-to-name resolution. For example, a domain name server might resolve the domain name www.freedonia.com into the IP address 204.62.130.117.

domain The name of a computer or a group of computers on the Internet. For example, the host name www.freedonia.com is made up of the domains www, freedonia, and com, with freedonia being a subdomain of com, and www being a subdomain of both freedonia and com (and also a host name). Domains are organized in an inverted tree structure called the *domain name space.*

e-mail Messages that are exchanged between computer users via a network.

Ethernet A networking standard for local area networks that carry data at 10 Megabits per second, or 1.25 Megabytes per second.

FAQ Frequently Asked Questions. Many Usenet groups have an FAQ: a list of frequently asked questions and answers to those questions. FAQ is often used to mean any informational document.

filename extension Two, three, or four characters at the end of a filename to indicate to computers without file typing what kind of file it is. For example, a filename ending in .sit indicates a StuffIt binary; a filename ending in .html indicates a file in HTML, or Hypertext Markup Language.

Finger A protocol that displays information about a user for a given system.

firewall A gateway that screens all traffic between an internal, protected network and an external network, and permits only authorized traffic to pass through.

form Forms, or fill-in forms, are the electronic version of paper forms, common on the Web to allow for user input and interaction. Although forms are created using HTML, they must be processed using some scripting or programming facility.

frame relay A digital network technology that provides high-speed connections over great distances. Data is sent over the network using "virtual circuits" between two end points.

freeware Software distributed without cost to the end user, although subject to licensing and redistribution restrictions.

FTP File Transfer Protocol. A method for exchanging text and binary files between computers on the Internet.

fully qualified domain name A domain name ending with a dot (.).

FYI For Your Information. Documents submitted to the Internet Engineering Task Force (IETF) that discuss topics related to the Internet of general interest. See also *RFCs*.

gateway A device that translates data between different protocols or networks.

GIF Graphics Interchange Format. A common 8-bit, 256-color graphics format developed by CompuServe. A 1989 update to the GIF format, GIF89a, added support for a transparency index and interlaced graphics.

Gopher A simple menu-based information service. Gopher clients present lists of items that can be downloaded or displayed, as well as items that are links to other directories or servers.

GUI Graphical User Interface. The Mac OS, Microsoft Windows, and the X Window system are all environments that take advantage of a graphical user interface, in which pictures are used instead of words to represent some elements of the OS, such as the file system. The Web is often called the GUI of the Internet, although there exist many text-based, command-line-driven browser users for which that statement wouldn't be true.

headless server A server without a display that is administered remotely.

host A computer on the Internet that allows users to communicate with other hosts, not to be confused with servers, which specifically serve information to clients. Every computer on the Internet able to connect to other computers on the Internet is a host, whether it's being used as a client or a server.

HTML Hypertext Markup Language. A simple markup language to set out a document's structure and relationship to other documents. Most documents made available on the Web are formatted in HTML.

HTTP Hypertext Transfer Protocol. The simple protocol used by the Web to transfer documents between clients and servers.

hub A device that connects multiple machines to a single network connection.

hypertext Text with links. Implemented as part of the Web via HTML.

IETF Internet Engineering Task Force. The organization that coordinates the operation and management of the Internet, through the development of appropriate protocols and architectures.

image map An image within a Web document that has "hotspots" defined, which are links to other documents.

IMAP Internet Message Access Protocol. A successor of POP, IMAP is a mail protocol that allows users to read and maintain mail using multiple mailboxes across a network.

Internet A network of networks using a common protocol, IP.

Internet Config The Internet Configuration System is a standard for the Mac OS which stores common configuration information, such as the machine owner's e-mail address, in one location, so that each Internet client or server that runs on the machine needn't ask for the same information.

Internic Internet Network Information Center. A managing body established by the National Science Foundation that performs, among other things, domain and directory services for the Internet.

invisible files Files on a Macintosh volume that do not appear in Finder windows. Depending on the intelligence of a server program, they may or may not appear as part of the volume's file structure to clients.

IP Internet Protocol. A network layer protocol that transmits data as packets. IP is used by all Internet services.

IP address The dotted decimal address, such as 192.0.0.1, for computers on the Internet.

ISDN Intergrated Services Digital Network. A standard for providing end-to-end digital connections, for both voice and data. Most ISDN connections have a maximum throughput of 64 or 128 Kbps, or .08 and .16 Megabytes per second, respectively.

ISO Latin-1 Developed by the International Organization for Standardization, a standardized character set for languages that use the Latin alphabet.

ISP Internet Service Provider. An organization that sells Internet connectivity and provides consultation and service to organizations and end users.

Java An object-oriented programming language that originated at Sun Microsystems, and that is currently being developed as a way of implementing cross-platform distributed applications on the Web. Java programs that run on the client's machine are called *applets.* HotJava was the first Web browser to include Java applet support.

JPEG Joint Photographic Experts Group. The name of the committee that developed the standard 24-bit image compression algorithm, designed for use with full-color or gray-scale photorealistic images. JPEG is commonly used to refer to both the compression algorithm and its standard file format.

LAN Local Area Network. A network that spans only a short distance.

leased line A private (nonshared) line for voice or data.

LISTSERV A UNIX-based program that allows for the mass distribution of e-mail messages. More generally, any list server.

list server Any program that batch distributes e-mail messages and allows the maintenance of e-mail list databases.

Local Area Network. See *LAN.*

log A file into which the actions or error messages of a server application is written, for reporting or troubleshooting purposes.

MacTCP A TCP/IP stack for the Mac OS, written by Apple Computer, and packaged as a control panel. MacTCP will eventually be superceded by Open Transport.

mail See *e-mail.*

mailbot A program that automatically replies to incoming e-mail, usually based on the content of that e-mail.

mailing list A list of e-mail addresses available through a single e-mail address, so that when a message is sent to a mailing list's address, each e-mail address on the list receives a copy.

MIME Multipurpose Internet Mail Extensions. A standard way of identifying data types; for example, a GIF file has a MIME type of image/gif; a μ-law sound file has a MIME type of audio/basic. When used outside the context of transporting these data types inside Internet mail messages, MIME types are often referred to as "content types" or "media types."

mirror A site that provides copies of some or all of the resources available at another site to improve their availability or to reduce network traffic.

modem Modulator/Demodulator. A device for sending digital information over analog lines.

MPEG Moving Pictures Experts Group. The name of the committee that developed several standards for the compression of moving pictures.

MTA Mail Transport Agent An e-mail server.

MTU Maximum Transmission Unit. The largest encapsulated network layer packet size that the physical medium will allow.

MUA Mail User Agent. An e-mail client.

multihoning The ability for a host to support multiple network connections using different protocols.

network Hardware and software used to exchange data between computers.

news News, or Usenet news, is a collection of threaded discussion groups, organized by topic.

Open Transport A networking system created by Apple Computer for the Mac OS. In addition to functioning as a TCP/IP stack with the included TCP/IP control panel (which replaces MacTCP), it also enables the use of AppleTalk, EtherTalk, and other networking protocols.

OS Operating System. The software layer that sits between a computer's hardware and a computer's applications.

packet A unit of data sent over a network.

Perl Practical Extraction and Report Language. A very useful cross-platform scripting language remarkable for its text manipulation capabilities.

pipe The physical or base protocol layer of a network connection. Also, under UNIX, a method of interprocess communication.

POP Post Office Protocol. A protocol that allows computers that may not be connected to the Internet at all times to receive mail via a "maildrop," in a fashion similar to a post office box at a post office.

port A channel for specifically addressing a single TCP or UDP connection.

PPP Point-to-Point Protocol. A protocol for transmitting data over serial lines. Unlike SLIP, PPP isn't limited to transmission of IP packets.

protocol Rules governing the exchange of data between processes, computers, or networks.

proxy A server that connects to another server on behalf of a client.

RAIC Redundant Array of Inexpensive Computers. A RAIC provides a single service, such as a Web service, through the use of multiple machines.

real time Information that is sent and received more or less immediately—a talk or chat session is considered to be a real-time conversation, while e-mail and Usenet news are usually far from real time.

relative path A file path beginnning from an arbitrary position in a file system, rather than from the root.

Reply-To: A line inserted into an e-mail message that indicates where replies to a given message should be sent, even if the message is sent from some other address.

RFC Request For Comments. Documents submitted to the IETF that describe Internet standards or proposed Internet standards.

root The topmost directory or folder. Under the Mac OS, the root is your hard drive's name.

round-robin DNS A domain name service capable of returning different IP addresses for the same domain name, for distributing load across multiple machines.

router A device that controls the flow of data from one network to another.

script A computer program written in an interpreted language, such as AppleScript or Perl.

SCSI Small Computer System Interface. A protocol that enables a computer and devices to communicate with one another on a common interface.

server An application or a computer that offers a service to a client.

shareware Software distributed on a try-it-then-pay-if-you-use-it basis. Shareware is different from demo software, in that shareware doesn't have any of its functionality removed and doesn't time-expire. Shareware is cool. Pay your shareware fees.

site An Internet server, usually referring to a single function of that server, not all the services provided through the one machine. For example, you might go to the Providing Internet Services via the Mac OS Web site, or <http://www.pism.com/>.

SLIP Serial Line Interface Protocol. A protocol for transmitting IP packets over serial lines; that is, using modems over telephone lines.

SMTP Simple Mail Transport Protocol. An Internet protocol for the delivery of e-mail.

SOCKS SOCKetS. A server running SOCKS acts as a proxy server that provides screening, authentication, and logging for application-level connections.

spam Flooding some place on the Internet with irrelevant or inappropriate data.

subnet A segment of a larger network.

subnet mask A bit mask that separates the portions of an IP address significant to the network from the bits significant to the subnet. For a class C address, a standard subnet mask is 255.255.255.0, which masks the first three bytes of the address, and leaves the last byte available to identify machines on the subnet.

T1 A network protocol that transfers data at 1.544 Megabits per second, or .193 Megabytes per second..

T3 A network protocol that transfers data at 44.746 Megabits per second, or 5.593 Megabytes per second.

Talk A protocol that lets two users talk to one another in real time via their keyboards. Unlike many real-time protocols, which transmit lines of text broken by carriage returns, talk transmits every keystroke as it's entered.

TCP Transmission Control Protocol. A transport layer protocol used by most Internet services.

TCP/IP The TCP protocol sitting atop the IP protocol.

Telnet A protocol that enables users to log in to remote hosts.

TLA Three-Letter Acronym.

token A string of characters (or a symbol) that represents some other value.

UDP User Datagram Protocol. A transport layer protocol that sits atop IP. Unlike TCP, it has no error checking.

UNIX (Derived from Multics.) A multiuser operating system popular as a platform for Internet servers.

URL Uniform Resource Locator. A standard for specifying resources on the Internet.

Usenet A network defined, suitably enough, as a collection of all the machines that carry and distribute news.

virtual hosting The ability for a server to answer to multiple names; for example, for www.freedonia.com and www.pism.com to actually be the same machine. This is complicated for Web servers by the fact that most people don't want the top-level directories of virtual hosts to point to the same information; a content provider often wants <http://www.pism.com/> to point to a different introductory page from <http://www.freedonia. com/>. HTTP 1.1 includes support for virtual hosts.

VRML Virtual Reality Markup Language. A platform-independent language being developed for use on the Web for the description of 3-D virtual worlds.

WAN Wide Area Network. A network spanning large distances comprised of multiple LANs.

Web A distributed information service built atop HTTP, which is supported by many graphical clients, called browsers.

World Wide Web See *Web*.

Index

Addison-Wesley Developers Press publishes high-quality, practical books and software for programmers, developers, and system administrators.

Here are additional titles from A-W Developers Press that might be of interest to you. If you'd like to order any of these books, please visit your local bookstore or:

FAX us at: 800-367-7198

Call us at: 800-822-6339
(8:30 A.M. to 6:00 P.M. eastern
time, Monday through Friday)

Write to us at:
Addison-Wesley Developers Press
One Jacob Way
Reading, MA 01867

Reach us online at:
http://www.aw.com/devpress/

International orders, contact one of the following Addison-Wesley subsidiaries:

Australia/New Zealand
Addison-Wesley Publishing Co.
6 Byfield Street
North Ryde, N.S.W. 2113
Australia
Tel: 61 2 878 5411
Fax: 61 2 878 5830

Southeast Asia
Addison-Wesley
Singapore Pte. Ltd.
15 Beach Road
#05-09/10 Beach Centre
Singapore 189677
Tel: 65 339 7503
Fax: 65 338 6290

Latin America
Addison-Wesley Iberoamericana S.A.
Blvd. de las Cataratas #3
Col. Jardines del Pedregal
01900 Mexico D.F., Mexico
Tel: (52 5) 568-36-18
Fax: (52 5) 568-53-32
e-mail: ordenes@ibero.aw.com
 or: informaciona@ibero.aw.com

Europe and the Middle East
Addison-Wesley Publishers B.V.
Concertgebouwplein 25
1071 LM Amsterdam
The Netherlands
Tel: 31 20 671 7296
Fax: 31 20 675 2141

United Kingdom and Africa
Addison-Wesley Longman Group Limited
P.O. Box 77
Harlow, Essex CM 19 5BQ
United Kingdom
Tel: 44 1279 623 923
Fax: 44 1279 453 450

All other countries:
Addison-Wesley Publishing Co.
Attn: International Order Dept.
One Jacob Way
Reading, MA 01867 U.S.A.
Tel: (617) 944-3700 x5190
Fax: (617) 942-2829

If you'd like a free copy of our Developers Press catalog, contact us at: devpressinfo@aw.com

Planning and Managing Web Sites on the Macintosh®: The Complete Guide to WebSTAR and MacHTTP

Jon Wiederspan and Chuck Shotton
ISBN 0-201-47957-5, $39.95 w/CD-ROM

This book, written by two acknowledged experts in the field, teaches you everything you need to know about using WebSTAR, the best known Mac HTTP server software and its shareware predecessor MacHTTP, as well as about writing CGI applications for your server. A special version of WebSTAR, plus tons of useful software are on the CD-ROM.

Web Weaving: Designing and Managing an Effective Web Site

Eric Tilton, Carl Steadman, and Tyler Jones
ISBN 0-201-48959-7, $24.95

Covering UNIX®, Windows®, and the Macintosh®, *Web Weaving* shows you how to install and configure Web servers, use authoring tools, implement security, and build structured, well-organized Web sites. The authors, experienced Webmasters, include tips for planning for growth, building in maintenance schemes, catering to your users' needs, and creating a logical, underlying infostructure.

Hooked on Java™: Creating Hot Web Sites with Java Applets

Arthur van Hoff, Sami Shaio, and Orca Starbuck,
Sun Microsystems, Inc.
ISBN 0-201-48837-X, $29.95 w/CD-ROM

Written by members of Sun's Java development team, *Hooked on Java* is a concise and practical introduction to using applets to add interactive capabilities to World-Wide Web sites.The CD-ROM contains a wealth of cool Java applets ready to plug into your home pages, examples of HTML pages that are already Java-enabled, Java source code, the Java Developer's Kit for Windows® 95, Windows NT, Solaris 2.x, and more.

The Internet Publishing Handbook For World-Wide Web, Gopher, and WAIS

Mike Franks
ISBN 0-201-48317-3, $22.95

The Internet Publishing Handbook takes you through the process of Internet publishing from beginning to end, using examples and advice gathered from Internet publishers around the world. You'll learn how to assess hardware and software server needs for your site; choose server setup options and features for World-Wide Web, Gopher, and WAIS; design HTML documents; implement digital cash, digital checks, charging, and more.

Growing and Maintaining a Successful BBS: The Sysop's Handbook

Alan D. Bryant
ISBN 0-201-48380-7, $39.95 w/CD-ROM

This book contains advice, tools, and tips from an industry expert on how to go from "up and running" to front runner BBS status. Alan Bryant's first book, *Creating Successful Bulletin Board Systems* covered the basics—this book takes you to the next level, covering topics such as discussions of why, when, and how you might choose to connect your BBS to the Internet; information on legal issues relevant to board content and sysop responsibility; online databases, and more.

Online Law: The SPA's Legal Guide to Doing Business on the Internet

Thomas J. Smedinghoff, Editor
ISBN 0-201-48980-5, $34.95

Written for the layperson, but extensively annotated for the experienced lawyer, *Online Law* provides clear guidance through the rapidly developing law of electronic commerce. Based on sound legal principles, this comprehensive handbook draws on the extensive knowledge of experienced attorneys at the forefront of today's emerging online legal issues.